D1196306

Padma Rangaswamy

NAMASTÉ
AMERICA

Indian Immigrants
in an
American Metropolis

The Pennsylvania State University Press
University Park, Pennsylvania

Library of Congress Cataloging-in-Publication Data

Rangaswamy, Padma, 1945–
    Namasté America : Indian immigrants in an American metropolis / Padma Rangaswamy.

        p.   cm.
    Includes bibliographical references and index.
    ISBN 0-271-01980-8 (cloth : alk. paper)
    ISBN 0-271-01981-6 (pbk. : alk. paper)
    1. East Indian Americans—Illinois—Chicago—History.   2. East Indian Americans—Illinois—Chicago—Social conditions.   3. East Indian Americans—Illinois—Chicago—Ethnic identity.   4. Chicago (Ill.)—Ethnic relations.
    I. Title.
    F548.9.E2R36   2000
    977.3'11004914—dc21   99-30458
                                                                                                            CIP

It is the policy of The Pennsylvania State University Press to use acid-free paper for the first printing of all clothbound books. Publications on uncoated stock satisfy the minimum requirements of American National Standard for Information Sciences— Permanence of Paper for Printed Library Materials, ANSI Z39.48-1992.

To the memory of my parents,
Saraswathi and K. G. Sivarama Iyer

CONTENTS

List of Figures ix
List of Tables xi
Preface xiii
Acknowledgments xvii
Prologue 1

Part I: Indians at Home and Abroad

1 The Indian *Oikumene* and Its Heartland 15
2 The American Context: From Pariah to Elite 41

Part II: The Chicago Community

3 The Attraction of a Metropolitan Region 73
4 The Quantitative Profile: Responses to a Survey 97

Part III: Voices and Countervoices

5 Astride Many Worlds: The Women 143
6 Caught in Limbo: The Youth 167
7 In Search of Security: The Elderly 193

Part IV: Strategies of Survival and Growth

8 Preserving the Core: Cultural Institutions 217
9 Building Infrastructure: Religious Institutions 245
10 Forging New Links: Business and Politics 273
11 Pursuing Special Interests: Professional Groups and the Media 301

Epilogue 329
Notes 337
Index 355

LIST OF FIGURES

1. A schematic view of select outliers in the migratory *oikumene* of India in the nineteenth and twentieth centuries — 17
2. Major Indian emigration destinations, 1830s–1990s — 19
3. Top ten countries with populations of Indian origin — 20
4. Indian immigration to the United States by decade, 1901–1990 — 48
5. Asian Indian population in the United States by major urbanized areas, 1990 — 55
6. Indian immigration to the United States by sex, 1964–1993 — 57
7. Indian immigrants admitted under "relative preferences" versus "occupational preferences," 1980–1993 — 62
8. Distribution of Asians in the Chicago region, 1990 — 81
9. Asian Indian population concentration in Chicago, 1990 — 82
10. Asian Indian population concentration in the Chicago Metropolitan Area, 1990 — 83
11. The Chicago survey: Demographic profile — 102
12. The Chicago survey: The professional dimension — 109
13. The Chicago survey: The social dimension — 113
14. The Chicago survey: The personal/familial dimension — 120
15. The Chicago survey: The religious dimension — 122
16. The Chicago survey: The national dimension — 125

LIST OF TABLES

1. Relative regional concentration of Indian population compared to total Asian population in the United States, 1990 ... 53

2. Selected social and economic characteristics for the Asian population, 1990 ... 58

3. Selected social and economic characteristics for Indians in the United States, 1980 and 1990 (includes Indians born in the United States) ... 64

4. Selected characteristics of foreign-born Indians in the United States by year of entry (excludes Indians born in the United States) ... 66

5. Distribution of Indians by county in the six-county Chicago Metropolitan Area ... 79

6. Population distribution of Indians in Illinois suburbs with 1990 population of more than 500 (in order of size) ... 84

7. Median income of Asian households in 1989 in Illinois by selected nationality and county (minimum Indian population of 1,000) ... 92

8. Indian immigrants over fifty years old admitted 1986–1993 ... 194

9. Industry distribution of self-employed Indian American men, 1990 ... 275

PREFACE

The idea for this book first struck me as I was strolling along Devon Avenue one summer day in 1990, marveling at the sights and sounds and smells of India. For a few moments, I forgot that I was in Chicago. The sight of richly embroidered saris in the windows, the sound of Hindi film music blaring from the video shops, and the smell of spices frying in ghee in the restaurants magically transported me back home; I felt I was in one of New Delhi's busiest bazaars in Karol Bagh or Connaught Place. I recalled that I had visited a lone Indian shop on this very street, twenty years ago, eagerly seeking out an Indian face in the crowd. Now it was the white face that had become a rarity. The transformation was historic indeed, and I went scurrying to the library to search for a book that would have told the fascinating tale of how Devon Avenue turned into Gandhi Marg. I could find no such record and I felt I had to create it.

Had I lived continuously in Chicago from the time I migrated to the United States with my husband in 1970, I would have been so much a part and parcel of this transformation, I might not have been so struck by it. As it was, after ten years of residence in the Chicago area in the 1970s, we had moved back to India in the 1980s, visiting Chicago every two years during that decade, recognizing afresh each time how much the Indian immigrant community had grown since our previous visit. In 1990, we came back to Chicago to resettle as return immigrants. This time around, I experienced a compelling and undeniable urge to explore this historic phenomenon of Indian migration. Thanks to the years I had spent in India, I felt I was distant enough from it to be capable of critical analysis, yet close enough to provide an insider's perspective. I became deeply involved in community life, trying to identify factors and understand processes of change that had shaped the community for three decades. Frequent visits to friends and relatives living in major metropolitan areas such as New York, Los Angeles, and Houston convinced me that other cities, too, were undergoing similar transformations, and the changes in Chicago were part of a larger, nation-wide scenario.

My attempts to chronicle the visible, outward transformations that were taking place among Chicago's Indian immigrants led me to a search for my own historic past. How did Indians like me, so firmly rooted in their own national traditions and so attached to India, wind up as immigrants in Chicago? What did it mean to be an immigrant? Back in India, the image of people who left their homeland to settle abroad was that of shallow oppor-tunists out to make a fast buck or hapless victims of circumstance con-demned to live in exile. One might travel abroad but one always came back home to stay. But in the 1970s, 1980s, and 1990s, respectable middle-class citizens, who were born in the aftermath of Indian independence and who thought of themselves as Indians—first, last, and always—were leaving India in droves, emigrating to Australia, England, and the United States. And far from being stigmatized, they were the envy of those who stayed behind. How were they different from Indians who had emigrated in earlier times?

I immigrated to the United States in 1970 with my engineer husband. Like thousands of other engineers, scientists, doctors, and their spouses, we answered America's call for skilled professionals to fill a gap in its labor market. Our entry was made possible by major changes in the 1965 immi-gration law, which opened up opportunities for nonwhite people from Asian countries. Even though we came on immigrant visas, we were con-vinced that we would return home after a few years of work and travel abroad. Yet we stayed for more than ten years, lured almost imperceptibly into becoming "permanent residents," enjoying financial success and living the "American dream"—that is until, in a fit of guilt and longing for the homeland, we returned to India in 1981 with our two daughters in tow, deter-mined to restore to them their rightful heritage as Indians. But we hadn't counted on the equally powerful pull of their American heritage, which led us back to Chicago in what must surely be one of the great ironic twists of our lives. Moving back and forth between India and the United States, we began to question our own identity. Who and what were we, Indians in America or Americans in India? How did immigrants like us, who were equally adept at putting down roots and tearing them up, define them-selves? In talking to friends we learned that even those who had never returned to India nevertheless yearned for the home country and were drowning in a morass of confusion and conflict. And if we were confused, how much more so our children who looked to us for help in developing their own identities? The search for context was at once personal and historical. It led me to abandon a long career in advertising and to seek out the University of Illinois History Department, where I found a wonderfully supportive team of professors. It also became the key to my understanding and coming to terms with my own immigrant experience.

In the process of researching the American historical context relevant to the post-1965 Indian immigration, I discovered that Indians have yet to be given their rightful place as players in modern American immigration history. Studies of Indian immigrants in the United States are very often relegated to the field of "third world" or "developing nations" studies or to an exclusive area of "South Asia" or "ethnographic" studies. I see Indian immigrants in America as one of the latest in a long line of immigrants to the United States and as a group whose story must be understood in the same context as that of the earlier European, African, or Asian immigrants. But Indians are also part of a global migration from India to other parts of the world and cannot be fully understood outside that context either. The story of how they built their lives in Chicago became connected to the immediate world around them in the metropolis, to the homeland whence they came, and to the rest of the world where Indians had built immigrant societies.

An ever expanding circle of connections and interconnections created for me a truly worldwide web, and helped me reclaim both my Indian and my American heritage. The two remain an integral part of me, sometimes reconciled, sometimes irreconcilable; at times distinctly separate, at other times fusing miraculously. But the important thing is that they are both accepted, never denied. That, for me, has been the ultimate reward in writing this book. I hope readers, too, some of whom may have undergone similar experiences in trying to reconcile their ethnic heritage with their American identity, will find this book equally rewarding.

ACKNOWLEDGMENTS

This study could not have been conducted without the cooperation and support of family, friends, and the Indian immigrant community in Chicago. But there is one person to whom I owe the deepest debt of gratitude and that is my mentor and advisor, Professor Leo Schelbert. He understood my ideas even before I had formulated them myself, gave shape to rough beginnings, helped to reshape several versions of the manuscript with infinite patience, and guided me through the occasionally painful but always exhilarating task of writing my first book. Above all, he believed in me.

I am grateful to the University of Illinois at Chicago for supporting me with a fellowship that gave the final impetus for the completion of this work. I am also indebted to the university for its intellectual environment, the variety of talent among its faculty, and the freedom they gave me to approach my subject from different angles. The quantitative analysis was conducted under the able guidance of Daniel Smith. Melvin Holli and Perry Duis provided me with fresh insights into Chicago's multicultural milieu, while Paul Hockings and Sylvia Vatuk gave important advice on the anthropology of Indian civilization. I am also thankful to Sumit and Tanika Sarkar of Delhi University for reviewing the chapter on India, to John Kelly of the University of Chicago for his input on Indians abroad, and to Arthur Helweg for his encouraging assessment of the manuscript. To Melvin Holli and Paul Hockings, I owe additional thanks. Melvin Holli was involved in the survey process from the very beginning and gave my preliminary findings valuable exposure by including my chapter on Asian Indians in the book *Ethnic Chicago: A Multicultural Portrait* (Grand Rapids, Mich.: W. B. Erdmans, 1995). Paul Hockings went over the manuscript with a fine eye for detail and gave it the polishing touches. The manuscript has also benefited from Lakshmi Menon's editorial skills and her meticulous search for the right word and the right phrase. Raymond Brod, geographer at the University of Illinois at

Chicago, produced the maps and some of the graphics. My editor at Penn State Press, Peter Potter, played a critical role in the transformation of my work from dissertation to book manuscript and provided his gracious support throughout the revision process. Would that all first-time authors could be so fortunate in their editor! I am also thankful to Rajeshwari Pandharipande of the University of Illinois at Urbana-Champaign and N. Gerald Barrier of the University of Missouri for their suggestions on sharpening the focus and tightening the presentation of the material, and to Mukul Roy for the generous contribution of her professional photographs.

I thank all those who participated in the survey and the many interviews and group discussions that constitute the foundation of this book. They are too numerous to thank individually but I want to express my deep appreciation of their cooperative spirit and the trust they reposed in me. I am especially indebted to Urmilla Chawla, who provided me with useful leads and contacts in the immigrant community, and Shobha Srinivasan, who helped fine-tune my survey. I owe thanks to my family members, including my sister Indira, who braved Chicago's blustery winter to distribute my survey, and my husband Rangy, who provided support and encouragement in myriads of ways that helped me stay the course and complete this work.

This book is dedicated to my daughters Priya and Anjali, who provided grist for the mill—sometimes unwittingly—when it came to second-generation experiences. It is also written for future generations of Indian Americans, who will no doubt be asking the same questions for which I sought answers. I hope this book will satisfy their need to know their past, inspire them to ask new questions about their heritage, and help them face the future.

PROLOGUE

When Sandeep, a young Indian mechanical engineer, first came to Chicago from Calcutta in 1968, he was so hungry for the company of fellow immigrants, he would greet any Indian he encountered on the street and invite him over for coffee to his cramped studio apartment on Broadway and Lawrence. Back then, Indian immigrants like Sandeep were a small, barely noticeable lot trickling into Chicago's North Side, lost in the city's diverse ethnic population. Almost three decades later in 1996, Sandeep was a well-established entrepreneur, regularly inviting scores of fellow Indians to lavish weekend parties in his tastefully appointed, custom-built home, set on a half-acre lot in the western suburb of Oakbrook. His experience was not unlike that of many other Indian immigrants in Chicago who had realized the "American dream" within a relatively short period of time. By the mid-1990s, Indians were a distinct, highly visible, and easily recognizable community, more than 100,000 strong, spread throughout the metropolitan region. Not only were they flourishing in many of the wealthier suburbs of Chicago, they were well-settled within the city, too, along the Devon Avenue shopping strip, which they had turned into the leading commercial center for Indian goods and services in all of North America.

The rapid growth of the Indian immigrant community in Chicago—as elsewhere in the United States—may have remained an easily recognizable but hard-to-assess phenomenon had it not been for the 1980 U.S. Census, which counted Asian Indians as a separate group for the very first time.[1] Thanks to this categorization, Indians placed on record a growth rate of 125 percent between 1980 and 1990, representing one of the fastest growing immigrant groups under the Asian American umbrella. They numbered 815,447 in the 1990 Census and were distributed fairly evenly all across the United States. A little more than one-third were located in the Northeast while the rest were spread over the South, West, and Midwest. Within each region, they tended to converge in major metropolitan areas. Of the 18 percent who were in the Midwest, most were located in the Chicago metropolitan area. There were 57,992 Asian Indians in Chicago and its six surrounding counties, an 82 percent growth over 1980. The demographic characteristics of Indians in America in the 1990 Census reveal some of the reasons why they have been so successful in building vibrant immigrant communities. They are young (median age 28.9 years) and an overwhelming majority (90 percent) are married-couple families. They have one of the highest median family incomes of any group (at $49,309, they rank second only to the Japanese and much higher than the national average of $35,225). They tend to hold mostly managerial and professional jobs in science, medicine, engineering, commerce, and real estate. Figures for the Chicago metro area show that Chicago's Indians share many of the same characteristics as the national Indian population.[2]

The Indian population is not only notable for its steady and continuous growth since the mid-1960s, it has become remarkably diverse within a comparatively short period of time. On the one hand, it is dominated by a highly educated elite of professionals who have six-figure incomes, live in sprawling suburban homes, drive late-model luxury cars, and send their children to Ivy League schools. They were followed in the 1980s by lesser-skilled relatives who moved into nonprofessional fields such as retail trade, food, and service industries. At the other end of the spectrum are the still-struggling newer arrivals who lack English language skills, need basic job training, and remain on the fringes of society. The number of Indians living below the poverty line steadily increased in the 1980s and 1990s, adding to the economic stratification within the community. These trends, which have been well-documented for the Chicago area, are fairly typical of all major Indian immigrant communities in the United States, no matter where they are located.

The heterogeneity among Indian immigrants is not confined to socioeconomic differences alone. Age-wise, they present a unique phenomenon. Within a short span of three decades of immigration, there are already four generations of Indians in America. Many immigrants who came in the 1960s have become grandparents themselves, but they have also sponsored their elderly parents from India to come and live with them. Indians come from every state in India, each with its own distinct language and cultural heritage. They also belong to many religious faiths including Hinduism, Islam, Sikhism, Jainism, Christianity, and Zoroastrianism. They differ, too, in their country of origin, hailing not only from India but from the global family of

Indians in other countries such as England, Canada, South Africa, Tanzania, Fiji, Guyana, and Trinidad. This variety is bewildering to Indians themselves, many of whom have no knowledge of their own long and checkered history of migration to the United States.

According to the records of the Immigration and Naturalization Service, the first lone Indian set foot in America in 1820. He was followed by a trickle of merchants, seamen, travelers, and missionaries amounting to no more than seven hundred up to the turn of the nineteenth century.[3] The first significant wave of immigration to the United States took place between 1900 and 1910, when more than three thousand agricultural workers, mostly Sikhs from Punjab, came to the Pacific Coast. They entered America at a time when anti-Asian sentiment was rampant, and though they tried to live peacefully, working on the Western Pacific Railroad and the lumber mills of Washington, they could not escape the racist attacks directed against all Asians, including the Chinese and Japanese. The Sikhs aroused the hostility and suspicion of white Americans, especially the Asiatic Exclusion League and the American Federation of Labor, who campaigned vigorously against the "ragheads" and "the Hindoo menace." Driven down the Pacific Coast, they were forced to seek refuge in the rural areas of California's Central Valley. Here they reverted to their agricultural traditions, and in spite of being discriminated against, became successful farmers and prominent citizens. There is a sizable Sikh community in California that traces its religious and cultural heritage to these first immigrants.[4] Immigration from India to the United States virtually stopped when the U.S. Congress passed exclusion laws in 1917 and 1924. It picked up again shortly after 1946, when the Asian quota was relaxed to allow limited immigration, naturalization of Indian residents, and nonquota immigration of family members. About six thousand Indians entered the United States between 1947 and 1965.[5]

After 1965, the number of Indian immigrants increased dramatically. According to Immigration and Naturalization Service (INS) figures, a total of 469,000 Indians were admitted as immigrants between 1961 and 1990. The increased inflow from India was a direct result of the changes in the immigration law in 1965 that abolished the national origins quota, provided for family reunification, and granted visas to those having skills or talents needed in the United States. This time around, the Indian immigrants were radically different from the earlier group. Not only were they well-educated, they came from all over India (not just the Punjab), they settled all over the United States (not just California), and the women came in equally large numbers as the men (there were hardly any women in the first group).

The unprecedented transformation of the American economy from industrial to postindustrial demanded the kinds of skills that Indians had in abundance, and the Midwest, as the traditional magnet for employment seekers, attracted Indians in large numbers.

The West has always held a certain glamour and mystique for the middle-class Indian. In the 1950s and 1960s, many Indians went abroad for higher education and on their return to India secured lucrative jobs. After 1965, immigration to the United States accelerated to the point where people began to talk of a "brain drain," a term used to describe the phenomenon of educated Indians going abroad and leaving India bereft of an intelligentsia capable of solving the country's problems. (In reality, India continues to produce highly educated and skilled manpower far in excess of its own economy's ability to absorb, so "brain drain" is hardly an issue.) The reasons given for the emigration of Indians to foreign lands are numerous, and the most commonly cited are the prestige of higher education abroad (a carry-over of the colonial mentality), the exasperating bureaucracy and corruption in India, the lack of employment opportunities for highly educated professionals, and the enormous disparity in professional incomes between India and abroad. Of course, the personal circumstances of migration differ from individual to individual, and for Indians, it was not just a matter of personal choice, but involved the entire family. Still, the lure of higher education and professional and business opportunities are the most common reasons given for the emigration of Indians to the United States.

But the paradigm of America as the land of golden opportunity is a partial and inadequate one for explaining the presence of Indians in Chicago and other cities of the United States. The question, Why leave India? remains unanswered until we examine the milieu in which the post-1965 Indian immigrants came of age in newly independent India. Those who had been reared on the nationalist ideals of Gandhi and Nehru, and the urgent need to build a strong and independent India, were convinced that their stay in America would be only temporary. They expected to return to their homeland where they belonged as soon as they had made some money. But as they became more and more successful in America, and as more and more of their compatriots joined them, they found it difficult to return. They also fit into America far more easily than immigrants from other Southeast Asian countries. Unlike the Koreans and the Vietnamese, Indians learned English in schools modeled on the British education system. This legacy of colonialism gave them a tremendous advantage and helped them gain a firm foothold in America, both professionally and socially. Many of them had also graduated from American-style engineering and medical institutions in India, and this experience enabled them to quickly become comfortable with the American professional culture once they landed in the United States. They began to accept America as their new home, nurturing their family ties, their religious and cultural traditions, and forging new links with their immediate environment. These are the foundations on which Indians have built their communities throughout the United States.

Even as they were accepting America as their new home, Indians refused to embrace the old-fashioned "assimilation" theories that once seemed convenient for historians trying to explain the immigrant experience. Since they were motivated primarily by economic considerations and did not come to America fleeing tyranny or pursuing some high ideals of liberty, they did not reject their past but made it very much a part of their present, trying consciously to recreate it in their new environment. They also move frequently between India and the United States, spending appreciable periods of time in both countries, thus adding to the already complex nature of their immigration. Thanks in part to their global interconnectedness, made possible by modern communications wizardry, Indians are able to accommodate paradoxes as well as conflicting and contradictory values. They are as far removed as can be on this earth from their original homeland, yet some of them visit their parents in Indian villages more frequently than do their siblings living in Bombay or Calcutta. They keep abreast of the latest technologies, competing fiercely with fellow professionals for top corporate positions in major multinational firms; yet they see no anomaly in consulting horoscopes cast by family pundits in the villages back home when arranging marriages for their children who were born and brought up in the United States. They partake of the material comforts afforded them in an industrialized, Westernized world, yet cling tenaciously to ancient Vedic rites handed down by their ancestors through the millennia. Other Indian immigrants who have come from England or Africa or other parts of the world (and who have already undergone a prior assimilation and globalization) bring still another dimension to the immigrant experience. The old paradigm where immigrants were seen as caught in an "either/or" dilemma, where they were forced to choose between the world of origin and the adopted land, is no longer valid. Indian immigrants are not willing to give up either. Neither do they have any illusions about some immigrant Utopia where they can blithely get the "best of both worlds." In the struggle to create a new meaningful identity, Indians draw upon a variety of resources, based upon individual inclination, family ties, religious affiliation, economic opportunity, and a host of other factors that can only be described as "historical context." This book attempts to set the Indian immigrant experience squarely within that historical context, using individual experience as the most important source for understanding the experience of the group.

The complexity of the immigrant experience can best be understood through the individual voices of the immigrants themselves. Among those who were interviewed for this book was a doctor's wife who expressed her frustration at not being accepted by "mainstream" society after having attained all the trappings of success.

> It's a WASP world. Let's face it. And it stings. I feel across the board, there's discrimination. It's not very obvious, but it's there. . . . We'll make money, we'll vote, we'll gain in political clout, but we will be a separate little ball, molecules in the same atmosphere, coexisting, but not part of the same big ball.

Or take the case of a young Indian, brought up in the United States and calling America home but bound by inexplicable ties to her native India, struggling to understand who she is.

> It's so hard to define what exactly an American is because we are such a diverse country. My dress is mostly American, my eating habits are mostly Indian. And I've become comfortable saying, "I don't have an identity." I don't have to have one. It sometimes frustrates me when people tell me I have to have an identity. I don't know. Maybe we're in a limbo stage when we're not going to have one.

The older generation, the parents of immigrants, who have decided to follow their children to America, have their own apprehensions. Here is an old man whose ambivalent attitude toward America reflects his uncertainty about his own future.

> Coming to America is good in one way, bad in one way. When we see that our girls get married or go astray, we still feel bad. Our children who were born and brought up in India came in 1965. We came only in 1980. It is different for us. If we are neglected and discarded by our children. . . . What do we need really? Only love and respect. God has given us everything else. When we need help, we turn to our sons, not even our daughters. It is the duty, the *karma* of the son.

How does one understand these words? How far back should one go in history to grasp the full import of what these immigrants are saying? Nothing less than an examination of the local, national, and international connections in the lives of these Indians will do because they seem to draw equally from all these different worlds in the day-to-day experience of building their lives here in the United States. Their links to the homeland of India, or some other part of the world from which they come to the United States, continue to be important as they create new identities without discarding the old.

When viewed from the homeland of India, the post-1965 emigration to the United States is only the latest manifestation of a wanderlust that has gripped Indians for centuries. Throughout the ages, Indians with diverse occupations and a variety of backgrounds have gone for a multiplicity of reasons to several other parts of the globe, including such far-flung lands as Fiji and the Caribbean. The commonly used collective term for all overseas Indians is "diaspora," and in many ways, the term is indeed a fitting one, describing as it does the scattering of seeds from a central source. It also suggests a condition of exile, as if Indians who live abroad are condemned to a permanent state of homelessness and can never return to the land of origin. What the term "diaspora" fails to capture, however, is the continuing connection to the homeland that Indians are wont to maintain, no matter where they live. An alternative term is *oikumene*, which connotes the formation of an extended household around a central *oikos* (a Greek word meaning "home"), and this may be more appropriate to the Indian emigrant experience.[6] In this image, the central source or homeland is as important to the emigrant as the outlying destination. The words "immigration," "emigration," and "diaspora" all imply movement only in a certain direction, whereas the word *oikumene* with its image of a central "heartland" and peripheral "outliers" is more accommodating of the idea of movement in several directions. Indians who emigrate keep returning to India for visits to the homeland. They also visit each other in the outliers, or migrate from one outlier to another. For instance, Sikhs migrated from India to East Africa in the nineteenth century, and their descendants moved from East Africa to England, America, and Australia in the twentieth century (see Fig. 1, page 17, for a graphic representation of the Indian *oikumene*).

In the search for a model that might be most useful for studying Indian immigrants in America, one is drawn to Asian American immigration studies. Until the 1965 Immigration Reform Act, any reference to "Asian" immigration was understood to include only the Chinese and the Japanese, but since then, other groups from East, Southeast, and South Asia have come under the Asian umbrella. Many scholars have detected a problem in including too many disparate nationalities under the rubric "Asian." For Indians, who may have no more in common with the Japanese than they do with the Irish or the Italians, this categorization is particularly problematic. Neither is a racial categorization any more helpful than the geographic one. Indians are neither black nor white nor can they be slotted in any of the commonly understood racial categories. Indeed, they are a mixture of many races and a civilization unto themselves. Whatever the limitations of putting Indians into the Asian category of American immigration history, this categorization has important consequences for the way Indians align themselves consciously along with other Asians as an ethnic group in America as they jostle for power and recognition in the larger society.

In some of the literature dealing with the turn-of-the-century Asian immigration, the grouping of all Asians in one category works in a limited way, because the only major influences portrayed here are white prejudice, public policies, and governmental action. And these factors affected all Asians regardless of national origin. Even in works that are obviously sympathetic to the plight of Asian immigrants, they are portrayed as oppressed in a race-conscious, color-conscious America. But there is now a call to abandon the "victim" approach, and to recognize the role immigrants played in directing their own destiny. Roger Daniels warned against what he called "negative history" or "history that recounted what was done to these immigrant peoples rather than what they did themselves."[7] And if the history is to be told of what Chicago's Indian immigrants did themselves, such images of dominance and subordination are too limiting, given the generally affluent and "upwardly mobile" nature of the group.

What, then, are other important ways in which we might look at Indian immigrants? How do they see themselves? In a more global context, what place do they occupy in the Indian *oikumene*? What is the nature of their continuing relationship with India? How does India view its people who reside abroad? How do answers to these questions help us understand their American immigrant experience? Scholars have attempted answers to each of these questions, separately and partially, but not considered them together in an interconnected way or woven them into a framework that can serve as a model for studying immigration.

Since the 1970s, studies have appeared of Indian immigrants in New York, Atlanta, Kalamazoo, and Los Angeles. Sociologists such as Paramatma Saran, who conducted the first major study of Indian immigrants in the United States, wrote from the conventional assimilation and acculturation angles, while anthropologists emphasized their linguistic and cultural diversity.[8] India's strong religious traditions and the attempt by Indian immigrants to transplant their religions in the United States have inspired detailed studies.[9] The extraordinary economic success that the Indian immigrants have achieved is the focus of another major study by Arthur W. and Usha M. Helweg, while Richard Brown and George Coelho have focused on the psychological aspects of identity-building among Indian immigrants in a stressful alien environment.[10] Additional works deal with the interaction between the first and second generations.[11] Transnationalism, the term used to describe the phenomenon of immigrants calling more than one country their home and spending appreciable periods of time in all of them, is also applicable to Indian immigrants.[12]

With these sociological, anthropological, and religious studies to draw upon, and with the passage of time since the first phase of the post-1965 immigration, it is now possible to attempt a historical interpretation of the Indian immigrant experience. In addition, there is also a substantial literature on Indians abroad from the mid-nineteenth century onward. Though they represent only between 1 percent and 2 percent of the total population of India, the incredible diversity in their migration and settlement patterns in different parts of the world at different times in history has given rise to a rich and varied literature. Recurrent themes in all these studies include the role of racism, ethnicity, and gender in shaping the histories of Indians abroad.[13] The history of Indian emigrants under British imperial rule classifies them according to how well (or more often, how badly) they are treated in the country of adoption.[14] The history of post–World War II migration from India to the industrialized nations of Australia, Canada, and the United States is less depressing, involving as it does a more diverse group of people, including highly skilled professionals, whom it is possible to discuss without constant recourse to the "immigrant as victim" model. There are sharp contrasts between the nineteenth- and twentieth-century emigrations from India, but there is a continuity in the history, especially for those descendants of the nineteenth-century migrants who have found their way to Chicago (say from Trinidad or South Africa), or those who are twice or thrice migrants themselves (say from Uganda to London to Chicago). It is important to be acquainted with this history, however briefly, to get a true sense of time and place in the lives of Chicago's Indians.

As far as more direct and contemporary sources of information on Chicago's Indians are concerned, comparison of 1980 and 1990 Census figures provides an excellent opportunity to track changes in the composition of the group. But macrolevel analyses of population reports have to be connected to the story of individual hopes and fears and frustrations in a meaningful way, and so other types of sources have also formed the basis of this book. They include a survey of 574 first-generation Indian immigrants in the six-county metropolitan area and scores of personal interviews and group discussions. The oral evidence allows one to probe below the generalizations and cover the real, day-to-day experiences of particular immigrants. The records of Indian organizations and associations, and the ethnic print and broadcast media in Chicago complement these data.

Using an interdisciplinary research methodology that combines the use of census reports, survey data, personal interviews, community records, and historical texts, this book traces the growth of Chicago's Indian community in the city and suburbs from 1965 to the mid-1990s by setting it in the international context of global emigration from India. It reveals how human agency, local circumstances, and international forces both extend and limit the world of Indian immigrants in Chicago. Though the study is of a microcosm, it is in many ways representative of the larger Indian population that tends to concentrate in major metro areas where their skills are most in demand. Indians in Chicago are similar to Indians elsewhere in the United States in their attempts to celebrate their differences from other urban ethnic groups, to maintain their connections with India, to link up with Indians in the global *oikumene*, and to build solidarity with their fellow Americans. Those Indians who live in far-flung or rural areas may have significantly different experiences, but they are rarely completely isolated from their fellow-immigrants in urban centers and may share many of the elements of the urban experience.

This work also focuses more on the upper-class, skilled elite who came in the first wave of immigration after 1965. Unlike some earlier immigrants to the United States, who thought mostly in terms of conformity, assimilation, and a rejection of their past, these Indian immigrants thought in terms of choice and compromise, of preserving their past so it was not lost to the future. However, they also had to face tensions generated by changing circumstances both within and outside the community: the influx of a second wave of less-skilled Indian immigrants, the coming of age of their children brought up in the United States, the immigration of their older parents, and increasing racial discrimination from the larger American population.

While it is hardly possible to examine in one work the entire range of social, political, religious, economic, and cultural factors that colors the immigrant experience, this book shows in a holistic way how some of these factors interact in a local, national and international context. Ultimately, this work is an attempt to explain, in human terms, how and why the lives of Chicago's Indians were changed by the decision to immigrate to the United States.

PART I

Indians at Home and Abroad

1

THE INDIAN *OIKUMENE*
AND ITS HEARTLAND

I was also fully aware of the diversities and divisions of Indian life,
of classes, castes, religions, races, different degrees of cultural
development. Yet I think a country with a long cultural background and a common outlook in life develops a spirit that is
peculiar to it and that is impressed on all of its children, however
much they may differ among themselves.

—Jawaharlal Nehru, *The Discovery of India*

Historians have long agreed that unless and until we understand the world
of origin of the immigrant, we can never fully grasp the nature of the immigrant experience in the adopted land. This is particularly true for Indians
who cling tenaciously to their roots, no matter how long they have been away
from the homeland. The Gujaratis of Kenya sent their children back to India
to be educated or married even after three or four generations in Africa.
V. S. Naipaul came back from Trinidad to his ancestor's village in India in an
agonizing search for roots.[1] Sikhs in England go back regularly to visit their
villages in the Punjab, even after years of living abroad. Chicago's Indian
immigrants shuttle back and forth, both physically and figuratively, between
the Old and New Worlds. They see the changes that India has experienced
over the years and sometimes bring the effect of those changes back with
them to Chicago. Indeed, they have been part and parcel of the change,
especially in their contribution to the globalization of the economy, the
transfer of technology, and the industrialization of rural areas in India. This
link with India is likely to grow even more as it becomes easier and easier to
maintain. A few dollars a month now buys Indian immigrants a subscrip-
tion to cable television, which brings news from India straight into their
homes on a daily basis. Relatives and friends from India visit the United

States regularly, and their give-and-take relationship with the Indian immigrants is based on the changing economic, political, and social conditions in India.[2] So the "India of Chicago's immigrants" is not a static world that they left behind but a changing world that has been undergoing its own course of development since they emigrated. The dynamics of immigration have been changed radically by the transportation and communications revolution of the second half of the twentieth century. They have also enabled immigrants to define who they are, how they see themselves, and to give new meaning to the word "immigrant."[3]

Indians in the *Oikumene*

The concept of an *oikumene*,[4] or a global household, is based on the fact that Indians all over the world are connected not just by some ineffable sense of "Indianness" but by real ties of family, commerce, religion, profession, and culture.

Figure 1 is a schematic representation of the Indian *oikumene* where India is the central heartland and the outliers are the major Indian immigrant communities of the diaspora. Drawn from the Greek word *oikos* meaning "household," the word *oikumene* describes much better than the word "diaspora" the true links between India and Indians who settle abroad. Like family members, they retain their ties to home, and with each other, leading separate lives in their adopted lands but never losing sight of where they came from. Not only are Indians in the *oikumene* connected to the fountainhead that is India, they are connected from one outlier to another. When Indians migrate from East Africa to England and thence to Canada or the United States, they are moving from outlier to outlier. They also move from outlier back to the central heartland, as in the case of return émigrés. Wherever they go, they are part of the global Indian *oikumene*, because their "Indianness" remains a part of them, generation after generation, thanks to the hold of their distinctive culture. It helps to think of Indians all over the world as part of a giant, interconnected web, a moving web, in which traffic never stops. Movement is heavy and concentrated at certain times in history, slower and more diffuse at other times, but the connection is always there. Another equally powerful image connected with the *oikumene* is that of a physical body, with the central heart of India pumping its lifeblood to its extremities and that same blood flowing back to the central heartland, bringing with it new nourishment for India and at the same time being

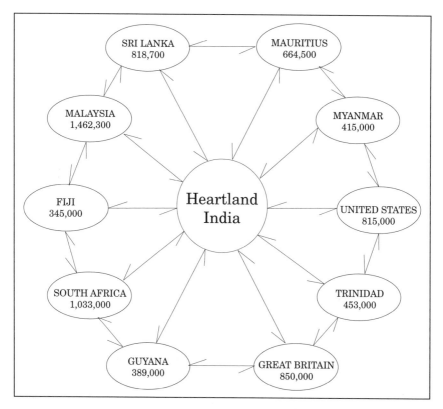

Fig. 1. A schematic view of select outliers in the migratory *oikumene* of India in the nineteenth and twentieth centuries

Source: Illustration adapted from Leo Schelbert, "Emigration from Imperial Germany Overseas, 1871–1914: Contours, Contexts, Experiences," in *Imperial Germany*, ed. Volker Duis, Kathy Harms, and Peter Hayes (Madison: University of Wisconsin Press, 1985), 126. Figures represent populations of Indian origin for different years (median year: 1988).

renewed and re-energized itself. Fanciful as these images may be, they help to convey the dynamics of migration for the Indian immigrants of Chicago.

It is difficult to estimate the exact number of Indians permanently settled abroad because the Indian government does not keep track of the figures. The Ministry of Labour has records for the number of Indians who require emigration clearances under different categories, but these are mainly for workers going to the Gulf countries.[5] Since emigration clearance is not required for professional and managerial workers, there are no official records regarding their emigration from India. The count of Indians abroad therefore comes mainly from the census of the country of destination of the emigrant Indian. As of 1987, the count of overseas South Asians (which includes all people of South Asian descent residing outside South Asia) from India, Pakistan, Bangladesh, Nepal, and Sri Lanka was 8.6 million, or less than 1 percent of the combined South Asian population of 1 billion.[6] They were spread fairly evenly across all continents—approximately 1.5 million in Europe, 1.4 million in Africa, 1.9 million in Asia, 1.3 million in the Middle East, 1 million in the Caribbean and Latin America, 1 million in the Pacific region and 0.7 million in North America (see Fig. 2).

A more recent estimate obtained from an official of the External Affairs Ministry in New Delhi (interviewed by the author in New Delhi in July 1995) put the figure of Indians abroad at 14 million, while another published source in 1993 made an "unofficial estimate" of 18 million.[7] Whether the figure is 10 million or 18 million, it still represents only between 1 percent and 2 percent of India's total estimated population of 919 million in 1994.[8] Despite their low numbers, Indian communities overseas continue to attract scholarly attention. Other overseas populations such as the Jews, the Chinese, the Africans, and the Europeans are much larger in number than the Indians, especially in comparison to their home-based populations. But because Indians are so widely spread around the world and have such divergent histories, they have much to tell about "international migration processes, social and cultural change, political development and ethnicity."[9] Figure 3 shows countries with the highest number of Indian overseas populations. The Middle East, where there may be as many as 2 million Indians, is excluded from this list since the Indian population there is more temporary than immigrant in nature.

It is convenient for purposes of analysis to divide the Indian emigration into two distinct phases—the nineteenth-century colonial phase and the twentieth-century post-independence phase.[10] Migrations from India in each of these two time periods are usually compared by scholars according to "types" of migration, circumstances of settlement, and the nature of community development in the adopted lands. While the divergent histories of these different migrations do tell us a lot about migration processes in general, what is also important here is how these histories affect Chicago's post-1965 Indian immigrants. This question cannot even be asked, let alone answered properly, without at least a cursory examination of the entire Indian *oikumene*.

The earliest recorded travels of Indians to foreign lands date back almost 2,500 years ago. Perhaps the first to go abroad in sizable numbers were the

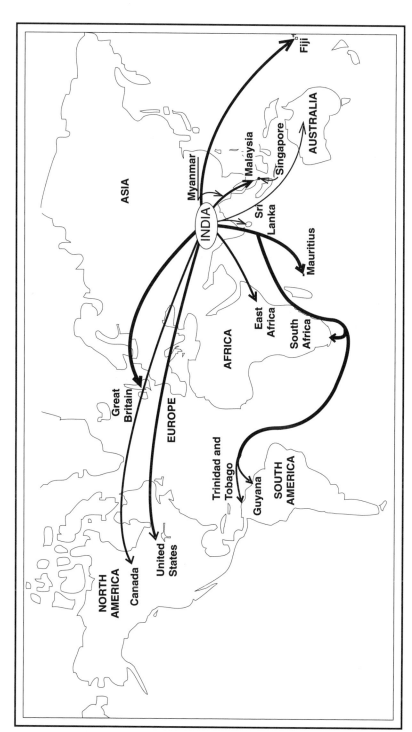

Fig. 2. Major Indian emigration destinations, 1830–1990s

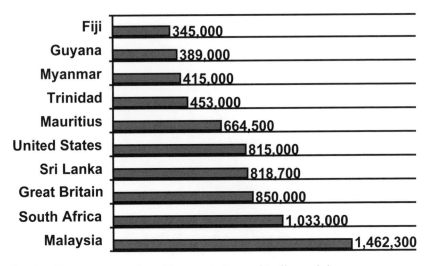

Fig. 3. Top ten countries with populations of Indian origin

SOURCE: The figure for Great Britain is from the 1991 UK census. Figures for all other countries are from *The Europa World Yearbook 1995* (London: Europa Publications, ltd.) and for years ranging from 1980 to 1994 (median year: 1988).

Buddhist pilgrims and missionaries who traveled to East and Central Asia to propagate the teachings of Buddha from the fifth century B.C.E. Indian merchants are known to have traveled to East and Southeast Asia and developed a thriving sea trade from the sixth century A.D. onward. Ancient South Indian dynasties held imperial power in the countries of Southeast Asia and the East Indies, including Thailand, Malaysia, Cambodia, and Indonesia. Looking westward from India, the Gujaratis from the west coast established trade connections with East Africans as early as the second century A.D. and traveled south to Central and South Africa. Some of these merchants left their wives and families in India and returned periodically to visit them, but even those who brought their families with them, such as the Ismailis, regarded India as their home.[11]

Indentured Migration

The first large-scale emigration from India that is recorded in history took place under British imperial rule. It was a direct result of the severe labor shortage in the European plantation colonies created by the abolition of slavery in 1834 and the subsequent emancipation of African slaves. Indentured labor from India was brought in as part of the solution to the plantation owners' problems not only in the British colonies of British Guyana, Trinidad and Tobago, but also the French colonies of Mauritius and Réunion, and the Dutch colony of Surinam.[12] Not only did the British replace African slave labor with Indian indentured labor, they found the indenture system so suitable to their ends that they introduced it into their colonies where no slave labor existed, colonies such as Ceylon (Sri Lanka), Malaya, and Fiji.[13] Indians also went to East Africa for building the railroads, along with the Chinese. A total of 1.5 million indentured Indians emigrated between 1834 and 1917. Indian recruiters, based in Calcutta and Madras, were sent into the hinterland to acquire emigrants to sign contracts for five years. These indenture contracts guaranteed the emigrants free or partly paid return passage to India, basic pay, food, accommodation, and medical care, but the conditions of indenture were so bad, Indians called it *narak* or hell.[14] It is obvious that terms such as "acculturation" and "assimilation" had no place in the lives of these indentured immigrants. Like the Africans who were brought forcibly to new continents and exploited for their labor, these Indians too yearned for their homeland but their economic circumstances and their bonded condition did not permit them to maintain any connections to India except in their minds and in simple, humble rituals woven into the daily grind of their existence. At the end of the indenture period, which was extendible to ten years, return passage was guaranteed but it was only grudgingly granted and many of those who returned to India did so penniless, benefiting very little from their exile.[15] But two-thirds stayed behind. Mostly they continued with the rural life they had always known, struggling in racially torn and capitalist-dominated economies. The indenture system was ultimately terminated in 1917 after vehement protests from Indian nationalists brought its ugly practices to light and forced the British authorities to shut it down.

Descendants of Indentured Immigrants

Descendants of the indentured immigrants who stayed on abroad now form communities of substantial size in Mauritius, South Africa, Fiji, Sri Lanka, Malaysia, Guyana, and Trinidad.[16] Though the circumstances of migration were similar in most cases, the present condition of Indians varies greatly from country to country.

In Mauritius, the Indians form over 60 percent of a population of 1 million. With the island being comparatively isolated from external forces, there is cultural preservation of Indian ways, with some families still speaking the mother-tongue.[17] The Fiji Indians were subject throughout the colonial period to laws designed to prevent them from becoming too strong both politically and economically. Today, they remain at the base of the economic pyramid in farming and trade occupations under a new political constitution that institutionalizes their political inferiority.[18] Guyana is the only country in the Western Hemisphere where people of Indian descent form a majority (51 percent) of the population.[19] But here, too, as in Fiji, Indians remained at the bottom of the class hierarchy even after the end of indenture. Class and race conflict have marred relations between Indian and African groups in Guyana and, to a lesser extent, Trinidad.[20] In South Africa, Indians became concentrated in South Natal, hemmed in by a policy of apartheid that placed severe restrictions on their physical movement and economic advancement. The majority are landless, unskilled or semi-skilled, and hardly better off than the blacks. Still, the perception persists among blacks that the Indians remain aloof and consider themselves superior. Nelson Mandela chided Indians because 70 percent of them had voted for white parties in the April 1994 elections.[21] There was also indentured immigration of thousands of Sikh and Punjabi laborers to British East Africa during the 1890s and 1900s to build the Mombassa-Uganda railway. The great majority of them returned to India after the period of indenture, but thousands of them stayed back and formed strong East African Sikh communities who later migrated to Britain during the 1960s.

Another type of contract labor migration, known as the *kangani* system and involving middlemen and financiers, took place between 1844 and 1938 to the neighboring countries of Burma (now Myanmar), Malaya (now Malaysia) and Ceylon (now Sri Lanka). Indians also went as middle-level bureaucrats of the colonial government to Southeast Asia and though their numbers are seen to be in "irreversible decline" their descendants have a specialized role in trade unions and education, and work in newspapers, schools, and universities.[22] In Malaysia, Indians are forced to live under a system circumscribed by restrictive quota laws. Indians in Singapore, by contrast, are well off. An enlightened political leadership has ensured them fairer treatment than they got in Malaysia or Burma, and as a result they have been able to contribute more to the Singapore economy.

The Legacy of Indenture

The historically relevant question to be asked with respect to the lives of Indians in most of these countries is: To what extent is their economic, social, and political status today directly derived from their indentured ancestry? Since their ancestors were geographically restricted to the plantation during indenture, and allowed to settle as "free" men only within the vicinity of the estates, they remained physically segregated. Very few had the economic wherewithal to travel back to India for visits, so contact with the motherland was minimal. Though they came from a very caste-conscious society, caste-consciousness waned with the years, and the caste system itself disintegrated overseas since it could not be sustained in an alien environment.[23] Most of the Indians were Hindus (85 percent) and shared the same regional background, and so they retained a high degree of cultural homogeneity in comparative isolation from the non-Indians. Sometimes a cultural divide between north and south Indians developed where they came in comparable numbers, for example, in Fiji and South Africa. Religious division along Hindu/Muslim lines was rare since few Muslims migrated. Relations have been smooth between the two groups, with each one taking part in the other's cultural celebrations. The majority of Indians in these communities are still rural residents engaged in some form of agricultural production, struggling in economies plagued by overpopulation and underemployment. In the case of Trinidad, an oil boom has brought sudden prosperity to the Indian community.[24] Generally speaking, the descendants of the indentured Indians are looking for better economic opportunities abroad, which often happens to be in Canada, Australia, or the United States.

The focus in most of the studies conducted so far on Indians in these countries appears to be on their separate and distinct identity, and the fact that their personal and political aspirations coincide with those of their own ethnic community rather than with the nation at large. The debate about whether Indians were "rejected" by whites and blacks from colonial days or freely opted to form a racially exclusive body is still hotly contested though hardly provable in conclusive terms. The truth is probably somewhere in between. A collective identity is both imposed upon and cultivated by Indian immigrants and what is obvious is that they remain segmented as a separate group. In all these settings, an organizational infrastructure developed to serve as a rallying point for communal sentiment. Some outstanding individual leaders emerged—Gandhi in South Africa, Ramgoolam in Mauritius, Jagan in Guyana are the best known—but more important were the many organizations which sprang up to provide religious activities and guidance in day-to-day matters, such as savings schemes and marriage and funeral services. There were also recreational and social centers, associations to promote links with India, and liaisons with other local organizations. These overseas Indians had a strong influence on India's foreign policy— even the imperial government was constantly debating issues of exploitation and discrimination against them. The size of the overseas Indian community was, of course, very important in its historical development. But majority strength did not automatically guarantee political power. The pejorative term "coolies" used to describe overseas Indians involved in disagreeable and low-paying jobs was popularized first in this era of indentured migration and remains, in many ways, the most telling comment on the history of a people herded from their native country under abominable conditions to serve colonial economic interests abroad, manipulated so that even after decolonization they would be denied a legitimate status in society, and then left to struggle for political and economic survival.[25]

Free Migration

As subjects of British colonialism, Indians had opportunities abroad only to the extent permitted by their imperial masters. When the British needed literate, middle-level functionaries to man the railways, telegraphs, steamships, rice mills, and other manufacturing industries in Burma, Malaya, and East Africa, they turned to the Indians. The reception accorded to Indians and their ultimate destiny in these countries stemmed directly from their role as "imperial auxiliaries." Hated, feared, tolerated, and ultimately expelled, they were circumscribed in their roles just as their indentured counterparts had been, even though they were technically free immigrants. In Burma, the rise of Burmese nationalism as early as the 1920s led to persecution of Indians there and an exodus in wave after wave. Today, Indians who remain live unobtrusively as shopkeepers or laborers, adopting Burmese dress and language, and staying out of the public eye.[26] Other places to which Indians went as employees of the British government include East Africa, Malaya, and South Africa.

Indians also went abroad, not for purposes of serving the British, but for their own interests of trade and commerce. They went to the same countries where their indentured countrymen had already settled and formed a ready clientele, such as Mauritius, Fiji, and South Africa. However, it was their presence in East Africa that attracted worldwide attention in the wake of the mass expulsions of the 1970s by Idi Amin. The Indian traders kept strictly to themselves, and did not fraternize much with non-Indians or even Indians of the other castes except for economic interactions; there was no intermarriage. Their affluence and proximity to India, compared to the indentured immigrants in the Caribbean and Fiji, enabled them to travel back to their homeland frequently and maintain ties with their families and their villages. Their caste consciousness remained high, and they perpetuated it by observing caste restrictions and building elaborate marriage networks through a caste nucleus in India. They were all concerned with safeguarding their separate identities, the "Jains, Goans, Hindus of various kinds, Sikhs of at least three categories, and several other Islamic communities of both Shi'a and Sunni dispositions."[27]

In fact, Indians were so cohesive in their own small groups, and such a self-sufficient and economically successful community that when African leaders of the newly independent East African countries looked for scapegoats to blame for the economically subordinate position of blacks in their own country, the Indians were the logical targets.[28] An exodus from Kenya began in the late 1960s and in Uganda, Indians faced mass expulsion by Idi Amin in 1972. The ensuing stampede from East Africa resulted in a world crisis that was resolved only through global cooperation. The exiled Indians were distributed, in a remarkably organized fashion, between several countries including India, Great Britain, Canada, the United States, and Australia. The residual Indian communities in Kenya and Tanzania are only a quarter of the size they were in the early 1960s, and they have almost entirely disappeared from Uganda.

The lessons of Uganda haunt overseas Indians who are constantly mindful of their "foreignness." They know that just as government legislation made it possible for them to leave India and enter a new country, they could just as easily be driven out by legislation. Even in a free country such as the United States, which has its own strong tradition of nativism and racism, Indians know that they are vulnerable. The treatment of Japanese Americans by the United States government during World War II, and, more recently, the reactions against Middle Easterners (when there were terrorist bombings in the World Trade Center in New York and then in Oklahoma in 1995) is a constant reminder of their own delicate position. Politically conscious Indian leaders in the United States try to remain vigilant and constantly warn Indians against discrimination and racist violence.

Another country of the *oikumene* in which Indians faced an uncertain future was Hong Kong. Indians first came to Hong Kong as part of a British colonial military expedition of 2,700 soldiers, many of whom died in the Opium Wars between Britain and China. In 1993, there were some 22,000 Indian businessmen, mostly Sindhis, who handled about 10 percent of all business activity on the island. Rumors of Sindhis from Hong Kong buying up land in Bombay or Bangalore in the wake of the transfer of the colony to mainland China fueled speculation in real estate and drove prices sky high. This provides yet another example of the rise and fall of outliers in the *oikumene,* and of how, even after centuries of living abroad, Indians in the *oikumene* continue to look to India as a home they can always return to in time of need.[29]

Post-Independence Migration

The Western, white-dominated countries of Great Britain, Canada, the United States, and Australia played host to Indian emigrants after World War II. Before Indian independence in 1947, the few Indians living in Britain were a middle-class group consisting mostly of students, scientists, doctors, and businessmen. The situation changed dramatically in the 1950s as Britain developed critical labor shortages in its booming industrial market. Largely unskilled workers from India and Pakistan came to fill the gap.[30] Even after several decades of settlement, in the 1990s, fully one-fifth of Britain's 850,000 Indian community is said to be at the lowest rung of the population in terms of wealth, with an income of less than 125 pounds per week. More and more Indians, however, tend to cover a wide range of occupations, including teachers and administrators. According to a study of the 1991 census conducted by social scientists at Manchester University, Indians were twice as likely as whites to be in professional jobs.[31] Still, racial discrimination based on color is a daily reality and reinforced and institutionalized by patterns of residential accommodation and employment practices. Indians are called "colored" and not much better off than the blacks in the racial hierarchy. The huge numbers of Indians and their constant interaction with the homeland in a jet age have enabled Indians in Britain to maintain their caste affiliations and resist cultural homogenization beyond a certain level. Most of the social organizations are instituted for the purpose of religion or community service, so religious sectarianism remains strong with little likelihood of all Indians submerging under some pan-Indian identity. Both the low-income levels and the entrenched British prejudice have combined to make the British experience for Indians quite different from the American one.

The Indian population in Canada is marked by even greater cultural and linguistic diversity than in Great Britain. The twice migrants in Canada are not merely from East Africa, but from many of the former colonies with sizable Indian communities.[32] Many Indians used Canada as a stepping stone to enter the United States because of the greater economic opportunities here while some found a welcoming climate in Canada and decided to stay put. Other countries that have received Indians in sizable numbers in recent decades are Australia and New Zealand. The 1977 population of Indians in Australia was 99,000, and in New Zealand 15,000. Again, some similarities with the immigration to the United States can be noted. They are a culturally heterogeneous group, live in urban areas but do not cluster in ethnic enclaves, nor do they conform to Australian society. Studies show that in their day-to-day choices they not only affirm their ethnic heritage but also show their commitment to life in Australia.[33]

Indian Jews have settled in Israel in significant numbers. There are only 7,000 Jews left in India while Indian Jews in Israel number 52,000. Their origins in India go back nearly two thousand years when their ancestors fled Palestine and settled on the coast of Maharashtra and Malabar, adopting the local language and customs as their own. Israel's Indian Jewish population, mostly Marathi-speaking, have integrated structurally into the society through service in the armed forces and employment in all areas of business and industry.[34]

An "NRI Culture"

The perception in the minds of many Indians who have never left India and never concerned themselves with migration is to lump all Indians who "live abroad" into one category, regardless of the nature of their stay abroad. The Indian government is partly responsible for this nondifferentiation since it labels all overseas Indians "NRIs"—Non-Resident Indians. The term is applied equally to the "Gulf Indians," who go to the Middle East on temporary visas, as well as to Indians who reside in the United States as permanent residents. NRIs are sometimes viewed as traitors who have abandoned their country and its problems in order to seek personal fortunes abroad. At other times, they are spoken of with pride because they have attained economic success and, through their professional and scientific achievements, given India a good name in their adopted lands. Indians from abroad know when they visit India that as far as the local resident is concerned, they are now the "other." Thus is born a community of NRIs whose culture differs from the culture of Indians in India. Yet they are very different in themselves also, because they reside in different parts of the world.

Despite their small numbers, NRIs are viewed with a lot of interest in India. Their economic role and relative wealth are considered to be important, especially in the form of foreign exchange remittances, and the Reserve Bank of India (RBI) manipulates the interest rate for its bank deposits in order to encourage the flow of foreign currency into India. Between 1986 and 1994, according to RBI figures, NRI deposits added up to $8.8 billion; but it is not known how much of this came from Indians in the United States.[35] On an average, India earns some $2 billion each year in remittances from Indians abroad.[36] There are no accurate, up-to-date figures for the extent of NRI investment in Indian industry, though it is expected to have increased with the economic liberalization of the 1990s. Sometimes, the infusion of NRI capital into India is seen as an attempt to destabilize Indian companies. For instance, the London-based NRI, Swaraj Paul's attempts to buy into the Indian companies of Escorts and Delhi Cloth Mills (DCM) were viewed with great hostility in India in the 1980s. At other times, NRIs are courted assiduously by central and state governments to invest in India. The relationship between India and her NRIs can be described as neither totally adversarial nor completely cooperative, but it is characterized by an awareness of mutual, overlapping interests and the kind of tensions that usually exist between members of an *oikumene*.

There are many other unquantifiable ways in which Indians abroad affect India—in the export and import of technology, in the exchange of ideas, and in the influencing of policies. There is hardly a family among India's elite today that does not have relatives abroad. There are influences at work in both directions, and in the present atmosphere of economic and cultural exchange between India and the United States, the opportunities for Indian Americans to serve in India have undeniably increased. "Coming home" is always on the NRIs' mind, no matter where they live outside India, even in a highly desirable place like the United States. They realize that a permanent return to India may not be feasible but they continue to look to India to help them develop their new identity as Indians abroad.

A Historic Sense of Self

Indians derive their identity and sense of self from a 5,000-year-old tradition that has maintained continuity but also has absorbed a variety of influences through the ages. Their culture has borrowed heavily from other civilizations, yet retained its own distinct character. But any attempt to glorify India's ancient past has to be tempered with sobering statistics. India is still one of the most populous and poorest nations in the world, with one of the highest rates of illiteracy. The paradox is that it is also a nuclear power and boasts of one of the largest pools of technically trained manpower even among the world's industrialized nations. Another complicating factor in the historical evolution of an Indian identity is that the different regions of India developed along different lines and came under different religious, political, and social influences at different periods in history. Since the immigrants in Chicago come from practically every region in India, it is important to acknowledge the diversity of their regional origins. The most numerous are the Gujaratis and the Punjabis, but almost every other major linguistic group is well represented among the skilled professionals in Chicago. These immigrants, regardless of their regional origin, share an outlook that, at its narrowest level, may be considered a product of their common upper-class origins in India. They came from families whose members were the agents of administrative and economic development in India and who provided the leadership for important movements of social reform and of the nationalist movement itself.

Most of Chicago's first wave of post-1965 immigrants were born in the aftermath of national independence. Throughout their growing years, there were proudly aware that India had thrown off the yoke of imperialism in a magnificent and path-breaking experiment in nonviolence. But they were also heirs to the institutions and ideas that the British left behind when they departed in 1947, especially the English-medium public schools. Thanks to the near-universal usage of English in urban India, the differences among the different linguistic groups were effectively bridged. Thus, a Tamil-speaking South Indian (say, a person whose father was in the Indian government service and likely to be transferred from one state to another) could attend school in Bengali-speaking Calcutta, college in Marathi-speaking Bombay, and find employment in Hindi-speaking Delhi, and not feel particularly alienated in any region, partly because all exams would be in English and English would be spoken everywhere. Chicago's professional Indians thus share a professional, middle-class ethos that has two apparently contradictory traits—a fierce pride in their pan-Indian identity and an easy level of comfort with a Westernized culture.

The political fallout of independence, the conflict between Hindus and Muslims after partition, was traumatic. Since then, the history of Indo-Pakistan relations has been punctuated by three wars, in 1948, 1965, and 1971, and the Kashmir issue has remained a festering sore between the two countries. If the Indian and Pakistani communities in Chicago are very often referred to in the same breath as "Indo-Pak" communities, it does not necessarily betoken a cohesiveness between them. Such an Indo-Pak identification would be unthinkable, indeed laughable, in both India and Pakistan. Conditions in the subcontinent always have, and will continue to, affect relations between Indians and Pakistanis all over the world, including the United States. Matters are complicated by the fact that Indian Muslims share a religious identity with the Pakistanis and a cultural and political identity with the Indians. Fortunately, in Chicago, Hindus and Muslims coexist peaceably enough, though they do lead somewhat separate social and religious lives. They share a commercial center on Devon Avenue, and see themselves as a minority with common interests in a larger, white-dominated world.

Another source of pride for Indians is the country's secular constitution whose flexibility and vitality have stood the test of time in much the same way as the American constitution has. Indians in America are used to the idea of an independent judiciary, and the separation of religion and state. They therefore tend to take fundamental rights and privileges for granted. They also understand the tensions associated with living in a multicultural society. In the 1960s, India was torn by linguistic and regional demands that threatened the unity and integrity of the country. Following violent demonstrations, the government was forced to concede the formation of new states along linguistic boundaries, amid fears of secession and balkanization. Today, India is made up of twenty-five states with eighteen official languages but still holds together as a nation.

It is important to understand the power of these regional and linguistic forces for several reasons. These diverse groups had to fight for the preservation of their language and their culture within India, and they were not about to give up that identity in the United States if they could help it. This explains why the Indian community in Chicago seems so sharply divided along linguistic lines. Many first-generation (and almost all second-generation) Indians in Chicago mistakenly bemoan it as a dangerous tendency. But when seen in the context of the way these tendencies were played out in India, and how they forced their political way into self-expression, it is possible to look at the linguistic structuring in Chicago as just a reflection of the way things are in India. Retaining a separate linguistic identity is important if Indians are to maintain their connections with the homeland. On the other hand, there is no denying the power of English in helping them adopt a more overarching Indian American identity. So far, there has been no true test of the cohesiveness of the Indian immigrants in the United States and of the strength of the inclusive Indian identity over the narrower linguistic loyalties. Only time will tell if it can stand up to a serious challenge, but indications are that it probably can, given the enduring character of the larger Indian identity and the way it has survived in India. There is no essential conflict in being Gujarati, Muslim, and Indian as long as one is not forced to choose between a regional, linguistic, religious, and national identity.

For almost twenty years following independence, the Indian state under its first prime minister, Jawaharlal Nehru, invested in steel plants, power and irrigation projects, and other heavy industries in which India's best-trained scientists and engineers found ready employment. But the early 1960s brought setbacks to the economy in the form of an unexpected surge in population, failed crops, and costly wars with China and Pakistan, all of which undermined the people's confidence in the government, and caused many of the skilled professionals to look for opportunities abroad. It was in 1965 when the first post-independence Indian generation was coming of age that the United States announced its new immigration policy. It welcomed those professionals who had the education and training to fill new jobs that were opening up in the United States, specialized jobs for which America itself lacked sufficient trained manpower. There were few constraints attached to immigration, no contracts to sign, no difficult conditions to fulfill. The only requirement was a professional degree, and a willingness to risk a future in America with only a few hundred dollars in one's pocket. (Because of India's poor foreign exchange reserves, Indians were allowed to carry with them no more than $400 at the time of emigration, after signing a bond promising to repatriate that amount, in dollars, before the end of one year.) Thousands of Indians answered the call. Still others were lured to Canada, Britain, and Australia. The combination of personal circumstance and external events propelled them into the migrant cycle just as they seemed ready to take the opportunity.

In subsequent years, Indian immigrants already in Chicago followed with interest new political developments in India, and as new immigrants came pouring in, they brought their own experiences of life under the administrations of Indira Gandhi, Rajiv Gandhi, and Narasimha Rao.[37] Other Indian immigrants coming to Chicago at this time from other parts of the world, such as England or Africa or the Caribbean, brought their own tales of racial prejudice, political oppression, and economic losses. It was during the 1970s when Indira Gandhi was prime minister that many of the Indians who had come to Chicago in the first wave of immigration after 1965 first returned to India to visit family and friends. They returned home laden with gifts of small appliances, saris, perfumes, and other consumer goods bought on Devon Avenue. The power of the dollar was such that travel itself was highly affordable, and most gift items that were cheap in the United States were prohibitively expensive or unavailable in India. Some of the immigrants who had spent several years in Chicago and made good decided that they would like to see their dollars invested in India to improve the Indian economy. It was both a gesture of attachment to the motherland and a hope for a sound economic return on their investment. But it was also a time when Indira Gandhi's left-oriented economic policies and red tape made business start-up in India a veritable nightmare. Not until Rajiv Gandhi entered politics and started economic liberalization did things look brighter for Indian immigrants who wanted to invest in their homeland. One Chicago immigrant, Satyen Pitroda, who had made his millions in the telecommunications industry in America, was encouraged to return to India and help modernize the Indian telecommunications system.[38] Other Indians renewed their contacts with India, setting up joint ventures, such as hospitals and factories, in their own home states.

In the 1990s, a government led by Narasimha Rao followed an even more liberal economic policy. Soon there was a flurry of activity by private investors looking for a niche in what has been termed the world's biggest middle-class consumer market. Multinational giants such as Coca-Cola, Pepsi, and McDonald's found a favorable economic climate and the volume of investment in India from Indian immigrants also went up steadily. With economic involvement came a ripple effect on family and friends and strengthening of cultural ties with the homeland. The bonds also grew because unlike many immigrant communities in the United States that are not supportive of the domestic and foreign policies of the country from which they originate (e.g., Poles, Cubans, Iranians, and Russians), Indians in the United States have been generally sympathetic to the Indian government.[39] The exceptions are the Sikh and Muslim communities, who have been sharply critical of the government's policies toward members of these communities in India.

Two incidents in particular have outraged these two religious groups and had a ripple effect on Indian communities worldwide—the storming of the Sikh's Golden Temple in Amritsar by Indira Gandhi's troops in 1984, and the demolition of the Babri Masjid mosque by rampaging mobs in 1992.

The Spread of Social and Cultural Forms

Social reform was much more difficult to implement than economic and political reform. In spite of all the legal writs that protected their rights in the new constitution, women, children, and the lower castes continued to suffer the effects of ancient discriminatory practices. For instance, divorce is still a stigma, especially for women. Dowry is a thriving practice in modern, urban Indian society. Female foeticide and infanticide are practiced in remote villages. Women in India continue to remain very vulnerable, as seen by the increase in rape of low-caste fieldworkers and by the burning of brides in dowry deaths, which assumed alarming proportions throughout the 1980s. Many of these practices remain limited geographically to India and are important to consider in the immigrant context only insofar as they reflect cultural and moral values that the immigrants carry within themselves. Such values have inherently profound significance because they gain a life of their own in the adopted land.

In the literature that seeks to explain the behavior of Indians in any immigrant situation, a common approach is to contrast the supposedly Indian values of group loyalty and family orientation, on the one hand, with the Western values of individualism and independence, on the other.[40] The latter qualities are depicted as desirable for immigrants wanting to flourish in an alien environment and the immigrant is depicted as torn between these two sets of values, caught between a rock and a hard place.

Indians are certainly a tradition-minded people in their respect for hierarchy, their concept of their "place" in life, whether in their own family or in society, but they do not necessarily see themselves as limited by it. One can hardly contend that Indians are not "individualistic" and do not value individualism. On the contrary, acquiring wealth, succeeding in one's career, being dedicated to one's job or to a particular cause—traits associated with individualism and Protestantism—are also highly valued by the Indian, whether Hindu, Jain, Muslim, or Sikh. Unfortunately, these traits are generally placed in direct contradiction to belief in group well-being and strict social control of the individual, which are also concepts that Indians value. The Indian's capacity to embrace apparently bipolar and contradictory values is viewed by Westerners as paradoxical, inconsistent, and sometimes even hypocritical.[41]

The following interpretation of "Indian values" is offered as a means of reconciling what are commonly perceived by Westerners as contradictory values in the Indian mindset. The interpretation is largely derived from Hindu philosophy, but is an Indian cultural value rather than a religious one. It is shared by large numbers of Chicago's Indian immigrants and practiced in their individual lives and their group activities. For Indians, belief in group well-being and belief in individualism are not necessarily incompatible or mutually exclusive. These beliefs only need to be prioritized and contextualized, so that while individualism is indeed valued, it is not valued above all else. What is valued, above all else, is the individual soul, whose path to salvation lies in following one's *dharma* or calling.[42] This belief in "duty," which often lies in obligation to some entity larger than the individual self (and in the case of Chicago Indians is generally to family, whether in India or Chicago or some other part of the world), is both deterministic and allows for free will. It lies in understanding what it is that one is "born to do" and then doing it the best way one possibly can. It encourages Indians to seek material success in a material world and be deeply religious and strive for spiritualism at the same time.

Family and Household Structures

One widespread feature of Indian society that cuts across barriers of language, caste and creed, is the ideal of the extended family based on an hierarchical system of kin relationships. There is no such thing as a standard Indian household because many different kinds of household arrangement exist in Indian society. For instance, there may be a widowed mother-in-law or destitute aunt living in an otherwise nuclear household consisting of father, mother, and children. Two brothers and their families may decide to make a home together, or live in contiguous homes for purposes of financial advantage or security. Many middle-class urban families in India became dual-income families in the 1960s and 1970s, when inflation forced educated young mothers to join the work force. Such families may adopt an extended household arrangement mainly so that their young children can have the support of elderly, stay-at-home kin. Generally speaking, extended family ties continue to be maintained because they still serve a purpose and are part of the rhythm of life in India.[43]

Indian immigrants in Chicago bring these attitudes with them, and follow many of the same practices in their daily lives as do their contemporaries in India. Dual-income families who are reluctant to admit very young children to institutionalized child care in Chicago generally sponsor their parents and siblings to immigrate under the family reunification immigration laws so that they will have family at home to care for their children. Even families without children welcome their relatives from India into their homes. Of course, the fact that the nuclear family is the predominant and accepted household unit in the United States, and apartment living is common, will influence Indian immigrants as they adapt to the ways of American society. But if business interests or family interests dictate that they adopt alternate household arrangements, they have a cultural background that makes it easy for them to do so successfully.

Hierarchy is another feature of family life in India. In the Indian family, formal authority is still determined by sex and age. Parental authority is supreme, which means a woman has to be a deferential wife, but can be an authoritative mother. A younger brother would have greater formal authority than his elder sister. Even in the markedly segregated worlds of men and women, each person can be dominant according to his or her rank, but must yield in the presence of higher family authority. Indian immigrant women of Chicago, who can be demanding and authoritarian in their professional work at the office, reveal themselves to be remarkably docile women in the presence of their husbands. What is important to know is that the behavior is governed by a set of deep-rooted traditions that persist even in the wake of immigration to a distant land. Public display of emotions is considered crude and there may be several subtle undercurrents in the family that are never openly acknowledged. Such restraint serves to keep the family intact by controlling potentially disruptive forces. In the United States, they have also served as repressive influences leading to strains and tensions that result in family breakups.

Whatever religion they belong to, Indians celebrate certain events in a socioreligious way. Birth, marriage, and death—these are milestones that are usually observed by ritual. In their essentials, the ceremonies are the same as they have been for thousands of years, and Indians deem it important to observe them, no matter where they might be located in the world. Thus, Indians in Chicago who would hardly classify themselves as orthodox or conservative, who eat beef and drink alcohol (even if it is prohibited by their religion), who might even approve of a "mixed" marriage, would still want weddings in their family to be conducted in traditional fashion. The flexibility of the rituals is that they allow easy incorporation of a wide variety of changes, so that if the exact same thing as prescribed in the orthodox position is not available, it can be substituted according to local convenience and usage. For instance, when a loved one dies in a Hindu family in India, the ritual is to scatter the ashes over a holy river, preferably the Ganges. A Hindu in Chicago would consider the ritual satisfactorily observed even if the ashes are scattered over Lake Michigan.

Just as religion permeates the life-cycle rituals of Indians, so also it inspires the classical arts. Both music and dance in India are devotional in nature and play out mythological events involving gods and humans. Appreciation of these arts is not confined to an elite patronage but enjoyed by the masses. It is no wonder then that the Indian immigrants of Chicago consider Indian dance and music an important form of self-expression and a part of their heritage worth preserving and perpetuating. Outstanding classical artists from India come on tour to Chicago but more important, the community has its own schools of dance and music that impart training to second-generation Indians. Pop culture, which includes the music and dance created for films and television, has a following that also cuts across class lines in India. In Chicago, Indian pop culture is big business—in the form of television shows, videos, and star-studded annual concerts, which are enjoyed by an audience eager to stay in touch with India. As fast as fashions and tastes change in India, they appear and disappear in Chicago.

Mass media, which got a tremendous boost in India in the 1950s and 1960s with the arrival of electricity and radio in the villages, became even more effective in its reach in the 1980s with the advent of color television. The televising of the epics *Ramayana* and *Mahabharata*, and historical romances such as *Tipu Sultan*, enjoyed tremendous popularity with rural and urban audiences in India as well as emigrant populations abroad. CNN and BBC transmit in India, and American talk shows and sitcoms are immensely popular. For Indians in the United States, Doordarshan (the Indian government-controlled TV station) and Asianet programs are now available on a regular basis, making it possible for all Indians, whether in India or abroad, to be watching the same programs at the same time. Being in the same physical setting is no longer a prerequisite for sharing of experiences.

Caste and Its Significance for the Immigrant

The caste system in India is not as rigid and inflexible as commonly understood by outsiders. What is mystifying to the Western observer is that caste is totally ignored and considered irrelevant by Indians in some contexts but treated as extremely important in others. There is no denying that caste is an elaborate system and a key element in the social structure of India but it is also dynamic and ongoing.[44] It exists among most of the religious groups of India, even when their religion specifically rejects it, including Muslims, Sikhs, and Christians. (It is also a common misconception that the caste system itself is outlawed in India. What is outlawed is *discrimination* based on caste or the practice of "untouchability.") One need not go into intricate details about *varna, jati,* and other such terms to get an idea of what caste means to an Indian; a broad understanding should suffice. The *varnas* (the word *varna* literally means "color") stratify Indian society into four major hierarchical groups according to ancient tradition: the *brahmins,* who formed the priesthood; the *kshatriyas,* who were kings and warriors; the *vaishyas,* who were the producers and the merchants; and the *sudras,* who performed the most menial tasks in society. The Untouchables are so low in the caste hierarchy that they are outside of it. Within the *varna,* people are further subdivided into *jatis* and this is the grouping Indians refer to when they talk of "caste." There is hierarchy within a *jati* as well as among *jatis,* but the groups have undergone considerable transition over the years through social mobility, religious movements, and absorption of new populations.

It is not possible to determine the caste categories of Indian immigrants in Chicago or even tell definitively whether they belong predominantly to the upper or lower castes, because no such records exist. But since privilege and education and wealth have been concentrated in the hands of the upper castes even in post-independence India, it is reasonable to suppose that most of the educated elite who came to Chicago also belonged to the upper castes. They do not cluster together or shun each other's company based on their caste. Neighbors and friends do not necessarily belong to the same caste. One aspect of life where caste remains an overriding concern, however, is marriage. Notwithstanding the hundreds of advertisements in the matrimonial columns that say "Caste no bar" (and this is true whether the location is New Delhi or Chicago), the very fact that the disclaimer is deemed necessary is a measure of the importance of caste in marriage. Generally speaking, Indians try to ensure marriage within the same caste because it ensures perpetuation of religious, cultural, and family traditions.

Strangely enough, while there may be no caste prejudice on a personal level, it has begun to acquire greater and greater political and social meaning in India. The politics of caste are based on the assumption that after years of undue privilege, it is time to even the score against the upper castes. Today, being a brahmin in India is roughly equivalent to being a white male in the United States in the context of a quota system. Ironically, some Indian brahmins in Chicago see themselves as having escaped discrimination and prejudice in their own land only to suffer the adverse effects of a quota system in Chicago! It often happens that a second-generation Indian American is denied admission to a coveted American university, despite his or her high academic achievement, because the university's "Asian" quota is filled.

The complex traditions described above persist to a remarkable degree in the lives of most Indian immigrants in Chicago. Barring the very rich who have no reason to leave their homeland and the very poor who have no means to do so, Indians from the entire "in-between" range of upper and middle classes emigrated to the United States. In order to understand them, it is best to follow the advice of Bernard Cohn who warns us against the dangers of overemphasizing regionalism and losing sight of important countervailing processes. The foregoing description is an attempt to capture that "pool of traditional Indian symbols, certainly Hindu symbols, which have been standardized through the nationalist movement and the emergence of an Indian nation state."[45] Cohn observes that just as sectionalism in American life has been replaced by a certain uniformity in American culture, India, too, may be said to have experienced the emergence of a new, uniform, middle-class mass culture. But even long before the existence of modern nation-states, when religious, cultural, and racial bonds were most important, Indians had begun to develop a sense of Indianness. As Nehru put it, "At almost any time in recorded history, an Indian would have felt more or less at home in any part of India, and would have felt as a stranger and alien in any other country."[46] In modern times, an emigrant might achieve a high level of comfort in a foreign land but the pre-emigration experience guarantees a certain sense of belonging in the homeland.

The cultural traditions set Indians apart far more so than their brief shared political history as a nation, but in order to understand why the Indian immigrants of Chicago make the choices that they do when ordering their own lives, it is necessary to consider both the ancient cultural history and the modern political history of India. Those Indians who come to Chicago from places other than India may have a different political history but their fortunes as global citizens of Indian origin are still connected to

India's political fortunes. Of course, not every Indian immigrant will sub-scribe to what is considered Indian "values" or Indian "philosophy," but in the very act of rejecting certain options, they are aware that they are either discarding centuries-old traditions or upholding them. That common her-itage or legacy of understanding is what constitutes "Indianness." In an alien environment, "Indianness" is not only inherited but also created in con-scious opposition to what is non-Indian. For some emigrants, the process of identifying one's "Indianness" and reinventing it may be too subtle or com-plex or even inexplicable. Indeed they resent having to explain it or identify it at all. They may not be able to explain why they value or enjoy what they do, but they do know that they can share it with other Indians from any other part of the world.

A New Paradigm

Historians, both Indian and Western, who study overseas Indians, whether in the colonial or contemporary phase, tend to examine Indians from the perspective of the receiving society. All have noted the phenomenon of dis-crimination, exploitation, and victimization of Indians in foreign lands. In rare cases where local governments have adopted a policy of multicultural-ism and multiracialism, as in Singapore and Canada, Indians are depicted as successful and welcomed for their contribution to the economy. In coun-tries where Indians are perceived as a threat, either by the local population or the dominant ruling elite, they are shown to have suffered an adverse fate, as in Burma and East Africa. It also appears that no matter what their occupation or their status on the socioeconomic ladder, the cultural distinc-tiveness of Indians always sets them apart and generates tensions. In the complex and variegated history of the overseas Indian, it is almost impossi-ble to separate the effects of race, class, gender, and cultural distinctive-ness. But it is important to examine how Indians responded to each one of these "givens" when studying their fate in their adopted lands. Then, as now, the choices available to immigrants were controlled by factors such as gov-ernment legislation (for example, in Fiji and in California, where Indians were severely limited in their ability to own land), or the limitations of trans-port and communications technology (as in the far-flung Caribbean islands from where there was no frequent or meaningful contact with the home-land). Ultimately, the personal and particular situation of the immigrants themselves determined the nature of the immigrant experience.

What remains largely unexplored is the role that Indians themselves have played in securing their own fate. Part of the problem is that the uneducated or poorly educated indentured Indians did not leave a record of their own experiences. It was left to their imperial masters and subsequent generations to reconstruct their history. But there is no doubt that, however adverse the conditions, Indians have survived as a separate and identifiable group. The question of nationalism and the processes by which Indians abroad construct a national identity, which may be based either on their religion or place of origin in India, must be considered in the context of changing circumstances in the heartland and the outliers. In each of the outliers, different groups of Indians have chosen to emphasize different aspects of their identity as Indians at different times in history, based upon their particular circumstances. For example, Hindus in Fiji have asserted their religious identity as a means of regaining national pride and fighting for Indian independence from the British in the 1920s. By contrast, Sikhs in England and Canada have used their religious identity for exactly the opposite reasons—to advance their secessionist demands for an independent Khalistan. The global nature of the Indian *oikumene* provides a wealth of opportunities to study issues such as territorial and extraterritorial nationalism.

Too often, Indians are studied only from the point of view of assimilation and victimization. If rejection and discrimination are indisputable facts in the overseas or immigrant Indian experience, as recounted in the histories of Indians in East Africa, Fiji, or England, the active role Indians themselves played in shaping their own destinies must also be considered. What did they do to change their status, if anything? If not, why not? Only by looking at immigrants as capable of making choices and being responsive to change can one begin to understand them as active players in their own history. Certainly, there is no other approach possible for the study of Indians in the United States. Some of them come from the most privileged and elite sections of society in India and have moved into the highest economic strata in the United States. Their confidence in themselves comes from their past, the atmosphere of hope and promise in which they grew up in post-independent India. But an historic awareness of the fate of other Indians in the *oikumene* is constantly brought home to Indians in the United States because of the regular traffic and communication between Indians worldwide. It is the individual and collective histories of these overseas Indians that hold the key to a more comprehensive understanding of Indian immigrants in the United States.

2

THE AMERICAN CONTEXT
From Pariah to Elite

The first Indian immigrants and the post-1965 Indian immigrants
are two separate worlds. It is a class thing. They came from the
farming, the lower class. We came from the educated middle-
class. We spoke English. We went to college. We were already
assimilated in India before we came here.
—"Second-wave newcomer," quoted in Ronald Takaki, *Strangers
from a Different Shore: A History of Asian Americans*

The first Indian in the United States is said to have been a man from Madras
who visited Salem, Massachusetts, in 1790 with a sea captain, according to
an entry in an eighteenth-century diary, but there is no way of determining
the accuracy of this report.[1] During the nineteenth century, there were a few
scattered adventurers, merchants, and seafarers who paid sporadic visits to
New York and San Francisco.[2] The records of the Immigration and Naturalization Service show a solitary Indian admitted to the United States in 1820
and a total of 716 arrivals from 1820 to 1900.[3] One of India's leading spiritual
luminaries came as early as 1893 to Chicago and introduced his message of
the universal philosophy of Vedanta to the West. Swami Vivekananda came
to the World Columbian Exposition and delivered his famous, electrifying
speech to the World's Parliament of Religions in what is now the Art Institute of Chicago.[4] Though Swami Vivekananda visited Chicago frequently in
later years, his visits didn't lead to any permanent Indian presence in the
United States until the Vedanta Society of Chicago was established in 1930.
Among these early Indians, there were also a few students and political
refugees who fled to North America to escape the wrath of the British. The
1900 Census of the United States counted 2,050 Indians, but one cannot be
sure how many of these were temporary visitors—or even if they were truly

Indian—because the records were based on place of birth rather than race or ethnicity.

The Punjabi Immigration

It was not until the turn of the century that the first significant wave of immigrants from India landed on the shores of North America. Most of the seven thousand or so Indians who came to the United States between the years 1904 and 1920 were not indentured labor; still, as illiterate peasants from Punjab, their experiences were very different from the experiences of the Chicago Indians of the post-1965 migration. It is important to briefly recount their history as part of the Indian immigrant legacy in the United States. Some of the themes that are relevant to both periods of immigration include the immigrants' origin in India and how it influenced their work and lifestyle in the United States, what tactics they used to struggle against the policies of the American government and white society; and how their identity as Indians in the United States was affected by their involvement with their homeland. Despite the obvious differences and contrasts, some important similarities also come to light when the "old" immigration is considered in the light of the "new."

In the late 1890s, farming in the Punjab became difficult as drought and famine took their toll, and changes in the British land-tenure system put the small landowner in a vulnerable situation. At about this time, Canadian steamship companies, acting on behalf of Pacific coast employers who were looking for cheap labor in their lumber mills, visited the villages of Punjab and distributed pamphlets, touting the economic opportunities in British Columbia.[5] Lured by such promise, thousands of villagers left Punjab, in search of fortune. At first they came as sojourners, hoping to make money in a short while and return to their families, so most came without their wives. They landed in British Columbia, in an environment already inflamed by white hatred for the Chinese and Japanese who had arrived before them in large numbers. Forced by racist attacks to flee Canada, the Sikhs made their way southward down the Pacific coast, working in the lumber mills of Bellingham and Everett in Washington state and then on railroad construction and maintenance crews, until they reached the warmer climes of California. Between 1907 and 1908, the Southern Pacific Railroad, the Northern Electric Company Railroad, and the Western Pacific Railroad employed between fifteen hundred and two thousand Indians.[6] The Sikhs remained culturally apart, and kept to themselves, cooking their own food in crowded camps on the outskirts of town. Their lifestyle was governed largely by the fact that there were few women in the group. Less than 10 percent of the single men married while in the United States.[7] Organized white groups, suspicious of the alien culture and resentful of the cheap labor provided by the hardworking Sikhs, launched violent attacks against them and ran a successful campaign to bar their entry to the United States. Their efforts resulted in the Barred Zone Act of 1917, which effectively cut off all immigration from India.

After the railroads were built, the Indians went to work in the Chico sugar beet farms, the fruit orchards near Sacramento, the vineyards of Fresno, and the San Joaquin delta near Stockton. They quickly rose from merely laboring in the farms to leasing and purchasing land, pooling their resources, and investing collectively. Many of them attained economic prosperity, developing the arid lands into profitable rice fields and becoming known locally as the "Hindu rice kings."[8] By 1930, Indians in the United States were mostly Pacific coast farmers, numbering roughly three thousand. There were another one thousand skilled workers, merchants, and traders in the eastern United States. Others in the Indian immigrant category included about five hundred students scattered throughout the United States, and twenty-five to thirty Swamis or holy men.[9] Immigration remained static throughout the 1930s and until the end of World War II.

In the general atmosphere of hostility toward them in the United States, Indians kept nationalist sentiments alive and invested much of their energies in revolutionary activities designed to win freedom for India from the British. Intellectuals and farmers alike came together to form the *Ghadr* party (*Ghadr* meaning "revolution" in Arabic). Activists such as Taraknath Das and Har Dayal published newspapers and founded societies to attract Americans to the cause. At first, they believed the United States would be a haven for revolutionaries but they were soon disillusioned. A group of Indians set sail from San Francisco to Calcutta in 1914 with the express purpose of fomenting an uprising in the Punjab, but the leaders were arrested in India and the movement quickly collapsed.

For a long time, historians portrayed the illiterate farmers from Punjab as helpless in the face of the anti-Asian laws that openly discriminated against them. It was believed that if there was any struggle on the part of the Indians for their rights, it came only from the educated elite of students and businessmen. But recent scholarship shows how the struggle for individual rights against both the government and white society was actually carried out on two fronts, by the illiterate farmers in their own and no less effective way than by the educated, well-to-do Indians in the legal arena. Antimiscegenation laws in California prevented the unskilled farmers and laborers in the West from marrying white women. So many of them married Mexican women and raised families of Punjabi-Mexican identity. The intellectuals in the eastern universities chose to marry white women, but they, too, had to face discriminatory laws and fight for their civil rights in court.[10]

The Alien Land Acts of California, first enacted in 1913 and strengthened in later years, were primarily aimed against the Japanese and Chinese, but they also prevented the Sikhs from owning land. Sikhs got around the system by using whatever legal and economic means they could to set up elaborate and complicated partnerships, at first with Anglos and later on with their own minor children who had citizenship rights, so they would always be able to control the land that they worked on.[11]

While the farmers worked around the system to get the better of it, the intellectuals fought head-on to change the system in the courts. In see-saw battles, the Indians learned that the judges provided their own free-wheeling interpretation of what constituted "white" and "Caucasian" and sometimes formulated opinions only to suit the public mood. The 1790 federal law that reserved citizenship for "whites only" effectively prohibited Asians from getting citizenship, but in landmark court cases such as *United States v. Balsara* (1910) and *A. Kumar Mazumdar* (1913), Indians were declared eligible for citizenship by the Supreme Court because they were "Caucasian" like the Europeans. About one hundred Indians were naturalized between 1913 and 1923. Then, in a dramatic reversal, in the *Bhagat Singh Thind* case in 1923, Justice George Sutherland ruled that being "Caucasian" was not enough to be considered "white" and Indians were not "free white persons" and therefore were ineligible for citizenship. Following this ruling, the U.S. government revoked the citizenship of some fifty Indians until Dr. Sakharam Ganesh Pandit, a lawyer himself and married to a white American, fought denaturalization proceedings successfully, and in 1927 won the right to retain his citizenship. While this case stopped the government from taking away the citizenship of those already naturalized, no further naturalizations were permitted. Aware that they were unwelcome in the United States, some three thousand Indians left for India between 1920 and 1940. Many Indians who had their citizenship revoked found themselves in dire straits, stripped of their property in the United States, their bridges to India burned. One such immigrant, Vaisho Das Bagai, even took his life in despair. The return migration was large enough to render questionable the idea of immigration as a one-way stream. Indeed, the "permanent" nature of immigration is liable to be revoked in the "outliers" of the *oikumene* at any time within the lifetime of the immigrant.[12]

One dramatic example of an individual who took full advantage of the rights of citizenship is Dalip Singh Saund. He was elected a member of the Eighty-fifth Congress from the Imperial and Riverside counties of California and served three terms from 1957 to 1963. He also served on the House Foreign Relations Committee and to this day he remains the only national elected political figure among Indian immigrants to the United States.[13] Saund, who earned a doctorate from the University of California, personally explained the effects of earlier discriminatory laws. "Few opportunities existed for me or people of my nationality in the state at the time. I was not a citizen and could not become one. The only way Indians in California could make a living . . . was to join with others who had settled in various parts of the state as farmers."[14] In the 1940s, the Punjabi immigrants of the early twentieth century were an all but forgotten group. Their numbers had dwindled to a mere fifteen hundred by 1946.[15] What prevented the Sikhs from either upholding their distinct culture in the United States or entering the mainstream were their small numbers and their illiteracy. By contrast, similar illiterate and disadvantaged Indians who went as indentured labor to the East and West Indies in the mid-nineteenth century did manage to retain a distinct identity but their numbers were much larger. Lack of formal education and low economic status have generally contributed to culture dilution among Indians. It is the upper-class elite who have functioned as the torch bearers among newer Indian immigrant groups and set the tone for the post-1965 immigration to the industrialized countries of Great Britain, the United States, Canada, and Australia. In 1946, the Luce-Celler Bill granted, among other things, citizenship rights to Indians and allotted India a quota of one hundred immigrants per annum. A gradual trickle of legal immigration began and continued through the 1950s and 1960s.

The 1965 Immigration

The watershed in the immigration history of Indians to the United Sates in the twentieth century is the 1965 Immigration Reform Act, signed into law by President Lyndon Johnson, which abolished the national origins system and replaced it with hemispheric quotas. The National Origins Quota Law is important in U.S. history because it sought to limit immigration from Southern and Eastern European as well as Asian nations, though Indians were already barred from coming to the United States by the Barred Zone Act of 1917. The 1965 law placed a limit of 120,000 immigrants from the Western Hemisphere (with no limits on any one country) and 170,000 immigrants from the Eastern Hemisphere, with a limit of 20,000 immigrants per country. Preferences were given to professionals and relatives of citizens and permanent residents, but immediate family members were exempt from numeric limits. In a 1976 statute, hemispheric quotas were abolished and a global limit of 290,000 was set with a cap of 20,000 for each country.[16]

After 1965, Indians arrived in record numbers and completely changed the dynamics of the earlier immigrant group, dramatically reviving the sagging, dwindling Sikh culture with an infusion of new blood. The new urban, professional, and well-to-do Sikhs were very different in origin from the old Punjabis and were far more eager and able to preserve their original ways. While the descendants of the older immigrants readily shaved their beards and discarded their turbans and proudly pointed to this as a mark of their assimilation, the newer immigrants were proud *not* to discard the outward symbols of their Sikh faith. Indeed, they sought to maintain a studied distance from the pioneer, rural, and less educated Punjabis whom they saw as diluting their culture.[17] Such differences are due in part to the totally changed circumstances of migration. Not only have the new immigrants come as family units, they live in an atmosphere that favors "pluralism" in the United States. New immigrants have also arrived in much larger numbers and have the economic wherewithal and group strength to sustain their distinct way of life. The re-establishment of traditional Sikh life by the new immigrants has thus affected the old immigrants and given them new options they did not enjoy before. The descendants of the old Sikh immigrants still farm in California, growing peaches in Yuba City or prunes, walnuts, and rice in Maryville, but claiming Indian identity is now a prideful experience for them.[18] As for the impact of the earlier Sikh immigration on the post-1965 immigrants, it may have alerted them to the dangers of losing their Sikh heritage and becoming rootless in the United States.

The policy of the U.S. Congress was intended to meet the country's need for skilled workers in a rapidly changing economy by drawing on global availability, but it may not have anticipated the rush of immigrants from Asia that resulted from the change in the law. President Johnson himself said, upon signing the 1965 Immigration Act, "The bill that we will sign today is not a revolutionary bill. It does not affect the lives of millions. It will not reshape the structure of our daily lives, or really add importantly to our wealth or our power." It was meant to correct "a cruel and enduring wrong in the conduct of the American Nation." The size of the Asian immigration took Congress by surprise. Asian countries had very short immigration lines at the time the law was passed, leading the Congress to believe that Asians were not keen on immigrating to the United States.[19] Among the groups that found it easier to come to the United States under the new law were Mexicans, who were not subject to quotas because they were in the Western Hemisphere, the Italians, the Greeks, and the Portuguese. But generally speaking, immigration from Europe fell, while that from Asia rose dramatically. Whereas between 1931 and 1960, four out of five immigrants had come from Europe, in the 1970s only one out of five was from Europe or Canada. Three-quarters of all immigrants came from Latin America and Asia.[20]

Several factors explain the drop in immigration from Europe. Economic recovery in Western Europe at this time was creating labor shortages which made many European countries *importers* of migrant labor and its people less interested in migrating to the United States. The Irish were interested in immigration but they didn't qualify under the new law since there were too few recent Irish immigrants to provide the kinship required to support chain migration. Poland placed restrictions on emigration of its skilled citizenry.[21] Only the Asian countries left their doors wide open. Many of these countries had a large reserve of highly skilled professionals who were eagerly seeking new opportunities and were well-qualified to enter the United States under the new law. In the immediate postwar years, many of India's professionals preferred Britain, but increasing racial tensions in Britain led to immigration restrictions there in 1962. More and more of those who left India from the late 1960s onward were bound for the United States. The number of Indian immigrants to the United States per year has climbed steadily since 1965 and has remained high, reaching a peak of 45,064 in 1991. In 1993, Indian immigration represented a record 4.44 percent of all immigration to the United States.[22]

The Limitations of a Causal Theory

In a 1975 classification of Indian immigrants by the U.S. Immigration Service, 93 percent of Indian immigrants were classified as "professional/technical

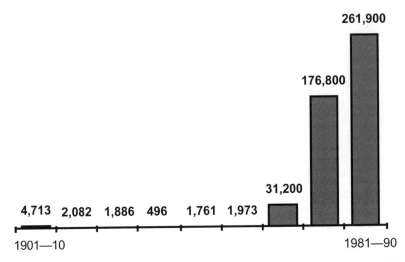

Fig. 4.   Indian Immigration to the United States by decade, 1901–1990

Source: Immigration and Naturalization Service Annual Reports

workers" or as spouses and children of professional/technical workers. Why would well-to-do professionals such as these leave the land of their birth and settle in a foreign land? There is no single cause or single explanation. While each immigrant usually has a variety of reasons for immigrating, there may be one or two overriding factors that appear more important than the others. If it is understood that "causes" and "types" of migration are concepts with limitations, one can free oneself to look at the individual lives of the immigrants and understand the nature of the immigrant experience.

It is also wrong to speak of immigration as happening at a single point in time in an individual's life. It is a process that is periodically and alternately affirmed and negated, repudiated, and endorsed by one's actions over a long period of time, sometimes several years, and sometimes in an almost subconscious way, so that without knowing how, why, or when, one has become an immigrant. This is not to deny the element of free will or conscious choice, but only to emphasize the subtleties and mysteries of the immigration process and to show that it differs from individual to individual. "America fever" did not grip middle-class Indian professionals until it became possible to immigrate. Until then, the United States (which had risen to world leadership after World War II and exerted a powerful influence on would-be immigrants worldwide) remained a distant and glamorous land to be experienced mainly through Hollywood movies and glossy magazines. In the 1950s, many families had relatives who had already received training abroad or been sent by the government on study missions. These individuals reported firsthand on conditions in the States so that when the opportunity for immigration arose after 1965, those who were considering it could consult their own uncles or elders in the family instead of relying only on the media or other published materials.[23]

Most of those who immigrated in the first post-1965 wave were urban, middle-class professionals, in their twenties and thirties, eager to explore opportunities abroad. The U.S. consulates in India had assured them that their technical skills were in great demand and they would easily find jobs. Very often, there were no qualms or serious misgivings about "immigrating" because there were no long-established careers to be sacrificed. Many of these immigrants had just graduated from major universities, had spent a few years on a job, and were looking for more rapid career enhancement than they could find in their current situations. They believed they had little to lose by making the move and everything to gain.

Of course, immigration was not a spontaneous or impulsive act for everyone. Many families debated the issue exhaustively and the decision to immigrate was arrived at only after considering all the issues. Who would look after the family's estate or business if the eldest son left? Who would care for the elderly parents? Would it be wise to send one son so that others could follow? Or so that others could stay? (Sometimes sending one son abroad and having him send home a regular income helped subsidize the family finances so that the others could stay on and fulfill their familial duties.) What about daughters? Did one dare send an unmarried daughter to the United States alone for higher studies? Or did one dare to give one's daughter in marriage to a bachelor who had emigrated earlier and perhaps succumbed to the "evil" ways of the West? Contrary to the European experience, the Indian immigrant's decision to leave usually involved the entire family and was rarely an individual decision taken in isolation. An increasing number of women went as the vanguard family member, especially if they had the skills traditionally developed among women in India, such as nursing and physical therapy, and much in demand in the United States.[24]

It is difficult to assess how far other factors such as economic instability or environmental degradation in Indian cities contributed to the desire of these professional Indians to make a move. Unemployment among qualified professionals in India is a well-known condition, but as mentioned before, it is not by itself severe enough to drive educated people to settle in foreign lands. For every Indian immigrant who professes to move because he or she can't find employment in India, there are thousands who stay and do manage to make a living. While it is possible to look at the post-1965 migration to the United States as a movement of labor from one area of opportunity to another, it must not be stressed to the exclusion of all the other factors.[25]

One could consider Malthusian-style theories that population pressures lead to migration by forcing an outflow from highly populated to less populated regions, but even within India, the flow of migrants from the villages to the already overcrowded cities makes a mockery of this theory. Inadequate services in the areas of health care and schooling in the cities of India may have encouraged some people to seek an environment abroad where such facilities are more easily available. The United States was portrayed in India by returning Indians as a place where schooling was "free" and living standards were high. When the first wave of immigrants returned for visits to India, they reported on how well they could live on their salaries as professionals in the United States. Their standard of living seemed so much higher and more easily attainable than what their counterparts in India could achieve. Indeed, many middle-class Indian professionals lived in supposedly intolerable conditions in the congested and under-serviced cities of India, where water and electricity supply is erratic and unreliable even in middle- and high-income localities. But for every emigrant who seeks an improved standard of living, there are other nonemigrants who think that giving up one's homeland for this is too much of a trade-off, and who prefer the emotional and spiritual comforts of a familiar environment. Corrupt government is still another factor frequently cited by Indians as driving them to seek a new home abroad. The legacy of a cumbersome bureaucracy from imperial days, coupled with an elaborate and restrictive system of controls that requires every small amenity to be licensed by the government, has led to the stifling of initiative and increasing public frustration. Professional Indians feel that their capacity for hard work and their desire for honest dealings, both in business and government, are more likely to be rewarded in the United States. Some groups, such as the Muslims and Sikhs and high-caste Brahmins, speak of discrimination by the government and government-sanctioned violence against them in India as the reason to seek sanctuary abroad.

Chances are that there are as many unique combinations and permutations of reasons for emigrating as there are individuals who immigrate; so historians must content themselves with understanding the contexts that make emigration possible and weave the stories of the individual immigrants into the larger picture. An examination of the professed motives of individual Chicagoans who were interviewed for this book shows how deeply embedded they are in the economic, political, and social conditions of their times, not only in India and the United States but the rest of the world. The only generalizations one may make have to do with the economic and social status of the immigrants. Most of them had enough money to make the journey without undue hardship; most hoped to capitalize on their high education and professional skills to do handsomely for themselves and their families by leaving for the United States.

The diverse geographical origins of Indian immigrants, whether they come from India or other parts of the world, make it even more difficult to generalize about motives. Besides Indians from practically every state in India, there are also those who have been supplanted from two continents before they came to call America home. For instance, there are about thirty thousand Caribbean Indians in the United States, descendants of the indentured laborers, who fled discrimination under black dictatorships in the 1970s.[26] Their motives have roots in political, economic, and racial discrimination that is quite different from the experience of Indians in India. Yet they, too, are "Indians," they, too, have professional skills and, when asked, give the same reasons for migrating to the United States.

The "cost" of immigration is not just to the individual immigrants but the country as well. The exodus of Indian professionals from India has been called a "brain drain," a phenomenon considered inimical to sending countries who are losing their extensive educational investment to the receiving countries. On the other hand, one should also consider the benefits accruing to India from this brain drain, in terms of remittances from abroad, investment in the home country, transfer of technology, and lessening of social and political pressures in the general population. The "national" cost and benefit are as difficult to quantify as the "personal." Most Americans prefer to see the professional successes of Indians and all other immigrants only in a positive light and congratulate themselves on providing immigrants with the right opportunities that are supposedly missing in the homeland. The reality is that since higher education is so heavily subsidized by the Indian government, there is a significant loss for the country. One head of an Indian research institute has estimated that in the past two decades, India has contributed at least ten thousand of its brightest science and engineering graduates to the United States through the productivity of a minimum of $10 billion to the U.S. economy.[27] According to a United

States Agency for International Development study, one-fourth of the graduates of India's medical colleges come to the United States annually.[28] But there are also hundreds of thousands of unemployed professionals in India, so it is not as though India is suffering from a dearth of brain power, either, as a result of the brain drain.

Settlement Patterns

To minimize the risks and hardships they would have to face immediately upon landing in the United States, even those who were married and were allowed to bring their wives with them came alone at first.[29] Unlike contract labor immigrants of the turn of the century, these professionals did not report right away to a would-be employer. They had to look around for jobs, and despite the rosy predictions, many of them could not find suitable employment upon arrival. Some of those who had advanced degrees had to take jobs well below their capabilities, others found that their degrees from India were not accorded the same importance as an equivalent American degree. They stayed with friends (generally from the same college or town in India) who had arrived before them or roomed in bachelor-type conditions until it was economically feasible for them to set up house on their own and send for their wives.

Compared to the other Asian groups, Indians are remarkably evenly distributed over the entire United States.[30] While the other Asians are more heavily concentrated in the West, Indians tended to go wherever their skills were in demand, that is, the industrialized metropolitan centers. Unlike the Punjabi Sikhs, who did not have the language or professional skills or the economic means to move about freely, the newer Indian immigrants are more self-assured. They do not tend to cluster since they are not from the same geographic region in India. Cheap transportation and its easy accessibility also contribute to the greater mobility of Indians and their greater spread over the entire United States.

The 1990 Census reveals that regional distribution of Indians follows the distribution for the general U.S. population more closely than any other Asian group. It shows a heavier concentration of Indians in the Northeast (35 percent) followed by the South (24 percent) and the West (23 percent). The Midwest or central region lags behind with 18 percent. It is also notable that the Midwest has lost its 1980 share of the Indian population (down from 23.1 percent in 1980 to 17.9 percent in 1990). The Midwest lost other Asian groups, too, except for the Japanese, so the Indians were following part of a more general trend. The West gained as many Indians as the central region lost between 1980 and 1990 (5.2 percent). Though one is tempted to explain the move by speculating that Indians have a preference for the warmer climes of the West or shun the conservatism of the Midwest, they may be doing no more than following the shifts in regional economic development. The general U.S. population, too, went West in 1990—the Midwest showed a 2 percent decrease while the West registered a 2 percent increase for the general U.S. population compared to 1980 figures. There is no reason to suspect that the Indians will not continue to concentrate in the urbanized, industrialized states, going where the general American population goes for jobs and desirable lifestyles.[31]

Other Asian groups are heavily concentrated in the West. Indians account for only 5 percent of the Asian population there, but represent between 18 percent and 21 percent of the Asian population in other regions. Nationally, Indians form 11.2 percent of the Asian population in the United States.

Within each state, Indians tend to gravitate toward the major metropolitan areas. According to the 1980 Census, about a third of the Indians live in the four metropolitan areas of New York, Chicago, Los Angeles, and Washington, D.C. For the years 1988 to 1991, between 27 percent and 32 percent of the Indian immigrants admitted to the United States declared these four cities to be their "metropolitan area of intended residence."[32]

The high technology-related industries that are concentrated in urban areas, such as the manufacturing industries of the East and Northeast, the

Table 1   Relative regional concentration of Indian population compared to total Asian population in the United States, 1990

	Asian Population	Indian Population	Indians as Percentage of Asian Population
United States	7,274,000	815,000	11.2
Northeast	1,335,000	285,000	21.3
Midwest	768,000	146,000	19.0
South	1,122,000	196,000	17.5
West	4,048,000	189,000	5.0

SOURCE: Statistical Abstract of the United States, 1992, table 24.

computer and petroleum mining and refining industries of the West and Southwest, the steel and automobile engineering industries of the Midwest, and the medical and scientific institutions in all these regions, provided the professional opportunities for the first wave of immigrants. Those who arrived later moved into the independent business sector and took advantage of the great diversity of employment opportunities in travel, real estate, and the hospitality industries. Some of this growth occurred in the urban areas, around the primary Indian immigrant population. Other immigrants served the general U.S. population, concentrating on newsstands and motels.[33] (Catchy phrases tying the "Patel" community to the "motel" industry abound even in the popular media.) According to the U.S. Census figures for 1980 and 1990, between 50 percent and 60 percent of the entire Asian Indian population is concentrated in less than a dozen urban and industrialized pockets—namely, New York–New Jersey, Chicago, Los Angeles, Washington, D.C., San Francisco, Houston, Philadelphia, Detroit, Boston, San Jose, and Dallas–Fort Worth.

Within the metropolitan areas there were discernible patterns of settlement. Indians seemed to prefer to live close to work or in neighborhoods where property values held up rather than to cluster together in a single area. The general tendency was toward dispersal in the white suburbs. Sometimes the development of a strong commercial complex in a specific area may have encouraged residential concentration in the same area, as in the case of Devon Avenue in Chicago, but the more affluent they became, the more Indians tended to get away from such concentrations. Unlike Indians and Pakistanis in Britain, who constitute the low-end workers in the textile and transportation industries and were confined to public housing, Indians in the United States had the ability and the means to avail themselves of a wide choice in locating in urban and suburban areas. Their education and income "prevented them from being pigeonholed into the ethnic social and spatial categories of an earlier era."[34]

Indians in the United States also moved around freely because of the relative absence of strong negative feelings toward them from the middle-class Americans in whose midst they lived. But where Indians clustered in the midst of lower-income groups who felt threatened by the prosperity of the newcomers, they have been attacked in a way strongly reminiscent of the earlier attacks on the Punjabis by Californians. In Jersey City, groups of working-class white youths calling themselves "dotbusters" ("dot" is for the decorative *bindi* that Indian women wear on their foreheads) have assaulted, and have even killed, Indians on the streets.[35] Whether changing

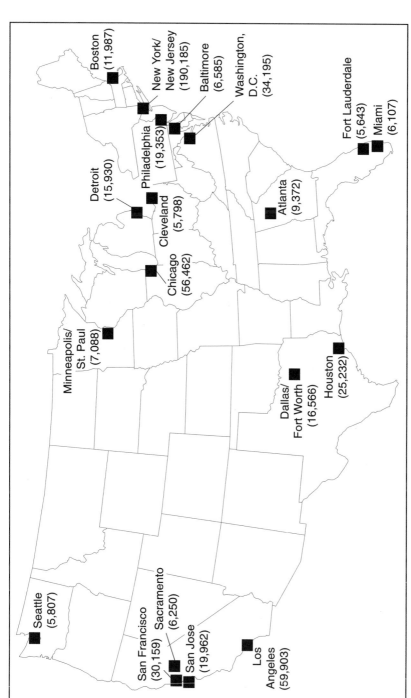

Fig. 5. Asian Indian population in the United States by major urbanized areas, 1990

demographics will affect the present dispersed pattern and cause Indians to "encapsulate" and retreat more within their own community for protection against racial attacks remains to be seen. For the present, spreading themselves spatially has helped Indians maintain a low profile and merge into the wider landscape, at least in the geographical sense.

Demographics

When looking at the statistics for the Indian immigrant population in the United States, it is important to keep in mind that the census statistics tell the story of the entire group, including those born in the United States. The 1980 Census showed that 70.4 percent of Indians were foreign-born, while the figure for the 1990 Census was even higher at 75.4 percent. The 1990 Census also showed that of the 75.4 percent of Indians who were foreign-born, 23.7 percent entered before 1975, 18.1 percent between 1975 and 1979, and 58.2 percent between 1980 and 1990.[36] To get a more accurate profile of the immigrants themselves (as distinct from the entire Asian Indian population that includes children of immigrants), one needs to look at immigration statistics. However, it is the census statistics that allow comparison of Indians with other groups, and provide a meaningful context for understanding their lives in the new environment. Thus statistics from both sources will be used throughout this section to examine variations within the community as well as to compare them with other groups in the U.S. population.

The Indian population in the United States is young (median age in the 1980 Census was 30.1 years, in the 1990 Census, 28.9 years). The median age for first-generation immigrants is, of course, likely to be significantly higher. One outstanding characteristic of the post-1965 immigration that has had far-reaching consequences on the socioreligious and cultural nature of the group and enabled it to maintain a distinctly Indian lifestyle is the gender balance. The male-to-female ratio of the immigrants improved steadily over the years. In 1966, the percentage of female immigrants was the lowest at 34 percent, while in 1973 and 1993, the percentage of female immigrants rose to its highest figure of 53 percent. The reason why the number of women immigrants surpassed the number of men in some years is probably due to the women joining their husbands who had arrived earlier or the previously arrived males bringing over new Indian brides.[37]

Another curious phenomenon is that visa restrictions on the entry of new brides from India has tended to influence marriage patterns of young

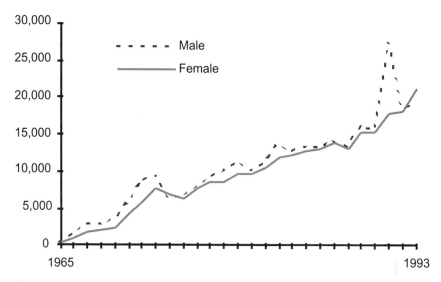

Fig. 6. Indian immigration to the United States, by sex, 1964–1993

SOURCE: Immigration and Naturalization Service Annual Reports, "Immigrants Admitted by Country or Region of Birth, Sex and Age." For exact number of male and female immigrants admitted by year, see Padma Rangaswamy, "The Imperatives of Choice and Change: Post-1965 Immigrants from India in Metropolitan Chicago," (Ph.D. diss., University of Illinois at Chicago, 1996), table 15, 520.

Indian men. Newly married wives of immigrants are forced to wait for long periods in India while their visa applications are processed. The result is that many men with training visas go home for a quick "arranged" marriage *before* they become eligible for green cards just so they will be able to bring their wives back with them. Most of the men and women were in the 20–39 age category, though their numbers have been declining in recent years as a percentage of total immigration. By contrast, the elderly population among the Indian immigrants has grown significantly as more and more parents of the earlier immigrants come to join their children in the United States.

Tables 2, 3, and 4 show select social and economic characteristics for Indians in the United States. Table 2, reproduced from *We, the American Asians*, compares how Indians stand in relation to other Asian groups and the general population in the 1990 Census. Table 3 compares figures from the 1980 and 1990 censuses that highlight some of the changes that have taken place in the profile of the Indian population over the course of the decade. Table 4 shows similar characteristics but only for the foreign-born population. This population has been divided by the census between those

Table 2 Selected social and economic characteristics for the Asian population, 1990

Characteristics	United States	Asian and Pacific Islander	Asian											
			Total	Chinese	Filipino	Japanese	Korean	Asian Indian	Vietnamese	Cambodian	Laotian	Hmong	Thai	Other
TOTAL PERSONS	248,709,873	7,273,662	6,908,638	1,645,472	1,406,770	847,562	798,849	815,447	614,547	147,411	149,014	90,082	91,275	302,209
AGE AND SEX														
Percentage under 5 years old	7.4	8.1	8.0	6.7	7.3	5.6	8.8	8.5	8.6	13.4	11.5	21.7	5.3	11.8
Percentage 18 years and older	74.4	71.4	71.8	76.5	72.6	81.5	69.1	70.0	65.9	52.7	54.9	38.7	75.0	64.5
Percentage 65 years and older	12.6	6.2	6.4	8.1	7.4	12.5	4.4	2.8	2.9	2.5	2.5	2.8	1.6	2.6
Median age	32.9	29.8	30.1	32.1	31.1	36.3	29.1	28.9	25.2	19.4	20.4	12.5	31.8	24.5
Males per 100 females	95.1	95.8	95.5	99.6	86.0	85.0	79.5	116.0	112.4	94.7	107.0	103.8	70.0	118.6
TYPE OF FAMILY														
Number of families	64,517,947	1,559,043	1,486,349	381,403	287,539	202,954	161,645	193,379	119,466	27,104	27,973	13,352	16,451	55,083
Percentage married couple families	78.6	81.2	81.6	83.9	78.3	83.1	83.4	89.2	70.6	67.2	80.5	83.4	72.6	78.5
Percentage female householder, no husband present	16.5	12.2	11.9	9.9	15.4	12.3	11.6	5.2	16.2	26.2	12.1	12.8	19.7	11.3
Percentage male householder, no wife present	4.9	6.6	6.5	6.2	6.3	4.6	5.1	5.6	13.2	6.6	7.5	3.8	7.7	10.1
Average number persons per family	3.16	3.80	3.79	3.62	4.02	3.09	3.60	3.83	4.36	5.03	5.01	6.58	3.48	3.75
NATIVITY, CITIZENSHIP, YEAR OF ENTRY, AND LANGUAGE														
Number of foreign-born persons	19,767,316	4,558,744	4,513,347	1,142,580	913,723	280,686	579,273	593,423	473,853	117,857	116,981	61,574	69,975	164,422
Percentage foreign-born	7.9	63.1	65.6	69.3	64.4	32.4	72.7	75.4	79.9	79.1	79.4	65.2	75.5	58.2
Percentage naturalized citizen	40.5	40.2	40.2	43.4	53.8	25.7	40.1	34.3	42.2	17.1	17.3	9.2	31.0	30.6
Percentage year of entry														
1980–90	43.8	57.5	57.6	56.8	49.1	54.6	56.4	58.2	61.8	88.1	79.5	75.9	42.6	65.9
1975–79	13.9	18.7	18.7	16.5	17.2	7.0	21.1	18.1	33.9	10.3	19.4	23.5	21.5	13.7
Before 1975	42.2	23.8	23.8	26.7	33.7	38.3	22.5	23.7	4.4	1.6	1.1	0.6	35.9	20.4
Number of persons in United States 5 years old and over	230,445,777	6,652,553	6,338,574	1,540,235	1,317,163	818,974	727,164	721,675	544,089	129,366	130,303	73,808	86,679	249,118
Percentage speak language other than English at home	13.8	73.3	75.4	84.0	68.4	44.0	81.6	77.8	93.8	96.0	96.8	97.4	80.1	67.6
Number speak API language at home	4,471,621	4,209,443	4,131,341	1,276,182	868,945	350,898	587,345	104,948	503,135	122,868	124,604	71,550	68,561	52,305

Percentage speak API language at home	1.9	63.3	65.2	82.9	66.0	42.8	80.8	14.5	92.5	95.0	95.6	96.9	79.1	21.0
Do not speak English "very well"	54.1	55.6	56.0	60.4	35.6	57.7	63.5	31.0	65.0	73.2	70.2	78.1	58.0	49.9
Linguistically isolated household	33.0	34.4	34.9	40.3	13.0	33.0	41.4	17.2	43.9	56.1	52.4	60.5	31.8	30.2
EDUCATIONAL ATTAINMENT														
Number of persons 25 years old and over	158,868,436	4,316,366	4,140,345	1,076,701	865,308	626,402	455,520	464,190	303,841	61,464	62,521	27,216	57,964	139,218
Percentage high school graduate	75.2	77.5	77.6	73.6	82.6	87.5	80.2	84.7	61.2	34.9	40.0	31.1	74.0	82.7
Percentage bachelor's degree or higher	20.3	36.6	37.7	40.7	39.3	34.5	34.5	58.1	17.4	5.7	5.4	4.9	32.8	41.7
Number of females 25 years old and over	83,654,171	2,282,675	2,194,033	551,414	492,955	350,125	269,165	207,657	146,899	33,463	29,888	14,078	37,699	60,690
Percentage high school graduate or higher	74.8	74.0	73.9	70.2	81.4	85.6	74.1	79.0	53.3	25.3	29.8	19.0	66.2	78.7
Percentage bachelor's degree or higher	17.6	31.8	32.7	35.0	41.6	28.2	25.9	48.7	12.2	3.2	3.5	3.0	24.9	34.2
LABOR FORCE STATUS														
Number of persons 16 years and over	191,829,271	5,403,615	5,167,530	1,309,042	1,078,817	724,683	579,867	576,157	423,121	85,500	87,683	40,649	71,907	190,104
Number in labor force	125,182,378	3,645,946	3,480,409	863,285	813,766	467,346	367,146	416,404	273,098	39,793	50,869	11,923	51,359	125,420
Percentage in labor force	65.3	67.5	67.4	65.9	75.4	64.5	63.3	72.3	64.5	46.5	58.0	29.3	71.4	66.0
Number in civilian labor force	123,473,450	3,603,080	3,444,188	860,688	790,869	463,770	364,680	415,346	271,587	39,704	50,703	11,890	50,717	124,234
Percentage unemployed	6.3	5.3	5.2	4.7	5.1	2.5	5.2	5.6	8.4	10.3	9.3	17.9	5.3	6.8
Number of females 16 years and over	99,803,358	2,810,588	2,692,480	664,384	599,208	399,585	333,225	260,532	199,310	45,754	42,044	20,265	44,917	83,256
Number in labor force	56,672,949	1,688,145	1,614,323	393,077	433,262	221,857	185,078	152,718	111,282	17,080	20,799	4,039	30,268	44,863
Percentage in labor force	56.8	60.1	60.0	59.2	72.3	55.5	55.5	58.6	55.8	37.3	49.5	19.9	67.4	53.9
Number in civilian labor force	56,487,249	1,684,082	1,610,906	392,696	431,564	221,299	184,719	152,621	111,170	17,080	20,786	4,039	30,201	44,731
Percentage unemployed	6.2	5.5	5.5	5.0	4.7	2.7	6.1	7.6	8.9	9.9	9.3	19.0	6.2	7.7
OCCUPATION														
Number of employed persons 16 years old and over	115,681,202	3,411,586	3,264,268	819,932	750,613	452,005	345,655	391,949	248,881	35,623	46,010	9,756	48,028	115,816
Percentage managerial and professional specialty	26.4	30.6	31.2	35.8	26.6	37.0	25.5	43.6	17.6	9.8	5.0	12.8	23.6	31.9
Percentage technical, sales, and administrative support	31.7	33.2	33.3	31.2	36.7	34.4	37.1	33.2	29.5	23.3	15.2	18.9	26.5	33.6
Percentage service	13.2	14.8	14.6	16.5	16.8	11.1	15.1	8.1	15.0	17.9	14.6	20.0	26.8	14.0

Table 2 (Continued) Selected social and economic characteristics for the Asian population, 1990

Characteristics	United States	Asian and Pacific Islander	Asian											
			Total	Chinese	Filipino	Japanese	Korean	Asian Indian	Vietnamese	Cambodian	Laotian	Hmong	Thai	Other
Percentage farming, forestry, and fishing	2.5	1.2	1.1	0.4	1.5	2.7	0.7	0.6	1.4	1.7	1.5	2.3	0.7	0.8
Percentage precision production, crafts, and repair	11.3	8.0	7.8	5.6	7.4	7.8	8.9	5.2	15.7	17.2	19.8	13.9	7.5	7.3
Percentage operators, fabricators, and laborers	14.9	12.1	11.9	10.6	11.0	6.9	12.8	9.4	20.9	30.0	43.9	32.1	15.0	12.4
WORKERS IN FAMILY IN 1989														
Number of families	65,049,428	1,577,820	1,506,724	398,818	293,229	208,165	163,149	192,836	118,309	28,185	28,592	14,374	16,710	53,357
Percentage no workers	13.0	8.3	8.3	7.9	4.1	8.7	7.6	2.8	13.6	38.1	26.7	49.9	5.0	7.7
Percentage 1 worker	28.0	26.2	26.2	25.5	18.1	33.2	31.8	27.7	25.1	20.7	18.7	28.0	26.2	34.5
Percentage 2 workers	45.6	45.7	45.7	47.6	48.2	42.9	44.8	51.8	40.0	27.7	35.7	15.4	53.3	43.4
Percentage 3 or more workers	13.4	19.8	19.8	19.0	29.6	15.3	15.9	17.8	21.3	13.5	18.9	6.7	15.5	14.4
INCOME IN 1989														
Median household (dollars)	30,056	36,784	37,007	36,259	43,780	41,626	30,184	44,696	29,772	18,837	23,019	14,276	31,632	30,010
Median family (dollars)	35,225	41,251	41,583	41,316	46,698	51,550	33,909	49,309	30,550	18,126	23,101	14,327	37,257	34,242
Per capita (dollars)	14,143	13,638	13,806	14,876	13,616	19,373	11,177	17,777	9,032	5,120	5,597	2,692	11,970	11,000
Number of families in poverty	6,487,515	182,507	171,816	43,184	15,267	7,131	24,037	13,964	28,131	11,872	9,207	8,885	1,806	8,332
Percentage of families in poverty	10.0	11.6	11.4	11.1	5.2	3.4	14.7	7.2	23.8	42.1	32.2	61.8	10.8	15.6
Number of persons in poverty	31,742,864	997,196	938,930	225,777	89,081	59,127	106,822	74,972	149,567	62,312	50,580	59,530	11,178	49,984
Percentage of persons in poverty	13.1	14.1	14.0	14.0	6.4	7.0	13.7	9.7	25.7	42.6	34.7	63.6	12.5	18.2

SOURCE: *We, the American Asians*, U.S. Census Bureau, 1993.

NOTE: Data for total persons, age, sex, type of family, occupation, and workers in family (1989) are based on 100 percent tabulations. Remaining data are based on sample tabulations.

who came before 1980 and those who came between 1980 and 1990. The advantage of looking at both sets of figures is that we can see the fine variations in the two sets of immigrant populations as well as understand how they contribute to the makeup of the overall Indian population in the United States that includes the 25 percent native-born. (The native-born, of course, are still mostly under twenty-five years of age and do not affect the labor and income statistics.)

In 1990, an overwhelming majority (89 percent) of Indians were "married-couple" families (with both husband and wife present in household), higher than for any other Asian group. Indians also had the lowest percentage of families with a female head of household and no husband present. This figure was 5 percent, and less than half the average Asian figure of 12 percent. Most of the population under eighteen lived with both parents, signifying a stable and secure family environment.[38] The average family size was 3.8 persons per household. This, of course, is in strong contrast to the high fertility of Indians in some parts of India, and is a result of the selective nature of the immigration process. Indians in the United States reflect the impact of class and education rather than ethnicity or national origin in their fertility rates.[39]

The naturalization rate of Indians in the 1990 Census was 34.3 percent, lower than the total Asian figure of 40.2 percent. But studies of Indians in the 1970s show that that they were naturalized at a much higher rate. Between 1969 and 1978, Indians had the highest rate of naturalization (81 percent) among all the Asian American groups.[40] This must not be attributed to a desire to break with the past or embrace "Americanization," though it does indicate a desire to enter American life as full participants. It is also a strategy to facilitate chain migration and bring in more and more relatives as fast as possible.

Indian immigrants put down roots quickly and, while maintaining contact with India, started to think of how their lives in the United States could be shaped anew. Bringing over more and more relatives was one way to transplant more of the world of origin. Taking full advantage of the family reunification clause in the immigration legislation that favored the immigration of spouses, children, brothers, and sisters in an elaborate system of preferences, many Indians sponsored their less educated relatives, who in turn sponsored more kith and kin in an extended chain of immigration that soon swelled the numbers and introduced an unexpected diversity to the immigrant population.[41] Between 1980 and 1990, the average percentage of immigrants admitted under "Relative Preferences" was 82 percent, with the percentages ranging from 76 percent to 86 percent.

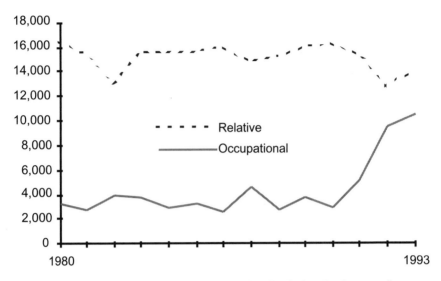

Fig. 7. Indian immigrants admitted under "Relative Preferences" versus "Occupational Preferences," 1980–1993

SOURCE: Immigration and Naturalization Service Annual Reports, "Immigrants Admitted by Class of Admission and Region and Selected Foreign State Of Chargeability under the Preference Categories Numerical Limitation," tables 5 and 6.
For years 1982–83, table IMM 2.1.
For exact number of immigrants admitted under "Relative" and "Occupational" Preferences, see Padma Rangaswamy, "The Imperatives of Choice and Change: Post-1965 Immigrants from India in Metropolitan Chicago" (Ph.D. diss., University of Illinois at Chicago, 1996), table 21, 529.

In the 1990s, these figures have dropped considerably while the percentage of those admitted under "Occupational Preferences" has increased. This suggests that the trend of the 1980s may be reversed as Indian professionals are once again being admitted in larger numbers than family members.

Educational and Occupational Diversification

The drop in educational levels among the late-arriving immigrant Indians has already been documented, even though it is a recent phenomenon.[42] More and more of those who came in under the family preference system were lesser educated brothers and sisters, sons and daughters of the earlier group and since they didn't qualify to come in as professionals in their own right, they had to depend on their relatives to sponsor them. Some of these Indians started to show up at checkout counters of grocery and department stores or in factories doing assembly line work.[43] Whereas the first Indian immigrants had worked only in the more exclusive professional occupations in medicine, science, and engineering, the newer Indians moved into the small business sector, opening up grocery stores, travel agencies, sari shops, and restaurants. Once the Indian community became large enough in a city, it could support fully its own stores, restaurants, and entertainment. Even those who were well-educated wound up in the small business sector, simply because the economy in the late 1980s couldn't offer them the same job opportunities that the previous immigrants had found or because they were discriminated against by their employers. According to the 1990 Census, one in every twelve Indians lives in poverty and 20 percent of those who arrived in the United States between 1987 and 1990 are struggling to survive.[44]

The level of "professional, technical, and kindred workers" reached a peak of 91 percent in 1971 and has been declining since then. However, the rise in employment-based preferences for the years 1992 and 1993 suggests that earlier trends may already be getting reversed. It seems that there is an increase once again in the early 1990s in the number of medical professionals from India, including many physical therapists. Like nursing, this is a profession in which Indian women are well-represented. Many married women in India have recently acquired professional visas and their husbands have accompanied them on the spousal visa.[45] Another field in which newer arrivals are well represented is the computer software industry. Every year, about fifteen thousand computer specialists enter the United States on three-year H-1B visas, and many eventually convert them to immigrant visas.[46]

By the mid-1980s, Indians had such an elaborate infrastructure that they could buy Indian groceries, eat in Indian restaurants, worship in Indian temples, buy Indian clothes, see Indian movies (at theaters and on video), attend Indian classical and pop music and dance concerts, and do practically anything they would be doing in India outside the work environment. This diversification represents a strategy to create a strong and sustainable subculture of Indian immigrants and is not merely an unintended consequence of sponsoring less-educated relatives. At first, many of the elite professionals decried the general lowering of economic standards in the community and bemoaned the entry of the nonprofessionals. But without

Table 3 Selected social and economic characteristics for Indians in the United States, 1980 and 1990 (includes Indians born in the United States)

	1980	1990
TOTAL PERSONS	387,223	815,447
AGE AND SEX		
Percentage under 5 years old	11.1	8.5
Percentage 18 years old and over	69.9	70.0
Percentage 65 years old and over	8.0	2.8
Median age	29.6	28.9
Males per 100 females	99.8	116.0
NATIVITY, CITIZENSHIP, AND LANGUAGE		
Percentage foreign-born	70.4	75.4
Percentage naturalized citizen	39.6	34.3
Percentage of persons 5 years old and over who speak a language other than English at home	68.9	77.8
TYPE OF FAMILY		
Number of families	97,596	193,379
Percentage married couple	91.0	89.2
Percentage female householder, no husband present	5.7	5.2
Percentage male householder, no wife present	3.4	5.6
Persons per family	3.45	3.83
EDUCATIONAL ATTAINMENT		
Number of persons 25 years old and over	238,684	464,190
Percentage high school graduates	80.1	84.7
Percentage 4 or more years of college	51.9	58.1
Number of females 25 years old and over	119,865	201,557
Percentage high school graduates	71.5	79.0
Percentage 4 or more years of college	35.5	48.7
LABOR FORCE STATUS		
Number persons 16 years old and over	278,359	576,157
In labor force	182,137	416,404
Percentage in labor force	65.4	72.3
Persons in civilian labor force	181,434	415,346
Percentage unemployed	5.8	5.6
Number females, 16 years old and over	139,653	260,532
In labor force	65,786	152,718
Percentage in labor force	47.1	58.6
In civilian labor force	65,715	152,621
Percentage unemployed	9.2	7.6
OCCUPATION		
Number employed persons 16 years old and over	170,855	391,949
Percentage managerial and professional speciality	48.5	43.6
Percentage technical, sales, and administrative support	28.0	33.2

Table 3 (Continued)   Selected social and economic characteristics for Indians in the United States, 1980 and 1990 (includes Indians born in the United States)

	1980	1990
Percentage service	7.8	8.1
Percentage farming, forestry, and fishing	0.9	0.6
Percentage precision production, craft, and repair	5.2	5.2
Percentage operators, fabricators, and laborers	9.6	9.4
	1979	**1989**
WORKERS IN FAMILY		
Number of families	97,596	192,836
Percentage with no workers	6.2	2.8
Percentage 1 worker	35.6	27.7
Percentage 2 workers	48.7	51.8
Percentage 3 or more workers	9.5	17.8
INCOME		
Median family (dollars)	24,993	49,309
Median household (dollars)	20,598	44,696
Male, 15 years and over (dollars)	15,799	N/A
Female, 15 years and over (dollars)	6,073	N/A
Per capita (dollars)	8,667	17,777
Number of families in poverty	7,188	13,964
Percentage of families in poverty	7.4	7.2
Number of persons in poverty	29,339	74,972
Percentage of persons in poverty	10.6	9.7

N/A = Data not available

SOURCES: Compiled from *We, the Asian and Pacific Islander Americans, Census Bureau, 1980. We, the American Asians*, U.S. Census Bureau, 1993.

this group of immigrants in the service sector—people like the chefs in the restaurants or the priests in the temples who provide culture-specific services, and even the travel agents who provide cut-rate fares to India, thus bringing travel within the reach of many lower-income Indians—it would not be possible for Indians to maintain their distinctly Indian lifestyle in the United States.

It is also important to note that those who came in the second wave, that is between 1980 and 1990 as recorded in the census, are not necessarily poorly educated or uneducated. Far from it. The same percentage (25 percent) have bachelor's degrees, whether they came before or after 1980 (see Table 4).

Table 4 Selected characteristics of foreign-born Indians in the United States by year of entry (excludes Indians born in the U.S.)

	Total Number	Year of Entry 1980–1990	Year of Entry Before 1980
EDUCATIONAL ATTAINMENT			
Number of persons 25 years old and over	449,495	239,014	210,481
Percentage with bachelor's degree	25%	25%	25%
Percentage master's degree	19	18	21
Percentage professional school degree	8	5	11
Percentage doctorate degree	6	4	8
Number of females 25 years old and over	200,632	108,765	91,867
Percentage with bachelor's degree	27%	25%	29%
Percentage master's degree	14	13	14
Percentage professional school degree	6	4	8
Percentage doctorate degree	2	2	2
LABOR FORCE STATUS			
Number of persons 16 years old and over	535,550	295,026	240,524
In labor force	395,734	206,178	189,556
Percentage in labor force	73.9	69.9	78.8
Civilian labor force	394,913	205,856	189,057
Percentage unemployed	5.5	6.7	4.2
Number of females, 16 years old and over	240,838	134,313	106,525
In labor force	143,481	73,038	70,443
Percentage in labor force	59.6	54.4	66.1
Civilian labor force	143,427	73,022	70,405
Percentage unemployed	7.5	9.5	5.4
OCCUPATION			
Number employed persons 16 years old and over	373,257	192,121	181,136
Percentage managerial and professional speciality	44%	35%	54%
Percentage technical, sales, and administrative support	33	36	30
Percentage service	8	10	6
Percentage farming, forestry, and fishing	1	1	1
Percentage precision production, craft, and repair	5	6	4
Percentage operators, fabricators, and laborers	9	13	6
Number employed females 16 years old and over	168,911	93,543	75,368
Percentage managerial and professional speciality	28%	20%	37%
Percentage technical, sales, and administrative support	33	30	36

Table 4 (Continued) Selected characteristics of foreign-born Indians in the United States by year of entry (excludes Indians born in the U.S.)

	Total Number	Year of Entry 1980–1990	Year of Entry Before 1980
Percentage service	9%	10%	8%
Percentage farming, forestry, and fishing	<1	<1	<1
Percentage precision production, craft, and repair	2	2	2
Percentage operators, fabricators, and laborers	7	8	5
INDUSTRY			
Number employed persons 16 years old and over	373,257	192,121	181,136
Percentage manufacturing	19%	19%	18%
Percentage retail trade	16	19	12
Percentage finance, insurance, and real estate	7	7	8
Percentage health services	16	12	21
Percentage educational services	10	12	8
	1989		
WORKERS IN FAMILY			
Number of families	187,916	83,383	104,533
Percentage no workers	3%	4%	2%
Percentage 1 worker	28	30	26
Percentage 2 workers	52	51	53
Percentage 3 or more workers	18	15	20
INCOME			
Median household income (dollars)	$45,309	$32,365	$59,976
Mean household income (dollars)	60,522	39,285	79,725
Median family income (dollars)	49,567	35,587	62,691
Mean family income (dollars)	65,725	42,665	84,119
Per capita income (dollars)	22,828	12,916	36,653
Number of families in poverty	13,372	9,637	3,755
Percentage of families in poverty	7.1	11.5	3.6
Number of persons in poverty	60,384	47,932	12,452
Percentage of persons in poverty	10.3	14.1	5.1

SOURCE: Compiled from 1990 Census of the Population, *Asians and Pacific Islanders in the United States*, tables 1–5.

Only the percentage of those holding master's, professional, or doctorate degrees (21 percent, 11 percent, and 8 percent, respectively) is higher in the "before 1980" group, than for those who came between 1980 and 1990 (18 percent, 5 percent, and 4 percent, respectively). In fact, the number of educated Indians is so astonishingly high that there is no fear of the Indian immigrant community losing its edge over other groups in this respect, at least in the near future. But a Bachelor's degree from an Indian university does not necessarily help the immigrant in the job market, which is why many Indians educated in India remain in the nonprofessional sector of the economy.

One change worth noting is that the number of Indian women with four or more years of college went up from 35.5 percent in the 1980 Census to 48.7 percent in the 1990 Census (see Table 3). Fifty-three percent of the immigrant women who came before 1980 had a Bachelor's degree or higher (29 percent Bachelor's, 14 percent Master's, 8 percent professional school, and 2 percent Doctorate), whereas only 44 percent of those who came between 1980 and 1990 had the same qualification (25 percent Bachelor's, 13 percent Master's, 4 percent professional school, and 2 percent Doctorate) (see Table 4). This could mean that many of the women from the 1980 Census acquired higher degrees during the course of their stay in the United States and thus contributed to the higher figure in the 1990 Census. The emphasis that middle- and upper-class Indians put on education and the selective nature of the immigration process both combined to give Indians the position of being *the* most highly educated group in the United States.

In the late 1980s, more and more entering immigrants were listed in the immigration records as having "no occupation." This does not necessarily mean they had no formal education. Together, the top "managerial and professional" and the second-level "technical, sales, and administrative support" categories still accounted for 71 percent of workers among those who entered between 1980 and 1990. For those who entered before 1980, the figure was significantly higher at 84 percent (see Table 4). Even in the 1990 Census, Indians still had the highest percentage of workers in the "managerial and professional category" (44 percent) among all Asian groups (see Table 2). Thus the comparative drop in occupational levels does not mean that a once economically and occupationally privileged community has turned into a blue-collar workforce.

Indians also had one of the highest levels of participation in the labor force in 1990, 72 percent compared with 65 percent of all Americans (see

Table 2). Asian Indian men had the largest participation rate of 84 percent. More Indian families (18 percent) had three or more members in the work-force than the general population (13 percent), but the figure was not as high as it was for the general Asian population. at 20 percent. What is inter-esting is that the figure has almost doubled from the 10 percent figure reported in the 1980 Census. Does this mean that Indian families are now beginning to conform to the immigrant stereotype where more and more family members join the "family business" and work long hours without pay? Not necessarily. Table 4 reveals that the growth in the "three or more work-ers" category actually occurred in the families of those who entered *before* 1980. This usually means that in these longer-established families, the chil-dren have become income-earning adults but are still living at home. The changing demographics thus reflect the changes in the lives of Indians in the intervening years, but do not allow ready assumptions about what these figures mean without reference to other factors and supplementary data.

Both the higher educational achievements and the greater number of family members in the workforce translate into higher income for Indians. Their per capita income in 1990 was $17,777, second only to that of the Japanese and much higher than the national figure of $14,143 (see Table 2). The per capita income for the foreign-born Indians is even higher at $22,828 (see Table 4). Again, there is a wide discrepancy between the figure for those who came before 1980 ($36,653) and those who came between 1980 and 1990 ($12, 916). The newly arrived immigrants are still working to secure a firm foothold in the economy.

It is, however, difficult to estimate whether the higher income for Indians, as compared to the general population, represents a fair reward for their higher education and greater skills. Some Indians assert that they have to work a lot harder and be much more highly educated for only a small increase in income, and that, compared to white Americans with the same education, they don't do well enough.[47] Statistics also show that Asian and Pacific Islander American males with four or more years of college earned less than their white counterparts. In the case of females, there was no such gap. Indeed, Asian females with higher education were likely to receive mar-ginally greater earnings than white females.[48]

Poverty rates for Indian persons, at 10 percent, is still among the lowest for all Asian groups and lower than the 13 percent for the entire nation (see Table 2). As expected, the poverty rate for the immigrants who arrived before 1980 is much lower, at 5.1 percent, than for those who came between 1980 and 1990 (14.1 percent) (see Table 4).

On the whole, the changes in the profile of the Indian immigrants between the 1980 and 1990 Census can be attributed in large part to the influx of the new immigrants, since they comprise almost 44 percent of the total Indian population in the United States.[49] The majority of these immigrants were also brought here in a conscious act of affirmation by the earlier immigrants, since most of them were family sponsored. In the act of bringing in their relatives (and indirectly, their culture and their Indian lifestyle), Indian immigrants showed what it was they held to be most important in their lives in the United States.

The contrasts between the turn-of-the-century and the post-1965 Indian immigrations to the United States bring home the importance of the historical context in understanding the immigrant experience. Changing historical contexts give immigrants new options based on something more than their ethnicity or a common land of origin. For the post-1965 immigrants, some of the most important options came from the freedom they enjoyed to choose their settlement patterns, the high economic value placed by the United States on their educational level and professional skills, and their ability to bring their families over from India. These options determined the socioeconomic characteristics of the Indian immigrant community and influenced the quality of life in the United States. It enabled them to avoid the ethnic clustering or ghettoization generally associated with at least the first phase of immigration for most immigrant groups, to bypass the slow and often agonizing transitional phase to economic prosperity; and to employ family reunification strategies that have yielded rich dividends in the form of a diverse, vibrant and interlinked national community of Asian Indians.

By 1995, the immigration laws in force came to be challenged. The Report of the U.S. Commission on Immigration Reform recommended drastic cuts in immigration and elimination of many of the family preferences under which Indians came in such large numbers. This will no doubt influence the dynamics of community development for Indians, but whatever the future holds for them, their numbers in the United States had already become sufficient for them to build a strong and solid foundation for the development and sustenance of a distinct "Indian American" subculture. They had also become significant enough for the "study of Indian immigrants and their offspring" to become "a necessary prerequisite to the proper study of America."[50]

PART II

The Chicago Community

3

THE ATTRACTION OF A
METROPOLITAN REGION

The social divisions and geographical dispersion of Chicago's
population along both class and ethnic lines has been a persistent
feature of the city. . . . Although (these) neighborhoods no longer
have the concentrations of people sharing a single national background that they once had, the identity of a culture with a place
continues to be important and celebrated.
—Gregory D. Squires, Larry Bennett, Kathleen McCout, and
Philip Nyden, *Chicago: Race, Class, and the Response to Urban Decline*

The early Indian immigrants to Chicago knew precious little about the city
before they got there. If they thought of it at all, it was as gangsterland, the
home of Al Capone. They knew nothing about its brash and gritty character,
its business, its politics, its neighborhoods. But it took them only a few years
to learn that, in order to be successful here, they would have to aggressively
seize the opportunities and challenges that the city offered to newcomers.
Gradually, they began to feel comfortable in an environment where people
spoke the world's many languages and belonged to several faiths. They began
to appreciate the city's peculiar combination of Midwest conservatism and
commercial opportunism until finally, they learned to call it home.[1]

The labels that the city has acquired over the years became more than just
that to the Indians, they were felt experiences. Indians knew that the
"Windy City" could send them scurrying for shelter in high winds and harsh
temperatures of ten below zero. A very few even learned that the city got its
name from its "windbag" citizens who were given to bragging about Chicago,
when it was first incorporated as a town with a population of about 350 in
1833, and experienced a spectacular climb to one of the world's great metropolises. On their visits to India, Indians themselves boasted about their city
that had the world's tallest building and the world's busiest airport. They

could also vouch for the fact that Chicago is the "City that Works." Businessmen on Devon Avenue learned that they could go to their alderman and get redress for their grievances, whether they related to parking problems or vandalism. They knew that "Machine Politics" did not die with Mayor Richard J. Daley and they would have to learn to work the system if they wanted fair representation for their own community. So they decked Mayor Jane Bryne in a sari, applauded Mayor Harold Washington when he appointed the first Indian on his Asian Advisory Council, and cultivated Mayor Richard M. Daley the son just as much as they had Richard J. Daley the father by contributing to Democratic coffers and working with other Asian groups to deliver the Democratic vote.

When Indians laid claim to the shops on Devon Avenue, they learned firsthand that Chicago was a "City of Neighborhoods," where ethnic groups jealously guarded their turf, and could intimidate and threaten those who dared to cross designated boundaries. However, amidst all the rivalry and competition, Chicago was also a "City of Festivals," whose citizens were happy to eventually recognize "Indiatown" and join in the celebration of Dussehra and Divali on the streets of Devon and in the temples scattered throughout the metro region. Chicago was the "International" city for Indians, thanks to the variety of other immigrants who had settled here over the years. There are at least thirty-three ethnic communities described in a handbook on Chicago's diverse cultures, and this did not include many groups such as the Pakistanis and the Bangladeshis.[2] There was always a model to follow for a national or ethnic celebration, whether it was a St. Patrick's Day parade on Michigan Avenue or a Chinese New Year's Day parade in Chinatown. Never mind the "Second City" label. Sure, Chicago didn't have as many Indians as New York or New Jersey, but neither did it have the problems associated with ethnic clustering and ghettoization. The "City of Big Shoulders" could carry its Indian population and recompense them for their hard work and struggles just as well as any other city in the world.

One area in which identification with the city is particularly powerful for Indians, at least among the professionals who came soon after 1965 and their teenage children, is sports. Indians, no less than other Chicagoans, love to watch Michael Jordan, tongue out, leap to the hoop in a soaring symbol of Chicago itself. They thrilled to the one and only Super Bowl victory that the Bears ever achieved in 1986 and sank into deep depression when the team started sliding downhill. Ultimately, Indians became Chicagoans because the city itself gave them so many good reasons to identify with it. They felt that the city embraced them, just as it had embraced its other ethnic populations such as the Irish, the Germans, and the Poles, all of whom thrive and struggle here just as the Indians do, and continue to celebrate their individual cultures long after they ceased to interact with the homeland. But Indians are also part of the hurly-burly of Chicago life, victims of the violent crimes that rock its neighborhoods, caught in the corruption and cronyism of its politicians, and sometimes crushed in the ruthlessness of its competitiveness. Any celebration of ethnicity in Chicago has to go hand in hand with an acknowledgment of the prejudices directed against immigrants and the odds they have to overcome in order to survive. Ultimately, Indians kept coming to Chicago because of its geographical location in the heart of the country, its excellent transportation hub, its fine educational and medical institutions, its research laboratories, its banking and insurance industries, its access to markets, and the multinational firms headquartered there. Thanks to this broad and diversified economic base, Indians knew they could find a job in Chicago even if they couldn't find one in Detroit or Pittsburgh or St. Louis. And even those who didn't necessarily identify with the "spirit" of Chicago or its neighborhoods or sports teams or politics still appreciated the economic opportunities here and the chance it afforded its new immigrants to make a living.

For many of Chicago's Indian immigrants, this city was not their first introduction to the United States. Before becoming immigrants bound for Chicago, many Indians had made earlier visits on business, visitor, or student visas. Intercity migration is also common among Indians, many of whom had lived in other parts of the United States before deciding to take up residence in Chicago. Some of them had landed in New York or San Francisco (which were the major ports of entry) or one of the other coastal cities before they found their way to Chicago either by air or by road. Most came via New York because that was the most economical route from India. Whichever mode of transportation they took, their first impression of Chicago could not have been particularly comforting or reassuring. The city's physical appearance suggested a tough and dirty town. If one came up around the south bend of the lake by road from the east, the dreary sight of a gray and ghostly silhouette, and the acrid smell of smokestacks were depressing enough to send a pang of longing in any would-be immigrant's heart for the vibrant atmosphere and teeming humanity of a Delhi bazaar. As one turned the bend and passed through the tangle of expressways ribboning their way around the Chicago Skyway, one became uneasily aware of the sheer size and urban sprawl of a modern metropolis. Out in the distance, the murky, smog filled-air hid the true contours of a giant city. And then it

hit you—the first impact of an awesome cityscape. The imposing craggy sky-
line set against the blue-green-gray waters of Lake Michigan conveyed an
unmistakable picture of commercial might. But then again, as you neared
central Chicago, the lakefront sent out mixed signals. On the one hand were
the decaying factories and weedy lots by the railroad yards clearly visible on
the near South Side. As one traveled further north, the stately museum
buildings, the sailboats on the lake, and the apartment buildings of the Gold
Coast suggested European-style elegance. It would soon become apparent
that Chicago was a city of contrasts and extremes, and as immigrants, Indians
would have to find their own space in it.

The most common approach for Indian immigrants was, of course,
O'Hare International airport. Those immigrants who landed there by night
possibly marveled at the array of twinkling city lights and diamond-studded
expressways. But for many other worldly types who had already stopped over
in London or Paris or Rome en route from India or lived in other grand cities
of the world, Chicago would not have struck them as particularly grandiose
or magnificent. It takes a long time to learn to love (or hate) a city like
Chicago, and for Indian immigrants, the process had just begun. The same
old magnet that had drawn fur trappers and traders in the late eighteenth
century and merchants and fortune-seekers throughout the nineteenth also
lured the Indian professionals and entrepreneurs in the twentieth century.
The engineers and doctors and scientists who came from India in the early
wave in the late 1960s and the 1970s hoped that corporate America had a
place for them in Chicago. The Midwest still had a strong manufacturing
base, it was poised as a springboard for industrial and scientific research,
and the transition to a service and information-oriented economy had not
yet taken place. The professional and technical skills that Indians had
acquired back home were very much in demand in this city. It enabled them
to fit right in and move along without even being noticed by the rest of the
population until their numbers swelled to noticeable proportions in the
1980s and 1990s.

"Indian Immigrants" and "Chicago"

Perhaps it is necessary to clarify which immigrants and which Chicago are
included in the term "Indian immigrants of Chicago." Indian immigrants
means immigrants from India alone, not those from other South Asian

countries, whose experiences are likely to be somewhat similar to those of Indians but also to differ in significant ways, based on cultural dissimilarities and political ideologies. There are many references to the "Indo-Pak" community as though they were one community, especially on store signs in Chicago, or in the ethnic newspapers, and radio and television programs that cater to both nationalities. (There is no great bonding between the two communities who live separate but peacefully coexistent lives in Chicago.) It is also very difficult to distinguish, based on outward appearance alone, between Indians and others of South Asian origin, such as the Pakistanis, Bangladeshis, or Sri Lankans. But the U.S. Census does differentiate between the different South Asian groups. The 1990 Census shows that the Pakistanis in Illinois numbered less than ten thousand, while all other Asians including those differentiated by nationality numbered less than eight thousand. Indians thus account for 80 percent of all South Asians in Illinois.[3] Many of the services provided by the Indian community organizations may be used by other South Asians also, and vice versa. They also have much in common with one other and these commonalties do set them apart from the larger American community. But the Indian immigrant experience as described here does not necessarily encompass the experience of all other South Asians.

A second point that needs clarification is the use of the word "Chicago" in this study. The sentiments expressed by other chroniclers of the city fit in so well with the Indian immigrants' understanding of the term "Chicago" that it is worth quoting them at some length.

> We mean by Chicago the entire metropolitan area, not simply the legal municipal unit. The modern metropolis, with its central city, suburbs, and "satellite cities," is a single historic and geographic entity. Today, it is politically fragmented, but in every other way it constitutes a functional unit. All of its parts grew out of the same historical roots; its present problems and prospects are interwoven; and all of its people will share a common future. At a time when so many see only a city divided between suburb and central core, or between black and white, the historian and geographer feel it is important to emphasize the shared heritage of all who live in "Chicago."[4]

Indian immigrants, whether city dwellers or suburbanites, also mean the entire metropolitan area when they talk of Chicago to outsiders. When they go back to India to visit, they refer to their home in the United States as

"Chicago." They may live in Oakbrook or Hoffman Estates but when they introduce themselves to people in Atlanta or New York or Los Angeles, they call themselves Chicagoans, not only because no one ever heard of Oakbrook but because their lives are so closely bound up with Chicago that it remains the source of their geographic identity. They may live in the city and work in the suburbs or vice versa. Even if they live *and* work in the suburbs, they come to the city for recreation and entertainment, whether it is a trip to Devon Avenue for grocery and sari shopping or a weekend trip to the museums and Water Tower Place. Indian community organizations draw their membership from the entire metropolitan area, which includes Chicago and its suburbs. This kind of suburban identification with the city does not necessarily apply to Indians in other parts of the United States, such as Los Angeles and New York. Given the immense sprawl of the Chicago metropolitan area, however, and the wide scattering of Indians, there is some segmentation between the northern and western suburbs.

This, however, does not mean that there is no difference between the Indians who live in the city and those who live in the suburbs. There is an ongoing dichotomy between the city and its suburbs that is reflected in politics, in business and industry, in racial and class divisions, and the Indians who live in the area cannot fail to be affected by it. One needs to distinguish between Indians who live in Chicago and those who live in the suburbs because there are marked differences in their income, lifestyle, schooling or residential patterns, but it must also be recognized that they are interconnected and integrated into a larger whole in a way that makes them all "Chicagoans."

Illinois Demographics

According to the 1990 Census, Indian immigrants comprise 5.3 percent of all immigrants in Illinois. Of all the Indians in Illinois, 97 percent live "inside a metro area," less than 1 percent live in a rural area, and 92 percent (89 percent in 1980) live in Chicago and its suburbs.[5] Table 5 shows the differential rate of growth of the Indian population among the six different counties in the Chicago area as well as the increase in Chicago and the suburbs between 1980 and 1990.

Table 5 Distribution of Indians by county in the six-county Chicago Metropolitan Area

	1980	1990	Growth Rate (%)
Counties			
Cook	23,062	39,225	+ 70
Du Page	6,381	14,172	+122
Kane	510	754	+ 48
Lake	1,012	2,257	+123
McHenry	130	305	+135
Will	763	1,279	+ 68
Total	31,858	57,992	+ 82
Chicago	11,209	16,386	+ 46
Suburbs	20,649	41,606	+102

SOURCES: 1990 Census of the Population, General Population Characteristics, Illinois, table 5; 1980 Census of the Population, table 15.

The Indian population in Chicago increased by only 46 percent while that in the suburbs went up by 102 percent. There are two and a half times as many Indians in the suburbs as there are in Chicago. Du Page County, which has a concentration of some of the wealthiest suburbs in the state, has seen more than a doubling of its Indian population, as have Lake and McHenry counties. These two counties, however, account for less than 2 percent of the Illinois Indian population, while Du Page has almost a quarter (23 percent) of the Indians in Illinois.

In Chicago, as elsewhere in the United States, Indians are perceived primarily as part of the Asian subgroup. The growth of the Indian population is usually taken note of as part of the growth of the Asian population. Indians represent 17 percent of all Asians in Chicago, 30 percent of all Asians in the suburbs, and 25 percent of all Asians in the metropolitan region. Indians are more numerous than any of the other Asian groups in the suburbs (Fig. 8). Chicago's City Hall and the state government in Springfield, tend to group all Asians under the larger umbrella of "Asian Americans." Since their own numbers are so small, Indians can claim their fair share of representation only by aligning themselves with the other Asian groups.

Table 6 shows that Indians are located in almost every suburb, and also that their population has increased dramatically in many of the north, northwest, and western suburbs. The suburbs that have registered the greatest economic growth are the same ones that have seen the most dramatic increase in their Indian immigrant population (see Figs. 9 and 10 for graphic representation of population distribution of Indians in Chicago and suburbs). The settlement of Indians all over the northwest and western suburbs, and the comparative lack of settlement in the southern suburbs is closely tied to the economic opportunities available to them in these areas.

It therefore becomes necessary to understand the economic conditions prevalent in Chicago at the time when Indian immigration started in order to see what choices were available to them and why they chose to settle in specific areas and not in others.

Economic Prospects

A brief overview of the changing conditions in Chicago from the mid-1960s to the present provides a framework for examining the Indian immigrants' responses to their particular situation. When the Indians arrived in Chicago, they found a city in transition. The postwar industrial prosperity of Chicago, fueled by the national surge in construction and manufacture of consumer goods, had peaked. Two different kinds of change were taking place that affected the professional Indians and influenced their employment and settlement patterns. One was the geographic shift from the city to the suburbs and the other was the business shift from the manufacturing to the service sector.

The first change was the shift in population from Chicago to the surrounding suburbs. Many of the industries that would employ Indian engineers and scientists had moved to the suburbs as early as the 1950s. "Lower land costs, a growing labor pool, a greatly expanded expressway system, a lower unionization rate, as well as the shifting consumer market, were all reasons why manufacturers and other businesses relocated to the new suburbs. . . . In absolute numbers, Chicago lost over 245,000 jobs in this decade (between 1970 and 1980) while the suburbs gained more than 540,000 employment slots."[6] Even though new immigrants were likely to arrive in the city and stay there for awhile until they got acclimated, they would eventually move to where the skilled jobs were located, and that was in the suburbs. Those areas that experienced the most substantial economic growth in the decade between 1970 and 1980 are the ones that also saw the highest increase in the population of Indians between 1980 and 1990, namely, northwestern Cook and Du Page counties. The band of research facilities and high-tech com-

Total Asians in the Chicago Region
 In Chicago: 95,123
 In Suburbs: 136,305
(Percentages in parenthesis represent ethnic group as percentage of total Asians in the Chicago region)

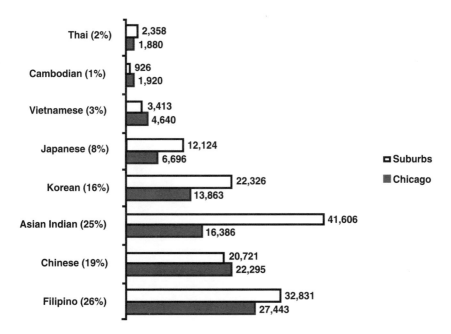

Fig. 8. Distribution of Asians in the Chicago Region, 1990

SOURCE: 1990 Census of Population Illinois, General Population Characteristics, table 6.

panies located in Du Page County, especially along the East-West Tollway on Route 88, reads like an employer's list for skilled professional Indians: AT&T, Bell Labs, Amoco Research Center, Argonne National Laboratory, and Fermi National Accelerator Laboratory. The phenomenal growth of the Indian population in Du Page County is due in part to the "230 percent increase in business establishments in Du Page County from 1965 to 1982."[7]

The other area of growth known as the "Golden Corridor" (that includes the suburbs of Elk Grove Village, Schaumburg, Rolling Meadows, Arlington Heights, Palatine, and Hoffman Estates) also saw a tremendous increase

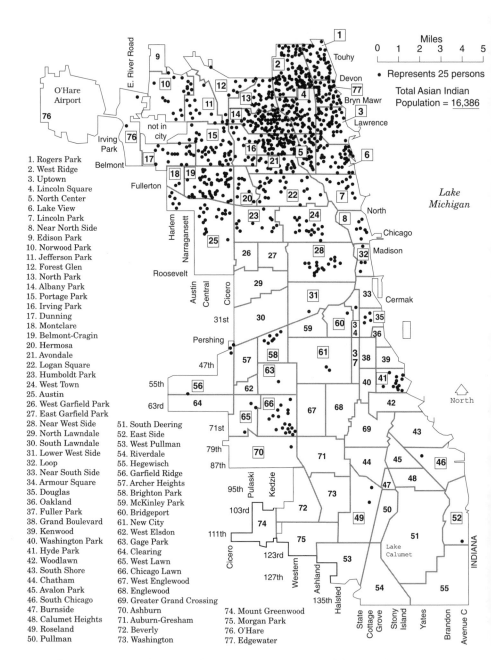

Fig. 9. Asian Indian population concentration in Chicago, 1990

Map legend and labels:

O'Hare Airport

E. River Road
Touhy
Devon
Bryn Mawr
Lawrence

• Represents 25 persons

Total Asian Indian
Population = 16,386

Irving Park
Belmont
Fullerton

not in city

Lake Michigan
Chicago
Madison
Cermak

North
North

Harlem
Narragansett
Austin
Central
Cicero
Roosevelt
31st
Pershing
47th
55th
63rd
71st
79th
87th
95th
103rd
111th
123rd
127th
135th

Pulaski
Kedzie
Cicero
Western
Ashland
Halsted
State
Cottage Grove
Stony Island
Yates
Brandon
Avenue C
INDIANA

Lake Calumet

1. Rogers Park
2. West Ridge
3. Uptown
4. Lincoln Square
5. North Center
6. Lake View
7. Lincoln Park
8. Near North Side
9. Edison Park
10. Norwood Park
11. Jefferson Park
12. Forest Glen
13. North Park
14. Albany Park
15. Portage Park
16. Irving Park
17. Dunning
18. Montclare
19. Belmont-Cragin
20. Hermosa
21. Avondale
22. Logan Square
23. Humboldt Park
24. West Town
25. Austin
26. West Garfield Park
27. East Garfield Park
28. Near West Side
29. North Lawndale
30. South Lawndale
31. Lower West Side
32. Loop
33. Near South Side
34. Armour Square
35. Douglas
36. Oakland
37. Fuller Park
38. Grand Boulevard
39. Kenwood
40. Washington Park
41. Hyde Park
42. Woodlawn
43. South Shore
44. Chatham
45. Avalon Park
46. South Chicago
47. Burnside
48. Calumet Heights
49. Roseland
50. Pullman
51. South Deering
52. East Side
53. West Pullman
54. Riverdale
55. Hegewisch
56. Garfield Ridge
57. Archer Heights
58. Brighton Park
59. McKinley Park
60. Bridgeport
61. New City
62. West Elsdon
63. Gage Park
64. Clearing
65. West Lawn
66. Chicago Lawn
67. West Englewood
68. Englewood
69. Greater Grand Crossing
70. Ashburn
71. Auburn-Gresham
72. Beverly
73. Washington
74. Mount Greenwood
75. Morgan Park
76. O'Hare
77. Edgewater

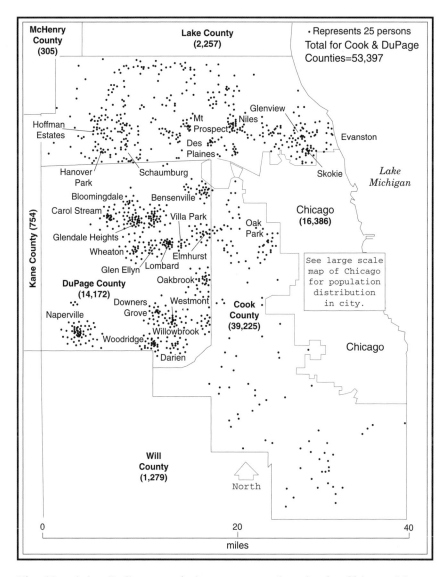

Fig. 10. Asian Indian population concentrations in the Chicago Metropolitan Area, 1990

Table 6 Population distribution of Indians in Illinois suburbs with 1990 population of more than 500 (in order of size of 1990 population)

Suburb	1990	1980	Growth Rate (%)
Skokie	2,292	880	+160
Naperville	1,468	327	+349
Hoffman Estates	1,347	497	+171
Mount Prospect	1,291	458	+182
Schaumburg	1,218	541	+125
Glendale Heights	1,177	593	+ 99
Addison	1,087	445	+144
Des Plaines	1,051	482	+118
Hanover Park	964	453	+113
Oakbrook	736	151	+387
Downers Grove	698	448	+ 56
Carol Stream	646	243	+166
Lombard	642	317	+103
Elk Grove Village	637	508	+ 25
Woodridge	637	290	+120
Evanston	632	314	+101
Morton Grove	622	223	+179
Bensenville	619	212	+192
Westmont	570	299	+ 91
Bolingbrook	566	406	+ 39
Niles	557	266	+109
Wheeling	545	150	+263
Forest Park	540	443	+ 22
Wheaton	531	261	+103
Elmhurst	504	277	+ 82

SOURCES: 1990 Census of Population, General Population Characteristics, Illinois, table 6; 1980
Census, table 15.

in employment between 1972 and 1982. The growth rate was 44 percent and
second only to Du Page, which had a 65 percent growth during the same
period. Again, many of the north and northwest suburbs such as Mount
Prospect, Schaumburg, Hoffman Estates, and Skokie registered the highest
increase in the population of Indians between the 1980 and 1990 censuses
(see Table 6). Major corporations such as Honeywell, Motorola, Western
Electric, and Siemens are located in that area. Most of the residents of this
area do not commute outside northwest Cook County for jobs, so it may be
assumed that the Indians who live in these suburbs choose to do so because
they work nearby. In contrast, those suburbs in southwestern and western

Cook County, such as Cicero, McCook, Bedford Park, Bellwood, Maywood, Melrose Park, Northlake, and River Grove, which lost jobs, do not have a significant Indian immigrant population. The wealthy suburbs of the north, such as Kenilworth, Glencoe, Winnetka, Wilmette, Highland Park, and Lake Forest, have a small but select Indian population, mostly doctors or entrepreneurs who have much higher incomes than the general Indian immigrant population.

A more recent trend in the geographical relocating process has affected Indians even more directly. New and expanding companies are now gravitating toward Asia because of the more favorable corporate environment there in the form of lower cost (and more exploitable!) labor and local government incentives to attract foreign capital. India is a major attraction because of its huge pool of skilled manpower, the newly freed market economy, and the potential consumer base in its burgeoning middle class. The flurry of activity by Chicago's business schools to introduce India as a manufacturing and consumer base is an indication of current and future trends. Northwestern's Kellogg Business School regularly conducts tours to India for its graduates, aided by immigrant Indian professionals and faculty members based in Chicago. Meanwhile, Indian immigrants in Chicago who know both the Indian and the Chicago environment intimately are seizing the opportunity to provide technical collaboration and initiate joint venture projects between the two regions.

Another noteworthy feature of the economy that affected the employment patterns of Indians is the shift in Chicago from manufacturing toward the service sector. This change hurt many of the Indian engineers who found themselves laid off *en masse* when factories shut down or relocated, such as Western Electric's Hawthorne Works Plant in Cicero. Sargent & Lundy, a consulting engineering firm that hired many Indian engineers, cut back its workforce drastically in the 1980s.[8] But the increasing orientation to nonmanufacturing sectors such as banking, finance, retail sales, insurance, and transportation has actually helped the second wave of family-sponsored Indian immigrants who did not have the skilled technical backgrounds in manufacturing that their predecessors had. They may not have been able to move as readily into the job market, but they oriented themselves to the new demands of the economy by acquiring marketing and computer-related skills, either before they left India or after arriving here. Many of them went into the retail industry that catered exclusively to ethnic populations while others opened small businesses that served the population at large. Dunkin'

Donuts franchises in the Chicago area, for instance, provide an excellent example of the Gujarati immigrants' response to the shifting economy and their ability to match their own skills with market demands. The service industry was also eminently suitable for those immigrants who started out in a modest way by serving their own community and were later able to expand to serve the larger community. Such success stories are to be found in the travel, insurance, and restaurant industries owned by Chicago's Indian immigrants and are explored in detail in Chapter 10.

Settlement Patterns

As is the case with the general population, the location in which Indians find employment has a lot to do with where they live. The settlement patterns of Indians in Chicago are particularly significant because Chicago has the reputation of being one of the most segregated cities in the United States. Any casual observer of Chicago city life can see how sharply demarcated are its neighborhoods, with one community separated from another by invisible yet effective walls of segregation. Each community has its own churches, its own civic and social institutions and its own businesses. Not only are whites segregated from blacks, European groups, too, live in fairly well-demarcated neighborhoods. There are the South Side Irish, the Milwaukee Avenue Poles, and the Hyde Park Jews.[9] The frontiers of these neighborhoods are also shifting as different groups jostle for the same space. Most Chicago neighborhoods are shared by more than one ethnic group, even as they are dominated by one ethnic group or another.[10] This is also true of "India town" on Chicago's North Side, which is shared by South Asians and Assyrians, Greeks, Russian Jews, Mexicans, and Koreans. In some cases, the boundaries are very sharp and crossed only at great peril. The African Americans who migrated from the south in the World War I era occupied the black belt on Chicago's South Side. Hemmed in on all sides by turf-conscious whites, they sought desperately to break out of the ghetto, only to be confronted by racial violence.[11] The south-side Back of the Yards was a Polish and Slavic neighborhood before it turned almost all black after World War II and then acquired a distinctly Hispanic flavor as more and more Mexicans moved in. Chicago's neighborhoods have been affected by economic forces, such as the closing down of the meat packing industry in the Back of the Yards, and the flight of industry from the city to the suburbs as well as by demographic change (such as the more recent influx of Mexicans).[12] The segregation is partly the result of the spontaneous impulse of its citizens to "live amongst their own," but is also due in part to the racist attitudes of the city's inhabitants, who have institutionalized segregation and narrowed the choices available to newcomers. Individual decisions do have a collective impact on the housing market, but it "pales in comparison to the impact of the large scale institutions whose single decisions about construction or investment can have sweeping and permanent consequences for thousands of people."[13] In Chicago, realtors and banking institutions have frequently been taken to task for "redlining" or practicing discrimination in the housing market. "Chicago style" means "suspicion toward outsiders, intolerance toward the unconventional" and a fierce guarding of neighborhood boundaries.[14]

How did Indian immigrants fit into a city whose inhabitants have always segregated themselves (or been segregated) by race and class? How did they fare in such an ethnically divided city? How did they use their own strengths and weaknesses as an immigrant group to fight the "unwelcome foreigner" syndrome? In their own unique way, it would seem—by both succumbing to the limitations of the system and rising above it. The dual pattern of settlement that Indian immigrants have followed, one within the city and another in the suburbs, is their response to the different choices available to them in two different environments. The response is also shaped by their own need as a community to develop a convenient commercial center, to develop a "neighborhood" where those who want to can gather together, and also to disperse and "merge" into the larger population in more affluent surroundings when their circumstances make it possible and desirable.[15] Differences in socioeconomic characteristics between city-dwelling Indians and the suburbanite Indians are apparent in a 1995 study on metro Chicago's immigrant community conducted by Chicago's Latino Institute and Northern Illinois University.[16] The study shows that Indians in the city have lower income, lower education, lower home ownership, and higher poverty levels than the suburbanites. Fewer of them are in professional occupations, and more of them are in sales occupations and the retail trade industry.

In the City

In a surprising number of ways, Indian immigrants in Chicago have followed the pattern set by other earlier immigrants such as the Irish, the

Germans, and the Swedes.[17] They made their first home in a "portal" neighborhood, where housing was affordable and occupied by other Indian immigrants who had arrived earlier. Sometimes three or four men, either bachelors or married men who had left their wives behind in India, would room in a two- or three-bedroom apartment. Occasionally a woman would arrive alone if she was single or divorced. Some women came with their children, leaving their husbands behind in India. For both men and women, the favorite locations for initial settlement were the mid-north and far-north areas on Broadway and Sheridan, going west along Lawrence and Devon avenues. Many Indian immigrants who went on to become vice presidents of major corporations and acquired million-dollar homes in Barrington or Oakbrook first got their start in this neighborhood. Others lived on the near West Side, or in the suburbs of Austin and Forest Park, if that was closer to the train or their workplace. But for the most part, the North Side was the first home of the newly arrived immigrants who sought out their own kind and looked for someone to show them the ropes. It was the place where they could experience the familiar while they tested the new and share their lives with others of their own class, race, ethnicity, religion, and even occupation. They could bide their time till they made enough money and plucked up enough courage to move on and strike out on their own in the suburbs.

Indian immigrants found the far North Side attractive for the same reasons as its other residents. It was a cosmopolitan urban neighborhood with a variety of other ethnic groups such as Soviet Jews, Mexicans, Vietnamese, Caribbeans, Chinese, and Koreans. Despite the diversity and the somewhat transient nature of the population, it was a stable neighborhood, with ample rental accommodation and many resident-owned small businesses, such as restaurants, shops, and services. It was well-connected to the Loop through the "L." Through the 1960s and late 1970s, it appeared that a ghetto was forming in the area, but vigorous efforts were made to attract the middle class and bring a quick turnaround. The population mix included both the elderly retired and the youthful students of nearby Loyola University, which had an institutional commitment toward retaining the vitality of the community.[18]

Best of all, the area had commercial strips that made it possible for many of the new ethnic groups to open shops and restaurants and attract patrons from far beyond the immediate neighborhood. The main commercial street in the area was Devon Avenue, which was built in the 1850s as Church Road. It was renamed Devon Avenue by English settlers for their native Devonshire. After World War I, it became the shopping center for the city's Jewish community.[19] In the 1970s, Greeks, Russians, and Assyrians started opening stores on Devon Avenue. The first Indian store to operate on Devon Avenue was India Sari Palace. Owned by India Emporium of Hong Kong and managed by Mr. Rattan Sharma (who was still manager in 1998), the store opened its doors on April 6, 1973, at 2538 W. Devon. (Uma Sari Palace, a store owned by Mr. and Mrs. Arora, started operations even earlier in February of 1973 but they were on Sheridan Road. In September–October of 1974, they moved to 2050 W. Devon Avenue before relocating again to their present store on 2535 W. Devon.) Mr. Sharma recalled the early difficult days when he had to endure the hostility of the Jewish merchants, who openly expressed their anger at the intrusion of the immigrants through acts of vandalism and threats of extortion. "But we stuck it out," said Mr. Sharma.[20] "We reported matters to the police, who were very cooperative. We were able to overcome those hurdles not only because of the police force but because we had the support of the North Town Chamber of Commerce. Mr. Irving Loundy, who was the head, was behind us 100 percent."

Part of the credit for Mr. Sharma's staying power must also go to his own support structure, for he was not a lone shopkeeper operating in a vacuum. He had behind him a parent company that had already opened a store in New York in the summer of 1971—"on 37, East 29th Street between Park and Madison" said Mr. Sharma, "and then we moved it to Jackson Heights, in Queens. Since then we have opened stores in Washington, D.C., and Los Angeles," he added proudly. In the 1970s, Jackson Heights became the most prominent shopping district in New York in much the same way that Devon Avenue grew in Chicago. As observed by the New York-based Indian historian, Madhulika Khandelwal, "To carve out exclusive Indian spaces and designate them as such is not a simple process."[21] In the case of Devon Avenue, the process started as early as 1973, and took the combined persistence of many store owners and managers, of whom Mr. Rattan Sharma was but one. It also took the cooperation of city authorities and local businessmen like Mr. Irving Loundy who helped the Indian merchants weather the rough periods and preserve the Indian commercial identity without destroying the interethnic flavor of Devon Avenue. In an urban environment like Chicago's, where different groups live cheek by jowl and interact with one another as they do on Devon, interethnic harmony is crucial to the development of a commercial center.

In the 1980s, when the second wave of Indian immigrants arrived, they saw an opportunity to cater to the commercial needs of a growing Indian population, just as the Gujaratis had done in England and East Africa. (It is worth noting that it is the merchant Gujarati community who have swelled the ranks of family-sponsored, second-wave immigrants in Chicago.) First came the grocery stores and sari shops, then the appliance and video stores, quickly followed by restaurants and banquet halls, and more recently, jewelry shops. Soon Pakistani and Bangladeshi merchants also joined the Indians and gradually took over the mile-long stretch between Oakley and Sacramento, pushing the Jewish merchants further west.[22] By the 1990s, Devon Avenue represented a kaleidoscope of ethnicity that gave it a truly international character. Between Ridge and Western were the Middle Eastern, Assyrian, and Pakistani districts. The central district between Western and California was Indian and Pakistani, while to the west, between California and Kedzie, were the Korean and Jewish businesses.

For Indians, the ability to open shop right where their customers were located was just the beginning of an exciting commercial success story. Soon, the Devon businesses expanded to serve a clientele that lived outside the area and in neighboring states. The growth of the Devon Avenue shopping complex into what its own merchants claim is the "biggest shopping center for Indian goods in all of North America," one that serves the entire Midwest, is typical of the growth of other enterprises in the city in other times. As a gateway city, Chicago has always nurtured the rise of trade and commerce not only with its own hinterland but with regions near and far.[23] The fate of the Indian business community, as indeed with any commercial endeavor in Chicago, is closely linked to the dynamics of national and international economies.

The growth of the commercial center on Devon Avenue is also closely connected to the development of Rogers Park into a predominantly South Asian residential area. The concentration of Indians here can be compared to the "clustering" of earlier ethnic groups who were concentrated in other neighborhoods, like the African Americans on the South Side and the Mexicans on the West Side. Institutions such as the Vedic Day Care Center and the Hare Krishna Temple on Lunt Avenue, that serve a purpose beyond the purely commercial, have sprung up in the area and given it many of the marks of a true ethnic "neighborhood," even an immigrant ghetto. There has not been drastic or marked deterioration in the area but there is constant talk of needing to "clean up the neighborhood." Certainly, those Indians who continue to live in Rogers Park are the ones who simply cannot afford to move out, those who need the comfort of an ethnic enclave, or those who see no need to give up the convenience of shopping nearby. Most of them also belong to the second wave of immigration.

The 1990 Census tracts 205 to 209, which comprise the West Ridge–Rogers Park area where Devon Avenue is located, show a predominantly white population with a significant concentration of Asian Indians. Asians number almost 25 percent of the population in these areas, and Indians constitute almost one-third (32 percent) of the total Asian population. Indians comprise the largest of all the Asian groups in Tract 205 (51 percent of 1,647 Asians) and 209 (47 percent of 2,389 Asians).[24]

Another recent trend among Indians in the city is that affluent young professionals are moving into the trendy uptown area and into exclusive high-rise buildings in downtown. As second-generation Indians graduate from the Ivy League schools and take up lucrative jobs as doctors and lawyers and business professionals in the service and high technology industries that are beginning to dominate in Chicago, they are also following the general tendency of upper-class Chicagoans to live in posh downtown locations. Luxury apartments in Water Tower Place, North Michigan Avenue's Magnificent Mile, and the Gold Coast, where second-generation Indian professionals live, are the obvious symbols of wealth concentrated in the city. A Gold Coast or lake view address is highly valued among these second-generation professionals who have formed their own social circles and groups in the city. However, they also have close ties to their immigrant parents, so first-generation Indians who had moved out into the suburbs find themselves being drawn once again into life in the city, this time at a much higher economic level than when they first started out on the North Side. Thus the interconnectedness between Chicago and its suburbs is maintained in the lives of the Indian immigrants, whether they are professionals or nonprofessionals, first or second generation.

Suburbia

Between 1960 and 1980, Chicago witnessed a more than 30 percent decline in the number of middle- and upper-income families while suburban Cook County saw a 30 percent increase in families in the same income categories. The increase was even greater in the other surrounding counties. Compared to other Asians, Indians have the highest percentage of their people residing in the suburbs. Of all Chicago area Indian residents, 72 percent live in the suburbs, compared to 64 percent Japanese, 62 percent Koreans, 56 percent Thais, 54 percent Filipinos, and 48 percent Chinese[25] (see Fig. 8).

Table 7   Median income of Asian households in 1989 in Illinois by selected
nationality and county (minimum Indian population of 1,000)

	State of Illinois	County			
		Cook	Du Page	Lake	Will
All Asian	$38,563	$36,418	$55,989	$55,561	$50,996
Chinese	$30,970	$28,606	$60,470	$66,724	—
Filipino	47,465	45,653	62,600	48,939	$61,408
Indian	44,354	39,118	55,366	63,728	61,108
Japanese	41,102	42,523	61,583	59,591	—
Korean	31,529	35,829	44,205	46,058	—

SOURCE: 1990 Census of Population, Social and Economic Characteristics, Illinois, 546.

Distinctions between the Indian immigrants who live in the city and those
who live in the suburbs are again remarkably similar to such distinctions in
the general population. Moving out to the suburbs has the same connotations for Indians as it had for previous immigrants of other nationalities, or
even for previous generations who have long ceased to think of themselves
in immigrant terms, such as the Italian Americans. In other words, a move
to the suburbs could mean that an Indian had made enough money to
invest in a home where property values would hold up, it could mean that a
young Indian couple was ready to start a family and wanted an environment
with good schools and a safe neighborhood. These are the very same reasons given by middle-class whites for leaving the inner city and going to the
suburbs.[26] Working in the suburbs would be a prime reason to live in the suburbs, but many Indian doctors work in hospitals located in the city yet still
prefer to live in the suburbs. The value of a home and its location are more
important factors for home-buying Indians than proximity to other Indians.

The most obvious distinction between city and suburban Indians is in the
income levels. The income level of Indians in Cook County is much lower
than it is for Indians in the surrounding counties, which holds true for all
other Asian groups as well (Table 7). These income differences are due in
part to occupational differences. They also result from the fact that the
more recent immigrants whose earning capacity has not yet reached its peak
are more likely to be located within the city.

Another factor that contributes to the divide between city and suburban
Indians is the nature of their day-to-day experiences. The Indians clustered
on Devon Avenue are much more likely to have neighborly relations than
those who live in the suburbs. The latter are more widely scattered, more

isolated, and in this respect, more like the white suburban Americans. Part of the reason why no alarm signals have been raised in the suburbs at the sudden appearance of Indians and other Asians is that they are seen to behave very much like their long-established, white, upper-middle-class neighbors.

There is always a danger that class distinctions within Chicago's Indians may become more and more powerful if the community should become more and more economically stratified, and may ultimately turn out to be far more divisive than the linguistic, religious, and regional differences that are the focus of study for most current observers of the immigrant scenario. There is also the possibility that with the increase in skill levels among the more recent immigrants and the rise of the second generation, economic differences may actually diminish.

The Unresolved Question of "Race"

Clearly, employment patterns have both contributed to, and been the result of, residential patterns of settlement among Indian immigrants. What is less clear is the role that racial attitudes have played in steering Indians toward or away from certain neighborhoods. How are Indian immigrants regarded by Chicagoans? The very word "immigrant" is often used in a negative context in Chicago as it is in other parts of the United States. Still, Chicagoans tend to discriminate between immigrants of different races and different nationalities. Surprisingly, Chicago media tend to portray Asians more favorably than they do immigrants of any other group, including Europeans. One study showed that "references to European immigrants (in the Chicago media) were 61 percent positive . . . and references to Asian immigrants were 65 percent positive," whereas "references to Latino immigrants were almost the opposite of Europeans and Asians, only 18 percent positive."[27] Part of the explanation for the favorable attitude toward Asians is the tendency of people to mix issues of class and race. The higher economic attainments of Asians compared to Latinos at this point may be making the Chicago media more favorably disposed toward Asians.

But the glorification of Asians as a "model minority" by the media and the public, in general, is a double-edged sword. Indians, like other Asian Americans, are becoming increasingly wary of this label that elevates them, on the one hand (model), and paradoxically relegates them to the fringes of society, on the other (minority). They are only too keenly aware that the label divides them along class lines (not all Indians are high-achievers), sets them against other minorities (so whites can ask "Why can't blacks and Hispanics achieve like Asians?"), and deprives them of the resources they feel they are entitled to (they get cut out of affirmative action programs because they supposedly don't need them). For the majority of the non-Asian population, Indians may be an ethnic group distinct from Chinese, Koreans, or Japanese, but the ability of Indians to buy homes and operate businesses in their neighborhoods is increasingly dependent on public perceptions that are influenced by such stereotyping of Asian Americans.[28]

Racial and ethnic demarcations do exist to some extent in the city for Indians but not in the suburbs. The exception in the city is the affluent downtown location where successful second-generation Indians mingle freely with whites. The reason why Indians have integrated with whites, at least with respect to housing patterns in the suburbs, is due in part to their economic success and the fact that they belong to respected professions. It also has something to do with race, with the fact that Indians are not classified outright as "colored" as they are in Britain. Nor do they carry the burden of colonialism as former subjects of the British. On the whole, Indians are generally lauded as a "model minority" who have achieved economic success faster than many other immigrant groups because of the high value they place on education. Their nationality or country of origin is the identifying factor not their race, which is much more difficult to place.

The confusion about what "race" Indians belong to harks back to the earlier immigration period in California, and the controversy surrounding "white" and "Caucasian" that was fought out in the courts but seems never to have been fully resolved. The assignment of a separate category of "Asian Indians" in the 1980 Census merely gave Indians an official minority status, it did not affect the American perception of Indians as a "race." The inconsistency in the census classification of some Americans by race (white, black), others by geographical origin (Native American, Asian/Pacific Islander) and still others by linguistic affiliation (Hispanic) is a reflection of the ambiguous attitudes prevalent in American society.[29]

Chicago's white communities have a deep-rooted fear of "losing" their neighborhood to the blacks. But Indians seem to have avoided the consequences of this attitude because they are seen more as an ethnic group than as a racial group. The following excerpt from *Chicago* shows the ambiguity of the Indian position.

Members of all ethnic groups can now be found in Chicago's suburbs. Some groups dispersed in outward directions fairly quickly, moving from the inner city to the city's fringes to the suburbs in just a generation or two. While white ethnic settlements have not altogether disappeared in the city, two factors have substantially changed their nature. First, the largest white ethnic groups now have a majority of their populations in the suburbs rather than in the city. Second, in the city race has come to be a far more significant characteristic for defining group membership and neighborhood residence than ethnicity.[30]

Indians seem to be following the pattern set by Chicago's other white ethnic communities, but this is contingent upon the whites continuing to perceive the Indians as a "Caucasian" race, however outmoded the concept itself might be. The only condition under which Indians appear to be in danger of generating tension and hostility is when they belong to a lower economic scale or cluster in concentrated areas (and the two usually go together) as they do in the city. Chicago provides a perfect example of how residential patterns are forced upon immigrants by a host society but can also be a matter of conscious choice on the part of the immigrants themselves. What is also important to consider is what it bodes for Indians as an immigrant group.

This dual residential pattern among Indians almost begs the question, what constitutes an Indian community? How important is geographical proximity when it comes to creating a sense of community? What do the suburban Indians have in common with city Indians? Do they share common interests and common institutions or do they patronize different institutions that serve the same purpose? What do the North Side Chicago Indians have in common with their own non-Indian neighbors on the block, such as the Jews or Koreans? What do they share with their suburban compatriots with whom they rub shoulders in the grocery stores or restaurants? The forces that both fragment and unify the Indian immigrants are what define their sense of community, and can be understood only through a detailed examination of their social, cultural, and religious organizations.

The ethnic neighborhood has always played an important role in Chicago's city politics and the aldermen of Chicago have often represented their own ethnic groups, but in the case of Chicago's Fiftieth Ward, which covers Devon Avenue, the representative is Alderman Bernie Stone. Democrat Stone created

some "political bad blood" when he beat an Indian candidate in the pri-
maries.[31] Many Indians in the area still cherish hopes that some day they will
be represented by one of their own. Devon Avenue can hardly be called a
political stronghold of Indians, it remains primarily a commercial center,
and Indians on Devon Avenue will work with people of other ethnicity as
long as their commercial interests are served. But it is also difficult to predict how long Devon Avenue will hold together as a commercial center.
Given that Chicago neighborhoods have always been changing, Devon
Avenue bears watching. Will it become a permanent "India town" like the
"Chinatown" of the near South Side, or will the opening up of new shops in
the suburbs where the Indians have moved in ever increasing numbers
diminish the importance of Devon Avenue and lead to its eventual decline
as a major hub of Indian immigrant activity?

Part of the answer lies in the changing demographics. Since Indians
migrate freely in and out of Chicago as and where economic opportunities
take them, much depends on how robust Chicago's economy remains. Part of
the answer is also in the attitudes of the Indians themselves toward each other.
What are the divisions within the community, and will they be exacerbated or
toned down—between the first and the second wave of immigrants, those
who belong to the upper and the lower economic classes, the city dwellers
and the suburbanites? A survey of Indian immigrants in the Chicago metropolitan area conducted in 1992 throws some light on these issues and is analyzed in detail in the next chapter.

4

THE QUANTITATIVE PROFILE

Responses to a Survey

> There is no disagreement that whenever it is appropriate, fruitful
> and possible, the historian should count.
> —Lawrence Stone, *The Past and the Present*

A statistical portrait of Chicago's Indian immigrants based on a survey is necessarily limited to what can be quantified but is not limited to the static. The variations within the community that are revealed by the statistical analysis are subject to change in the dynamic movement of history. Thus demographic factors such as age, gender ratio, differences in income levels, and length of stay in the United States, factors that change over time, determine to some extent what choices are available to Indian immigrants at a given point in their history. The "sheer numbers" in each category also influence what elements of their heritage Indians may choose to emphasize and what they may choose to discard or forget as they recreate their ethnic identities in an alien environment. The use of quantitative data to understand basically unquantifiable issues pertaining to culture or religion is admittedly debatable, but attitudinal surveys on these issues are useful in pointing the directions in which research may delve further. Generally, the survey analysis serves as a reliable indicator of some of the values of the immigrants, certain elements of their lifestyle, and how they position themselves vis-à-vis their own ethnic group and the larger American society.

To the outsider, Indian immigrants of Chicago probably present a solid, monolithic front. There is no doubt that, given their position in an alien environment so far away from their homeland, what they have in common far outweighs their differences. The survey data, time and again, reveal broad areas of agreement and solidarity, especially in religious and cultural values. However, as the years go by, and more and more Indians arrive in the United States, the differences among Indians grow sharper and sharper, and have more room for expression. As with other immigrant groups such as the Catholic and Lutheran Germans, the divisions that exist in the home country are maintained in the United States. The priorities in the immigrants' lives also change with time, depending on what stage of the life cycle they happen to be in—whether they are single or heads of families or "senior citizens." While the survey highlights some of these differences, it also underlines the fundamental unity of Indians, and helps to build a cohesive picture of the Chicago community as a whole.

The Statistical Approach

In the search for a theoretical model on the basis of which the survey results might be analyzed, one has to consider the many theories that have been developed about how immigrants react when they find themselves in the alien environment of the host country. Reactions could range from total rejection to minimal adaptation to a more balanced acculturation or complete assimilation. This last goal remains a difficult one to achieve, and at least as far as the newest immigrants from India are concerned, perhaps it is not even a desirable one. These choices may change over time for the same individual, and will certainly change from one generation to another. Of all the theories of assimilation and acculturation that have been postulated over the years, two are particularly relevant to the Indian immigrant situation. Horace Kallen, in the 1920s, rejected the "melting pot" assimilationist theories that were prevalent during his time and maintained that immigrant and ethnic groups, far from losing their distinctive identities, would perpetuate their heritage and maintain autonomy in a kind of "cultural pluralism." He envisaged America as a loose federation of different nationalities who would have enough in common to maintain a cohesive political identity but would remain culturally disparate.[1] In the 1960s, Milton Gordon argued that "cultural pluralism" remains an unrealizable ideal because along with the maintenance of ethnic subsocieties, there is also a massive trend toward acculturation of all groups to American culture patterns. He saw two opposing trends in American society, one toward "Americanization" or homogenization, and the other toward cultural separatism. Gordon suggested that "the various ethnic varieties of Americans, excepting the intellectuals, tend to remain within their own ethnic group and social class for most of their intimate, primary group relationships, interacting with other ethnic and class varieties of Americans largely in impersonal, secondary group relationships."[2] He called this "structural pluralism."

Assimilation theories such as those Gordon outlines have fallen out of favor with some historians who consider them too simplistic and ahistorical. But there is no reason why the assimilation model cannot be used as a framework for understanding how immigrant groups fit into the larger American society, always keeping in mind the particular time and place and cultural milieu in which the study is undertaken. Gordon believed that while "structural pluralism" was particularly applicable to immigrants of lower middle-class backgrounds, it also encompassed the great majority of immigrants of higher-class origins. However, he thought they were "less likely to arrive in large numbers."[3] The post-1965 Indian immigration has both disproved his suggestion about the likelihood of upper-class immigrants arriving in large numbers and at the same time given us a chance to examine whether the idea is, indeed, applicable to immigrants of higher-class origins.

The statistical approach is thus designed in part to test Gordon's "structural pluralism" model. Though Gordon had mostly Catholics and Jews in mind, the theories he outlined continue to have some validity for Chicago's Indian immigrants in the 1990s. The data analysis addresses six different dimensions: the demographic profile, the professional, social, personal/familial, religious, and national dimensions. It provides systematic statistical evidence as to how far Indians are acculturated in different aspects of their lives by comparing adaptation levels in different spheres. It also reveals in what areas Indians are willing to submerge a strong ethnic identity, and in what areas they choose to emphasize or underscore their being different from other Americans. Within each dimension, four different perspectives are presented: an overall perspective that gives a composite picture of the whole population, and three different "subperspectives" that try to capture variations within the population—variations relating to gender (male/female), income (low/middle/high) and length of stay in the United States (the first and second wave).[4]

The statistics tell us where the fault lines of division lie within the community. Generally, they appear to be more along class lines than gender lines. Since higher income is generally the result of higher education and more advanced professional skills, it is possible to see the class division as a division between professionals and nonprofessionals. Both income and length of stay seem to be positively correlated, meaning that a longer stay in the United States generally corresponds with higher income. This suggests that whatever differences exist among high- and low-income Indians and the first and second wave of Indians are likely to be blurred with time, with people moving from one category to another.

A Note on Methodology

A random survey was deliberately avoided because response rates for such surveys are historically very poor for immigrants from all countries. It was therefore decided to administer the survey to cover as wide a range of potential respondents as possible, so that the sample would be large, and could be studied as a reliable measure of some segments of the general population. Five thousand surveys were distributed in the Chicago metropolitan area, by mail and direct handouts at community gatherings and Indian shopping centers, between September 1992 and January 1993; 574 responses (a response rate greater than 11 percent) were received by February 1993. There was hardly a suburb in the six-county Chicago area that was not represented in the survey. The analytical method adopted was to first divide the thirty-seven survey questions into separate categories, with responses in each category being used to indicate the level of assimilation in a particular dimension of an immigrant's life. The survey analysis highlights differences based on gender, income, and length of stay but also emphasizes similarities.

Based on the broad demographic profile of Indian immigrants, it was feasible to examine whether there was any relationship or measure of association between one variable and another. The analysis showed that the later arrivals tended to have lower incomes and lesser education than the earlier arrivals. It appeared that length of stay could be treated as an independent variable for purposes of analysis, since it seemed to have a bearing on at least two other important variables. It could be seen as an indication of an immigrant's lower status at the time of immigration, and could reasonably be expected to influence assimilative tendencies. Gender, on the other hand, did not seem to significantly affect any of the variables concerned with demographic features. However, its value as an independent variable when analyzing attitudes and opinions cannot be discounted, so it was decided to keep gender as another independent variable when analyzing the data. It also seemed worthwhile to examine in detail what differences in attitudes and behavior existed between the different income groups. Analysis of variance techniques were used to determine the significance of each of these variables on immigrants' attitudes toward assimilation in different spheres.[5]

Demographic Profile

The 1990 Census shows that the male population of Indians in Illinois was slightly higher (33,955 or 53 percent) than the female (30,245 or 47 percent). Among survey respondents, the ratio was even higher (69 percent male to 31 percent female from a total of 574 respondents). Fully two-thirds of the respondents were in the 35–54 age group, with the mean age for men being 45 and for women 42 (Fig. 11-a). An overwhelming majority (90 percent) were married. About 80 percent of the survey population had between one and three children, while almost half (47 percent) had two children. The mean age of the first child was 16 years, second child 14 years and the third child 11 years. The statistics clearly indicate that a large proportion of the Chicago Indian immigrant population was busy raising children who were poised on or had crossed the threshold of adolescence. The most pressing issues in their lives concerned their families, which included not only their children but also their siblings and their parents. Many of the immigrants surveyed were worried about passing on the torch to the next generation, and their energies were focused on building the infrastructure necessary to create and preserve a special way of life for them.

The survey captured a population with a wide range of income levels. The highest percentage of respondents (28 percent) were in the middle-income range of $50,000 to $100,000 per year. Twenty-one percent reported an income between $20,000 and $50,000 while 10 percent said that they earned less than $20,000. As for those in the high-income brackets, 19 percent earned between $100,000 and $200,000 while an impressive 18 percent reported an income above $200,000 (Fig. 11-b).

Most of the respondents (68 percent) came to the United States before 1980. A slim majority (51 percent) reported that they had actually intended to return to India rather than stay here permanently when they first came, but most of them had passed that period in their lives when they were uncer-

Figs. 11-a–d. The Chicago survey: Demographic profile

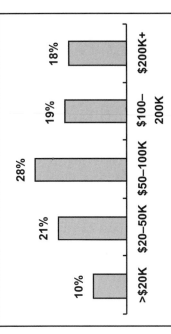

Fig. 11-a. Age

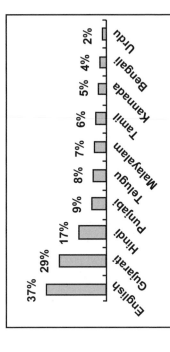

Fig. 11-b. Income

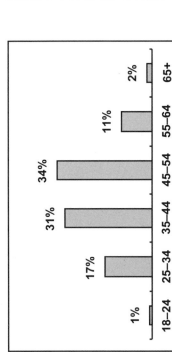

Fig. 11-c. Reasons for immigrating

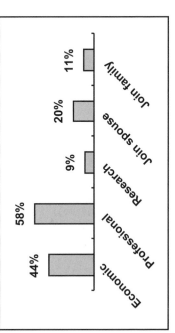

Fig. 11-d. Languages spoken at home

NOTE: Total number of survey respondents = 574. The number of people who responded to each question varies. Percentages do not add up to 100 due to rounding or missing values that are not shown separately.

tain about staying on as permanent settlers. Eight percent still planned to go back "definitely," while another 5 percent wanted to go back but didn't think it would work for them. While almost all immigrants cherish what may be no more than a pious hope for a return to India, 5 percent of those surveyed had made it a reality. But they had also come back to the United States as second-time immigrants. Their first stint in the United States could have been either on a temporary visa or a permanent immigrant visa. A significant 55 percent continued to believe that they might return to India "later, but not now." Interestingly enough, a greater percentage of men (57 percent) than women (51 percent) thought they might go back to India at a later date. Earlier research has also indicated that Indian men have a stronger yearning for the homeland than the women.[6]

The average length of stay in the United States for Chicago's Indian immigrants was fifteen years (median: seventeen years). About two-thirds of the survey respondents (66 percent) had been in the United States for between ten and twenty-five years, while 27 percent had been there less than ten years. Thus, in the twenty-seven-year period of growth of the community from 1965 to 1992, there was both stability and change in the population. Some immigrants had been in the United States long enough to build institutions and plan for long term growth, while fresh infusions of immigrants lent renewed vitality and kept reshaping the community according to new imperatives.

Most of the immigrants said they came for professional or economic reasons (58 percent and 44 percent, respectively), though many also came to join their spouses who were already here (20 percent). Most respondents gave more than one reason for their move, giving further credence to the view that motivation is always complex and many-sided. Of the 113 respondents who said they had come to join their spouse in the United States, 27 percent were men. They were joining their wives who had emigrated on their own steam and were the pioneers for the rest of the family (see Fig. 11-c).

Language

All survey respondents who spoke English at home also reported speaking an Indian language that is their mother-tongue, any one of the sixteen different languages reported in the survey.[7] The largest number (29 percent) were the Gujarati-speaking group. The other major language groups were Hindi (17 percent), Punjabi (9 percent), Telugu (8 percent), Malayalam (7 percent), Tamil (6 percent), Kannada (5 percent), Bengali (4 percent),

and Urdu (2 percent) (see Fig. 11-d). Other native languages of Chicago's
Indian immigrants include Marathi, Sindhi, Konkani, Oriya, Marwari, and
Kashmiri. In India, one normally differentiates between the "North Indian"
and the "South Indian," with people from Gujarat (in the west) and Bengal
(in the east) being conveniently categorized as "North Indians." According
to this differentiation then, approximately three-fourths of the Indians in
Chicago are North Indians, compared to one-quarter from the South.

A survey conducted in New York in the 1980s reported that 34 percent of
the Indian immigrants came from Gujarat, 20 percent from Hindi-speaking
states and 22 percent from the four states of South India.[8] In Kalamazoo,
Michigan, too, the dominant linguistic group in a survey was Gujarati (26 percent). Other North Indian languages were represented by 41 percent, while
South Indians made up 23 percent of the population.[9] The makeup of the
Chicago population is thus similar to that in other U.S. cities in this respect.

The complex relationship between language, regional identity, and ethnic origin among Indians is based on a long history of movements of peoples and the intermingling of cultures, not only within India but also in the
rest of the world. Supposedly, Tamilians speak Tamil and hail from the state
of Tamil Nadu, yet Indians who have never lived in Tamil Nadu and do not
speak a word of Tamil (like some of the Tamils in Fiji or Réunion) might
still call themselves Tamilians, because their ancestry is Tamil and this is the
only way they can differentiate themselves from people who belong to other
parts of India. Then again, Gujarati-speaking Ismailis may prefer to down-
play their linguistic relationship with Gujarati-speaking Hindus and emphasize their Islamic ties with non–Gujarati-speaking brethren. Different aspects
of the ethnic identity are emphasized by different groups, or by the same
group, at different times or at different stages in their lives. But language
and religion always remain integral factors in the identity-building process,
at least for first-generation Indian immigrants.

More than one-third (37 percent) of the survey respondents spoke English at home, reflecting the special place of English in their lives. The Indian
immigrants' knowledge of English is a carryover from imperial times. It is
also one of the most important factors responsible for smoothing their transition to life in the United States. Indeed, many first-generation Indian
immigrants, educated in public schools in India and abroad, speak and
write more grammatically correct English than their second-generation
children growing up in the United States. What sets them truly apart from
their children and even each other is their accent, which ranges from
clipped British to sing-song "Indish." This term refers to both the accent

and the turn of phrase in the usage of English which varies according to one's native language in India. The cultivated Indian ear can easily tell which region of India a person hails from just by listening to the way he or she speaks English. A Bengali speaks English very differently from the Gujarati or Tamilian, and sometimes all are equally unintelligible to other Chicagoans! Some first-generation Indian immigrants who came in the second wave and learned their English in the United States are distinguishable by their exaggerated American accent, which doesn't quite match that of the second-generation Indians but tries hard to imitate it. Schools that work at accent elimination and teach pupils how to acquire the requisite American accent do brisk business among Indians, especially among those who have faced bias or feel they need to improve their job prospects.[10]

An overwhelming majority of respondents (88 percent) said they spoke the mother-tongue at home. About 3 percent of the respondents reported having more than one mother-tongue. Between 20 percent and 52 percent spoke the mother-tongue at home *all the time*, with the low-income group having the highest percentage. A majority (51 percent) spoke the mother-tongue at home some of the time and only 4 percent reported that they rarely speak their mother-tongue at home. It is with the second-generation Indians that the loss of ethnic language skills becomes apparent. Sixty-one percent of the respondents reported that their children spoke the mother-tongue at home, with only 18 percent reporting "Good" to "Excellent" fluency. It is the lower-income and later-arriving immigrants whose children have greater proficiency in the mother-tongue. The basic dilemma for many Chicago Indians, especially the professional, public school-educated ones in the first wave, was that they were more comfortable with English than with their mother tongue. They did not speak or think in their native language, though they were surrounded by its culture. They became reconciled to language erosion among their children in the United States, and rather than taking steps to arrest it by pushing language classes, they tried to develop an alternative, English−language-based Indian culture. This group tried to ensure that the priests in the temples explained the meanings of rites and rituals in the language that the second generation could understand easily, and in relevant terms that they could identify with. Such transformations and modifications in the practice of Indian culture take place over and above the protests of those who insist that Indian culture cannot survive without its traditional linguistic roots or is unacceptably corrupted in an Anglicized version.[11] But new developments have presented the Indians with a host of options and imperatives. The arrival of the second wave of immigrants whose English language skills were not so well developed and who preferred to speak the mother-tongue at home meant a resurgence of native language use in the community. The presence of non-English speaking grandparents also added to the pressure on second-generation Indians to learn the mother-tongue. Some of the older college-age children, searching for their roots, wound up taking Indian language classes in an effort to understand themselves and their heritage. For many Indians, knowing or learning an Indian language became a conscious way of affirming or denying a particular aspect of their ethnic identity.[12] The demand for Indian language classes, especially Hindi, Urdu, and Gujarati, among the Indian immigrant population is seen in the increased enrollment at universities where these courses are offered, including the University of Chicago's South Asia Department and community colleges such as the College of Du Page. But the immigrants themselves have felt that the preservation of language is primarily their own responsibility and only the first step in the much larger agenda of preservation of an entire culture. Language classes offered at the temples of Chicago reveal the commitment of the community toward language preservation, but responses to survey questions also reveal the extent to which language erosion is taking place in the community. American-born Indian children know that the "mother-tongue" is useless in communicating with their American peers, and so often refuse to speak it.

The loss of language skills among second-generation Indians is also connected with a strong desire on their part to acquire a nonregional, pan-Indian identity. Many second-generation Indians have grown up in Chicago area schools identifying strongly with other Indian children, no matter what their linguistic backgrounds. They dislike the fact that their Gujarati parents move only with other Gujaratis and not with Punjabis or Tamilians. They are determined that their own Indianness will be nonreligious and nonsectarian in nature. Thus the postcolonial language predicament of first-generation Indian immigrants is carried over in complex and troubling ways in the lives of their children. One second-generation woman wrote: "Although English was my mother's tongue, I cannot bring myself to call it my mother tongue."[13] The statistics, which point to both language retention and language erosion among first- and second-generation Indians, reflect this on-going dilemma in the lives of English-speaking Indians.

Property Ownership

In keeping with the image of the thrifty, hardworking immigrant, Indians tend to save up and buy a home as quickly as they can afford to. (The first investment is generally toward education, the second one toward a home.) They also tend to buy where property values hold up since they see their home primarily as an economic investment. As could be expected of a highly educated, high-income group, a majority (77 percent) owned their own homes. Only 49 percent of the low-income people owned their homes compared to 93 percent of those with high income. Less than half (49 percent) of the later arrivals owned homes compared to 89 percent for those who had come before 1980. A survey conducted by the publication *India Abroad* of Indians in New York in 1985 showed that 69 percent owned their homes while 23 percent owned investment property in India.[14] In the Chicago survey, the lower-income immigrants owned property in India by a greater percentage (39 percent) than did the higher-income people (24 percent). Also, the later arriving immigrants were more likely to have property in India than the earlier (42 percent to 22 percent). It appears that the Indians who had been here longer may have divested themselves of their real estate connections in India. It is also possible that the land-owning classes of India were among the group of low-income or later immigrants.

Citizenship

Since the survey was directed at first-generation Indian immigrants, almost all (96 percent) are U.S. citizens or green-card holders. The legal rights of green-card holders are similar to those of U.S. citizens, the main difference being that only citizens have the right to vote and sit on juries. Some Indians choose to retain their Indian citizenship for sentimental as well as practical reasons, since India does not allow them to hold dual citizenship. Overall, 57 percent are U.S. citizens and the percentages for women and men are identical. However, twice as many high–income-level Indians, 70 percent, are citizens as compared to 35 percent for the lower-income group. The same disparity is seen between the earlier arrivals of whom 72 percent are citizens, and the later arrivals with only 23 percent. It is easy to explain the disparity since it is necessary to have held a green card for at least five years before one is eligible for citizenship.

Among those who are U.S. citizens and eligible to vote, an overwhelming majority, 91 percent, reported that they do exercise the right to vote. This high level of participation is true for all groups. Only among those who came after 1981 does the percentage drop to 83 percent. Any attempt to explain this overall high figure must draw upon a wide variety of factors such as historic immigrant voter patterns and motivation and perhaps even a tendency for people to exaggerate past voting experiences.[15] Suffice it to note that the Indians in the sample reported an extraordinarily high voting rate. This image is somewhat offset by the general impression in the Indian community that Indians are too apathetic to vote, have no political savvy, and are naive in matters of lobbying and acquiring political clout. The truth is that they are still too small in numbers to make a significant difference as a voting bloc, but are intelligent, wealthy, and motivated enough to produce influential individuals in government.[16]

The Professional Dimension

Work patterns among Indians show that most were employed and many were dual-income families (Figs. 12-a–d). Eighty-eight percent of the Chicago sample population was employed. In terms of group differentiation, the figures ranged from a low of 79 percent for low income to a high of 94 percent for the high-income group. Eighty-two percent of the women were employed as against 91 percent of the men. Ninety-one percent of those who came before 1980 were employed compared to 82 percent for those who came after 1981. Approximately one half of the total sample (48 percent) reported dual income. The highest percentage of dual-income families was in the middle-income group (62 percent). The high-income group had only 60 percent dual-income families. The low-income group had the fewest number of dual-income families, at 43 percent.

These figures support the view that Indian women work mainly for economic reasons, since most of them in the survey belonged to the middle-income group. Previous research also indicates that when Indian immigrant women joined the workforce in significant numbers and pursued active careers, they did so as a family endeavor, not merely to realize a personal goal or fulfill their "individuality." This has also been interpreted as the reason why some educated urban elite women were able to combine careers and family with far less inner emotional conflict than their American counterparts because they saw their career as an extension of their role within the family rather than independent of it.[17] A career was usually pursued with the consent and cooperation of the husband and even the in-laws. When faced with hostility or opposition from the family toward their career pursuits, even the educated Indian women were likely to compromise their careers in the larger interest of family harmony.

Figs. 12-a–d. The Chicago survey: The professional dimension

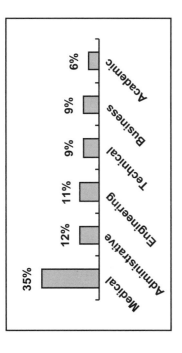

Fig. 12-a. Highest level of education

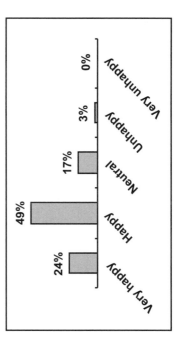

Fig. 12-b. Occupation

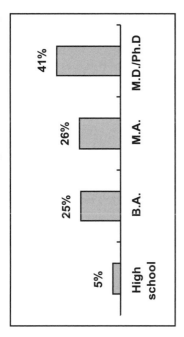

Fig. 12-c. Professional satisfaction

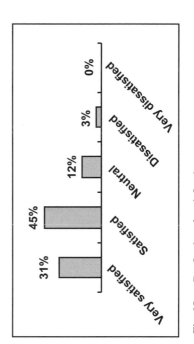

Fig. 12-d. Happiness on the job

NOTE: Total number of survey respondents = 574. The number of people who responded to each question varies. Percentages do not add up to 100 due to rounding or missing values that are not shown separately.

Education

The immigrants' background in India had prepared them to some extent for life in the United States. Almost half (47 percent) were pursuing the same occupation here as they had in India, and of these 59 percent belonged to the medical profession. Most of the highly skilled professionals, especially the doctors and engineers, received their professional education and training in India. A large percentage, 41 percent, had advanced degrees of M.D. or Ph.D., while 26 percent of the survey respondents had a Master's degree and 25 percent had a Bachelor's degree (see Fig. 12-a). An overwhelming majority (91 percent) of those in the high-income bracket had Masters' degrees or above, while the figure was 70 percent for the middle-income group and only 38 percent for the low-income group. (The 1985 *India Abroad* survey also indicated similar high educational levels for Indians in New York, with 90 percent being college graduates, and 70 percent holding post-graduate degrees.[18]) Due to the nature of the Immigration Act, which permitted lesser educated kin to immigrate at a later stage, a much larger percent of those who came before 1980 (70 percent) had advanced degrees compared to 47 percent for those who came later, after 1981. Indian immigrants are very keenly aware of the value of a U.S. education, and whenever possible, even those with advanced degrees from India, go on to acquire an American degree. More than half the survey respondents (56 percent), especially the physicians, had received education and training in the United States. The average number of years of American education they received was five years. This also reflects market conditions and the choosiness of employers who insist on credentials from an American academic institution. In some cases, as in the medical and nursing professions, state certification is mandatory.

Occupation

Survey respondents were predominantly in the professional and technical categories of workers (82 percent), and in this respect they approximated closely the national Asian Indian population characteristics as reported in the 1990 Census with 77 percent in the professional and technical categories (see Fig. 12-b for occupational distribution). Most of the professionals were in the middle- and high-income brackets while the administrative or sales workers tended to be in the lower-income bracket. The distribution for the different professions was a reflection of current wage and salary scales in the various employment fields. The low-income group had the highest proportion of people in administrative/sales (19 percent) and technical fields (15 percent), the middle-income group had the highest proportion of engineers (22 percent) and academics (11 percent), and the high-income group had the highest proportion of doctors (67 percent) and business people (10 percent).

The medical profession also dominated among the early-arriving immigrants (44 percent). The percentages for the other professions, both among early- and later-arriving immigrants, was so widely distributed, ranging from 6 percent to 17 percent, with such few cases in each category, that generalizations cannot be made. The statistics accurately reflect the pronounced occupational diversity among Indians, even though there is a heavier concentration among the professionals. Indian engineers and scientists work quietly and successfully in the corporate environment, in places such as Fermi Labs, Argonne National Laboratories, AT&T, Bell Labs and Amoco. Many individuals, such as the late Nobel Laureate Chandrasekhar of the University of Chicago, have gained top honors in their fields. Indian physicists figured prominently in the team of scientists who discovered the top quark at the Fermi National Laboratory in Batavia.[19] The more enterprising among the immigrants who lacked professional qualifications opened restaurants, grocery stores or travel agencies. Fully 10 percent of the Chicago survey respondents reported "business" as their occupation. (In Chicago, Indians have the second highest percentage of entrepreneurs among Asian Americans, next only to the Koreans.[20])

The variety in occupations amongst Indians is also linked to the diversity of the clientele they serve. Whereas the first wave of professionals looked for jobs in the mainstream sector and served the larger American public, the second wave of immigrants had another option—a growing Indian clientele and an ethnic market to cater to. Jobs opened up in the Indian grocery, clothing, jewelry, and restaurant business in the 1980s that did not exist in the 1970s. Those who didn't speak any English but knew a "Belgian cut" diamond from a "Bombay cut" diamond could make a decent living in Chicago. The sprouting of temples all over Chicagoland created the need for sculptors and priests, many of whom would not have dreamed of venturing out of their villages or towns in India but for this new demand for their skills. They came on temporary visas but stayed on to merge into the Indian community. Some moved on to other cities to find jobs in their fields, some found new occupations in Chicago.

Job Satisfaction

Responses to all questions dealing with job satisfaction were highly positive for all categories. The general tendency was for higher-income Indians to be more satisfied with their jobs than lower-income Indians. Professional satisfaction levels were very high. Overall, 76 percent reported they were "Very satisfied" or "Satisfied" in their professional work (see Fig. 12-c). The widest range of responses was between those with low income (74 percent) and the high-income group (92 percent). Overall, 73 percent reported they were either "Very Happy" or "Happy" in their job (see Fig. 12-d), with percentages ranging from a low of 70 percent for the low-income group to a high of 89 percent for the high-income group. Across the board, Indians felt they were economically better off in the United States than in India. The overall figure was 83 percent with the lowest percentage among the late-arriving immigrants (78 percent). There doesn't seem to be any doubt about the economic and professional rewards that Indians are reaping in the United States. The only unsettling aspect has to do with discrimination on the job, which is discussed in the following pages.

The Social Dimension

As reflected in Figures 13-a–c, the social sphere of the Indian immigrants of Chicago is a dichotomous one. There is the larger social world of all Americans, and then there is the other subethnic social world in which only other Indians (and perhaps some other ethnic groups) are players. A nearly 100,000 strong community in Chicagoland is bound to have many layers of special interest groups, and it is difficult to predict which particular social setting respondents may have had in mind when they answered the questions with the word "social" in them. Also, social patterns in India are very different from those in the United States. Family, lineage, caste, as well as personal accomplishment give a person a sense of social standing in India, and there is a solid sense of belonging, no matter what one's caste or creed. In the United States, immigrants are not only bereft of the familiar social framework, they don't have another framework that they can step into readily, at least in the first phase of immigration before a substantial immigrant community becomes established. Indian immigrants judged themselves and were judged by American standards, which generally meant by their wealth.

Figs. 13-a–c. The Chicago survey: The social dimension

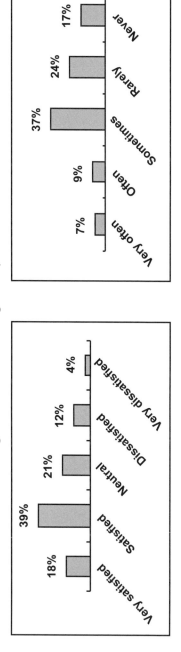

Fig. 13-a. Social satisfaction

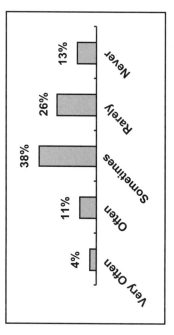

Fig. 13-b. Feel discriminated against at work

Fig. 13-c. Feel discriminated against socially (outside work)

NOTE: Total number of survey respondents = 574. The number of people who responded to each question varies. Percentages do not add up to 100 due to rounding or missing values that are not shown separately.

There are indications that the Indians are "coming of age" as an ethnic group in Chicago and beginning to judge the members in their own community according to their own standards. They have their own elite who provide community leadership and gain "social standing," and this group may have nothing to do socially with the larger society. They may be recognized as volunteers in temple activities, or valued for their services in conducting language and dance classes for second-generation Indians. Many of them do not speak English well, and might not have been successful, either socially or financially, if they did not have a large ethnic population to cater to. Such nuances were not explored in the survey, but their existence must be kept in mind when we analyze the responses.

Social Satisfaction

Compared to the scores for professional satisfaction, there is a distinct drop in scores when we examine levels of satisfaction in the social sphere. Overall, 57 percent reported they were "Very satisfied" or "Satisfied" with their social life (see Fig. 13-a). Percentages ranged from a low of 31 percent for the low-income group to a high of 71 percent for the high-income group. Thus, also in the social sphere, income levels seem to have a bearing on attitudes and levels of satisfaction. Dissatisfaction levels were also higher than in the professional sphere, with almost one quarter (23 percent) in the low-income group reporting that they were "Very dissatisfied" or "Dissatisfied" with their social life.

A majority (57 percent) said they did not have a better social standing in the United States than in India. Only a little over one-third (36 percent) of the population said they did, the rest did not respond or said "Sometimes." Again, the high-income group had the highest percentage of those who said they had a better social standing in the United States (41 percent), confirming the association of social standing with income levels.

Discrimination

The most frequently reported response to the question "Do you feel discriminated against in your job?" was "Sometimes" (see Fig. 13-b). Overall, 37 percent reported they were discriminated against sometimes, the middle- and high-income groups had the highest percentage (43 percent each) of those who were discriminated against sometimes. But the low-income group experienced the most severe discrimination. The highest percentage of those who reported they were discriminated against "Very often" or "Often" were in the low-income group (21 percent). Overall, 16 percent of the sample reported they were discriminated against "Very often" or "Often."

It is worthwhile examining the rate of "Rarely" and "Never" responses to this question of discrimination in some detail. Overall, 24 percent said they were rarely discriminated against on the job, while 17 percent said they had never been discriminated against. The highest percentage of "Never" responses was for those who had come after 1981 (30 percent). This could mean that their occupation was such that they did not encounter as much discrimination on the job because they interacted more with their own ethnic group than with the larger society, or they were not perceived as a threat by others if they were still in low-paying jobs. Yet there are no pat answers for how, why, and when an immigrant experiences discrimination; what one can capture in a survey is the immigrants' own perception of how they are treated by the host society.

The responses to the survey question on job-related discrimination could be interpreted two ways. One could look at the bright side and say that a large number of respondents, between 40 percent and 53 percent, reported they had rarely or never experienced discrimination on the job. On the other hand, it would be naive to ignore the fact that between 47 percent and 59 percent reported that they had felt discriminated against sometimes, often, or very often. What is most significant is that all groups, at the rate of between 31 percent to 43 percent, felt discriminated against sometimes. In a society that upholds ideals of equality and nondiscrimination, the least signs of violation of the ideal are worth noting.[21] One must conclude that while Indians were indeed remarkably assimilated in the professional/occupational sphere, their ethnic background and adherence to their own religious and cultural practices still sets them apart and makes them vulnerable to discrimination.

When asked if they felt discriminated against outside work, the largest percentage (38 percent) responded "Sometimes" (see Fig. 13-c). Percentages ranged from a low of 33 percent for the later arrivals to a high of 43 percent for the mid-income group. The earlier arrivals were more likely to have experienced social discrimination (59 percent reported "Very often," "Often," and "Sometimes") than those who came after 1981 (47 percent). The longer Indians have been here, the more time they have had to be discriminated against, hence the higher figure. Indians with higher income were also more likely to experience discrimination (56 percent) than those with lower income (50 percent), showing that affluence does not necessarily protect the Indian from discrimination. Fifty-eight percent of the middle-income Indians perceived social discrimination at least "Sometimes." The "Very often" and "Often" responses ranged from 13 percent to 17 percent, with an overall figure of 15 percent. "Rarely" and "Never" responses ranged from 38 percent to 42 percent.

On the whole, these figures point to a fairly unified response from all Indians no matter what their gender, income, and length of stay. The levels of discrimination they have experienced vary somewhat according to income and length of stay, but variations noted among the different groups are not large enough to permit one to say definitively that social experiences of discrimination are different for different groups.[22] The range of responses shows that discrimination was felt by the wealthy (many of whom reported feeling deliberately excluded from certain mainstream social circles) as well as the middle and lower classes. Some lower-income Indians, especially those who have been in other "closed society" countries such as the Middle East and Britain, find Americans very open and friendly. A temple priest at the Balaji Temple in Aurora said he was welcomed everywhere he went, from the grocery store to the gas station, even when he was dressed conspicuously in his traditional *dhoti*.

Communication

Familiarity with the larger American world or insularity from it can be measured to some extent through analysis of survey responses that dealt with their affiliations to nonethnic organizations, readership of magazines and newspapers, and willingness to communicate with others regarding personal problems. More than one-third (40 percent) of the total population belonged to American organizations. However, the organizational affiliations were for the most part at the professional not the social level. Only 20 percent of the low-income group and 22 percent of those who arrived after 1981 belonged to American organizations. More than half the respondents (61 percent) read American newspapers for their daily news. The readership levels were lowest among the low-income group (49 percent) and those who came after 1981 (51 percent), and highest among the high-income group (68 percent) and those who came before 1980 (66 percent).

It is necessary to compare the above figures with corresponding figures for involvement in the ethnic community to get a balanced idea of assimilation levels. Indians may be in touch with the American world around them but it appears that they were even more attuned to what was going on in their own ethnic subculture, through the ethnic media and ethnic associations. Between 54 percent and 83 percent of Indians read ethnic newspapers for news about India (the overall figure was 71 percent), while between 43 percent and 72 percent belonged to Indian community organizations. Here again, the lowest figures were for the low-income group and those arriving after 1981. One might expect that ethnic affiliation as evident from ethnic newspaper readership and membership in community organizations would be higher for the later arrivals and the low-income group since they are historically seen to be in a tighter ethnic circle. As it turns out, it was the high-income Indians who had the highest readership of ethnic newspapers (83 percent) and highest membership in ethnic community organizations (72 percent). Sometimes even ethnic or community organizations were professionally oriented, such as the American Association of Physicians from India. This organization both furthers the professional interests of the doctors and provides a forum for their families to socialize at gala annual events.

Survey respondents were asked to name up to three Indian community organizations and three American organizations to which they belonged. Sixty-one percent of the respondents said they belonged to Indian community organizations. The largest number of organizations named were regional, cultural, or language-based organizations, such as the Kannada Kuta or Tamil Sangam (37 percent), followed by religious (26 percent), professional (15 percent), women's (6 percent), pan-Indian (5 percent), and social service (4 percent). Approximately 40 percent of respondents said they belonged to American organizations. Of the American organizations, an overwhelming majority (75 percent) were professional, and over half of these were in the medical profession. The other categories were engineering and science. Among the nonprofessional organizations named (22 percent) were the Rotary and Lions Clubs, PTA, local school board, political organizations, ACLU, and Amnesty International.

With respect to more intimate areas of communication, respondents were asked who they would turn to for help if they had problems with their marital life, their jobs, their children, and their parents. The possible range of responses to these questions and the numeric values assigned to them (in parentheses) were: "Only native" (1), "Mostly native" (2), "Both" (3), "Mostly American" (4), "Only American" (5), and "Neither" (6). Respondents took full advantage of the range of options to respond in a variety of ways. The mean responses (higher means indicate more reliance on American counsel, lower means indicate heavier reliance on Indian advice) show that Indians generally stuck to the middle of the road, but had a tendency to lean more toward the ethnic community in resolving issues dealing with marital life (2.50 mean) and parents (2.11 mean). When it came to their children (3.09 mean) and their jobs (3.39 mean), however, they leaned toward the counsel of their American friends.

One aspect that seemed worth investigating was whether Indian women were more likely to stay within their own ethnic world, and how their behavior might differ from that of the men. For marital problems, 28 percent of the women said they would seek only or mostly Indian help compared to 37 percent of the men; for problems with parents, the figures were: women 36 percent, men 49 percent; for problems with children, women 16 percent, men 24 percent; and for job-related problems, women 4 percent, men 5 percent. It appeared that the *men* and not the women were the ones more likely to stay within their own ethnic group for help on all kinds of problems. Yet the women did not lean too heavily on the American side either—they differed from the men by only a small margin in preferring American help. However, they were more likely than the men to be balanced and seek the help of both Indians and Americans for all their problems.

The experience of immigrant community leaders and social workers of Apna Ghar, a Chicago-based shelter for battered Asian women, indicated that Indian women were not very open or forthcoming with their problems, especially marital problems, but when they did feel the need to discuss such problems, they often preferred the anonymity associated with seeking help outside rather than within their own immediate ethnic social circle. Reports from Apna Ghar also indicated that many cases go over the brink simply because Indian women do not seek help in time. In India, very often marital problems are simply suppressed because of family pressures or work themselves out with the help of extended family support. The basic difference between the situation in India and the situation for immigrants in the United States was the lack of immediate involvement of family elders and friends in day-to-day domestic issues.

Among the different income groups, the low-income group tended to look more toward their own ethnic kind for help than did the high-income group, no matter what the nature of their problem. Those who came after 1981 also leaned more heavily on Indians than those who came earlier.

The analysis so far suggests that Indians as a whole were more inclined toward ethnic affiliation in the social sphere, and affiliation with the mainstream world in the professional sphere. Everything points to an affirmation of Milton Gordon's "structural pluralism" model whereby a community seeks its primary, intimate group relationships among its own kind. Only in areas related to job and children do Indians reach out to Americans, and that, too, not to the exclusion of their own ethnic group.

The Personal/Familial Dimension

The innermost sanctuary of the Indian immigrant's life is the home, the place where important decisions regarding personal relationships and the observance of religious practices are made. Here, too, is the point at which tradition and culture are upheld and perpetuated on the one hand, or discarded and forgotten on the other.

Dating and Marriage

The tradition of arranged marriages is something most first-generation Indian immigrants have experienced firsthand, since the practice is still alive and widespread in India. It is a practice that they approve of, but it is not clear how successful they will be in implementing it for their children. The issue of dating is also a thorny one among Indian families who are wrestling with the question of how much latitude to give their children in these matters. The second generation of Indians has grown up in American schools celebrating "choice" as a birthright, while the first generation is worried about mixed marriages and culture erosion. Too often, they fail to see each others' viewpoints. But many Indian parents try very hard to accommodate their children's perspective. The result is an ambivalent and often unresolved attitude toward dating and marriage for their children.

Almost one-third (30 percent) of the respondents "Disapprove" or "Strongly disapprove" of their children dating an American, though a larger percentage (35 percent) were neutral on the issue. The overall percentage for those who "Approve" or "Approve strongly" of their children dating Americans was 24 percent (Fig. 14-a). The disapprovers ranged from 24 percent among the high-income group to 35 percent among the low-income group. No such disparity existed between those who came before and after. They disapproved more or less equally (30 percent to 32 percent, respectively) of their children dating an American. Among the approvers, the women presented a surprise. The percentage of those who "Approve" or "Approve strongly" is higher (31 percent) among women than among men (20 percent). It was also higher among the high-income group (33 percent) than among the

Figs. 14-a–b.   The Chicago survey: The personal/familial dimension

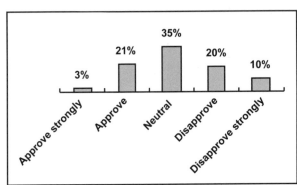

Fig. 14-a. Attitude toward their child dating an American

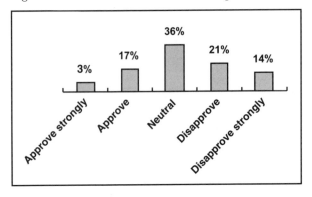

Fig. 14-b. Attitude toward their child marrying an American

NOTE: Total number of survey respondents = 574. The number of people who responded to each question varies. Percentages do not add up to 100 due to rounding or missing values that are not shown separately.

low-income group (14 percent). Those who came before 1980 approved of their children dating Americans at a higher rate than those who arrived later (26 percent to 19 percent). Still, the largest percentage, between 30 percent and 41 percent, were neutral on the dating issue.

A majority (71 percent) of the total population approved of arranged marriages. Group-wise, the lowest percentage was among the women (66 percent), while the highest percentage (76 percent) was among the late-arriving immigrants. The fact that Indian women approved of arranged marriages to a lesser extent than the other groups challenges the fallacy that women are more tradition-minded than the men. But many of them may also perceive arranged marriages as heavily weighted in favor of a patriarchal system that forces women to fall in line with the wishes of their husbands and in-laws. Other women may be more in touch with their children than the men and may empathize more with their children's views on dating and marriage. Attitudes toward issues such as dating and marriage can be understood only in a culture-specific context. Indian parents tend to permit group dating as a way to allow their children to develop social skills, but frown upon it as a "spouse-hunting" exercise, since they still believe in the advantages of arranged marriages. They also believe that dating will lead to marriage, hence they tend to have the same attitude toward both dating and marriage as seen in the survey results. Historically, as immigrants, they have not inter-married with members of the host society, being bound by sanctions of caste and religion to endogamy. At the time of the post-1965 immigration, the image of America as a permissive, sex-crazed society is deeply embedded in the minds of Indian parents who fear that dating generally leads to pre-marital sex, and they are afraid to let their children loose in such an environment. Needless to say, the children themselves, especially those of high school age, are straining at the leash and are likely to make their own decisions.

Overall, 35 percent of Indians disapproved of their child marrying an American. Thirty-six percent were neutral and only 20 percent approved or approved strongly (see Fig. 14-b). A higher percentage of men (38 percent) than women (31 percent) disapproved or strongly disapproved of their child marrying an American. The highest percentage of disapprovers were in the low-income group (40 percent). There appeared to be more hostility than active approval of intermarriage between Indians and Americans, though there was also a certain degree of tolerance or neutrality on the issue. In written comments on the surveys, some respondents indicated they wanted further definition of the word "American" to see if it included other ethnic groups or only whites, but most seemed to take the term to mean "non-Indian." (The attitude of Indians toward other colored groups was not explored in the survey.) Only between 10 percent and 20 percent of the sample population had an immediate family member married to an American, so intermarriage with Americans would be a new experience for most of them.

The Religious Dimension

No official figures are available for the breakdown of the Indian population in the United States by religion, but the Chicago survey figures correspond quite closely to the distribution back in India. An overwhelming majority

Figs. 15-a–d. The Chicago survey: The religious dimension

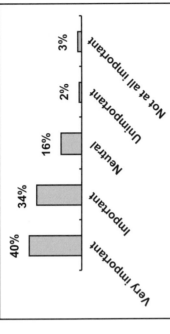

Fig. 15-a. Religion

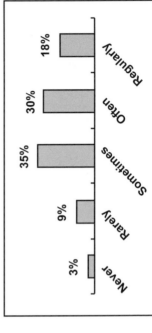

Fig. 15-b. Importance of religion

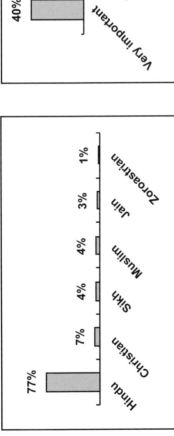

Fig. 15-c. Celebrate religious functions

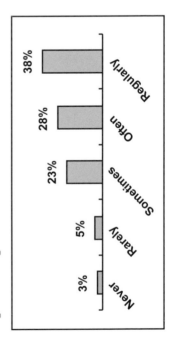

Fig. 15-d. Visit place of worship

NOTE: Total number of survey respondents = 574. The number of people who responded to each question varies. Percentages do not add up to 100 due to rounding or missing values that are not shown separately.

(77 percent) of the survey respondents belonged to the Hindu religion. There were small minorities of Christians (7 percent), Muslims (4 percent), Sikhs (4 percent), and Jains (3 percent) (see Fig. 15-a). In India, Hindus make up 80 percent of the population, with all the other minorities accounting for the remaining 20 percent. The Chicago survey figures also correspond roughly to figures for other American cities such as Kalamazoo and Atlanta.[23] All major religious groups are present in Chicago in large enough numbers to have built their own elaborate houses of worship in the Greater Chicago area. Responses to survey questions dealing with religion show how much store Indian immigrants set by their religion. Many observers of the Indian immigrant situation have remarked that even those who were not particularly religious in India become more conscientious about practicing their religion in America for the sake of passing on the heritage to the children.

The highest percentage (40 percent) of respondents reported that religion was "Very important" in their lives, while the next highest (34 percent) said it was "Important" (see Fig. 15-b). Nor was there much variation between the different groups on this issue. The highest percentage of those who said religion was important or very important was in the middle-income group (77 percent), and the lowest (70 percent) in the high-income group. Indians also celebrated religious functions on a regular basis. Again, overall, the highest percentage (38 percent) reported that they celebrated religious functions "Regularly" (which was the top option denoting the highest frequency). Twenty-eight percent said they celebrated religious functions "Often" (see Fig. 15-c). Again, there were no great disparities between the different groups. It is worthwhile noting that the highest percentages for those who celebrated religious functions often or regularly were among the early immigrants (69 percent) and the high-income group (68 percent), while the lower percentages were among the late arrivals (61 percent) and low-income group (64 percent). This indicates that the high-income, early-arriving groups support religious activities more than the other groups. A study of Indians in California, too, concluded that "the higher expressions of ethnicity, measured by support of and participation in religious and/or linguistic associations and activities, came from the earlier, professionally-oriented immigrants such as doctors rather than from the more recent self-employed immigrants."[24] The Chicago survey suggests that this is true for Chicago also.

Indians do not necessarily equate "going to church" with being religious. Many of them pray regularly at small altars in their homes, or get together for group worship or singing of *bhajans* (religious songs), especially if they

find it inconvenient to visit a temple because of time and distance constraints. However, a large number do visit a place of worship often or regularly. Overall, 30 percent reported visiting a temple often, and 18 percent
said they visited regularly. The highest number (35 percent) said they visited
a place of worship "Sometimes" (see Fig. 15-d). Once again, there were no
significant differences between the groups. Middle-class Indians were the
most frequent temple-goers. Fifty-two percent of them reported visiting a
temple often or regularly. Many Indians go to the temples to avail themselves of cultural opportunities, not all of which are associated directly with
religion. Indian religious functions, whether Hindu, Christian, Muslim,
Sikh, Jain, or Zoroastrian, have a strong social character that acquires even
greater significance in the immigrant context. The study of Indians in
Atlanta also concluded that while Indians do carry out some form of individual worship, prayer, or meditation in the home, they also take part in
group worship for reasons that are not necessarily religious.[25] Group worship is more important for the monotheistic Muslims, Sikhs, and Christians,
than for Hindus. Given the difficulties involved in trying to assess the true
significance of religion in a person's life from survey responses, and given
the variety of religious practices among Indians, the only generalizations to
be made from the survey are that religion was very important to Indians,
they celebrated religious functions and visited houses of worship regularly.

The National Dimension

Most of the responses dealing with the national dimension showed a positive attitude toward India, with over two-thirds and up to three-quarters of
the respondents indicating a strong attachment to the culture and traditions of their homeland. While the later arrivals swelled the ranks of Indians
and made mass cultural celebrations a reality, it was the older, more established immigrants who provided the individual leadership and the financial
contributions that laid the foundation for cultural continuity.

Links to the Homeland

Nationalist feelings are also kept alive through frequent visits to the homeland. Almost two-thirds (62 percent) of the respondents visited India at least
once in three years and one-quarter (25 percent) visited once in two years.

Figs. 16-a–d. The Chicago survey: The national dimension

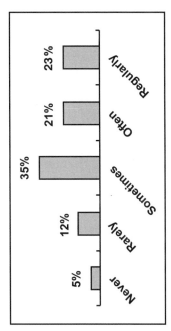

Fig. 16-a. Visit India

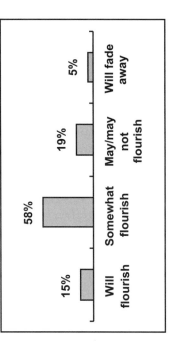

Fig. 16-b. Keep in touch with India

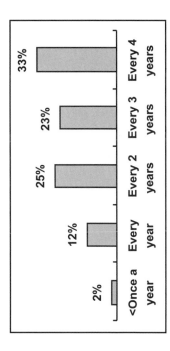

Fig. 16-c. Attached to India

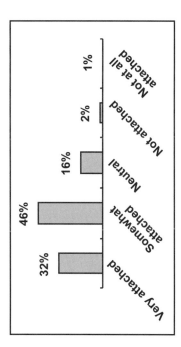

Fig. 16-d. Believe Indian culture will flourish in U. S.

NOTE: Total number of survey respondents = 574. The number of people who responded to each question varies. Percentages do not add up to 100 due to rounding or missing values that are not shown separately.

One-third (33 percent) visited once in four years or more (see Fig. 16-a). Women and men visited at almost the same rate (65 percent and 61 percent, respectively, visited once in three years or oftener). Fifty-one percent of the low-income group visited once in three years compared to 71 percent of the high-income group. The figure is 74 percent for early arrival immigrants compared to 60 percent for the later immigrants. Even the lowest figure of 51 percent represents a high level of contact with the homeland, given the distance involved and the expense of such visits.

When asked if they keep in touch with developments in India, 44 percent said they kept in touch "Often" and "Regularly" and 35 percent said they did so "Sometimes" (see Fig. 16-b). The percentages did not vary much among the different groups, fluctuating from 32 percent to 40 percent in the "Sometimes" response and 40 percent to 48 percent among those who answered "Often" and "Regularly." It would seem that all groups kept in pretty close touch with developments in India. Apart from visits by family and friends, Indians had a host of publications and cable television channels to tune in to if they wanted to keep abreast of developments.

Attachment to the homeland is something that fluctuates for all immigrants and depends as much on events in the home country as on how well they fare in their new land. Both success and failure in the new country can breed nostalgia for the old. More than three-quarters (78 percent) of the total population said they were "Very attached" or "Somewhat attached" to India (see Fig. 16-c). The percentage was even higher for women (83 percent) than for the men (76 percent), and ranged from 76 percent to 80 percent for the other categories. Between 12 percent and 17 percent said they felt "Neutral" toward India, while only 2 percent to 4 percent said they were "Not attached" or "Not at all attached." Since the respondents are all first-generation immigrants, such strong attachment to the homeland is only to be expected. What is particular to the Indian immigrant situation is that such attachment combined with the wealth and talent in the community led to the rapid establishment of a new ethnic, distinctly "Indian American" subculture.

The majority of respondents (58 percent) believed Indian culture would live on in the United States. Percentages of those who believed this among the different groups ranged from 53 percent to 62 percent. Between 11 percent and 18 percent believed Indian culture would flourish in the United States (the highest figure of 18 percent was in the mid-income group), while hardly any (between 2 percent and 8 percent) believed it would totally fade away (see Fig. 16-d). The great majority in all the groups felt that Indian culture and traditions have a future in the United States.

The survey asked Indian immigrants to make a choice between whether they thought of themselves as more Indian or American. Slightly more than two-thirds (68 percent) said they thought of themselves more as Indians than Americans. The least identification with being Indian was among the high-income group (60 percent), while the low-income group and those who had come to the United States after 1981 had the highest percentages (77 percent) of people identifying themselves as more Indian than American. Economic success and longer stay in the United States seem to increase identification with the adopted land.

General Life Satisfaction

The problem with surveys is that they force a respondent to sum up, with one mark, the totality of one's life experiences. The fact that respondents continue to oblige is, of course, the surveyor's good fortune! Over two-thirds (69 percent) of the overall population were "Satisfied" with life in the United States. Fourteen percent were "Somewhat dissatisfied," while 7 percent wished they were "back in India." Nine percent said they were "Thrilled" to be here, while 1 percent didn't "like it at all." The largest percentage of "Satisfied" immigrants was in the high-income group (75 percent) and the lowest was in the low-income group (59 percent). Only 40 percent of the overall population believed that they had reached their peak potential in the United States. (Given that the mean age of the population is only forty-four, this is hardly surprising.) Another indication that America still holds promise for the immigrants was that only 19 percent of the later arrivals and 24 percent of the low-income group felt they had reached the peak. A majority (54 percent) of the high-income group, however, believed they had reached the peak. The percentage of women who believed this was slightly lower than the men (35 percent to 41 percent).

Another resounding vote of satisfaction with life in the United States is that 84 percent of the immigrants had no regrets about having immigrated to the United States. The range of percentages, from a low of 81 percent for late arrivals to a high of 89 percent for the high-income group, showed no significant discrepancies between the different groups on this issue. Indians also felt that as an ethnic community of Asians, they were well thought of in the United States. The overall figure for those who believed in this positive image was 75 percent, with percentages ranging from a low of 65 percent for the low-income group to a high of 84 percent for the high-income group.

Conclusions

What kind of a general profile of the Chicago Indian immigrant community emerges from this analysis of the survey data? It appears that Indians have achieved their highest level of satisfaction in the professional sphere. The one aspect in which there could be undercurrents of dissatisfaction in that domain has to do with discrimination. This was experienced only "rarely" or "sometimes" for the most part; still that may only mean that it is too subtle or sophisticated to be easily detected. It is also difficult to tell whether discrimination was felt more in professional or nonprofessional occupations. From the survey responses, it does not appear to be a major irritant right now, but certainly has the potential to develop along those lines.

On the issue of social assimilation, Indians again appear well satisfied but that satisfaction does not necessarily stem from becoming assimilated into American society. It may well be due to the development of a parallel ethnic society, in which Indians are happy to fulfill their needs for social recognition. They still have a strong allegiance to their own culture, but they stay in touch with the American world, especially because of their work and their children. On the personal front, there is much ambivalence as they struggle to arrive at some resolution and reconciliation of their own position and that of their children, especially on issues of dating and marriage.

As for the variations between the different groups, it appears that class differences are far more pronounced than any other differences. The influential high-income sector of the Indian population, those who arrived earlier in the United States and to a lesser extent, the women as a group, tend to veer toward the direction of greater Americanization. Pulling in the other direction are the low and middle-income Indians, the later arrivals and the men as a group who tend to be more conservative than the women. One can hardly say that a battle is joined for the causes of "assimilation" and "structural pluralism" because the differences between the various groups are not wide enough. One can, however, say that discernible differences do exist within the community that could lead to tension.

If, as the statistics suggest, the widest differences are between the low and high-income groups, and if the earlier immigrants differ considerably from the later arrivals, there could be greater homogenization or greater polarization within the community, depending on whether income differences even out gradually or become more pronounced, and whether fresh immigration from India is brought to a halt or if immigration continues for years to come. If immigration ceases, all the new immigrants would soon become "old" immigrants and there would be no new ones to take their place so that the divisive tendencies might be reduced. Of course, it could also be that whatever the internal tensions between the groups, they might dissolve in the face of a common threat such as racism or discrimination. Test results suggested that class might be the most important factor in influencing variations between the different groups, followed by length of stay.[26] Gender seemed to have the least overall effect though its effect was somewhat pronounced on certain issues.

The above analysis suggests that some generalizations can certainly be made on the basis of a statistical study about this rather elite group who have immigrated to the United States under circumstances quite different from those of the stereotypical immigrants. The general impression about Indian immigrants—that they are a homogenous group—is borne out by this study. For the most part they share certain characteristics, attitudes, and patterns of behavior, and they do things in a collective way, which distinguishes them as an immigrant group. What they are not is monolithic. In other words, variations do exist within the community, but the differences as seen in the statistics are not wide enough to tear the community apart. Though levels of assimilation and acculturation do differ according to income level and length of stay in the United States, Indians are held together by a strong common bond: the heritage of strong religious backgrounds, belief in common cultural forms and a collective effort to perpetuate them in the United States, as well as a firm and continuing connection to the motherland. Some of the gender differences that undoubtedly exist in any community are somewhat obscured in this study because many of the characteristics that normally differentiate women from men, such as lower education and reduced participation in the workforce, are not found in this population. As the demographic profile revealed, these women are as highly educated as the men and as involved in economic activity and at the same professional level.

In the years ahead, many aspects of the Indian immigrant community will no doubt change, and many of the agents of change will be beyond the immigrants' control. For now, it appears that there is an affluent, highly qualified and successful section of the community in Chicago that is seriously committed to building its own future in the United States and has consciously shaped its own destiny. All Indians, whether high or low income, early or late arrivals to Chicago, are interdependent in the creation of a viable community identity. The early immigrants may have more money and exercise leadership authority, but it is the later immigrants who have swelled the ranks and made the subculture a reality. It remains to be shown how the Indian immigrant community went about the task of building the ethnic institutions that help sustain a special way of life for themselves and for future generations.

An Indian bride in wedding attire, including a traditional Indian sari and Indian jewelry as well as a veil, which shows that she is Christian. Indians have always blended their religious and cultural identities, so that whether they are Hindu, Muslim, Christian, Sikh, Jain, Zoroastrian, Jew, or Buddhist, the stamp of their Indian culture is readily apparent. Photo courtesy of Mukul Roy.

A pre-wedding "Tikka" ceremony at the home of the bridegroom (May 29, 1998, Chicago). The tradition of arranged marriages, often misrepresented in the West as a coercive practice that forces children to marry against their will, actually covers a wide range of matchmaking options, and generally allows the couple to have the final say. Regardless of what brings a couple together, the traditional cultural ceremonies remain an essential element of the wedding day. Photo courtesy of Mukul Roy.

Higher education is greatly valued by both first- and second-generation Indian immigrants as a means toward success in the larger community. Pictured here, a mother and son after a graduation ceremony at the University of Illinois at Chicago (May 1998). The mother, a professor at the medical school, conferred a medical degree on her own son. Photo courtesy of Mukul Roy.

The preservation of the cultural core of an immigrant community is achieved through dance and music. Here, *Bharatanatyam* dancers of the *Natyakalalayam* dance school rehearse for a Ravinia Festival performance (1997). This ancient classical dance form is taught in dance schools throughout the Indian community in the United States as a way of nurturing Indian culture and values in a new land. Photo courtesy of Mukul Roy.

A *Raas Garba* performance, at the Federation of Gujarati Associations of North America (FOGANA) dance competition, Paramount Arts Center, Aurora (July 17, 1998). The *Raas Garba* is popular among Indian teenagers, whose parents encourage participation as a means to stay in touch with their heritage. Photo courtesy of Mukul Roy.

Hindu Temple of Greater Chicago (Lemont, 1998), the oldest of the religious institutions built by the post-1965 immigrants in Chicago's western suburbs. Both North and South Indian styles of worship are apparent within the temple's building, which accommodates many different deities under one roof. Many Hindu leaders view this synthesis of faiths as an important symbol of Hindu unity in North America; however, the construction of new temples to different deities exemplifies the desire of different religious groups to worship their own gods individually. Photo courtesy of Mukul Roy.

Top: Opening ceremony of the Balaji Temple (Aurora, 1985). The Sri Venkateswara (Balaji) Temple was built in a purely South Indian style and its congregation prides itself on the "authenticity" of its rituals, seen here in the traditional attire of the ceremony participants. Photo courtesy of Mukul Roy.

Bottom: Women marching on Michigan Avenue to celebrate the opening of Swaminarayan Temple (August 1992). The temple is supported almost exclusively by Gujaratis and in part represents a proliferation of temples to gods who are particular favorites on India's west coast. These few examples of Chicagoan temples demonstrate the vast diversity of religious organizations among Chicago's Indian immigrants, while the traditional celebrations illustrate the pride Indians hold for their cultural institutions. Photo courtesy of Mukul Roy.

Judy Barr Topinka at the First India Day parade on Michigan Avenue (1985). Parades are important to Indian Americans, who use them to invent and reaffirm their ethnic identity, but "parade politics" have also resulted in wrangling and infighting among self-styled community leaders and have turned people away from participating in parades. Photo courtesy of Mukul Roy.

Indians march on Devon Avenue protesting Indira Gandhi's assassination (December 1, 1984). As cultural traditions and religious institutions evidence Indian immigrants' strong ties to the culture of the homeland, so too do immigrants remain firmly connected to the political goings-on in India. Photo courtesy of Mukul Roy.

An advertisement for satellite TV, which enables subscribers to watch programs on TV Asia and Zee Network. These cable stations connect immigrants daily to the homeland with broadcasts primarily in Hindi, Urdu, and English, and also in key regional languages (*India Today*).

The post-1965 Indian community has the wherewithal to make its presence known in the political arena, though it has yet to muster up the votes to elect an Indian-American to national office. Pictured here, the senate campaign for Carole-Moseley Braun on Devon Avenue (October 1992). She was guest of honor at the annual dinner dance of the Club of Indian Women held in May 1993. Photo courtesy of Mukul Roy.

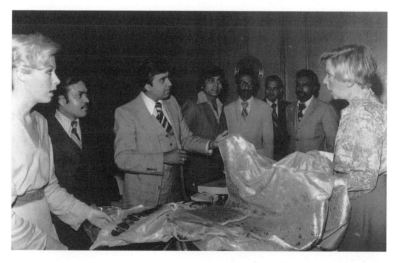

Ranjit Ganguly (Indo-American Democratic Organization [IADO] president) and Rattan Sharma (India Sari Palace), accompanied by members of Chicago's Indian immigrant community, visit Mayor Jane Byrne in City Hall and suggest that she wear a sari to IADO's first banquet in 1980. Foreground, left to right: Kathy Byrne (the mayor's daughter), Ranjit Ganguly, Rattan Sharma, and Chicago Mayor Jane M. Byrne. Photo courtesy of the Office of the Mayor, Chicago, Illinois.

Success in business, achieved by targeting many groups, is exemplified in the Patel Brothers grocery store, which caters to both the Indian and Pakistani communities. Patel Brothers began as a small grocery store in the 1970s and has expanded into the nation's largest Indo-Pak food retailer. Photo courtesy of Mukul Roy.

Indians generally do not cluster in ethnic enclaves, preferring to invest in homes in suburbs where property values hold up. But as more and more of them approach retirement age, they are attracted to the idea of living among their own. This ad from *India Today International Edition* targets a specific audience of NRIs and offers the allure of a "home away from home," an Indian retirement community in Florida.

PART III

Voices and Countervoices

5

ASTRIDE MANY WORLDS
The Women

We are a little hesitant in making decisions and taking bold steps.
I'm trying to get over it but I do carry my Indian values. My family
comes first, but I have also become more aggressive about fighting for my rights—both within the family and outside. So there is
an exchange of values. I'm trying to take what's best for me and
suits me.

—Indian immigrant woman interviewed for this study.

The core of human history and the nucleus around which the story of civilizations is reconstructed is the personal experience of the individual. It
may be impossible to separate the individual experience from the collective
experience, though it is customary to assign the study of the individual
experience to literature, mainly fiction or biography, while the study of the
collective or group experience is considered the legitimate field of history.
A historian cannot afford to forget that whatever choices people may make
as a community, the inspiration for their actions comes from individual, personal experience and is guided by personal interest. Yet the personal experience is so closely entwined in the group experience that one can hardly tell
which is which. Oftentimes, "what actually thinks within a person is not the
individual himself but his social community."[1] Some of the elements of the
"social community" thinking may be so deep-rooted and ingrained in a culture, they form part of the collective consciousness and span across succes-
sive historical eras. Some of those elements of the historical Indian
consciousness are described in Chapter 1 and, together with the statistical
portrait of Indians drawn in Chapter 4, should help us interpret the individual experience explored in the interviews. Looking into the hearts and
minds of people, no matter how much one presumes to understand their

thinking, is a daunting task, intimidating to the psychologist, sociologist and anthropologist alike. It is no wonder, then, that historians are often tempted to "lose" the personal dimension and bury it in the general discussions about political, social, religious, and cultural forms.

What follows is an attempt to capture the secret sources of migration in the individual voices of Indian immigrants in Chicago, voices that have so far lain submerged behind the quantitative data. Scores of individual interviews and three focus-group discussions were conducted between 1992 and 1995 and form the basis of the following chapters. The overall interview and discussion strategy was to pose a number of different open-ended questions relating to certain key issues and to allow each interviewee or group participant to pick up a line of answering that suited him or her best.[2] Because every individual is unique, what is captured here can hardly be called representative, it is only a sampling. But even as the voices speak of their individual experience, one can look beyond and through the uniqueness and discover the dynamics of intercultural contact in the group experience. Sometimes, immigrant voices speak in unison, and occasionally it is possible to detect what it is that makes them all members of the same community. At other times, their individuality predominates, defying the stereotypical images and forcing us to recognize that though all Indian immigrants in Chicago may have faced a similar set of historical circumstances, each one has reacted to those circumstances in his or her own way.

Three different groups of Indian immigrants were chosen for exploration of the personal, experiential dimension—the women, the younger generation (who came to the United States when they were still under ten years old or had spent some part of their childhood in India), and the older generation (parents of the adult immigrants). Some of the issues confronting these special immigrant groups are particular to their gender or age, and are only rarely explored in immigration history from their own specific vantage points.[3] The story of women immigrants tends to be subsumed in the larger history of the ethnic group, or told from the viewpoint of their "contributions" and "achievements" rather than day-to-day realities. Because the presence of Indian immigrant women has been so crucial in shaping the experience of the entire Indian immigrant community, it is particularly important to hear them tell why, how, and when they made important choices and changes in their lives, and how it affected the lives of those around them. The second group, the younger generation of immigrants, faced challenges quite different from those of their parents—they were more limited and confused in their choices as youngsters, they had few role models to emulate, but as adults they had a wider range of options to choose from, whether in their careers, their marriage partners or their lifestyles. As for the third group, the parents of the adult immigrants, most of them were caught in the trap of tradition and were unable to reshape it to suit their new circumstances. The choices they had to make to adjust to the demands of a new environment were particularly heart-wrenching because, sometimes, they were hardly choices at all.

The Cultural Context

Indian immigrant women in the United States in the 1990s are at the center of the issues of race, class, and gender that affect every individual in any multicultural society. But the cultural baggage they bring to the immigrant experience is uniquely Indian and their common heritage is a paradoxical one. They have seen a female prime minister, numerous female cabinet ministers, governors, and ambassadors, but they have also seen their society tolerate shameful practices toward women such as dowry deaths, police rape, female infanticide, and child marriages. The question of female infanticide and foeticide, especially, has disturbing, long-range consequences.[4] The unspoken laws governing Indian society that most Indian women subscribe to without much question, at least until they reach adulthood, are drawn from the *Smrtis*, which were composed as long ago as 200 B.C.E. and serve as commandments for many sections of society in India to this day. The most famous of the *Smrtis* dealing with the role of women is *Manusamhita*. Also called *Manusmrti*, it defines a highly restrictive role for women, keeping them in total economic, legal, and moral dependence on men. Manu enunciates the ideal of wifehood as the negation of the wife's personality. A woman can gain salvation only by virtue of her total obedience and devotion to her husband.[5] "In childhood, a female must be subject to her father, in youth to her husband and when her lord is dead, to her son. A woman must never be independent."[6] Another image of womanhood that has a profound effect on the Indian psyche is that of Sita, the heroine of India's most beloved epic, the *Ramayana*. Sita's chastity, obedience, and unflinching loyalty to her husband represent the ideal path for an Indian wife. This ideology survives even among modern, upper-class Indian women who defer to their husbands in an almost instinctive way. But it would be wrong to think of Indian women as merely submissive. Though all the myths and legends are created to make women internalize the idea of subordination to man, Indian culture and the Hindu religion also abound in images of female dynamism and power, as seen in Kali, the goddess of destruction, or Lakshmi, the harbinger of wealth and prosperity. Partly because of this cultural background, women in India do not necessarily think in purely dichotomous terms of man as strong and woman as weak, and despite all the rules and customs restricting their freedom, they sometimes manage to break out of the roles traditionally assigned to them.

As India approaches the twenty-first century, women in India enjoy many of the same rights granted to women in the most "advanced" countries of the West—the rights to inheritance of property, to vote, to divorce, to remarry, and to get an abortion. Independence in 1947 brought rapid reform and political gains at an almost dizzying pace. Article 15 of the Indian Constitution prohibits discrimination based on religion, race, caste, place of birth, or sex. This overt promise of equality is not available even to American women who saw the Equal Rights Amendment defeated for lack of ratification by state legislatures even though it was adopted by Congress in 1972. However, many of the laws live more in the books than in the streets or homes of India. The importance given to virginity and chastity ensures early marriage; divorce is still frowned upon and can be obtained only after years of separation. Both social opprobrium and economic hardships discourage Indian women from seeking divorce. The practice of dowry is so widespread and controversial that no amount of legislation is able to eradicate it. The patriarchal system still defines the limits within which reform can be sought. Many Indian women believe, along with Mahatma Gandhi, that "home life is entirely the sphere of woman," "man is supreme in the outward activities of a married pair," and though "woman is gifted with equal moral capabilities" she will not make her contribution to the world by "running a race with man."[7]

This background is important for understanding how far Indian immigrant women in Chicago will go when it comes to managing the demands of home, career, and raising a family. They have enough education, skills, and sophistication to enter the American workforce with relative ease (as shown by the survey data), but their upbringing discourages them from straying too far from their primary homemaking duties. There are many factors that differentiate the Indian women in Chicago from one another. Their experiences are colored by their background in India, which could be rural or urban, small town or cosmopolitan. Also, when and how they came to the United States is important. Did they come as single or married women, to work or to study? Their educational level is one of the most important distinguishing characteristics because it is what gains them entry into the job market and serves as the foundation on which they build their lives here.

The Historical Context

The significance of the role of Indian women in shaping the community is highlighted when we compare the circumstances of the post-1965 immigration with those of the immigration to California at the turn of the century. The one outstanding characteristic of this early immigration was the absence of women. By their very absence, women had a profound effect on the character and stability of the Indian immigrants' lifestyle. The men led shabby, itinerant lives, crowding together in rooming houses and wooden shacks, grouping in bands of twenty or thirty for cooking and sleeping arrangements. They lived frugally and spent very little on food, clothing, and entertainment, saving all their money to send back home.[8] This reinforced the prejudicial attitudes of the whites who thought of Indians as dirty and unhygienic. During the peak years of the early immigration wave, it is estimated that only one in seventy-five was a woman, and this figure itself might be an exaggeration.[9] Whether Indian women failed to come because of restrictive immigration laws or because the men chose to leave them behind is not clear, though both might have been good reasons. We should also remember that some Indian women did migrate as indentured labor under the colonial system. It was not until U.S. immigration laws changed in 1946 that it became possible for Indian women to enter the United States more freely. The survival of Indians as a distinct community in the United States is attributed to the large numbers of women and children among the approximately twelve thousand Indian immigrants who were admitted to the United States between 1947 and 1965 under quota and nonquota categories.[10]

The post-1965 Indian immigrant women are a different breed altogether from their sisters of earlier times. As articulate and organized professionals, they have expressed themselves in literature and recorded their immigrant experiences for posterity.[11] Still, they have not received their fair share of focused attention from historians even though they represent half the immigrant population. In the following excerpts from taped interviews, the women speak in their own voices about why they came to the United States, their experiences in Chicago, their joys and sorrows, their triumphs and travails. They speak of their loneliness and the sense of "not belonging" that many first-generation immigrants experience. But they also speak of their pride in their work and their career, and how economic independence has contributed to their development and sense of self-worth.

Why Come? Why Stay?

Five of the women in the study were married and came to the United States through marriage, either along with their husbands or later. Some saw themselves as free agents of their own destiny, others as being swept along by circumstances. Two women were single. One of them remained unmarried after almost twenty years in the United States. The other was a recent, younger immigrant but both the single women had struggled through the immigration process, emotionally or financially. Both saw emigration as "a difficult decision" or "fighting an uphill battle."

> This was 1976 and I had to make a decision whether to go back to India after my studies in Chicago or stay on as an immigrant. I was single and getting older. It was a difficult decision and there were so many issues to be considered, I started seeing a therapist. In India I could have had a comfortable life financially even if I didn't work. I was not committed to staying here because of a husband or a family. It was very much an individual decision. But doing nothing in India even though I didn't need the money was not very attractive. I had to have something to involve me, for me to feel good about myself. On the other hand, I missed the family, I missed Indian culture. At times I thought I would be better off with my family in India. My parents were not pushing me to come back. But they were questioning me because I was the only one in the family here. Also, I felt a sort of commitment to India, I felt like I was betraying a country in which I had grown up. I had been very happy, very contented, had very good friends in India. . . . But there is always ambivalence. One can always think back and say, "What would have happened had I gone back?" I think there are always questions that are open.

> I was born in Himachal Pradesh, lived all my life in Delhi, did my Master's in Delhi University and got married at twenty-two. I saw my

husband only after the wedding. He was doing his residency in Lucknow. We stayed there three years while he finished and then we came to England. My side of the family has been living in America and England for many years since the 1950s. England was only a means to come to America. Even in India this is where we wanted to come eventually. We were in England two and half years while he did his ECFMG [Entrance exam for Foreign Medical Graduates]. Then, in 1971, we came to Worcester, Mass. That was our first stop, then we came to Chicago, we've been here ever since, at Mercy Hospital till 1975, then we moved to the suburbs.

We were middle-class, not very high, we always aspired to be more. The idea of coming to the U.S. has been there ever since we got married in 1976. My husband wanted to study here, do his post-doc, but he realized he could not get into the U.S. except by immigration. My brother got his citizenship in 1981, sponsoring us took seven to eight years and we finally got here in March 1989. We never had any fears or apprehensions, we thought all it would take was hard work. I can never forget the moment when the four of us—my husband and my two boys and me—got down in Chicago with a bag in our hands. The past was haunting us, the future was totally a question mark. We felt so lonely, it was a turning point. A major change could also have happened in India but being here and without family, in a new culture, it definitely added to the experience.

I see it as mobility of labor. You get educated, you want more education, you go where you can get it. Qualifications get you jobs. You get mesmerized by all the comforts, your emotions are not drained off yet. The career, the goals, the glamour—that is what economic growth is. You don't worry about parents, you think money will make international distances shorter, you can make phone calls. You think you can conquer all that. Only later, when you've had it all, when your parents are getting old there and you've had your fill here, that the intersection point comes. I still don't ask myself what I'm doing so far from home. I've still got my goals going. But I'm not done, though I'm open to retiring in India. Because at that time, my emotional needs from the family will be greater. I will be torn between here and there with my children here, but if I can travel to both places, I will. The emotional pain is there—more so for the sons. Because to us, if we can serve our husband and children, our duty is done. But for the husbands, if they are not able to take care of their old parents back home, it's a heavy emotional toll for them. But they get so busy with work, they are able to suppress it and carry on. But they do carry it within themselves. That is the biggest toll of immigration we are carrying.

When we came here, we came as a batch of medical students. So it really wasn't a conscious decision. It didn't strike me at the time, what we were doing. It seemed the way to go. But as time has gone and the children have grown up, I see their Indianism is gone. You can teach them music, culture whatever, but the Indianism is gone. That seems to bother me but not to the point where I would want to go back to India, because I don't want to lose my independence of thought and movement which is restricted in India. There is a tradeoff and things have weighed toward my decision to stay on. But I had a definite say in the decision. I chose my citizenship but I did not consciously think then as I do now. But if I were given the choice, I don't know if I would be fit to go back. I have my own views. I don't know if I could live independently in India.

My husband was offered a scholarship at the University of Illinois for his Master's. He was here three years before I came. I married him and I came. He did tell me when we got married that if he chose to live in America leaving family behind and had no intention of coming back, I had to think. He already knew life in America. But in a way I had no choice because my father had already chosen him for me. It was his decision. I couldn't say much. But anyway I don't have any regrets. In India, we are moneylenders and landowners. Due to legislation we lost much of our lands—my husband's family as well as my own. So our only outlet was more education. I was born rich but by the time I was marriageable age, we had nothing in our home. We had lost everything. The same thing happened to my husband's family. Since our parents were too old to go out and do anything different, they had always been moneylenders, the sons had to get more educated. That was what brought us here.

I knew exactly what I was doing when I came here. In fact, I was the only one who had a say in this. I didn't "fall" into it, it was an uphill battle for me. I was equally independent in India and I think I'd fit in even if I went back to India. I was educated in Bombay. I was teaching for three years. I was bored out of my mind. I was working two jobs, I felt I needed to do something more with my life. My father would not let me take a job in industry. He said okay to government jobs, teaching, that's fine. I couldn't work in industry over there. Then one day somebody suggested to me—a professor—he said, "You're wasting yourself. You're too bright to be here. So go." Then I started thinking about it. I took my GMAT. There was a war at home. "How do you think you're going to go?" my father said. "Who's going to give you the money?" For the longest time he wasn't going to help me but eventually he did. When I was ready to come, he did help. He said, "Okay, if you're that determined, I don't want to stand in your way."

I was born in Calcutta. I am the oldest of three children, the only girl. I went to a Catholic convent school, St. Joseph's, and I did my Master's in geography. My marriage was arranged in 1974 and I came here on November 14, 1974. My husband was here as a student in 1968, he got a job, came back to India to get married, and we came back together again. I was always in love with America. And his was the only proposal from America. We got married in six days. My mom said, "Don't get married now, wait awhile, get to know him." But I wanted to get married. We lived in an apartment in Wheeling and one of the things that stood out was the lack of people. It was winter, very cold. I wasn't used to living by myself in an apartment and I also did not like the closed air. I'd have the windows open with the heat on very high, and the electric bills were very high—it did not sit well with my new husband. But he was making good money and I had no problems with living conditions or food. I just had to get used to things. For me it was a big deal. I was cold all the time. I used to get cramps every night, just wasn't used to being alone. I didn't want to take a shower if my husband wasn't home. I had this horror that somebody would get in the house when I was in the shower. It was an overwhelming feeling of loneliness I wasn't used to. I come from a very large family with a lot of people around you in Calcutta, lot of street noises. There was absolute silence here and that was deafening. I found it very oppressive. In 1975 we moved to Libertyville, more into town, in a building with mostly older people, all Americans. My experience with American people when I first came was actually very positive. Looking back, Libertyville is actually supposed to be a WASP area but most people there were very nice to me, very friendly. One woman who took me out everywhere used to call me her Indian princess. She'd say, "Dress up in one of your silk saris, we'll go out." We'd go out a lot.

Home and Career

Indian women are taught from childhood to view marriage as a sacrament, and the traditional role of wife and mother is respected enough to keep them motivated as homemakers. "Family values" consists of working toward family unity, accepting one's place in the family hierarchy, and pursuing a career only for the sake of the larger good of the family, not for "individual" fulfillment. Sometimes an Indian woman's behavior is perceived as inconsistent, hypocritical, or even schizophrenic by American standards. She may be assertive and even overbearing at work with her American colleagues, if she feels the situation demands it, but completely submissive and unprotesting toward her husband or even her children. This capacity for "dual" or even "multiple" behavior patterns has sometimes helped Indian immigrant women successfully combine work and career, and avail themselves of new opportunities without discarding the advantages of a traditional value system. Whereas American women, who are also sometimes equally loathe to fully abandon the "homemaker" role, feel the conflict and contradictions between home and career, Indian women see the pursuit of a career as an extension of their homemaker's role, not as an alternative to it. The interests of family generally take precedence when they clash or are at cross purposes with career interests. Indian women are thus more willing to seek reform within their own cultural traditions and less willing to embrace a militant feminism. In a pilot survey of thirty-seven Indian women immigrants (which was conducted by the author before the larger Chicago survey for this study), 70 percent believed that a man's career is "sometimes," "often," or "always" more important than a woman's. But 82 percent of the women also said "No" when asked, "Do you believe a woman's place is in the home?" The general sentiment appeared to be that women did belong in the home, but not *exclusively* in the home, and that the needs of the home ought not to be sacrificed to the woman's need for self-expression.

But not all women achieve the ideal of a happy balance. Beneath the veneer of economic and professional success, beneath the figure of the well-adjusted immigrant, there lurk unfulfilled expectations and dissatisfactions. Sometimes the problems are obvious. Domestic strife, caused as often by the presence as the absence of extended kith and kin, has led to breakup of families. As in American society, women bear the brunt of the consequences of such tragedies. Apna Ghar, a shelter for battered women in Chicago, has unfortunately seen its clientele grow from year to year. Generally, most Indian men, especially those reared in a strong patriarchal tradition that sharply demarcates male and female spheres of activity, do not help with household chores. A large number of Indian women, especially the nonworking ones, themselves support this stance. This may be changing for second-generation Indians, but first-generation Indian women continue to do most of the housework after putting in a full day at the office and bear the major responsibility for rearing the children. As such, they experience the physical and emotional hardships and frustrations that go with fulfilling traditional roles while trying to explore new paths. The orthodox Indian role of submissive wife and dutiful daughter-in-law is an irksome one for many of the highly educated and professional Indian immigrant women, whether of the first or second generation. Working outside the home is at once an escape and a trap, but Indian women continue to hold their own against increasing stresses and pressures of the immigrant situation.[12]

I was psyched up to work after my Master's. I took up a job as a lecturer in a college in India and my father didn't talk to me for six months. He thinks I defied him. I wanted to make money. But your value system inside—you feel you have to take care of your husband. There is no money for us to go to college in America. Your husband has to establish himself first. My life got derailed from the day I got here. Whenever I try to get back on track, I find the rails are rusted. We are not primary earners, we are secondary earners. When you go out into the corporate world, they expect you to work like it's your primary job.

In India, we were always being told, "Don't do this because you're a girl. Whatever you want, if your husband lets you do it after marriage, you can." If my goal was to get educated in America and have a career, my only passport to achieve that was to get married and come to America and then do what I wanted to do. I enjoyed staying home with my son but now I want to go out and work. For me, that is becoming a lot more important. . . . I think Indian men would be happy to keep us at home, come back from work and get a hot meal. When they see their wives spreading their wings and going out, they do feel threatened. Because the opportunities that were offered to them are now offered to you and they're afraid of how much advantage you're going to take of it. Most of the Indian men are supportive, especially on the outside. But the job I'm going into now, I have to work in the evenings and my husband's asking me, "Why don't you get a 9 to 5 job?" We had a spouse interview for the job at which he was very agreeable and my manager said, "Oh, your husband seems very nice," but though he's supportive on the outside, he does feel threatened on the inside. He's thinking, How many evenings is he going to have to baby-sit our son? What else is expected of him? When I worked 9 to 5, I still dropped our son off at school and picked him up, still cooked all the food, getting him settled before my husband came home for dinner . . . he realizes all that is going to get disrupted.

My husband was sure he would find work in America with his education and experience (with a pharmaceutical firm in India) but he wasn't getting a break. He had to pass some exams. I was fortunate to get a job within one month. My friends were not in the same position or in the same field to get me work. It just so happened I got my job through an Indian. But I'm sure if I had been willing to work hard, put in eight hours at Jewel or McDonald's, I would still have managed. Our basic aim was to become independent and stand on our feet as quickly as possible. I'm sure that hard work is the only thing that will get me ahead. I enjoy working. I would like my work to be more appreciated. I have seven people working under me. As immigrants, we are in need of a job, and I think one side is taking advantage of us. I don't say I'm not needy but I can recall instances very clearly where I feel I was taken advantage of. Immigration by itself need not be so traumatic, but I had to struggle to find a job. I was thrilled to come here. I thought I was very lucky to be here. I wouldn't blame the country. America didn't call me here. I wouldn't blame the American way of life for my problems. It was just the circumstances. To start a life all over again at middle age, and knowing that whatever you did for fifteen years in India, you struggled and achieved so much success but that meant nothing in this country. We are not recognized. Those things bothered you. Maybe with time, it will be behind me like it is for the others.

I tried to learn about computers. I took a course, but my children were growing up. I never pursued it fully, never took up a job, so it got kind of forgotten and forgiven. I stayed a housewife all my life. Fortunately, my husband has provided me all I needed. I never felt the need to go out and get a job. We also decided amongst ourselves, as long as the children were in school, I would be home. I found an outlet and challenge in art, doing some social work. I'm working with an interior designer now, but I'm not doing it full time. I'm basically an artist and designing is an outlet for me. I used to spend a lot of time on household work but not now. Throughout my life, I have done social work, been involved in some project or another. For a year or two I took care of my mother who was bedridden until she left to be with my brother. I feel that I have to be doing something physically all the time. I'm not a person who makes friends easily but I had no trouble getting on with my husband's colleagues. Other physicians in India have a more luxurious and less stressful life. They have servants. Here we are working harder. Coming to America has enhanced my life, broadened my thinking. In India I would not have matured the way I have. I would have been less exposed. Interference from other family members would have taken up more of my time.

My husband wanted me to find a job as soon as I had come. Growing up, being brought up in India, you never think you have money value. You have a degree but you don't realize you can earn with that degree. So I went to Libertyville National Bank and applied for a job. And they said I couldn't work until I wore a skirt. I didn't feel comfortable in a skirt in those days so I didn't get the job. I was very upset. There was another opening in a novelty shop called "Things Beautiful." I got the job. It was $100 a week at that time. I was very happy in the job but my husband said, "You've got to find another job." I got a job in inventory control at Baxter. Then my husband decided it was time for me to go into computers. He was making all my progress for me. I used to be very happy but he'd decide it was time for me to move on. At that time, it was always like "for our own good," but each time I felt added pressure. Then my husband said, "You've got to apply at Harvester." The money was very good but I didn't like doing it. I hate change, I find it physically upsetting, but it was either that or you put up with the constant nagging at home. You gotta change, you gotta change, you gotta change. In the long run,

financially it was a big boost but it was still a big tension. Because you
get used to people at work, you're happy. I never settled down from
the time I came to this country. There was never a time off.

So, like many nonimmigrant women, Indian women, too, are caught
between their responsibility for running a home and their need for a chal-
lenging career outside. For some, it is a matter of personal choice and they
find homemaking "enriching," "a career in itself," and improving the "quality of life." But they also feel subtly pressured to do something outside the
home and become more than "just" housewives. This ambivalence between
home and career is managed by each woman in her own way but their deep-
seated unease with the inevitable compromises is apparent.

Family

Indian women, regardless of their religious background, share a common
attitude toward preservation of the family unit. As one Chicago resident,
Dr. Marilyn Fernandez, who is an Indian immigrant herself and has conducted research among Indian immigrant women put it, "It doesn't matter
what your religion is. I was brought up a Catholic. I was taught to believe
that every Hindu was pagan. Christianity was *the* religion. I went to Jesuit
convent schools, my entire upbringing was Catholic and I'm amazed at how
Indian I am. It's not Hindu. It transcends religion. I think exactly like my
Hindu friends in some respects, even though they are steeped in Hindu philosophy." What Dr. Fernandez describes as typically Indian is women's ability
to harmonize roles, to solve problems through a distinctive coping style that
seeks to accommodate the demands of all family members. (Dr. Fernandez
also believes that the "average" Indian man is not capable of such adjustment, the woman is the only one capable of sacrificing for the larger cause.)
The driving principle behind the actions of most Indian women is the commitment to keeping the family together.[13]

> Our respectful family traditions—we should keep those. Americans
> miss out on that. Indian families are struggling in this effort. Parents
> would like to keep more control over their children, have their chil-
> dren brought up the way we were brought up. On the other hand, the
> children are fighting for their own identity, a place of their own. We

had differences when my kids were in high school. That is the toughest time. They are living in the house, they are part of the family, yet they want the independence of grown-ups. We had many arguments over it, but now they are grown up, both are in college.

I miss all the weddings, all the births, all the deaths. I'm not there, I've no idea how my relatives are growing up. I do talk to my parents, because inside here, I feel something, but the distance is taking its toll. Five years from now, I don't know. The cousins I was so close to, my uncle's kids that I practically brought up, that I stayed with for months. I don't even know what grade they're in right now. My uncle just passed away. I couldn't go. I had to call and say how sorry I was, but I couldn't pay my respects. I would have gone to Delhi from Bombay had I been in India. Friends are only friends, family is family. That's blood. It's different. If my sister was sick, I'd take leave and go look after her for a week. I don't know if I'd do that for my friends. It helps to have the emotional support of the extended family. I do try to fill the gap with friends but it's not really the same. I feel friends here are very superficial. Friendship you can spoil with one little thing. A relative you can't get rid of like that. I realize the value of family even more after coming here. There you never stop to think about it. Here you stop and think so much. The bond here has strengthened but the link is weakening because of the distance. I have no brothers. I'm the eldest of three sisters and my parents don't expect me to provide for them. They won't touch a dime from me but I feel I should be there for them. Ten years from now, when they are retired, all the children will be here. My younger sister is already here and the youngest will come sooner or later.

Our need as immigrants to keep up our ties with our families is much greater than their need to keep up their ties with us. Of course, once the parents go, the ties might weaken. One thing my kids miss here is the emoting, the freedom to express their feelings physically, the hugging, the touching. It's not their fault, it's just the society here. Our kids are told they should not be touched in a particular way, so they lack that kind of emotion. I also dislike the way my children state their own views. Sometimes they cross the borderline, especially with the grandparents. Either they are not aware of it or we are just not letting them know their limits. But in a way I also admire their freedom. I guess it's better to have children speak up and put things in front of you and keep communicating than have them do things behind your back. Our kids can't be expected to be like us. We do teach them respect but our understanding of it is different. People from India see outspokenness as disrespect. We don't.

In India, you're somebody. Just being born into a certain family gives you status. We all come from rich families, by and large. I came here, it was riches to rags, as my husband said. He was a student on an assistantship. I was just the wife of a student. I wasn't even allowed to work or go to school. It was a rude awakening. You have to start from scratch, travel by bus. Nobody recognizes you, knows who you are and even once you are introduced, nobody cares. In a way it's a learning experience. You have to relate to all kinds of people. The difference is that in India, I was known for whose daughter I was, whose wife I was. Here I'm known for myself, the person that I am, which for me is a personal growth.

I didn't come from a rich family. I came from an upper-middle-class family. We could afford certain things but my family was not known even in Delhi. My family were already immigrants in Delhi from the south, my background was in Bangalore. When I came here, it didn't bother me. We were brought up to do everything. I adjusted easily. I feel I've risen in social status here.

My mother-in-law stayed with us. Things seemed fine but they really weren't fine. I felt cornered by my mother-in-law. I don't know how other Indian women go through this. She just came for a visit but there were always questions like how much money I was giving my family. It was little things like that. I almost had a nervous breakdown finally. I was expected to take her shopping. I hate shopping. Malls and shopping centers give me headaches, but it was always my duty. People were glum if I didn't come through. This family politics was rather difficult. . . . I'm not the one who asked for the divorce. It took me a long time just to get used to the idea. It was a gradual disillusionment. When we first got married, I had a different idea. But the chemistry was never there. After awhile, it was never right. I had no confidence in myself. If there had been no interference from the family, from my brother-in-law and mother-in-law, we would just have coexisted. There was no spark. . . . But the families are allowed to break a marriage. A lot of times the woman sees it, but not the man. For one who grew up sheltered like me, my divorce is a bit of a personal victory. As an Indian you just don't think of divorce. You think marriage is forever. I feel sometimes I should have stood up earlier. But I felt my parents have given everything in marriage to me. My mom was a widow. If I get turned out on the streets she can't keep me. It'll be a shock to her. These things were going through my head. There are many reasons why people stay in a marriage till you can't take it any more. I have a new man in my life now. I should call him my partner because he's not my spouse yet. I like him very much, however you define love. I think love is like when somebody makes you feel good. I get a lot of pleasure out of my children, that's why I love them.

The women acknowledged that the absence of extended kin in the United States had its advantages and disadvantages. Raising children without the support of extended family called for a delicate balance between freedom and discipline and the development of new standards more in tune with the American environment. For the married women, it was important to place family interests above all else but there was also an awareness that they had to sacrifice their individual interests for the larger good.

Society

Accepting their own differentness was considered the first step in understanding American attitudes toward Indians which are sometimes prejudiced and discriminatory. But the women knew they had to overcome these problems and find their own place in a white-dominated, multiracial society.

You're slotted and you have work extra hard to be considered an equal. We are not brought up to be aggressive. But we have to learn to be more assertive. If you don't speak up, you're a dead duck. If you voice your opinion, they respect you and listen to you. As a doctor's wife, we knew where we stood in their estimation. I'm at the top notch level, on the board of doctor's wives, but even at this level, you can mix with them only so far. For sixteen years I've been on the board, but they've never put me on a committee. The whites are together. We've invited every doctor in the hospital, but only two or three have invited us back. They'll play golf, tennis with you but never invite you socially. I do get invited out sometimes but that's because my husband is a cardiologist and he has done a heart job on them. We meet them at Christmas, but it stops at that. We haven't grown in friendship the way we do with our Indian friends. We'll make money, we'll vote, we'll gain in political clout, but we will be a separate little ball, molecules in the same atmosphere, coexisting, but not part of the same big ball.

I don't know if I want to call it discrimination. I just want to call it something different. Like if there are eight of us Indians and one Chinese woman sitting here. I know she's different. And she knows it. But I'm not discriminating against her. In social situations, you sometimes feel you're an Indian, you're a woman and you're not white. My friends are those I made in India and who have come here since. They are not new friends I made here. We all have friends like that. You feel like you've never left them. You see them after fifteen years and it feels like you saw them yesterday. With Americans, there's a subtle difference. They don't understand us as well.

I think there are cultural differences. We Indians think nothing of imposing on others. That's an Indian trait. Like "Can I borrow your car? Can you give me a ride someplace?" You'd think twice before you'd ask an American family that. They'd say, "Why don't you take a cab?" It has a cultural implication. It's just the way they are. It has nothing to do with being close. I think you can unload emotionally, share emotions quite a bit, but in terms of small points of dependence, they tend to be much more self-dependent than we are. When you borrow a dime from an American for a coffee machine, he expects it back. That's the difference. The Indian wouldn't even take it back. He'd think you're insulting him. If I were to borrow a stamp, and this has happened to me time and time again, you don't expect an Indian to give you back a borrowed stamp or give you twenty-nine cents. But an American will give it back, and you take it back, too. If you give them thirty cents, they insist on giving back one cent. In America, there's no such thing as a free lunch. Even clients know very well, "This is my money that's buying the lunch." Someone always pays, but in India, you're not taught that, you're not aware.

I see us Indians as being just as racist as any other group. In this country, you would have to be deaf, dumb and blind not to be aware of race. In England, we would be in the colored category. Colored includes Indians, blacks, Pakistanis. In America, they make a difference. Blacks are blacks. And really, they don't have a word for us. They don't call us blacks but we are not totally white either. We all make distinctions. I don't think we are any more racist than the others. It can work both ways—you can feel superior, you can feel inferior. I think it comes into play more in a society which is white-dominated. The fact that we are not white makes us much more self-conscious about it. In India it gets played out on an individual level—all those matrimonial ads for fair wives—so there is a color consciousness in India. Here, it is attached to an hierarchy. You have to come to terms with it. You are living in a society where there are different colored people and there are implications. The danger is that you may feel "Oh, I'm an Indian. I'm being discriminated against or fall backward and say, "Oh, I'm so American. I will not meet any Indians." The most important thing for me was that I could make professional choices and changes that the Indian situation would not have allowed for. I would have had much more difficulty there. This is not just America, but the intellectual, international environment that this community has provided me here. I feel mentally very alive here, very stimulated. Things are more structured here, you can do things easily for yourself. In that sense, I can be more independent here. The downside to that is that you can become isolated. When you put out a hand and ask for friendship, you get it. But if you don't, they leave you alone and you can become isolated. In India, just by being a member of the family, you get included in family activities. You get invited because you are someone's aunt or cousin, whether they like you or not. I've built different kinds of ties here."

"When my children were very young, they were going to public schools. We used to live in an all-white neighborhood. We were the only Indians there, they felt some discrimination. My daughter was called "brownie" and she became very shy. My son overcame that feeling by "buying" his friends (spending money on them). But once they moved to a private school with more Indians, they became more comfortable. We are not involved in local community affairs, only on a professional level are we involved with Americans. Indians tend to be involved only with Indians. I have more ethnic friends than American friends, mostly Indian. My children have all kinds—white, American, Greek. My children have sometimes accused me of being racist. When I notice my kids in a photo with a friend, I say, "Oh, he's black," and they'll immediately ask, "Why do you say that? You shouldn't label people by their ethnic identity." They also get upset at the attitude Indians have amongst themselves. When we talk of Bengalis and Gujaratis, they say you shouldn't identify them like that. My children don't like the Indians in Chicago. They think we are all hypocrites. No matter how hard we try we don't come up to their expectations. But it's true, when we were first here, we would greet an Indian in the store and just acknowledge that he was Indian. Now we are so many and we have all these regional organizations and associations—Jain and Kannada and five Gujarati associations—we are just as divided here as we are in India.

I have two kinds of friends here. Some friendships are two decades old. Those kinds of friendships you don't have to work on. My husband's music circle has helped me make more and more friends. In fact, we have to put a stop somewhere. Quality and quantity-wise I have more friends here than in India. In fact, I have so many, I have never felt the desire to go out and seek white American friends. I'm sure if I were to try I would have made them. I've never felt the need. Or maybe it's the time. I just don't have the time to make new friends. I haven't gone out to look for them. I don't care if they are black or Hispanic but my present circle is so satisfying. . . . But I don't think it is necessary to be good friends with them to live among them. One can still live here without moving in their circles. . . . My major Americanization is yet to come. When my children grow bigger and expect us to understand their American ways, that's the time. Right now, we're still influencing them. I can see it coming. They will be moving with different cultural and moral values. I'll have to change myself at that point and it will be hard. . . . I do not like it as a parent— for them to be so aggressive and answer back. That's not the way we were. But if they are going to be here, I don't want them to be mild either. Because basically, they are going to spend three quarters of their life with these people, outside, not with us, so they have to learn, from the school or the media. When they first came here, they were so mild and meek. I could see how hurt they were when they dealt with boys of their age. I don't like it, but it's okay, they need it to survive—as long as they stay within their limits with us.

On the whole, it appeared that Indians socialized mostly with other Indians, and they saw their lack of involvement in the wider society as stemming from their own volition. They were more comfortable among their own kind and didn't have the time to pursue new friendships, sometimes to the chagrin of their own children. But there was also an awareness that they could become branded and isolated, not only from mainstream society but from the second generation growing up in the United States.

India

India occupies a special place in the hearts of these women, though none of them would consider a permanent return to India at this time. Some of the ways in which they remain connected to the homeland are visiting regularly, maintaining close ties with family and friends, and helping the less fortunate in India.

I don't have many relatives in India any more. In certain ways, we've outgrown the style of living there. I do visit, practically every year, or a year and a half, but the way I see things is different from them. I don' think I'll ever be able to go back and live there. But I'll keep going to India because I love it, it is my native country and I have affection for it. I have a sister who is a nun. I like to visit her. I also like to travel, to get away from here to a different environment, to restore myself or freshen up mentally. I'm a totally different person there. I go there, I enjoy myself there and I come back. Why India? Maybe that's my comfort zone.

After the divorce is over, we might all go to India, my partner and his family, me and my family. We would all like to go, take his daughter, take my boys. My brother is still there. I don't think he wants to come here. I've been trying to work on him so he sends my nephew over at least. I still think it's better here. I love India, but it's not the India I left. Sometimes, when I go it's like the shattering of the image I had. It's sometimes painful but it's also nice. I meet my old friends. Right now, I see my life here. Both the boys are Americans. This is their home. For me, my place is here.

There's something about India. I can't quite figure out what it is. I just feel good when I go there, the streets, the smell. So even if my family is not there, I might just go back if I feel the need. The kids too, they have our genes. It's like ducks in a pond. They are going back to their natural environment. The love and affection they get from their cousins in India, you don't get here.

Even when I travel from the north to the south in India, I never feel lonely. There's a sense of belonging, you can never get it here. Going to the temple here is not quite the same as going to the temple in India. It has to be planned, the temples are forty miles away. In India, I don't have to make sure my kids are okay, that one of them doesn't have a test the next morning, the other doesn't have a fever, that my husband doesn't have music practice, that he is available to take us in the car. In India, the atmosphere is different. You can hear the bells ringing, you can see the temple up on the hillock, you have a bath and take a walk down and say your prayers. My boys would just go and do a *shastang pranam* (prostrate themselves in prayer) at the temple, and everyone else would also be doing it. It is never the same in America—it can't be. You have to tell yourself, you have to do this or that. In India, nobody has to tell you, you just do it. The need to define one's identity is not there. It just *is*.

Conclusion

What discernible patterns emerge from these accounts of individual experiences, and how do they compare with earlier research on Indian immigrant women? In the first major study of Indian immigrants in the New York metropolitan area, Paramatma Saran found that Indian women still operated within the traditional framework of husband-wife relationships and were not particularly influenced by American trends or the immigrant experience to step out of their traditional roles.[14] Saran's survey of 345 households in the Greater New York Metropolitan Area included 285 women. Twenty-six percent of the married women had postgraduate degrees at the Master's level and above, and most of them had completed their education in India. Among the married women 40 percent were working full-time, 10 percent "occasionally," and 7 percent part-time. The single women were evenly distributed between the professional and technical categories of employment but the married women worked mostly in clerical positions and sales. "Even in those areas where wives seem to have greater freedom, they are still in essentially a subordinate position. Generally Indian women are less assertive than their American counterparts, and the majority feel that relations cannot be changed by being too assertive. They recognize that being assertive and demanding is not the right approach to correct things."[15] Apart from the unwarranted editorial comment on what is the "right approach to correct things," the Saran study reveals an obviously male perspective. The Chicago interviews show that Indian immigrant women make a fine distinction between being "aggressive," which they classify as an "American" value, and being "assertive," which is what they feel they must become in order to survive in the United States. Saran further concluded that women were better adjusted than the men because they had greater control over their own lives and the lives of their husbands than they would have had in India since they were free of family interference. Also, "in Indian tradition women are better prepared psychologically to break ties from their parents after marriage."[16] The Chicago interviews show that pressures and obligations prevalent in India are not necessarily absent in the immigrant situation. In fact, many new tensions emerge, such as having to deal with increased workloads, new roles and responsibilities in an alien cultural environment, and lack of supportive kith and kin. Also, breaking ties with their own family is not always accepted by the women as a natural corollary to marriage. Women realize that keeping up and nurturing ties with their own family even after marriage can be a matter of personal choice for them, especially if they are working women with an income of their own.

Another work entitled *On the Trail of an Uncertain Dream* is worthy of mention because it is by a woman, Sathi Das Gupta, and contains a chapter on the experience of Indian immigrant women.[17] Some of the conclusions reached in Das Gupta's study may have been true for a newer immigrant population but they are not always borne out by the Chicago research. She concluded that Indian women have low self-worth and can never have a genuine sense of well-being in the United States because their long-established, enduring relationships built in India are lost to them forever and they are cast adrift in a friendless sea. The subjects of Das Gupta's study conducted in 1981 were also upper-class Indian immigrant women but, unlike the Chicago women, they lacked confidence and a true sense of independence that may be due to their lack of marketable skills. Das Gupta also contended that the Indian women were engaged in "status competition" with other Indian families and their effort to "keep up with the Joneses" prevented them from developing new friendships. Her final conclusion that "their gains are minuscule compared to their losses" is rather dubious. The voices of the Chicago women tell a far different story. Some of these women are confident of their ability to cope, to break out of traditional molds, or even to go it alone. Being single or divorced may not be an ideal state, but they prefer it to being unfairly dominated or abused by men. Other images of Indian immigrant women emerge from the writing, such as the works of novelist Bharati Mukherjee and they are mostly of conflict, pain, and near or total disaster.[18] The only way for many of Mukherjee's heroines is to discard the past, totally and irrevocably, and embrace total Americanization. Other works show Indian immigrant women exploring their sexuality and alternative lifestyles, and struggling with inner demons of isolation and cultural displacement.

Many of the above described images are sometimes reinforced, sometimes contradicted, by the Chicago study and any attempts at generalization are perilous since every individual woman has her own destiny and her own way of coping with it. While struggle, pain, and compromise are an integral part of the immigrant experience, many of these women do not necessarily see total Americanization or rejection of India as the path to wholeness. They may have accepted America as their home, but their yearning for India and sense of loss is also accepted as an inevitable corollary of immigration. Most of all, these women see that the world of their children is very different from their own. They anticipate the challenges they will face or are already facing as their children's world intrudes more and more upon their own comparatively safe and secure lives, and forces them to make new choices. In the following chapter, we shall see that world through the eyes of the children, the second-generation Indian Americans.

6

CAUGHT IN LIMBO
The Youth

Your parents made a decision to immigrate and you've grown up
here. It wasn't your choice to leave and become one or the other.
You can't change your ethnic heritage. I was born in India, I have
two Indian parents, and I've been raised with an Indian mind-set.
I'm Indian, there's no question for me. But my friends tease me.
They say, "You're the most Americanized Indian I know." So
where's the answer? I don't think there is one for me.
——Indian youth interviewed for this study.

The children of Indian immigrants to the United States are referred to as
"the second generation" regardless of the land of their birth. Most of them
were born in the United States, and are still barely out of their teens. The
children of the pioneers who came in the late 1960s or early 1970s have
reached adulthood by the mid-1990s, and some even have children of their
own. There is still another group of young Indians who were born in India
and came to the United States when they were already five or six years old—
the so-called "1.5" or "knee-high" generation, because they were knee high
when they first came to the United States. These children have had many
years of school and college in the United States, but unlike their American-
born counterparts, they also have a storehouse of Indian cultural experiences to draw upon. The youth themselves make fine distinctions between
these different categories. Those who were born in India and spent a few formative years there tend to speak their mother-tongue, retain more of their
culture, and appreciate Indian music and art forms more than do the
American-born Indian youth.[1]

Perhaps the most significant difference is between those youth who grew
up in an earlier era when Indian immigrants in Chicago were still an invisible minority and there were no temples, *Bharatanatyam* classes, religious

summer camps or Hindi movies to shape their experiences of growing up, and those who grew up in the "institutional" Indian culture that had developed in Chicago by the late 1980s. The former youth lack the sense of connectedness and bonding as a group that the latter developed through shared Indian cultural experiences. Going through adolescence and attaining adulthood as a shared experience in the midst of people with the same ethnic background colors the ethnic experience and opens up far more options for immigrant children, especially when it comes to socializing, campus life, or choice of marriage partner. Teenagers for whom the searing question is "Who am I?" or "What am I?" tend to resolve their basic identity issues in different ways depending on how many true peers they can count in their midst.

The 1990 Census figures show that 125,000 or one-sixth of all Asian Indians in the United States are between the ages of fifteen and twenty-four, and 92 percent of all children below eighteen live with their parents.[2] Thus, most Indian youth are still very much under the influence of their parents, and family relationships play an important role in the development of their identity as Indian Americans. Indian parents in Chicago, while generally approving of the American educational system and goading their children to academic success within that system, try very hard to counteract the American social influences at school, especially dancing and dating. The free socialization of boys and girls, particularly during adolescence, is frowned upon by Indian parents and is a perennial source of tension in the Indian immigrant family. Indian parents who believe that dating leads inevitably to sex and who automatically associate "American culture" with promiscuity, AIDS, drugs, and divorce try to inject massive counter-influencing doses of "Indian culture" into their children through celebration of Indian festivals, visits to temples, and enrollment at summer camps for prayers, meditation, Indian dance, music, history, and philosophy. While some Indian children enjoy these opportunities to understand their heritage, others strongly resent Indian culture being "rammed down their throats." Many teenagers who cannot conform to the temple/mosque/*gurdwara* culture and who feel disenfranchised by the majority community create a subculture of their own by mixing elements of the old and new. One example is the "bhangra-reggae-rap" culture that has grown rapidly in Canada and the United States among Punjabi teenagers.[3]

Indian teenagers see hypocrisy in pretending to be "American" at school and "Indian" at home, and are unable to switch roles on and off in the way their parents manage to do. The contradictions between the values they must adopt at home to get along with their families and what they must adopt in the outside world in order to be competitive are seen as too severe and irreconcilable. They also complain that they do not know if they must identify with a nonviolent Indian independence movement or a bloody American revolution. The acronym ABCDs (American Born Confused Desis—"desi" meaning "belonging to the native land or India") has gained wide currency in the Indian community throughout America and India because it encapsulates the dilemma of the Indian teenager growing up in the United States. Generational conflicts combine with cultural conflicts that are inherent in the immigrant situation and add to the confusion and turmoil that are a part of growing up, no matter what the circumstances.

Indian youth realize that their parents are also caught up in the learning curve as they try to adjust in a new American environment that is so different from the Indian one. They feel their parents have not embraced the new country in full earnest, and that they are still living in the India of their past. They see them as novitiates, too, and so are unwilling to accept any received wisdom from them about America. Most of the second generation feel that their parents have no true understanding of American culture, and that they resort to stereotyping of the unknown American mainly in order to influence and control their children. Parents see challenges to their authority as "typically Americanized" behavior and demand that their children be "Indianized" and respectful and unquestioningly obedient. Children, in turn, brand their parents' demands as "emotional blackmail" and consider their outrage totally unwarranted. Yet they feel a strong sense of affiliation with their Indian background and have no desire to shake it off totally. Stresses and strains resulting from miscommunication or even total lack of communication between Indian parents and their children may remain suppressed for a long time but sometimes erupt into confrontations or lead to catastrophic results. Indian psychiatrists report seeing more and more Indian patients as teenage suicide and juvenile delinquency begin to affect the community. One teenager, Anjali Gupta, who was completing her electrical engineering degree at the Illinois Institute of Technology in Chicago, committed suicide by plunging her car into Lake Michigan on April 6, 1993. Hers is only one of several teenage suicides that have shocked the Indian community in the United States. Though there is no evidence that emotional disturbance among teenage Indian children is any higher than for any other ethnic group, such incidents, which are widely reported in the Chicago ethnic media no matter in which part of the nation they occur, force the community to take stock of parental attitudes toward their children and examine the "cultural identity" factor in personality development.[4] How parents influence their children during the adolescent years determines to a large extent how Indian youth face the issues that confront them on the road to adulthood. Those issues can be broadly categorized as identity resolution, career issues, and choice of marriage partners.

In the following excerpts, Indian youth of Chicago speak in their own voices of their experiences of growing up in the United States, their search for an elusive "identity," and their hopes for the future.

Who Am I?

Just as the immigrant parents sometimes felt resentful that only in America did they need to have a defined or discernible "identity" (whereas in India they could just "be"), so also second-generation Indians felt that they were being unfairly forced to define who they were, where they were from and how they perceived themselves, while the American whites and blacks were required to do no such thing.

The very legitimacy of the identity question is challenged by the youth, many of whom fear that the assertion of an Indian identity is automatically construed as a rejection of an American identity and vice versa. Trying to define themselves as either Indian or American often leads to contradictions and paradoxes. Sometimes they operate from an Indian "base," sometimes from an American one, depending on their particular situation, and they want to accept both as equally valid.

> I graduated from the University of Illinois last year in Computer Science. Right now, I'm working for a consulting firm. I speak Tamil at home. I came here when I was four years old and since then I've been back to India four or five times. Last time was four years ago. If I were to describe myself, I'd say, I was raised with Indian values but my behavior patterns are American. So I think I'm both Indian and American. I wouldn't try to characterize myself as either one. I get values from both sides, but my sense of duty, it's definitely Hinduism. In Hinduism, your sense of duty is stressed more. I personally owe America more for what I am today because I was raised here. I feel pride in both countries but ultimately, if I had to choose, I'd choose America because I feel I owe them more for what I am.

I'm twenty-one, I've just graduated from U of I with a degree in math education. I speak Sindhi, a little broken Hindi. I've been to India four times, the last time about two years ago. When you look at the basic important things, I think I'm very much Indian. It's not how you dress or what you eat or how you speak or who you associate with—that's all environmental in terms of proximity—but in terms of the basic things, I'm very much Indian. I want to be cremated, not buried. In some ways, I feel very different from other Indians growing up in India. But in a lot of ways, like music, surprisingly, we listen to the same music. . . . I feel we're definitely stereotyped by Americans because we are second-generation Indians. In a college environment, half the Indians are engineers, the other half are pre-med. Another stereotype is that Indians study very, very hard and when they let loose, they go crazy. You have a lot of women in college, smoking for the first time. I've seen how that is, they have a few beers and they're like three sheets to the wind. Big stereotype that you can't hold your liquor and get carried away because it's so rarely that Indians do drink. For the first two years, freshman and sophomore, everyone said, "Haresh is a really difficult name. Why not change it to Harris?" So the first two years everyone called me Harris. And my friends said, "Why are you changing your name? Your name's not that hard." And I said, "You don't have a difficult name, you don't know how hard it is." Then it seemed really stupid to me. This senior year I was resident advisor in the halls. I changed it back to Haresh. . . . Now, even when I order pizza, or have a haircut, I say, "My name is Haresh, let me spell that for you, H-a-r-e-s-h."

I graduated in December of 1991. I'm a mechanical engineer and I work for the Electromotive Division of GM. . . . At a professional level, I just see myself being comfortable with everyone, because at work I have to deal with Americans and Indians. It's a process, as I've gotten older, I've gotten more adjusted to more people. My closest friends are Indians because I had my upbringing over there.

I have a Bachelor's in social work from U of I. I have an older brother. I went to India last time in 1990 in the summer. I've really become comfortable with not having an identity. You ask any person and they're going to have a different answer about how they define identity. Some people are going to say it's the type of clothes you wear, the kind of music you listen to, the kind of people you hang around with. Other people are going to say, it's your values, your attitudes, your general approach to life. Other people are going to say, it's your heredity, who your parents are, what your religion is. It's a hodge-podge, a mixture of all that. My heroes are Gandhi and Mother Teresa. My college experience was spent in trying to change people's views. They know I'm not a typical Indian. But when I went to India for the summer, I don't know what happened. It got turned around, I was everything Indian.

I work as a stockbroker in downtown. I'm twenty-three and I have a sister. I went to India two years ago to attend her wedding. I speak Telugu, and understand and speak some Hindi. I understand Hindi pretty well from watching movies. When I was in grade school, socially I was just going to other Indian family parties. That's all I had exposure to so I think I was more Indian at that point. I went to a very big high school and I didn't get along with a lot of Indians in high school because they were so—in simple terms—so geeky. They were also very bookish. I got more Americanized in high school. When I was in grade school, kids tended to pick on me more. But it wasn't necessarily easier when I was in high school. We lived on the north side of Chicago near Norridge.

I was born in Chapel Hill, North Carolina, and then we moved to Chicago. At the end of fifth grade, I went to India for summer vacation, liked it and stayed there till I finished my tenth standard. Then I came back here. In the beginning, I hated it. Now I'm pretty much used to it. I graduated from U of I in 1991. I understand Marathi, Gujarati, but if I speak it even to a *dhobi* (washerman), he'll be laughing. I stayed in India with my aunts. Everybody there kept saying, "Go back to America, go back to America." My parents were here throughout and so were my two younger brothers, five and ten years younger than me. Everybody was like, "Go back. Go back." So I came back. I had lived here, I knew there wasn't any magic in it but to everybody else, there's a lot of magic in America. I consider myself American for a very simple reason. I was born here, I've been brought up here and I'm going to die here. I know I lived in India for five years. . . . Being in India brought about a pride of being American. Before that, I would have been very happy to be called Indian. But when I went to India and lived there, I realized I was not Indian. I think like them and have the same values but I'm American. . . . Over here, my sensation is like being a child with one black parent and one white parent. Am I black? Am I white? So I've had to take a stand.

"I graduated in 1991 from Drake University from Des Moines, Iowa, in public relations and advertising. I'm currently unemployed. I'm looking for a position. I speak and understand Kannada. My family is from another part of Karnataka where they speak another language called Tulu, which I can understand if you don't talk too fast. I can speak it at the level of a four-year-old. I visited India last in 1990. When I'm in India and my family asks, "Who do you identify with?" that's putting you in a very bad situation. They're asking you to make a decision and that's very hard. . . . When I think of my Indian heritage, part of that is art and culture. I learned dance for seven or eight years. To me that is the most distinct and rich and incredible part of our culture. And that is something I'd love to keep alive. But part of me wants to blend in with the mainstream, the part about what I do for a living, where I live. I think that's fine as far as mainstream America is concerned. But as far as my art and culture is concerned, I want that to stay alive. If you ask me who my closest friends are, people I trust the most, outside of my family, it would be Americans.

I graduated from UIC and got a job selling life insurance and financial planning. I can understand Malayalam but I cannot speak it. I have a younger sister, age sixteen. I was in India in the summer of '86. I grew up without a single Indian adolescent influence till I reached college. I knew no Indians at all—not a one. Never hung out with one. When I got to college, I was always the "American-acting" Indian in the Indian crowd, and I was always automatically associated with the Indian crowd by the Americans because in college, all ethnic background people hang out with their own, Indians, Ukranians, what not. I became on the outside, looking in, in each circle. Then by virtue of hanging out with my Indian friends which I got in college, I assimilated some Indian culture, but I'm very American. The things I thought were American I could probably trace back to my parents. So there's no reason for me to identify them as American or Indian. The consciousness came about only in college. Let me put it this way. If I were to walk into a room with all Americans, I would feel way more comfortable than if I walked into a room with all Indians. . . . My Indianness is a matter of timing. When I'm at work, I don't think India at all, no way. When I call on an Indian client, I go, "This is Aah-jit. If it's an American client, I go, "This is A-jit." You have to be cut-throat in business. My dad says, "In India, people are so nice to you. People you don't know are friendly toward you." And here, they're not. They're a bunch of. . . . If you can't do anything for them, you're nobody, they don't want to talk to you. That's exactly how I operate when I do business. But when I'm in a social situation, when I go to a cultural function, I'm not like that at all. My boss told me, because a lot of my work is on the phone and you're fighting to get in front of someone, "Why don't you just call yourself A.J.?" Because they'll know I'm Indian when I say Ajit. "Ajit? What the hell is that? No, I won't talk to you." But I'm still Ajit at work. I refuse to compromise the integrity of my name, but the pronunciation, I'll accept. We got called names when we were kids—teepees, camel jockeys, Hindus. I got beat up plenty of times. I think guys got beat up more than girls. Once I walked home from high school. A car pulled up. Three seniors got out and proceeded to beat the living crap out of me. Right there on school property. Just because I was Indian. I was a junior in high school in Mount Prospect. It's in the city, except it's at the edge, almost in the suburbs. A white, middle-class neighborhood, so it's not the heart of the city.

Education and Career Choices

The high level of academic excellence among Indian youth is almost legendary, as seen by their prominence in merit scholarship lists and dean's lists in high schools and colleges throughout the country. This success has been attributed by sociologists to a solid work ethic and "family values." But when it comes to career choices, Indian parents feel that they know better what is good for their children. Success-oriented as they are, and already comfortable in their own medical, engineering, or scientific professions, parents try to encourage their children to follow the same paths. Certain fields such as elementary or secondary school education and social work are not highly regarded by Indian immigrants, mainly because they are not lucrative. Children who try to break new ground by choosing these fields are often pressured to pick alternative careers that pay better. In some cases, the children professionalize their "mom-and-pop" operations, so that they are no longer "motel owners" but executives in the "hospitality industry." Financial returns remain an overriding concern in the choice of a career; the children of doctors who follow in their parents' footsteps look forward to private practice, not socialized medicine. Those who can't afford to go to medical school in the United States go to one of the many colleges in India that set aside seats for the children of NRIs in return for hefty premiums also known as "capitation" fees, ranging from $25,000 to $50,000. Tuition and other costs range from $65,000 to $95,000.[5] Sometimes parents choose to send their children, especially daughters, to be educated in India not for monetary reasons but to shield them from the "corrupt" ways of American society.

> About our studies, me and my brother, we got straight As. It wasn't something particularly good, just normal. When I come home with a 95 percent, it's not "You did a good job," but it's "Why didn't you get 100 percent?" I'm serious. "Why did you miss 5 points?" And when Indian parents say success, they mean money. It's purely materialistic. They want me to be well off so I can take care of my family. . . . I'll always be grateful to my parents. I don't think I will ever be in financial hardship thanks to my parents. I sincerely believe I'm better off.

> When my parents knew about my wanting to be an Education major, there was a huge rift. They forced—no, that's not the right word—they encouraged me very strongly to go into engineering. So I went down to Champaign to do engineering for a year and half but I didn't like the classes. I want to be a high school teacher. I got my degree and for these last few months I've been working in this low-income project with blacks and Hispanics. My parents see what I want to do and have come to terms with it.

> It was so painful growing up here and our parents were so busy going to work, they missed what we were going through, all that pain. Maybe in India getting straight As means you will be popular but here you have to be doing other things, socially you feel so isolated. They didn't even understand we were going through that. My mother would say, "Today, you're going to Show & Tell, and you're going to talk about *Divali.*" I don't think she knew how embarrassing it was for me.

Parents from India spend too much time working. It's easy enough for our parents to say, "I don't understand you." But they don't take the time like American parents do. I think Indian parents are too busy being productive and trying to be successful in their lives. They think, "My kids need to get straight As. That's all they need to do. It's not important to mold and shape their lives and understand that they mature properly." I don't know if I can say it's their Indian heritage because in India it's not happening the same way.

When I was growing up my parents would spend every single night helping me with my homework. That's what they were raised to do and I did great in school because of that. We forget that they gave us a lot based on what they could give. But I think my parents want me to succeed so they can brag about me. Even in the field I'm in, I make decent money, I can survive, I feel happy. But they don't like the fact that I didn't get my Master's or do engineering. Some of the things I do I'm very proud of, but they never brag about that stuff. It took me awhile to have enough self-esteem to say, "I don't care."

Our parents want us to be successful because you have to be successful to avoid discrimination. The more money you have, the less people will discriminate against you. They like you because of your money.

What hurt me most in my four years of high school was that my father came to watch me perform in school and did not even look up from the book he was reading. I'm afraid to tell my Dad that the only master's I'll ever consider is in education. Because I think it'd kill him. He'd be like, "Why can't she just be like everyone else?"

The reason we came to America was because both me and my brother were flunking out of school. Once our parents saw us getting Bs, Cs and As, they were ecstatic. Because over there, in India, it was mostly Fs and Ds. So there was a little bit of pressure from our parents to study, but not too much. They were just happy to see we were doing okay.

My father always went to my sister's violin concerts, her debates. He had to go to another school to do that. I used to play a lot of sports, and those events like the regionals, they took place over the weekend.

To a sports person that means a lot. But my Dad never once came to see me play because he didn't think that was important. For eleven years, he's never seen me play. My Mom, she's never seen me play.

Parents

The generation gap is compounded for immigrant children who must also contend with the cultural gap. The fact that they visit India frequently with their parents complicates the picture further since it introduces the possibility of ever-changing and ever-broadening perspectives. Different perceptions of India and America and what constitutes "Indian" and "American" collide in the lives of these Indian Americans and become important value-laden concepts when used to define what is "good" and "bad."

Notions of "progress" and "Westernization" are inextricably bound up with happenings in India and the United States. The result is that that the homes of Indian immigrants with grown up children are turning into virtual cauldrons of conflict.

When my Dad came over, it was to give his children a good education, and he thought we'd get educated and still be totally Indian, isolated. He totally underestimated the effect the American culture would have on us. He thought he'd keep us totally isolated and Indian—like what Indian kids were like twenty years ago.

My father came to California. He had a job out there and he stayed with an American family and he was just so charmed with them. So he came back to India and he said, "The people over there are outstanding. Let's move over there." So I think we are different, atypical. My Dad thinks American people are very spirited. He can get along well with everyone, but there is a much bigger jump that they have to make in America. It's hard for our parents to find common ground with the Americans. They've spent twenty-five to thirty years of their life over there. My parents have been very open with rules about our socializing but that could be because they have two boys. It would have been very different if they had had a girl.

My father is a complete wanderer, he can't stay put in one place for more than a year. At that time when he had just graduated from medical school or a couple of years after, they tried to segregate people in India according to caste. An affirmative action kind of thing was going on in India. He thought of going to Australia, but here in America there was democracy. Nobody has democracy except here.

My parents didn't even try to make friends here with Americans. I agree that they grew up in India twenty, twenty-five years. But if we were to go back to India now, would we not at least try to relate to the people there, to reach out and adapt? Our parents' generation is really scary, the way the Indian community reacted to that boy's suicide. Rather than consoling those who'd lost their son, there was a lot of speculation, "Oh, he must have been on drugs, he probably had a girl friend." Rather than being a support system for the family, they said, "Oh, the parents must have been bad people." They were comparing the boy who committed suicide to his older brother, the achiever. That was scary, that they weren't there for each other, there was no unity. We are so competitive amongst ourselves. You can be best friends with the family, but it's always a competition as to whose daughter is going to go further.

I think Indians are more segregated and stay within their own linguistic community in America because you don't have so many barriers to cross. I can understand their fears, not being comfortable with someone brought up in a totally different society. But this north Indian/south Indian segregation is so disturbing to me, it really is. Our parents have a real stake in these organizations and institutions. That's their social life, basically. I've learnt to forgive my parents a lot because when I went to India I realized that it wasn't that they didn't trust me, it was that they didn't trust the American environment. But I thought they gave me pretty good values. They said they had a good daughter. The restrictions they put on me was because they said they didn't trust the environment. Communication among the family is not encouraged even in India. My parents came from an extremely poor family. They were worried about what they would eat the next day, not about whether they could communicate. They had to learn those skills, they're not socialized that way.

My father got a scholarship from his job to come here and do his Masters. And after he finished his Masters, his professor was like, "Why don't you do your Ph.D.?" He tried to get an extension of leave from his work but they didn't give it to him, so ultimately he just stayed here. He got a job, he got money. He's a psychologist. It's easier to be a psychologist here. My Mom says, "There's more crazy people here than in India," which is not true. Americans try to get help and are more able to pay for it. I'm upset with my parents for not being able to grow after they left India. They stopped, back in 1965. I think that's retarded not only me and my brothers, it's also retarded them. One of my cousins in India, he's living with his girl friend, another cousin eloped, got married to this guy, stayed with him for two or three years, then decided she couldn't stand this guy any more and she moved back home. This is in India and her parents accepted it. But my parents are like, "Oh my God! What are we going to do with our daughter? She's in America, she'll do that too!" In India they gave me so much freedom. My parents have moved around in the Chicagoland area, they got tired of all the Hindu associations, they've moved away from the mainstream.

I've asked my Mom why she and Dad immigrated to the United States and she said, "to follow the American dream." My parents came because of the opportunities they assumed to be available here. Better life, better job. Our parents came here at a certain time, and they continue to live in the India of that time. They don't realize how much India has progressed. My parents' friends are not even from south India, but Kannada, only Kannada. They're from Udipi, they've been all over India, but in Bombay, they have only Udipi friends. Here in Chicago, we live in a very big metropolis and because of this our families can afford to fall along linguistic lines. . . . I would like to see my parents have Indian friends who speak other languages. The only American people my parents know and occasionally socialize with are people my Dad works with.

These organizations our parents belong to, everything is so corrupted, not just the religious activities, the social and cultural activities, using it for their own advantage, for economic and social status. . . . You're going to see a lot of turnover in these organizations.

Dating and Marriage

Marriage is serious business for both parents and their children since it is fraught with long-term consequences for the community as a whole. A survey of Indians who got married in the United States showed that 24.6 percent of the men and 8.3 percent of the women got married outside their "race."[6] Generally, news of an impending "interracial" alliance is greeted with dismay by Indian parents. There is much soul-searching: What did we do wrong as parents? Is this an act of rebellion against us? The first reaction is always one of "tears and fears." Indian friends are prone to commiserate with the affected family, treating it almost like a tragedy and openly discussing how they can prevent this from happening to their own children. Marriage to a white American is less undesirable than marriage to an African American. Part of the disappointment for Indian parents is that they look forward to acquiring a new Indian family when their children get married and that doesn't usually happen with Americans who see it as more of a personal or private affair between two people. Americans who marry Indians are also not quite prepared to accept the fact that they are marrying not just the individual but the entire family.[7] Usually, intercultural weddings are held two ways—the couple goes through an Indian religious ritual as well as an American Christian or Jewish ritual.

Alarmed by the growing number of interracial marriages in the community, first-generation immigrants have taken significant steps to reverse the trend. Religious and cultural institutions provide Indian youth with an exclusive environment in which to mix with others of their own faith and find their match. As teenagers "hang out" together at temple functions, Indian parents fondly hope that their children will find their life partners from this crowd. The Gujarati community also holds "matrimonial events" at which the main purpose is to bring eligible boys and girls into contact with each other. The First Annual Charotar Patidar Samaj Convention of the Midwest, held on Memorial Day weekend at the College of Du Page in Glen Ellyn made arrangements for four hundred eligible candidates to "mingle," to learn more about each other at "one-on-one matrimonial meets," and for "parents and youth to meet jointly and separately." Theme parties for the youth and lectures by adults stressed "the importance of marriage within the Charotar community."[8]

An elaborate worldwide network has also been established in the matchmaking business that caters to the needs of eligible Indians living abroad.

Apart from the regular matrimonial columns in the Indian newspapers in India and the ethnic Indian newspapers in all parts of the globe where there are sizable Indian communities, there are computerized databases available for families to review in complete privacy. Among the vital statistics of eligible people that are computer verified are horoscope match, educational level, caste, religion, occupation, height, weight, age, income, number of members in the family, unmarried brothers and sisters, property ownership, and place of residence. One matchmaking service in California boasts a database of six thousand candidates that is continuously updated. Another hot item in the marriage market that uses state-of-the-art technology are video matrimonials. Once they have been able to verify essentials such as financial status, family backgrounds, and matching of horoscopes, the candidates judge one another's physical appearance and demeanor through specially prepared videos before making a final decision. If one candidate is in the United States and the other is in India, or some other continent, this becomes a particularly cost-efficient approach. Such business-like transactions are greeted with horror by many second-generation Indians, but appear to serve as a satisfactory alternative for a large number of families settled abroad for whom the traditional networking system of matchmaking has broken down.[9]

The arranged marriage system has even piqued the interest of the American media. On 10 March 1994, the *Oprah Winfrey Show* worked with an Indian computerized matchmaking service and arranged for a young Indian man from England to meet, for the first time, on stage and on camera, an Indian girl from the United States and consider her as a prospective bride. The television show generated much discussion on the pros and cons of "arranged marriages," with a University of Chicago anthropology professor suggesting that it might even be a good course for Americans to follow if they could only understand its merits. Lively and heated debates on this issue continue to be the stuff of drawing room conversation in Indian immigrants' homes. Other matchmaking services have sprung up that deal directly with young professionals instead of going through their parents, catering to the Americanized tastes of the second-generation Indians who prefer to act on their own.

How do young Indian men and women regard each other when it comes to marriage? It appears that Indian teenagers, when they do date, prefer to date non-Indians, but when they reach marriageable age, prefer to marry Indians. College-going Indians themselves estimate that about 50 percent of them are sexually active, but such relationships are generally with non-Indians because of the fear that word of inappropriate behavior quickly circulates within the Indian community and ruins one's chances of a suitable marriage, particularly for women, since chastity is still highly prized among Indian families.[10] Young Indian women, who have been brought up to be independent and career-minded, complain that their parents expect them to revert to age-old standards of feminine and "housewifely" behavior. They expect more egalitarian treatment from their husbands than what their mothers got from their fathers. Indian men often employ a double standard, preferring to date American girls or feisty Indian girls but choosing subservient and submissive wives from India, modeled more after their own traditional-minded mothers.

On the whole, the second generation appears to be working toward a middle ground, with more and more of its members anticipating that they will probably marry another Indian, perhaps someone their parents might introduce them to but definitely someone they themselves would be comfortable with. In other words, the ultimate choice will be their own, but their parents' views will be taken into consideration when they make their choices. There is neither wholesale acceptance nor rejection of Indian traditions as their parents might have experienced them in India, rather a tendency to modify them to suit new circumstances.[11] Most Indian teenagers growing into adulthood see that their greater exposure to different languages, cuisines, and cultures is an enriching, not a limiting, experience; but first, they have to negotiate some difficult terrain in their adolescent years.

These are such sensitive issues that most second-generation Indian Americans would rather not discuss it with their parents at all. Most Indian teenagers date but in secret and over the objections of their parents. Peace has been bought in the Indian immigrant household at the expense of honesty, and the youth have accepted it as the only possible way to deal with an impossible situation. The youth who were interviewed expressed a variety of opinions on premarital sex but on the whole, they do not approve of it or think it desirable. They were angered and frustrated by parental pressure on the issue of arranged marriages, but were open to the idea of family involvement in the selection of a spouse as long as they were free to make up their own minds and were given ample time to make their decision.

> When we were dating, we did everything we could to keep it from our parents. Boys can do much more than girls, you can't argue with that, it's etched in stone. It goes back thousands of years. According to my

Dad, when you're twenty-three years old, you're not supposed to enjoy life. You read, you study, that's all you do. Then, only when you're in the householder stage . . . he really thinks that, that's it's a realistic possibility, I don't even try arguing against it. My mother would think she's a failure raising me if I told her I was dating. I don't even want to tell my Mom because she would take it real badly. As for pre-marital sex, I'd say that if I'm convinced I'm going to marry a person, I'm not going to wait till the wedding. And I would marry an Indian. I think in an ideal world, I would have no problems with an interracial marriage, but I've seen too many problems in interracial marriages to put my children through that. I also have a lot of faith in myself. When I decide to marry somebody, it's not going to be a frivolous decision, and I honestly don't think I'm going to make a mistake.

There's this one girl in Champaign. Her older sister is twenty-four and she's marrying an American guy. So before the marriage, the parents are sending off the younger girl to India so she can be married, pulling her off her sophomore year in college, sending her to India to be married within a week. So the family won't suffer because of the low reputation of the older girl. Just because, after the older sister gets married, she won't have a chance. . . . I'm very much of the opinion that marriage is till death unless you have some extenuating circumstances. The whole thing about compromise in a marriage though, I think with Indian women it undermines their self-reliance. Always it is the woman who is compromising and the men just don't budge. . . . I would rather have my wife work outside the home, because you get more of an equal relationship. . . . But if she's very involved in her career, and you're very involved in yours, I think that's very detrimental to the kids. . . . What I would have a problem with would be lack of attention for the kids. Unfortunately, they're connected. If the man is always on the run and the woman is also always on the run, say you have children, who's gonna deal with that? Whoever makes the most money gets to work? I'd agree with that.

I meet enough Indian boys. I know I can find Indian men on my own. I don't need my parents to introduce me to Indian boys. I can probably find someone on my own a heck of a lot better than them, but there's not an Indian man in Chicago I can get along with. Take the case of my friend. The first person that her parents chose for her was at least ten or fifteen years older than her. She showed me a picture, a pretty unattractive guy. She had nothing in common with him. I could see her being completely depressed and unhappy for the rest of her life. And it was only near the wedding date that she broke it off. But the next time, she chose someone her mother liked, but that was because she didn't want to displease her parents. She married this guy whom she had met only once. When she came back from seeing him, I asked, "What's his name?" and she said, "I don't know." Oh my God, you don't even know his name! Even if I did marry a non-Indian, he would have to understand my culture, he would have to love it. I know a white boy, he speaks Hindi with my mother over the phone, he makes Indian food, he watches Hindi movies by himself. He understands what it is to be Indian, probably more than what Indian boys do. That's great, if I can find that in an American, and he would want to pass it on as much as I would.

I waited until college to start dating. When I was at home, I found it too much of a hassle to find someone to date, and the people I was interested in dating, it was too much to put them through because I'd have to hide it from my parents. To your parents, you're not an adult till you're married. Even now, they tolerate my dating, but they don't accept it. They found out I date, I don't keep it a secret any more but they only tolerate because they know I won't listen to them if they tell me not to date. I wouldn't have any problem with pre-marital sex but living with someone isn't as common as it used to be, even among Americans.

We did date but we desperately didn't want to hide it from our parents. That doesn't mean we told them we were dating, but we talked in generalizations. We would argue and argue and argue about why they wouldn't let us date, even though we were already dating. Because we didn't want to hide it, we wanted to have an open relationship with our parents and share it with them. But it wasn't until late high school that I was able to share it with them and they were okay with it. And NETIP [Network of Young Indian Professionals]. I'll tell you frankly. The reason it exists is because people are looking for husbands and wives. I'll say it's the hidden agenda for NETIP. As we assimilate more and as our children assimilate and have interracial marriages or whatever, there won't be any need for NETIP. What

I'm finding an interesting phenomenon is happening now. My friend's mom recently asked me to introduce her to boys. That was unheard of a few years ago. The parents are coming to a point where they are going to help with our marriages, pushing us to date Indian men. It's an interesting switch. Now they're encouraging the dating, as long as it's Indian men. . . . I feel an incredible ambivalence in the sense that in order for me to feel successful, I have to have a busy, driven life, but the guilt of not focusing on a family and a homemaking lifestyle is driving me crazy. My parents constantly tell me how I can be a proper wife. . . . I'm scared because I've seen a lot of Indian men, first-generation Indian husbands alienate themselves from their own wives because their wives choose to have busy lifestyles, driven in that sense, and it scares the heck out of me.

I started dating, then stopped for awhile, then started again, at sixteen. No way would I be allowed to go to the prom. My brother came from U of I and told my mother, "I'm going on a road trip to South Dakota." I wanted to go on a road trip to Memphis with a girl who had parents who lived there. But my parents said, "No! You can't go to Memphis." But sure, my brother can go to South Dakota. I'm sure he was just drinking along the way. From my personal viewpoint, I believe if you love somebody, pre-marital sex is okay. I don't believe in one-night stands, and I don't believe in casual sex, but in a love relationship, it's fine. I did have one American girlfriend that lived with her boyfriend, and I think we all learned a lesson. It didn't work for her, I'd say, even with my American friends, I don't see a whole lot of them living with boys.

I decided that I would be good and wouldn't date as long as I'm under my parents. It wasn't that I was bad once I left home. It was different. It's awful to say this but I found it too much of a hassle. The way I see arranged marriages, your parents expect you to have a conversation with someone on the phone and then you have to decide whether to marry him. It's what my parents have done on several occasions over the past two and a half years. You're told to meet so and so and make a decision. I'm out of college and I don't work, therefore I should be married. And that's the natural progression. I'm a talkative person, I talk on the phone. Quite frankly, the three people I've talked to so far have had nothing to say back to me. And my parents are like, "Well?" "Well, what?" I said. I don't know how I'm supposed to respond. I don't know how to respond to this. I guess love is supposed to be blind. Blind, deaf and dumb.

We knew better than to discuss dating with our parents. If my girlfriend were coming over, I'd just say, "Mom, get ready. Here's someone I want you to meet." When they know it's not just a friend, then the meeting's a little different. It was expected that I wasn't going to date. So I rationalized, I'll just be good and I can go away to college. That way, I can do what I want without really hurting them. Because they're not gonna know. We didn't tell them but they found out in weird ways. Usually, it's a mistake, a slip of the tongue. In my case, they saw a picture. Thank God my ride showed up to take me to Champaign and I said, "Gotta go!" and I weaseled out. It's something parents don't want to know. Avoid confrontation at all costs. As for marriage, I see no problem in your parents introducing you to people, but I feel ultimately, it's your decision. And divorce, I'd be forced to consider it if . . . it depends on how severe the violation was of your trust that got you mad. I understand there's something to be said for the effect on the kids, but I also think that staying in a bad marriage will have a bad effect on the kids too. So I'd much rather explain to them why you're doing what you're doing and get separated.

Religion

Most of the youth in the study had grown up without the influence of the religious institutions that were only beginning to take concrete shape in the 1980s. So their views on religion came mostly from their personal and family experiences rather than from any formal education or affiliation with religious organizations. For some, this led to lack of awareness about the significance of religious rituals and hampered their ability to identify with their own religion. Still, they took pride in their religious heritage and sought ways in which to keep it alive for their children.

I was completely overloaded with religion when I was young, and it's an equal and opposite reaction when you grow up. I tended to drift away from it during my formative years during high school and college. I was talking to some other Indian adults who grew up in other countries and their response to it was, as a family they tended to come back and be more religious. And I can see myself doing that. I didn't know a lot about Hinduism as I was growing up and I'm learning more just as a lay person. I'm more exposed to it now. I don't see myself being involved in the religious, social, and cultural associations that our parents are involved in. But I do see myself getting involved in the economic ones, where we want to bring some more wealth back into India, improve the lot of the poor.

I have this talisman around my neck. I love it when people ask me about it at American parties. I always have it out and I explain it. Not that this is going to change their ideas about Hinduism, but they understand when I say, "It was given to me by our Swami and our family believes in it." I think it's real important to keep that, to keep disseminating those ideas.

My Dad was extremely religious. He taught us Sanskrit when we were little, he reads that everyday. Although my Mom was religious, I just did what she did without understanding. I went to India and saw the circles people did around the altar. I never understood how many times you were supposed to go around and my cousin said, "It's simple. You have to do it only in odd numbers." Your parents don't even tell you that.

My dad is the high priest of Zoroastrians. I chose my religion, I know it and also because my father's the high priest. Whenever we went on road trips anywhere, out would come the prayer book. But not only that, he read all the translations, so I knew all the translations by heart. I knew the *sadma* and the *hasti*, he taught me what all that means. It's a shield to protect you. In Zoroastrianism, good and evil are at odds with each other, and of course, good always wins. I'm on the Board of the Temple right now, but next month, I'm giving my resignation. I'm so sick of it because of all the politics. In my religion, Zoroastrianism, my friends are pretty much marrying Americans. I'll definitely be passing on my customs to my children. No matter who I marry, my children will be in my religion. But for that, I'd have to marry a Parsi.

India and the United States

There is a vested interest in seeing India prosper and pull itself out of want and poverty but the connection is far more fragile that it is for the parents. The youth are more concerned about their career opportunities in the United States and the barriers they will encounter in their climb to the top.

I'm the only Democrat in my family. My brother and my father are Republicans. You have to become a citizen if you want a voice in this country. You can't change what you don't like unless you join in. My brother, he works for Henderson, he's on the partner track. Working hard and having connections is important not just for Indians, it's for the Americans too. Most of my American friends don't have jobs.

If I go to my friend's house and see any Indian newspapers lying around, I'll start reading them. I just notice Indian articles in American newspapers and just try to look for them. If our involvement in India propagates violence, I don't think it's appropriate to send money there. I've talked to a lot of Irish about this. They support the IRA but what about all the kids over there dying for a cause they don't even know. You should know that if you give money to India it is not going for killing other people or making nuclear bombs. What we need is an Indian voice in America which we don't really have. I'd like to pass on some technology to India that India is lacking in. I see myself going back to India only in a worst case scenario, when people like us are persecuted for some reason.

I keep in touch with what's going on in the United States. When it comes to India, I don't because a lot of times it's so confusing, there's so many different opinions and I don't feel there's any honest opinions coming out of India. Here I get all points of view and I can tell . . . whereas with India it's hard to pick the signs. I'd like to see India-U.S. relations improve.

I'm a very great champion of democracy. I'm very anticommunist, antidictatorship. I look around and see so many undemocratic countries and India is democratic and I see Ayodhya as. . . . It's just ruining a house, as a danger to democracy. It would be a great thing to have a lobby for India-U.S. relations, to help India get more money, to help India solve some of its problems. We're Democrats, my family came here during Carter's election. Career wise, in the beginning I expect to get ahead, but in the end when that Board of Director's chair is very near, I don't expect to get into it. I see myself going through life with values that my parents gave me, but not necessarily on the track my parents would want me to be.

When bad things happen in India, it hurts, when good things happen, I'm happy. But I see it almost as an outside person. I don't know how to explain it. What happened in Ayodhya was scary. I'm a Democrat, much to the chagrin of my incredibly Republican friends. We're concerned about our generation as a whole, not just being Indian, but people our age. Five years ago when I went to college I would have said, we have an absolutely bright future. But I see a change that's going to make this whole generation different from the last generation, regardless of our ethnic heritage. Statistically, we're the first generation that's not as well off as the generation before us since World War II. As a woman in my field, I totally expect to encounter a glass ceiling but for different reasons than my father. I don't think my opportunities are any less because I'm Indian, but there's something different.

I didn't become a U.S. citizen until Russia collapsed. Because the affiliation was Russia-India, U.S.A.-Pakistan. I never became a citizen till that influence of Russia and Pakistan diminished. I wanted to retain the right to go back, I didn't want to have the Indian government be able to deny me a visa as a U.S. citizen because of U.S. affiliation with Pakistan. I'm a Democrat. I have a mild interest in what's going on in India. As far as connections and networking are concerned, we're not privy to that much information. Personally, I think your career prospects depend on what you do. If you're in a corporate environment with a Board of Directors that's been monopolized by a certain sect, yes, there's a glass ceiling for a while. But working hard is very important. It is the American way.

Conclusion

For the Indian youth, the search for an identity in America is a more fluid and frightening process than it was for the parents. Their first-generation immigrant parents came to America in their adult years, with their allegiance to Indian traditions fairly well set. When these parents encountered what they regarded as a clash with American ways, they had a firm point of reference from which to make their choices. The youth, on the other hand, felt constrained to make choices without having had a chance to develop a sense of belonging as either Americans or Indians. Though there were no children of mixed marriages among the interviewees, studies show that they are also resentful and confused, feeling forced to "pick" which race they belonged to, and being stuck in a racial category because of their obviously white or black or Indian appearance.[12] Indians from the Caribbean of mixed Creole parentage had a particularly hard time in the United States, feeling alienated from both African Americans and Indian Americans, no matter which group their physical appearance slotted them into.[13]

In addition to being at odds with the outside world, the young Indians were also at odds with their parents. Indian "values" were constantly cited as the sacred mantra, they were asked to accept them unquestioningly, and to defer to parental authority. They wanted to decide things for themselves (independence generally being considered an "American" value) instead of bringing the whole family into the decision-making process (an "Indian" value). The normal generation gap was compounded by cultural rebellion, but it was also tinged with a genuine desire to please their parents whom they saw as hard-working, if sometimes misguided and inflexible, folk willing to make sacrifices for their children.

The youth could not identify with India or feel the same sense of belonging and closeness to the old country as their parents did. However, once they reached college age and attained a certain level of maturity, it seemed that after years of hating who they were, they were able to look upon their Indian backgrounds more positively, with greater confidence and self-esteem. The youth also took pride in many aspects of Indian culture, especially music and dance, though religion remained both a mystery and an area of legitimate inquiry. Here, again, their parents' unquestioning faith is frustrating and difficult for the youth to comprehend. When it came to marriage, both sexes were prepared to make compromises, but the women were far more wary and skeptical of the men's ability to follow through and keep their end of the bargain. The age-old dilemma of family versus career continued to loom large even for the younger generation. They saw the challenges of getting ahead in their careers, not just in terms of their ethnicity, but as something that affected their entire generation. In this respect, they identified with their American self more than with their Indian heritage. Of course, many of their concerns were directly related to their age and their own life stage, and would no doubt change with the passing years, but they managed to convey through their voices that for now, they were existing "in limbo," as it were, to use their own terminology, until they should find themselves and where exactly they belonged.

7

IN SEARCH OF SECURITY

The Elderly

My coming here was not my personal decision. My children grew
up and came abroad. I retired and my son asked me to join him
here in the U.S. I said, "Let me first build my own house in India.
What if I don't like it in your town? Where will I go?"
                              —Elderly immigrant interviewed for this study.

The elderly Indian population in the United States has two kinds of immigrants. The larger group of elderly consists of the parents of those who
came in the post-1965 wave of immigration. These elderly Indians spent
their most productive years in India and came to the United States after
retirement, entrusting their future in the hands of the children who sponsored them. This is the group that was interviewed for this study. The second
group consists of the aging primary immigrants themselves who spent their
most productive years in the United States. The latter are much better prepared, financially and emotionally, to face the challenges of old age in
America simply because they went through the initial adjustment process in
their younger years and had plenty of time to prepare for old age. Their situation is also discussed later in this chapter.

The Parents of Immigrants

The number of elderly Indian immigrants entering the United States has
been growing steadily since 1986, and shows no signs of abating. The average
percentage distribution for immigrants fifty years and older who entered the

Table 8   Indian immigrants over fifty years old, admitted 1986–1993

Year	Total Persons	Age 50–64	Age 65 + years	Older Immigrants as Percentage of Total Immigration
1986	26,227	3,757	1,428	20%
1987	27,803	3,716	1,552	19
1988	26,268	4,166	1,621	22
1989	31,175	4,397	1,821	20
1990	30,667	4,774	2,002	22
1991	45,064	5,366	2,114	17
1992	36,755	5,259	2,124	20
1993	40,121	5,519	2,232	19
Totals	264,080	36,954	14,894	
				Average distribution: 20%

SOURCE: INS Annual Reports, "Immigrants Admitted by Selected Country of Birth, Age, and Sex," 1986–93.

NOTE: Between 1965 and 1977, the average distribution for this age group was 3 percent, ranging from a low of 1 percent to a high of 7 percent. Parmatma Saran and Edwin Eames, eds., *The New Ethnics: Asian Indians in the United States* (New York: Praeger, 1980), 147.

United States between 1986 and 1993 is 20 percent. Between 1965 and 1977, the corresponding figure was only 3 percent (Table 8).

Researchers in the Indian community estimate that there are about 100,000 Indian senior citizens in the United States.[1] Of these, about 60 percent are not eligible for any Social Security benefits because they have not worked in the United States. Neither are they eligible for Medicaid, which provides for the elderly indigent, because they have not fulfilled the residency requirement after obtaining the green card. About 13 percent receive Social Security benefits and approximately 19 percent receive Supplemental Social Security Income (SSI). Anti-immigration forces have noted that immigrants nearly tripled as a percentage of SSI recipients between 1963 and 1993, rising from 4 to 12 percent. But whether this is due to abuse of the system or is a result of changing demographics is impossible to determine.[2] Within the Indian community, there is much debate as to whether elderly parents, who do not have any dollar income or assets of their own in the United States and who technically qualify for SSI, should avail themselves of these benefits since their well-to-do children are able to support them. In the Indian culture where children are dutybound to care for their aged parents, such issues acquire greater moral complexity.

In metropolitan Chicago, the percentage of Indians sixty-five years and older to the general Indian population is about 3 percent. The two major social service institutions that address the needs of seniors in the Chicago area are the Indo-American Center and Asian Human Services. Another agency called Suburban Family Services provides help at home for elderly couples, especially for those in the northern and northwest suburbs of Evanston, Skokie, Niles, Wheeling, and Schaumburg.[3] A survey of the elderly done by Asian Human Services in 1993 shows that the majority are Hindi- and Gujarati-speaking, though other linguistic groups are also represented. Out of a total of 132 elderly South Asians from India, Pakistan, and Bangladesh who were surveyed, 34 spoke Gujarati, 31 spoke Hindi, 16 spoke Urdu, and 6 spoke Punjabi. The remaining language groups had only 1 or 2 elderly represented in the survey. Many have no English language skills, access to transportation, or any interaction at all with the mainstream society. Their problems range from isolation and boredom to severe financial difficulties exacerbated by poor health and lack of independent income. The Chicago Department of Aging runs a kitchen on Devon Avenue where balanced and nutritious meals conforming to the strict dietary habits of South Asians are provided at very low or no cost to the indigent elderly. Other activities associated with the lunch programs include English language tutoring, citizenship classes, health screening, and recreation.[4] Though there are state- and community-sponsored efforts to reach out to the elderly, many of them never manage to make the adjustment from a traditional setting in India, where old age is equated with wisdom and privilege, to an American environment, where old age is generally held in low esteem. They continue to live as misfits in the United States or return to India in despair. A few, especially those who made the transition to America in the early years after their retirement from active employment in India, do manage to create a new life for themselves in the United States.

The role of the elderly in contributing to the remarkable successes of the post-1965 Indian immigrants in the United States has not been fully recognized or even acknowledged by the community. This success has usually been attributed to the high educational levels of the immigrants themselves, their professional skills, and their solid family values, but the fact is that many of the immigrants could not have done it without the presence in the United States and the active cooperation of their elderly parents. Sometimes the contribution is obvious, as with the baby-sitting, the housekeeping, or adding to the family income. At other times the elderly have contributed in unquantifiable ways that have enriched family and community life—through language retention among the second generation or through conflict resolution in family relationships. Above all, they have provided historical and cultural continuity to their children who are struggling to find their own niche in a new land.

Most of the elderly parents in the United States came under the family reunification clause of the immigration rules. They came to live with their children for a variety of reasons, ranging from their own desire for sightseeing to a need to help out their children with baby-sitting and household chores. Some came because they had no one left in India who could provide them the support they needed in their old age. The circumstances of their immigration determined to a large extent the nature of their experience in the United States. One study concluded that certain factors such as sex, reasons for coming to the United States, living arrangement, access to transportation, self-assessed health, finance, number of friends, and frequency of meeting friends are important in explaining the variance found in life satisfaction among the elderly.[5] Were they financially independent in India, and could they transfer their financial resources to the United States? Did they find employment after arriving here and did they have their own dollar income? (Very few do and financial dependence in turn leads to a host of other problems.) Did they come voluntarily or did they feel pressured into immigrating by their children? How old or young were they when they first came? Did they know the English language back in India, learn it upon their arrival here, or did they lack English language skills completely? Were they used to an urban metropolitan life or did they come straight from an Indian village? Did they take on a useful role in the household or did they feel they were a burden on their children? What was their health condition? Given the prohibitive cost of health care and the fact that even legal immigrants do not qualify for Social Security medical benefits because they have never contributed to the system, this remains one of the most problematic issues in the lives of the Indian elderly. Did they come with their spouses or were they widowed? Did they have an active social and professional life in India that they could never hope to replace here satisfactorily, or were they happy in the United States with their bridge clubs or their *sat sang* (prayer) gatherings? The variety in the circumstances of the elderly is bewildering indeed, reflecting as it does the variety in the status of the immigrants who sponsored their parents, and defies generalization. But two separate points can be made about the reasons why the elderly emigrated, and one or the other of the two reasons is applicable in most cases of elderly Indian immigration to the United States.

Because of the peculiarity of the American immigration laws and the waiting periods for different preference categories, it was easier and quicker for an immigrant who was a citizen to sponsor a sibling for a green card by first sponsoring his or her parent and having that parent in turn sponsor the sibling. With immigration to America being considered the golden key to prosperity, sibling sponsorship was deemed almost a family obligation. As a result, many parents acquired the green card whether they wanted it for themselves or not, and once they had fulfilled their goal of sponsoring the sibling, they were free to return to India. But the choice was not always an easy one. Having already spent long years in waiting in the United States, many had lost touch with India or burnt their bridges there in order to finance their own passage or that of their children. They felt they had no option but to stay on as immigrants, whether they liked it or not. This group of immigrants was not easily reconciled to their life in the United States and many of them felt that they had to sacrifice familiar surroundings in their old age for the material prosperity of their children.

The other valid generalization about the elderly has to do with Indian culture, and the special motivation it provides for the elderly to emigrate to America. Most Indian male immigrants, like their brethren in India, feel an obligation to take care of their parents in their old age. Though this sense of responsibility is particularly applicable to Hindus, it does cut across all religious lines and applies to other religions as well. If it were not for this universal Indian moral law, parents would not have followed their children halfway across the world from India to the United States, uprooting themselves from the only life they knew and risking their future in a strange environment. Of the eight people invited to the focus group discussion for this study, six said they would have preferred to continue living in India (mostly because of a "better social life" and "independent living") but felt that in their old age their place was with their sons in the United States. The feeling that Indian parents and sons have of wanting to live together is mutual. The male immigrants wanted to absolve themselves of the guilt of not being able to care for their parents in their old age, so they invited them over to America. The parents were also afraid of being left in India without the support of their children. It is a rare immigrant indeed who decides to pack his bags and return to India for the sole purpose of caring for his parents in their old age, so it was generally a one-way street.

This cultural norm must be understood in the context of changing attitudes in India about responsibility to the elderly. (The change in India is
slow, it may be confined to the upper-middle-class urban families and has
not undermined the beliefs of the immigrants who left India long ago.)
Indians in India who sent their children to primary schools in the 1980s and
early 1990s did not necessarily expect to be taken care of by their children in
their old age. But however much they were reconciled to fending for themselves in their old age, they also realized that any solutions to the problems
of senior citizens must emerge from within the matrix of the family and the
community. The increasing number of elderly in India's population has led
to a call for expansion of public support systems. The over-sixty population is
expected to increase from 60 million in 1990 to 150 million by 2020, according to a report by the Population Research Center in Dharwad, India.[6] But
the idea that the Indian government might provide some social security as is
done in the United States is considered laughable by the middle class since
the government cannot deliver even basic civic services. There are some institutions that care for old folk who have no family in India, but conditions in
these places are deplorable. To have prosperous sons abroad and not be able
to live with them was considered the ultimate indignity in old age. All the
immigrants in the focus group took it for granted that their sons would look
after them. "Why should our brothers and sisters look after us?" said one
woman. "After all, it is our sons who inherit our assets."

The possession of a green card or resident-alien visa was not necessarily
indicative of true immigrant status for elderly Indians. Some of them
acquired the green card for travel convenience—they could avoid the long
lines at the embassy for a new visitor's visa every time they wanted to visit the
United States. Others hoped to qualify for government benefits available
only to residents. Thus, despite the "permanent resident" status, elderly
green-card holders were in the United States only temporarily until they
had fulfilled certain objectives. Others shuttled back and forth intermit-
tently, still uncertain about their permanent stay in the United States. Still
others distributed their time among several children in different cities in
the United States and Canada and other parts of the world. Generally
speaking, because of the cost of travel, the elderly stayed on for extended
periods once they arrived in the United States. The cumulative effect of
these extended stays was seen in their collective impact upon the immigrant
community.

Among the elderly in the United States were those who definitely considered themselves birds of passage. Such people were generally happy to be

visiting their children for long periods but were not ready to give up their lives in India completely. They understood the ethos of the nuclear family, and were able to accept the fact that their children did not want them in their homes on a permanent basis. They also realized that their children would not drastically revise their own lives in order to accommodate them. No matter what the future held for them, they felt that their place was in India and they had the financial means to support their dual lives.

In the voices of the elderly immigrants who were interviewed for this study, one can detect a strong adherence to the age-old values of Indian civilization, the values that Indians cherish most and want to pass on to their children, generation after generation. Occasionally, there is fear that some values may be lost irretrievably in the immigration process, at other times there is a firm optimism that new solutions will be found for emerging problems in a new environment.

Why Come? Why Stay?

Elderly Indian parents consider it almost a natural law that they must follow their children, especially their sons, to the United States. As such, they see the decision to emigrate as out of their hands, yet India continues to exercise its hold on them. Leaving India and staying in the United States are difficult and agonizing decisions and made only because they believe it is in their own best interest and the interest of their sons.

I wanted to come here in 1952 for further studies. I couldn't come then. Then I got a chance to send my son here for further education. I came here to enjoy my life with him. It was my own desire to understand America. I did my M.Sc. in Physics, taught science in an engineering college in India. After World War II especially, I became more interested in America. I would never miss the chance to come to America. There are so many things one can learn here and enjoy.

I had a hip problem. I needed surgery and though I had good surgeons in India, I was afraid of infection. When I first came I was very happy. I met ten or fifteen of my former students . Each one of them came to visit me and said how happy they were to see me. They even said their home was open if ever I wanted to come and stay with them. I was in management. I know how to talk and get along, it was because of my profession. I also have a daughter in Houston. I feel that for my children this country is better, atmosphere is healthier. I also have attachments in India, but that is like toward a daughter who's married off and not your own anymore.

We always want to be with our children in our last days—whether they are in Bombay or Delhi or here. The children wanted to come here. After your son gets married, you have to rediscover him, what kind of bride he brings. Would she like us to live with them? Fortunately for us, she gave us love, she wanted us to live in her home. Even in India, we would have liked to live with them. Because in your old age, there are many problems, which no one other than your children can solve for you. When you are ill, only your children can help you whether they are good or bad. But if the children don't desire it, we don't want to live with them. They should also want it, to give us love and respect. If not, we would prefer to live in India.

I have four sons and one daughter. The eldest son is an engineer. My second son is also an engineer, he was crazy to come to the United States. My third son is also an engineer. Quite brilliant. At first, he didn't want to come, and I was also not particular. But at the last moment, he also came. Then, after my sons were married, I came for the first time in 1981. My youngest son was a medical student and very keen to come here. Although I was not very keen, I had to take my immigration to sponsor him. He was very adamant. After making sure my son had his green card, I went back to India. I like several things here, very good government, good schools, good foodstuffs, but still I was missing something. I came and went for many years, then I decided I would go back. There was no point in living here. I still have one son and one daughter there. But if all my children come here, then I have no alternative. I am very close to my daughter. I had almost decided to settle down in India when my wife suddenly had a heart attack. The medical treatment there was not so good so I had to send her here. She has had a bypass so I am going to be here for the next four or five months. I'm absolutely undecided about my permanent home. I don't know. Sometimes I feel like going back, sometimes I feel it's all right, I can continue for some more time. Somehow I keep myself busy.

Coming here was my own decision but it was a very difficult one on my part. My son came to the United States. in 1986 to do his Master's. Six months later, my husband had a heart attack and he died. I was working in India. I waited for my son to finish his studies and come back to India but I wanted to see where he would settle. I stuck to my job. In the meantime, I was coming here on vacations. My son got married in India, his wife also came back here with him and did her Master's in Computer Science. I was also growing older and having health problems. I decided that it is better that I should resign my job. My son wanted me to be here. My parents are there and my in-laws are there but my only son is here. He said, "Mom, come here and we can all live together." That was a very important point in my life. Then I resigned from my job in 1991. I was still only fifty-one and had nine more years to go with my job. But I thought this is the time for me to resign and go to the United States. I can study, I can do whatever I want. I still had some funds in India. I went back to collect them.

Thus, many elderly immigrants found themselves caught up in a spiral of circumstances over which they had little control. Some took full advantage of conditions in America, especially in health care. Those who came to America for medical treatment found themselves forced to stay on beyond their initially planned period. Some were too old when they came here to build their lives anew, others enjoyed financial independence as well as the opportunity to socialize and keep their days filled with activity. They were generally the best adjusted to their new circumstances.

Work

The range of occupations among the elderly is truly astonishing. Some were particular about wanting employment only in their own field, but others were willing to do anything to remain employed. Those in financial need worked as cooks, baby-sitters, tax-preparers, or helped with the family business. Generally, the menfolk were more likely than the women to find an occupation outside the home. Volunteer work appeared to be the most satisfying alternative for the able-bodied elderly immigrants who could not find employment. They enjoyed religious, social, and cultural activities that gave them an opportunity to show off their own expertise in certain areas. Through temple and other cultural organizations, they taught the younger generation about their mother-tongue and their scriptures, gave them lessons in Indian arts and crafts. The sense of passing on a legacy made them feel they were contributing to the life of the community in significant ways. They also claimed to spend more "quality time" with the grandchildren than did the parents, and were convinced that child care centers could never take the place of a family member when it came to nurturing and protecting the very young. They saw their role as facilitators in family relationships, helping smooth out the rough edges of life. Other, less fortunate, immigrants were aware that their children considered them an interference and a nuisance. Some of them came to the United States in direct response to their children's frantic cries for help in raising a family. Indian mothers who would never entrust their infants to crèches or child care centers while they pursued a career were quite comfortable leaving their children with their parents or in-laws and continue going to work. The elderly, just like women and children—and this is true not only for immigrants but for society as a whole—go largely unrecognized for their work because it remains unquantified for dollar value. Generally speaking, the women had more continuity and stability in their lives than the men, especially since most women of that generation were housewives and their lives revolved around home and hearth even in India. The women who had worked outside the home in India or had active social lives there felt that it was much harder for them to find suitable work in the United States than it was for the men.

Though some elderly immigrants were highly qualified and had previous experience of work in India, their advanced years made it difficult for them to find gainful employment in the United States. Their children, too, preferred that the elderly parents lead a comfortable, retired life and be involved with family life. Only one couple had managed to turn a hobby such as palmistry into employment that was not only gainful but positively lucrative.

> I was working as a professor of physics in India. I took to physics because of my interest in metaphysics when I was barely twelve or fourteen years old. I was blessed with know-how of palmistry, astrology, and numerology. I have continued practicing astrology, palmistry and numerology here since 1985 and have been completely self-sufficient. I go to Canada, St. Louis, visit different parts of the country. I am self-sufficient economically, socially, and politically. I enjoy my work and I keep myself busy. It used to be a hobby for me in India.

When we decided in 1984 that we were going to live here, I took voluntary retirement since I had worked for more than twenty-five years. When we came here, all our friends knew of my husband's talent for palmistry and asked, 'Why don't you start it here?' But we never thought it would take off the way it did. We go to many psychic fairs. Here it is very organized, we even had to sign legal documents. In India, we would have done the same thing after retirement but we wouldn't have done it for money. We didn't take money even here at first but our friends told us, "Here, in America, if you don't charge money for your services, it has no value." So we started charging for it. People recognized us as Indians because of my sari. They also know that Indian astrology and Indian philosophy is much superior to all others. We were invited to be readers in the fair, along with other clairvoyants, tea leaf readers and sand readers. We were so successful that other promoters invited us to San Francisco, Florida, New York. Now we have so much business that I have to act as his secretary. He only does the reading. I have to make his travel arrangements, coordinate his meetings and now I'm also fully involved in it.

We were retired from service when we came here. We knew nobody would give us a job. We tried but we could not get one even though we would like to be working. We had a very good status there. We cannot do physical work here, we have come at the age of fifty-eight to sixty after retirement. If we had come at the age of forty or forty-five, we would have had different conditions. We could perhaps have gone to work for four or five hours, doing simple things like bagging groceries but our children would not like it, they would not allow it. I took an income tax course and could have done some work there, but I don't drive and that is a problem. I would have had to drive out fifteen to twenty miles. Our only anxieties are about our children. Because they have better opportunities here, they wanted to come over and we helped them to come.

When I came, I wanted to work. But my son said, "Dad, you have worked for forty years of your life. You have educated all your children. Why do you want to work now? Enjoy the evening of your life." It's very nice of him, very good thought. At this age, we only want love and affection from our children. But the day something goes wrong, then we have a problem. The reason is, back in India, we have others who know us and will help us. I used to drive but then I had one or two accidents and so I gave up. My son doesn't want me to drive. I don't feel I can start a new career at this age. What is the point, working so hard all your life. Here I want to spend my old age reading novels or enjoying myself.

After my surgery, I was home all day. What to do? Everyday I analyzed myself. What have I done today? Then I devoted myself to my grand-children. I devoted myself to volunteer work and made myself avail-able for twelve hours a day. That gave me great inner satisfaction.

I was teaching in a college in India. I published two books on Indian culture, about Indian festivals, in Gujarati. Now I'm working as a vol-unteer in the community college, teaching English as a second lan-guage, but I'm still looking for a part-time job. My daughter-in-law may have a baby in which case I want to stay home and look after her.

My life is very similar to what it was in India. I never worked at an out-side job there. I worked hard in the kitchen all my life. Here I don't do much work. I'm leading a retired life.

I used to work with arts and crafts in India. I had my own embroidery, cutting, and sewing company in Chandigarh. I tried to start some-thing here, but my son said, "Don't tell anybody that you can do these things." He put a stop to everything. I don't even do much cooking. The children only like to eat pizza and American food.

The Value System

While the elderly immigrants provided a bridge between India and America and enabled their children to hold on to their careers and their heritage, they also brought with them a host of problems and dilemmas, not only in increased health care costs and other financial burdens, but in irreconcil-able differences in the clash of Old and New World cultures.

As the years went by, life in America began to sour for many of these immigrants, and the initial euphoria was replaced by a growing disillusion-ment. At first, the weekend social visits to friends' homes, or the shopping sprees and festival celebrations at temples were exciting, as were the "the clean living, the good food, the excellent medical care" in the words of one immigrant. Gradually, they began to miss their life in India. They found themselves isolated at home while their sons and daughters-in-law were at work all day. They were irked by the cooking of beef in the home or their inability to follow some of their own orthodox ways that involved the observance of rites and rituals. They saw that their own children no longer had the ability or the means to accommodate them in the face of growing pressure from the grandchildren. They realized that as their grandchildren grew up and brought American ways into the house, they would not be able to change some of these ways and would have to learn to deal with them. Their grandchildren, who adored them when they were toddlers, had grown into rude teenagers who "talked back," "didn't respect their elders," and were obsessed with dating and fashions. Television did not amuse these elderly immigrants any more, and the American culture seemed more and more alien to them. Those who had not visited India for a long time found their nostalgia for the homeland ever more painful to bear. Some who had burned their bridges behind them made earnest efforts to adjust, creating their own social circle with card clubs or *bhajan* gatherings or volunteer work, but there was a distinct sense of loss in their lives at having abandoned the land of their forefathers.

For other elderly immigrants, matters were much worse. Their misery came not merely from being isolated or neglected but from being exploited quite mercilessly by their children. Horror stories abound in Chicago about how the elderly have been abandoned in shopping malls, disowned by their children, and generally maltreated by them. Some children are known to have grabbed their parent's Social Security income and denied them any access to it at all. The sense of resentment and deprivation amongst this population is profound enough to cause severe psychological problems for some. It has even motivated a social worker who helped found Apna Ghar, the shelter for battered women in Chicago, to start a program to deal with elder abuse.

> People of our generation, we want our children to be comfortable here but we still want them to retain Indian values. Our children are reconciled to their children becoming American but we are not. Once you come over at a certain age to this country, you will have to take its good points with the bad. Children who go to school here are bound to develop new values.

Most of our children who come here work like donkeys. They don't come home at 5:30 or 6 when they are tired after a day's work. They keep on working. It is there in the national symbol of the American political parties—the donkey and the elephant. Work like donkeys and eat like elephants. As a father, I do feel, "What has happened to my children?" When I see all the excesses. . . . Our children don't have the time to instill their religious heritage in their kids. The Muslims are very particular, they do their *namaz* (ritual prayer), no matter what. They observe their strict dietary laws. Have you ever seen a Jew celebrating Christmas or a Muslim eating pork? I have yet to see it. But we Hindus are willing to do anything, eat anything, celebrate all festivals. We are too liberal.

I have met thousands of Americans and many of them know more about Hinduism than we do. They are inquisitive. They have studied it thoroughly. Only the media here has trashed Hinduism. Even if our children do not propagate or observe it, Hinduism will survive.

There is always an in-law factor. Every individual family has different circumstances. Some daughters-in-law are very good. But not all. I shouldn't say this but we do provide valuable services. Whether our daughters-in-law are good or bad, they know that we look to proper functioning of the kitchen, we provide 100 percent baby-sitting, much better than any other, because we provide love and care as no one else can. I have also seen that when the children become ten and fifteen years old and no longer need baby-sitting, the grandparents have been made to cry and driven out of the house. This is the truth.

I wouldn't like to live away from my son if I am in the United States. I had that chance in India. I opted to live here with him. Still, I'm scared. In America, children always talk of moving out of the house. My daughter-in-law may also be feeling that all her American friends are living on their own while she has to live with a mother-in-law. Today, we may get along with our daughters-in-law. Tomorrow, we may not. My daughter-in-law lives in a different world in American society. Her friends may ask, "What! Your mother-in-law lives with you?" There is a saying that if your repeat a lie a thousand times it becomes the truth. What if the daughter-in-law also begins to believe that it is wrong to have your in-laws live with you?

Indians who are building new homes here are thinking of a separate in-laws' portion. That way, we also get the feeling that we are in our son's home but separate. We as a society will have to face this. That is why I try to contribute in my own way by volunteering at the temple.

In India, we are economically independent. If we are unhappy in our son's house, we can always say, "You be happy in your own home. We'll be on our own. We've got our pension, we have our own money." But if we are unhappy here, we have no option. We have to stay in our children's home and learn to be happy with them. If our children say something to us or hurt us even slightly, where can we go? If the government or some cooperative housing society would give us housing and we could live on our own for a few dollars, we would definitely like to live on in America. We have good medical facilities here. We have also made friends here in the last twelve years. Our friendships in India are also diminishing. Our children would also like it if we are nearby and safe and if they can phone us regularly. I know of a family in Canada where the old parents live separately and the children go and visit them regularly.

As an immediate answer to our need to live alone, I suggest that since we have four or five temples here, a few rooms could be constructed for us senior citizens. We could live there. We don't want to be bothered with buying groceries. Our meals could be cooked for us. We could live there for eight or ten or fifteen days, not for always. Right now, we have no other home to which we can go in America.

The sense of alienation in America persisted even among the highly educated Indian elderly, especially the unemployed who could not build their own social circle independent of their children. The general perception was that older Americans were on totally different wave lengths from the Indians, and there could never be a meeting of the minds. Their grandchildren, the new generation that was born and brought up here, did many things that they themselves found distasteful, especially dating, staying out late and behaving irreverently, but they felt it was beyond their control and something that their adult children should handle. They seemed reconciled to the fact that coming to America had changed things irreversibly for their children.

What they themselves wanted was to be given some options in their own lives—better transportation, better referral services so they could avail themselves of all the benefits set aside for them by the city, state and federal agencies, and the opportunity to socialize through clubs and other institutions. They felt that other ethnic communities such as the Chinese and Koreans had done a lot for their elderly in Chicago while the Indians lagged far behind. The community, by not involving the elderly fully, was losing out and denying itself the services that they could provide. Most of all, the elderly wanted the chance to live independently and with dignity. The American norm of the nuclear family looms as a threat over the lives of these elderly parents who are insecure in their sons' homes. There is also a recognition that Indian values generally are being eroded in the lives of their children. Limited in their options by their lack of economic independence, the elderly are nevertheless anxious to devise new strategies with respect to housing and living arrangements that will keep them close to their children but not impose a burden on them.

Grandchildren

Ties to the grandchildren are strong and loving, but there is also a sadness at the drifting away of the children as they grow older and more independent. Unlike first-generation immigrants who would like to influence their children's choice of a spouse, the elderly grandparents are more detached and reconciled to the inevitability of change and new influences in their grandchildren's lives. Their relaxed attitude comes, no doubt, from not feeling any direct responsibility for the welfare of their grandchildren.

> Do you know the saying that the interest is more precious to you than the principal? That is the way it is with us. Our grandchildren seem even more precious than our children. We do sometimes feel that we missed out on our children. Where did the twenty years go? Suddenly they have grown up, got a job. So we are closer to our grandchildren because we have more time to spend with them now.

> My grandchildren always want to know if I will be home when they come back from school. They say, "We don't like it when you go out. You aren't going out anywhere today, are you?" But these children

aren't as close to their parents as our children were to us. Maybe it is a generational thing. Each new generation is less attached to their parents. Children who are three, four, seven years old spend more time with their grandparents and are closer to them. There is more bonding, until about ten or so. But when they turn seventeen or nineteen and twenty, then it is different.

In 1942, my brother-in-law married a Spanish girl and was thrown out of the house. But times have changed, that doesn't happen any more.

We can't control our grandchildren. Our children are our responsibility and if we have Indian spouses for them we are happy. Being married within your own caste is okay, but it's not that important. It's also okay if our grandchildren want to marry Americans. It's their life. What our grandchildren do is their business. Even my brother, thirty-six years ago, did not marry a Brahmin, he married a Kshatriya. It is our children who will have to weigh the plus and negative points for alliances for their children. What our grandchildren do, we can't influence them.

There are some advantages to being married in your own caste. In my community, we had seven subcastes. We had a network of relatives to rely upon. We had many marriage offers for our son. Our only requirement was that she be a Punjabi and a Brahmin. We felt that a girl from among our own kind would understand our ways, our eating and living habits. If she is from Assam or Bengal, it will take her that much longer to learn our ways. Being a Brahmin was most important. First, it was important to be a Brahmin. Then from the same region.

I feel that the institution of marriage itself is obsolete and should be destroyed. We should not stick to old ways of thinking and seeing. We should come out of that.

Socializing

Among the elderly parents, those who were employed held favorable opinions about Americans; the unemployed had limited opportunity to mingle with Americans but that did not prevent them from forming their own ideas about American society. The predominant feeling was of alienation and discomfort with other Americans and of being discriminated against because of their culture.

> In my work as a palmist, I come in contact with a lot of Americans. They are very helpful, considerate, the youngsters are very helpful. My work and social life are connected. My clients become like family members, a bond is created. We get very good treatment from Americans. The psychic fair promoter always makes sure that we are lodged at the same hotel as he is because he knows we don't drive and don't have transportation. In my ten years here, I have never had to pick up my own bag. Indians have never helped me with my bags, but Americans always have. I have a very high opinion of Americans. Our clients are all highly educated doctors, engineers, scientists.

> The Americans who are above fifty they don't come forward, they don't disclose themselves. Their society is different. For us, once we are married, we are married for our whole life. But they are different, their involvement begins and ends with "Hi." Americans don't want to come out of their shell. Look at the way we talk to each other. They don't communicate like this even among themselves. Because I did volunteer work, I was able to build some bridges. Younger Americans are different. In the Lemont Temple, it was a pleasure to talk to the younger groups, the environment was different. We had to tell them what we Hindus stand for, what is our heritage, why we built the temple.

> The general situation is this. Our children are doctors, engineers, they have their own friends at work. But we move in our own circles. Americans look at us and feel we are different. They see Sardarjis amongst us with turbans, they see our clothes are different, they think our cooking stinks. They don't want to socialize with us and our children. Even if we are better educated and better placed in life than they are. They also say that when we move into their neighborhoods, it lowers the value of their property. I don't know how far this is true. About ten years ago, when we moved to Westchester, it was an all-white community. At first, they considered themselves superior. When we bought our house, they were worried that property values

would drop. It so happened that we had Indian doctors for neighbors who were very happy to have us. Our Polish neighbors had to convince everyone on Cromwell Street that we were a highly educated community and that our minimum education was a Master's. Still, there was slight discrimination there also. The idea was already in their heads about us.

One day we were walking our grandchildren to school and some Americans met us and asked, they asked my wife, how long she had been married. She said, "Forty-five years." And they said, "To the same husband?" Imagine saying that in front of the children. How will it affect their young minds? We have always told our neighbors, if ever you need baby-sitting, send the children to our home, we are always home. That is the only way to reach out to them. But still they look at life through their own glasses.

If you go for a job interview dressed like an Indian, they will not hire you. Even if that is not really discrimination, it means they are uncomfortable with another culture.

The Immigrants Themselves

The aging primary immigrants, the true pioneers of the post-1965 Indian immigrant saga, may be likened to the so-called "sandwich" generation. They were the first to come and face hardships on their own, they established the foundations of a society that future immigrants and future generations could build upon, but they also have to provide solutions for the very special problems posed by their aged parents. By the 1990s, they had constructed temples, founded religious, cultural, and professional institutions and shaped a legacy that the second generation would inherit. For the first two or three decades after immigration, they were preoccupied with providing for their young but in the mid-1990s, their thoughts turned increasingly to their own impending old age. The increased attention paid to the elderly at Indian gatherings, both formal and informal, is a sign that old age issues will loom larger and larger on the Indian immigrant agenda.

What fuels the entire process is that the American elderly are such a powerful, organized, special interest group. Indian immigrants who turned fifty were wooed just like other Americans by the AARP (American Association of Retired Persons) and subjected to a barrage of information about legislation concerning Medicaid, Medicare, and SSI. To the extent that they had access to information circulating in the mainstream society, the aging Indian immigrants were no more nor less at risk of being hurt or benefited than the general American population. What ultimately sets the aging Indian immigrants apart is the effect that their special culture has on their future. Will they enjoy the respect of their children in a society that worships youth and physical beauty and that is in sharp contrast to their native culture that venerates old age? Have they taught their children to look upon them any differently than other American youth look upon their aged parents? In other words, was there a value to being Indian in America in old age?

Another relevant question is whether Indian immigrants in America will build a wide network of relationships so that they are not dependent solely on their children for support in their old age, as their own parents are now. How will they balance the role of institutions, ethnic or mainstream, with the role of the family in the care of seniors? What role will religious institutions play in the care of the aged? Temples and mosques and churches in Chicago have shown a remarkable capacity to innovate according to the need of the hour. If they can hold SAT coaching classes and career fairs for the youth, what is to prevent them from sheltering the aged on their premises, as one elderly immigrant suggested. Other ideas to cope with this issue are already being implemented. Advertisements appear in the Chicago or International edition of Indian American newspapers and magazines, touting the attractions of retirement communities in Florida where elderly Indians can live in a culture-friendly environment.

Since the immigrants have shown extraordinary commitment to building institutions and forming organizations in order to bring about desired changes in their lives, there is no reason to doubt that they will do the same when it comes to meeting the special needs of the elderly. Class divisions and regional identity may play a big role in determining future options for Indians. Though the Chicago Indian population is extremely diverse, there is an increasing concentration of Gujaratis and middle/lower class nonprofessionals in the community. If solutions to the problems of the elderly come from this section of the Indian community, they are likely to retain strong elements of Indian culture. But they will also take full advantage of the state-supported provisions for elderly care that are available in the United States but which were not available to them in India.

Conclusion

The elderly share certain characteristics of the immigrant experience with the youth and women. For one thing, they were all following or accompanying or joining other family members on their trip to the United States. Some women did come on their own as independent agents, but the youth were brought by their parents, and the elderly came to live with their adult children. This involuntary nature of their migration made it harder for them to adjust to difficult circumstances and to accept the challenges of a new life. For the elderly, their work options were particularly limited not only because of their lack of marketable skills or their infirmity, but also because their children refused to allow them to work at certain jobs which they deemed unworthy of their status. Home and family relationships for the elderly were both rewarding and frustrating. They took great pride in their children's achievements and successes, but were also reconciled to their inability to control them or their grandchildren.

In the voices and countervoices of these three different groups of immigrant Indians—the women, the youth, and the elderly—one can detect echoes of what was described in Chapter 1 as part of the "historical consciousness." The same concerns about family, obligations to fellow human beings, and one's place in society are viewed by the individuals in the study from their own unique circumstances but their perspective is always informed by a similar set of ideals and beliefs that may be called "Indian." The fact that these beliefs are shared by all Indians, regardless of gender, generation, region of origin, or religious faith is what distinguishes them from other members of the societies in which they live and makes them part of the global *oikumene*.

PART IV

Strategies of Survival and Growth

8

PRESERVING THE CORE
Cultural Institutions

Personal adaptation involves empowering the self to cope with change. In this process of self-transformation, communities play a vital role in providing social supports and rituals for preserving tradition and celebrating change.
—Richard Harvey Brown and George V. Coelho, eds., *Tradition and Transformation: Asian Indians in America*

It is only natural that when traditional networks of association that exist in the home country are no longer available for immigrants in a foreign land, they will form new associations to replace the old ones. But the institutions built by Chicago's immigrant Indians are hardly replicas of what exists in the homeland. Instead, they are responses to new conditions and constantly changing imperatives based on the immigrants' need to forge an identity that draws from both Old and New World influences, at first for themselves and later for their children. In the process of building this infrastructure for a new society, the immigrants discover themselves afresh, reshaping their old selves into new forms.

The process of rediscovery for Indian immigrants involves digging into their own national consciousness and retrieving a repository of knowledge accumulated not only during their own lifetimes but generations past. It means drawing upon myths and legends, folklore and history. It also means getting organized because unless they act as a group they cannot hold on for long to either the outward symbols of their identity such as language, food and dress, or their inner, mental symbols such as their morality, religion, and family values. Institutions thus both reflect and shape a complex sense of identity, which must be created anew by the immigrant if he or she is to survive the immigrant experience.

For many Indian immigrants, this is a long, slow, and painful experience. Being Westernized, educated in American ways and belonging to the upper class have their own dangers. Some of the postcolonial Indians, especially the "brown sahibs," who are sometimes more "British" than the British themselves, feel that they are so well accepted by white American society that, in order to truly "belong" with them, they must set themselves conspicuously apart from their lower-class compatriots in Chicago. They are often dismayed to find late in life that they have hit the glass ceiling or been denied entry into the country club. At that point, some of them turn to the Indian community with whom they share the same skin color and a common past, realizing that their Indianness can never be shed, only recast and reworn. Other immigrants who live in the cocoon of their own immigrant community and never climb the economic ladder of success wonder why they gave up their homeland at all if they cannot reap the economic benefits of immigration, such as they are, and why they must continue to live on the fringes of an alien society. Whatever one's occupation or class, gender or ethnicity, no immigrant can go long before being forced into some soul-searching for a meaningful sense of time, place, and self.

To give all Indians a single sense of identity and see them, as the U.S. Census does, as belonging to a single ethnic group, is to give them skin but no flesh and blood and bones. Indians cherish many different aspects of their ethnicity and choose to emphasize them in different ways, and while they are all important, each in its own way, the organized form is what concerns us here. Other, nonorganized networks such as personal friendships developed through individual and family contacts are even more important for immigrant Indians. These networks are not the visible pillars of the community and do not speak the unified language of the institutions, but they are nevertheless shaped by them. Indians get together regularly at private parties and social gatherings in homes. Other basic institutions such as marriage and family are common to most societies, and though they are not discussed in this chapter under separate headings, they are also deeply affected by and shape the religious, cultural, professional, and other formally organized Indian institutions that are discussed here. These associations enable Indians who are widely scattered geographically, not only all over Chicago and the suburbs but all over the nation and the world, to come together and act as a "community." The word "community" is used in its metaphorical sense, which "labels thousands of individuals, unknown to one another, as though they lived in the same village and conversed regularly.[1]

Whether a social entity is an "institution," "organization," or "association" is a matter for debate and the distinctions are not particularly relevant here. What may be a fragile "association" today may grow into a rock-solid "institution" in years to come and vice versa. What is important is that Indian immigrants use these forms to come together for a common purpose under a common label, ready to follow certain rules and regulations concerning their conduct, and they do this because they wish to be recognized as a separate and distinct entity. It is not uncommon for an Indian immigrant to belong to half a dozen or so such separate entities. It is also important not to see these identities as competing and conflicting but complementary. There are also Indians in Chicago, among them Parsis, Jews, and Christians, some of whom have American spouses, who opt to have nothing to do with Indian organizations and only have American friends. They are most likely to have arrived before 1965, as students, and established their friendships with Americans before the large scale post-1965 immigration.

When Indians choose to emphasize certain aspects of their identity in an organized fashion, it is not necessarily because those aspects are the most important but because they feel that these aspects require this particular form of public expression. In a democratic society such as the United States where pressure groups are formed out of political necessity, Indians learned quickly the need to be organized and to articulate their interests in a collective voice that could be heard above the fray. In a field as crowded and raucous as Chicago's, a group's very survival may depend on its ability to organize. But unity remains an ideal to strive for rather than an achieved reality among Chicago's Indian immigrants. The disparate linguistic, religious, and regional backgrounds of Indians in Chicago are so dizzying to contemplate that Indian immigrants themselves use organizational affiliations to understand each other and "place" each other in the larger spectrum of their overall Indianness.

Patterns of Development

Despite the confusing variety and range of the scores of organizations and associations, some general themes emerge that are fairly typical and characteristic of most of them. One is the pattern of growth from a small, intimate group to a formal, registered organization with a broader, dues-paying membership. Since these associations were called into existence by the forces of immigration, they are specific to a particular time and place and change according to the needs of the community they serve. Many of the early associations were formed in response to loneliness and alienation and answered the psychological and social needs of a small and somewhat scattered population. They were formed in the 1960s and early 1970s when immigrants eagerly sought each other out no matter what part of India they were from, gathered in each other's basements or got together for picnics, and chatted nostalgically of things Indian. Organizations such as the India Forum were born in such an atmosphere and thrived as long as the immigrants were concerned only with their own social and intellectual needs.

But as the population grew and the immigrants started raising families, their priorities changed. There was regrouping based on a variety of factors such as life stage imperatives, parochial interests, or geographical concentration. There was a need to teach Indian children who were growing up in America and learning only American ways something about their own Indian heritage and religion. Indian parents were often alarmed at the prospect that their children would become completely alienated and consider their own parents "weird" if left to the influences of the outside world. They would drive for miles across state lines for a Sanskrit teacher who could teach their children verses from the *Ramayana* or the *Mahabharata*, although they themselves did not know a word of Sanskrit or much about the scriptures! Teaching Indian children about Indian values also became important so that the "evil" and "corrupt" influences of American society could be kept at bay.[2] It was around the mid-1970s that the idea of building houses of worship and conducting language and scripture classes first took root. The growth of the second generation in America coincided happily with the arrival of large numbers of new immigrants from India, so even as these institutions took form, they were continuously shaped by influences from the home country.

As the numbers grew, so did the opportunity for Indians to express themselves in their narrower Indian identities. Whereas earlier a pan-Indian organization such as Association of Indians in America satisfied their need to express an ethnic identity, now they could choose to be Gujaratis, or Tamilians, Bengalis, or even Hyderabadi Muslims. The Bihar Cultural Association or the Association of Rajasthanis in America and other such language or state-based organizations sprang up in the late 1970s and early

1980s—almost overnight it seemed—giving their members the opportunity to share a cultural life with others who spoke their own language, ate the same kind of food, and dressed in like fashion. In later years, these associations broadened their mission to promote their own culture aggressively by staging elaborate entertainment shows or sponsoring artists from the homeland.

Geographical concentration also played a part in the development of these organizations. The Skokie Association of Indians came into being only when enough Indians became concentrated in that suburb. Other developmental changes took place with the maturing of the community. The "Youth Wing" of the Hindu Temple of Greater Chicago was formed only when the second generation came of age. Such adaptation to changing circumstances has meant prolonged growing pains but it has also kept the institutions thriving and vital.

Though the institutions are broadly divisible into categories according to their main focus, they are also multifaceted in their activities and their goals. Many of the so-called cultural institutions use "culture" as a catch-all term, and conduct such a variety of religious, social, political, educational, and family-oriented activities that it is difficult to place them in a single category. This is especially true not only of the language and state-based associations, such as the Bihar Cultural Association or the Chicago Tamil Sangam, but also of more specifically defined associations. For instance, a professional association of doctors whose main aim is safeguarding their professional interests will plan a cruise for members and their families as part of a medical convention and thus fulfill their social needs. A Hindu temple will conduct dance classes or SAT (Scholastic Aptitude Test) coaching sessions or even run a marriage bureau, while a social service agency may conduct "culture awareness" workshops for Chicago-area public school teachers. Such diversity has meant uncontrolled and sometimes unfocused growth, but also dynamism, innovation, and change that has kept the community vibrant. The Chicago Indian immigrants have a wide range of organizations to choose from when planning their social calendar. Some Indians are so bewildered and confused by the available options that they choose to stay away altogether and not join any of them!

Another general characteristic of these institutions, at least the more self-conscious and forward-thinking among them and those most likely to survive, is that they have realized the importance of the second generation. Youth wings and second-generation groups have sprung up like branches or appendages of the main institutions and seem poised to break off from the main trunk or take it over in due course. The first-generation immigrants realize that unless they grant greater autonomy to their children in running these institutions, all their foundation building may come to naught.

Members and Leaders

If it were not for the activities of these organizations, the Indians who live in Chicago and those who live in the suburbs might never have come together. The people who run these organizations and benefit from them, the members, the donors, the workers, and the volunteers, are drawn from both the city and the suburbs. These organizations also bring together members of the diplomatic community and prominent politicians and businessmen from India, thus promoting continuous interaction among people of Indian origin whether from the homeland or around the world. They bring together not only the first and second generations of Indians but also the parents of the immigrants. Most of these organizations keep in touch with their members via regular newsletters and by advertising their events in the ethnic media. Such coming together of a diverse population has also meant increasing clashes of special interest groups within these organizations, often resulting in the emergence of new organizations. Personality conflicts are most often the reason for such friction, but more recently, discord has been attributed to class conflict between the earlier arriving professionals and the later arriving nonprofessionals. Sometimes the squabbling has reached such a pitch that many members have turned away in disgust. Lack of moral leadership is an issue that plagues the community and the fight for power and control in these institutions is constantly played out between individuals, between generations or between classes.[3]

The role of women in the Indian ethnic organizations is highly visible, variegated, and vital. Not only have they been at the forefront by donating funds and taking active part in the planning and implementation of programs, they have done so without abandoning the traditional role assigned to them by a patriarchal Indian culture. It must be noted, however, that the top posts in these organizations, especially the religious ones, are dominated by the men. (However, in a precedent-setting move, a woman, Sudha Rao, was elected head of the Hindu Temple of Greater Chicago in 1996. The Indo-American Democratic Organization was also headed by a woman,

Ann [Lata] Kalayil, in 1998.) When faced with crises or required to respond to the special needs of their own gender, the women have formed separate associations of their own. If the pulse of a community can be gauged by the participation of its women, the Indian immigrant community in Chicago is indeed bursting with health.

Research conducted in the 1970s and even early 1980s among the Indian immigrant communities in the United States recognized only four or five kinds of associations—the campus-based students' associations, the language or region-based associations that conducted social and cultural events, the religious, the professional, and the pan-Indian associations. But in the 1990s, these categories are no longer sufficient. The rise in popular entertainment, political activity and social activism has spawned a plethora of organizations. Some of them are, strictly speaking, commercial organizations formed mainly to fulfill financial objectives, but because they fulfill a "cultural" or "social" need, they cannot be seen in a purely business light. To keep from drowning in the sea of organizations and associations that reflect the life of the community, it is necessary to divide them into broad categories. By examining in detail some of the major institutions in each category and acknowledging the existence of many others, it is possible to build a fairly comprehensive portrait of Chicago's Indian immigrant infrastructure and track its growth since 1965.

Chicago's Indian immigrant institutions are divided into several groups and discussed under separate chapters. This chapter deals with the all-India organizations, the linguistic or state-based organizations, and the performing arts organizations that are aimed at helping Indians preserve the core of their immigrant identity. Other chapters deal with religious infrastructures, business and politics, and professional and special-interest organizations. These last also include social service organizations and the media, which are more worldly in their approach and driven by an agenda that is not primarily religious or cultural. They provide Indians with a vehicle to reach out and create new connections to the world around them.

All-India Umbrella Organizations

These organizations were among the earliest to be established and served the Chicago immigrant community well as long as the community was small and the interests of its members were broad enough to be included under a single umbrella. With the passage of time and the growth of linguistic and regional institutions, their relevance was called into question. In the 1990s they find themselves struggling to represent Chicago's Indians in a national forum by bringing them together with Indians from other parts of the United States.

Association of Indians in America (AIA)

The Association of Indians in America, headquartered in New York with an Illinois chapter in Oakbrook, is the oldest national association of Indians in America. Founded on August 20, 1967, and incorporated in 1971 as a tax-exempt, nonpartisan and nonpolitical organization, it claims to be a grass-roots organization with members spread across the nation. Its thirteen chapters constitute a loose federation and do not have to follow any set agenda or report to headquarters. Its goal is "to provide a forum of common action to all whose Indian heritage and common commitment offer a bond of unity." Its most notable achievements are the reclassification of immigrants from South Asian countries as Asian Pacific Americans, obtaining minority status for them for civil rights purposes, and getting separate enumeration for them as an independent category for the first time in the U.S. Census of 1980. The organization addresses issues of bias and discrimination against Indians in America, setting up legal aid funds for the defense of victims of ethnic and religious bigotry and violence.[4]

The Illinois chapter of the AIA was started in 1976 and regularly conducts seminars and workshops, youth activities, social and cultural programs, and an annual banquet in the Chicago area. Its significance to the Chicago area residents has diminished considerably in recent years. "It was quite active until about 10 years ago," said Dr. Nayeem Shariff who was elected president for 1995 and 1996. "Two to three years ago, the AIA almost died in Chicago because there has been such a proliferation of organizations here, nobody has the time or energy to get fully involved in more than one or two." AIA in Chicago has about two hundred members (of whom forty to forty-five are life-members) drawn from the city and all over the suburbs. Dr. Shariff hoped to revive the organization by getting it to collaborate with other associations instead of trying to go it alone and merely diluting the community's resources. But without a distinctive agenda and without offering benefits to its members that no other organization can duplicate, AIA faces an uncertain future and its survival depends heavily on the quality of individual leaders. "When our membership is not committed, and that does happen often because so many come and go, our activities dwindle," conceded Dr. Shariff. AIA may become a victim of the "adapt or perish" trend among Chicago area institutions unless it responds more aggressively to local needs.[5]

National Federation of Indian American Associations (NFIA)

The NFIA, also New York–based, was started on May 23, 1980, to promote the interests of people of Indian origin and claims to be the "largest Indian-American organization." Its regional and biennial national conventions are supposed to provide a format through which all its member organizations can function in unison. It claims to be issue-oriented and conducts seminars on such a wide variety of topics that nothing is excluded from its purview. The following is a list of topics covered at the Seventh National Convention held in Atlanta, October 2–4, 1992: "The role of Indian-Americans in the corporate community, human rights violations, film festivals, emerging economic opportunities in India, managing stress, Indian American youth, hotel-motel industry, franchising, the aging population of Indian Americans, influence of Indian American heritage on youth, investment and business opportunities in USA."[6]

In Chicago, NFIA comes into the limelight only when the city is chosen as the venue for a national convention, and back-room politics are exposed to the glare of publicity. The three-day Eighth National Convention of the NFIA was held over a Labor Day weekend (1–5 September 1994) in the plush halls of the Hyatt Regency O'Hare with prominent keynote speakers from the Indian American community. Speakers also included Senator Larry Pressler and Congressman Gary Ackerman who, in the manner of all politicians seeking the support of the Indian community, duly praised the contribution of Indian Americans and vowed to fight pro-Pakistani and anti-India legislation in United States government. But the management of the conference by Indians in Chicago came in for sharp criticism in a section of the local ethnic media that said that the conference had done nothing to promote Indian unity or progress and everything to expose a self-serving leadership.[7] Another development is the holding of the "First Biennial Second Generation Conference" on a concurrent basis in 1994. The discussion topics showed that though the second generation had some issues that they shared with their parents, theirs was a distinct agenda: "Campus Issues, Careers and Networking, Cultural Awareness, Indian Artistic Expressions, Perceptions of Indians in the Media and Political Participation."

Federation of India Associations (FIA); Alliance of Midwest Indian Associations (AMIA)

The FIA and the AMIA are best known in Chicago as the warring parties in a long drawn-out feud as to who is to represent the Indian immigrant community for the annual India Independence Day parade on Michigan Avenue, a feud that came to an end only when the City limited the parade permit to one per ethnic group in 1993 and forced the community to speak with one voice.[8] Parade politics has often descended into petty bickering of "egomaniacs" (as they are contemptuously called by critics in the immigrant community) and tarnished the image of the ethnic community not only in its own eyes but in the eyes of city officials who are fully aware of the questionable tactics used by these groups to gain undue advantage.[9] Parades are important to Indians, as they are for other ethnic groups in Chicago, because they help them *invent* ethnicity and differentiate them from the more inclusive cultural identity that embraces all South Asians. Because parades are the public expression and celebration of the national spirit of an ethnic group, the dissension in this sphere is taken more seriously by the Indian community than infighting in other areas.

The format of the parade, which had been the same for many years, underwent some significant changes in 1995. The Mayor of Chicago was usually the Grand Marshall (accompanied by some minor local politicians) and a series of floats representing different Indian associations and organizations paraded down Michigan Avenue. But the parade has become less meaningful over the years, especially for the upper-class suburban Indians who do not see them as a symbol of their identity as Indian Americans. They also find themselves far outnumbered at these events by the second wave of immigrants. Now Chicago personalities are no longer enough to draw the crowds; instead film celebrities from India are especially invited for the occasion in order to encourage attendance. In 1995, the parade venue was shifted from Michigan Avenue to Devon Avenue, the Grand Marshall was no longer the Mayor but an Indian film actor who spoke in Hindi to the crowd. Attendance in 1995 was mostly from the local inhabitants of Devon Avenue and hardly representative of the entire immigrant community. Whereas in earlier years, shoppers on Michigan Avenue stopped in curiosity to watch the parade and got to know that there was a significant Indian population in Chicago, now both spectators and participants are limited to Indians. Such changes may indicate that the community is drawing away from the mainstream and more into itself, reaching out to its own immigrant population or trying to reflect the interests of the community. Leaders who organized the parade on Devon Avenue said that the purpose was to give a boost to the merchants of India Town and create a tradition whereby the neighborhood would acquire the same level of recognizability as Chinatown in Chicago and come to be associated permanently with Indians. Constant exhortations in the local media by parade organizers ("Be there—Be proud to be Indians") show that attendance at these parades is still a matter of concern.[10] The Mayor's Office hosts a traditional reception for prominent Indian Americans, and being on that list of invitees is still considered a feather in the cap by the social climbers in the community.

The AMIA, having given up the parade-organizing role to the FIA, hosted the banquet and cultural program in connection with the Independence Day celebrations in 1995. It hosts other charitable events during the year such as its now traditional Thanksgiving feast. At its seventh feast in 1994, over one hundred volunteers gathered to feed over one thousand disadvantaged Americans at Truman College.[11] Such outreach programs are undertaken with the specific purpose of boosting the image of Indians and showing their involvement with other Chicagoans, and to counter accusations of exclusiveness.

The ILA Foundation (Formerly The India League of America)

The ILA traces its history to the first organization of Indian immigrants in America of the same name, formed in the early part of this century. It is a Chicago-based, pan-Indian association formed in 1972 when a group of Indians revived the name to represent the interests of the newer immigrants. It changed its name to ILA Foundation in 1981 when it saw that the language-based associations were more successful in attracting Indians for social purposes and felt compelled to redefine its own role. The ILA nurtured the birth of the FIA with the specific purpose of uniting all the disparate associations and changed its own role to that of a funding institution.

The ILA's major political activity was to oppose AIA's attempts in 1976 to gain minority status for Indian Americans. ILA argued that if Indians were classified as a minority group, their economic opportunities would be limited to the small percentage or quota allocation for such groups. (This has indeed happened in the case of Indians seeking admission to Ivy League schools that deny otherwise qualified Indian students admission on the grounds that their minority quota is already full.) A special study authorized by the ILA in 1976 resulted in the Elkhanialy-Nicholas survey of Chicago area immigrants. The goals of the survey were to "determine which racial terms the immigrants prefer as self-designations, and also the extent to which they have experienced racial discrimination."[12] The results showed that 70 percent of the 159 respondents preferred to call themselves "brown," not "black" or "white," and approximately three-quarters preferred minority status. ILA's attempts to forge a Caucasian identity for Indian immigrants so that they would merge with the whites resulted in failure, while AIA's victory in gaining a separate minority status for Indians has had far-reaching consequences for their future as an ethnic group. It affirmed their need to be separate and distinct, indicated their rejection of the melting pot style of assimilation and, paradoxically, opened up opportunities for them to participate in the American political process by building pressure groups and garnering votes based on their growing numbers. Formal organizations such as the AIA and the ILA thus determined what options were available to Indians in the identity-building process even while they took their cue from the attitudes and beliefs of the individual immigrants themselves.

Since the function of these umbrella organizations is to give Indians in the United States a strong unified voice, they must be judged by the quality of their leadership and their ability to pull together a diversified group. Such leadership has so far proved uneven at best, and an embarrassment at worst. Some amount of conflict and infighting among groups is inevitable, especially in such a large, pluralistic, diverse community as the Indian community in Chicago. While all would-be leaders have "egos" and some are bound to be self-serving, what is disconcerting is that so many different organizations exist supposedly to serve the same purpose and are unable to galvanize all Indians under one banner.[13] In some cases, making speeches, inviting prominent politicians, and presenting awards to each other is the main activity of a select coterie of organizers. Well-meaning individuals exist in every organization but so far no outstanding leader has emerged in Chicago who can profess to speak for all Indians. Divisions, while they may be taken in stride in other religious and cultural organizations, are anathema to umbrella and pan-Indian organizations like these whose main mission is to unite. Like the India of the 1990s, the Indian immigrant community of Chicago has a fragile social fabric that reflects all the nuances and problems of the homeland. Thus resolving differences will continue to pose a challenge, no matter how the community shapes up in the future. Today, just getting the community to hold one parade instead of several parades represents a high water mark. But if some day Indians in Chicago are called upon to speak in unison on serious issues that affect their economic and political well-being, one or more of these organizations should provide them with the platform.

Language or Regional or State-Based Organizations

Scholars have long debated why certain immigrant groups under certain conditions at certain times in history have maintained the parochial differences that exist in the homeland and at other times submerged them in a national identity. In the case of Indians, a clear distinction can be made between the indentured and the free-passage emigrants. Those who went in the nineteenth century to Guyana, Trinidad, Mauritius, Fiji, and South Africa had no means of maintaining ties with the homeland or of retaining their caste and linguistic differences under conditions of indenture, hence they were forced to adopt a pan-Indian identity. It is also argued that the nationalist movement in India of the 1920s sent emissaries to these countries that fostered among the Indians a fused sense of unity and nationalism.[14] On the other hand, the independent entrepreneurs who emigrated at their own expense to Great Britain, East and South Africa, and Fiji continued to be rooted in the homeland even after emigration, mainly because they had the financial means to return to India for marriage and religious reasons. They formed associations based on natal language (many of them knew no other language and were not comfortable with English), religion, and sometimes even caste. They may have toyed with the idea of a permanent return to India at some point in their lives but gave it up as their economic ties and the involvement of their children in the adopted land grew more and more difficult to break. But their affiliations to India were strengthened with the passing years, especially for the Sikhs and Gujaratis, both Hindu and Muslim, in Africa and Great Britain.

The Indian immigrants in the United States, and more particularly, the professional immigrants of Chicago, do not fall into either of the above categories. Their fluency in English is such that they do not need a language-based association to communicate with others of their own region in India. They are hardly particular about caste, except when it comes to marriage, because they had grown up in an India where discrimination based on caste was denounced as divisive folly. A permanent return to India looks more and more remote with each passing year, so there is no need to keep the differences that exist in the homeland. Even if they did go back, it would probably be to one of the major metropolises where parochialism is more *passé* than it is in Chicago. Why then have Indian immigrants in Chicago formed more than twenty-five language-based associations? Why are these associations more active and popular than the pan-Indian associations? Are they to be viewed as a strength or weakness of the community?

The structure of these associations suggests that they may not be as narrow in scope as the word "parochialism" suggests. Many of them are loosely federated with other language-based organizations around the country and even around the world. There is the Federation of Tamil Sangams of North America with which the Chicago Tamil Sangam conducts joint literary events. When the World Gujarati Samaj held its convention in New Delhi in September 1994, over four hundred delegates from local organizations in America, England, Canada, Africa, Australia, Singapore, and Pakistan participated.[15] When the Maharashtra Mandal of Chicago celebrated its twenty-fifth anniversary in July 1994, it proudly proclaimed that it was presenting local, national, and international talent.[16] Parochialism, in the case of emigrant Indians, is truly global in its scope. The reasons for the global networking are many and varied—from matchmaking for the second generation to establishing business contacts and holding alumni meetings.[17]

Other associations, though language-based, are national in scope, such as the Telugu Association of North America (TANA). TANA seeks to promote not only Telugu culture but also welfare projects in the home state of Andhra Pradesh, such as setting up educational institutions, providing drinking water, and sponsoring health-care centers. With wealthy members in the medical and business sectors of the economy, the Telugus in North America are involved in a wide range of activities whose only common denominator is the Telugu language. As with other national associations, its impact on the Chicago community is greatest when the city is chosen as a convention site, as it was in 1995.[18]

Language-based associations have sprung up in Chicago and elsewhere in acknowledgment of the fact that no culture can survive if its medium—the language in which it is expressed—is allowed to die. "Indian" culture has no meaning without its constituent language-based cultures, though it is also more than the sum of its parts. Indian culture is both more and less than a Gujarati culture or a Tamil culture or a Bengali culture, but Indian culture propagation is not possible without coming down to its language-based specifics, especially for popular culture. Whenever a community had the financial means and the numbers required to sustain a language-based culture at the local level, a Chicago association sprang up to support it. These associations are best understood as the "keepers" of their culture.

The diversity of India, which is so well represented among the Chicago immigrant population, finds expression in these associations and their celebrations. Festivals and art forms are particular to certain states of India and can be celebrated in Chicago only through these language-based associations. *Onam* (a harvest festival) is celebrated by the Kerala Association, *Durga Puja* (a religious festival that celebrates the triumph of good over evil and where images of the Goddess Durga are taken in a procession and immersed in water) by the Bengali Association of Greater Chicago and *Pongal* (also a harvest festival of the South) by the Tamil Association. Gujaratis organize a *Garba Raas* celebration (a festival of folk dances) as a month-long event, holding annual national dance competitions in Chicago.[19]

There is an additional value to these events that goes to the heart of the identity-building process for Indians. They can eat, dress, and talk exactly the way they do back in India. They can do it in a public forum that comprises other Indians and without necessarily exposing themselves to the larger American public eye to whom their ways might seem strange. Far from conflicting with their truly public identity in the workplace—whether they are doctors or janitors they have to observe dress codes laid down by the host society—this "semi-public" identity allows them to express another side of themselves. For instance, wearing a sari or an Indian dress in public has very important connotations for the Indian woman. It is an expression of her nationality, her modesty, it is the way her husband might like to see her dressed, and it allows her to proclaim to the world that there is a certain part of her that has not been erased because she has emigrated to a new land. Such symbolism goes far beyond practical considerations and the simplistic dichotomy between outward and inward symbols of identity. It also had only limited scope for expression in the early 1970s when a sari could be worn only in the seclusion of one's home or at private gatherings. Today, Indians walk down Devon Avenue or attend gala fund raisers at events organized by these associations, dressed like Indians. On such occasions, they are a majority group and behave with the self-confidence and self-assurance that comes only from belonging to the majority.

Another question that must be asked about these associations is, Why do certain languages or states have more than one association? Surely it is not the size of the population that warrants it? The Telugus and the Malayalis do not make up more than a small fraction of the Indian population in Chicago but both groups have at least three associations each. The Gujaratis, who amount to approximately one-third of the Chicago population and whose population is growing at a much faster rate than that of the other Indian immigrant groups because of their tendency to sponsor large numbers of relatives, have five or more associations. These numbers do not include religious organizations such as the Gujarati Muslim Association of North America and the Council of Kerala Churches of Chicago. Some of these are breakaway groups formed when there were differences among the original members, so loyalties became divided. Those who belong to one Telugu association do not belong to another. Sometimes it is a matter of geographical convenience, with some associations concentrating in the western suburbs, others in the northern suburbs or in city neighborhoods. Among Gujaratis, different associations focus on different activities, so members may belong to more than one organization. The Charotar Patidar Samaj are a caste-based group who hold grand annual conventions that are more like marriage fairs. Marrying within their own caste is a high priority for them and they organize for this specific purpose. The 1995 Charotar Patidar Convention in Chicago held May 27 and 28 at the College of Du Page in Glen Ellyn had "one-on-one matrimonial meetings" and "theme parties for young adults." There was a different individual (all named Patel) to represent each one of the following subsects: Six Gam, Vansol Vibhag 27 Gam, Bavis Gam, Chovia Gam, Five Gam, and Satyavis Gam.[20]

In Chicago, the general trend has been toward the formation of associations with narrower and narrower focus among those with lesser economic means and a lower level of formal education. The more well-to-do, established professionals, while they do belong to the language-based associations, also try to maintain a broader focus and interact with the mainstream, identifying new areas of involvement such as education or politics.

The Chicago Tamil Sangam

Tracing the history of one of these associations, identifying its membership and its range of activities reveals growth patterns that are common to many associations. The Chicago Tamil Sangam began with a group of Tamilians getting together over pot-luck dinners and discussing Tamil culture and language issues. Over the years it grew into a formal association with a constitution and bylaws, biennial elections, a Board of Directors, and various committees to oversee specific activities. Meetings are generally conducted in the homes of office bearers. Though individual leaders have given the association a certain impetus or a thrust in a particular direction, the growth of the association does not depend on outstanding leadership but on group involvement. It has a dues-paying membership of about three hundred, but some of its more popular functions are attended by over one thousand people. The membership is drawn from all over Chicagoland. Mr. N. Aathimoolam, the president of the association for 1995, pointed out in an interview with the author that there were no obvious lines of division in the community. "Unlike the Gujaratis, we did not bring over our uneducated brothers and sisters to work here for $5.00 an hour. Most of us Tamilians have the same high educational level, we are a fairly homogenous group in terms of income also. Our association is open to all who have some Tamil affiliation, but our events are also attended by some who don't know any Tamil, like the spouses of some Tamilians here."

The main events the Sangam celebrates are *Pongal* (the Tamil New Year), *Deepavali* or *Divali* (India's most celebrated festival of lights, which celebrates the return of Rama of the epic *Ramayana* to Ayodhya after his fourteen-year exile), and *MuttuTamil Vilam* (a special event to promote awareness of the written, literary word that is so different from the spoken Tamil word). The Sangam conducts a Children's Day in November and holds other family-oriented functions throughout the year. It prides itself on the rich Tamil culture, especially the literature and music, and tries to promote them by inviting artists from India to perform in Chicago. When asked why the Sangam duplicated the efforts of other organizations, Mr. N. Aathimoolam replied, "It's a question of taste. The Tamil artists that the India Classical Music Society sponsors are not necessarily the kind we enjoy. Also, Tamilians like to celebrate *Deepavali* in their own way, among the people who speak their own language. We do collaborate with other groups for national events, but for occasions that have particular significance for the Tamil people, we celebrate separately." Though the Sangam has no functions of the type performed by mutual aid societies, it has occasionally helped its members in distress, such as showing a wife how to cope with funeral arrangements if a husband passes away, and provided other such support. Its connection with national federations is limited to attending the annual conventions where literary events are promoted on a national scale.

The Tamil Sangam also provides an example of how participation in a language based organization can broaden one's awareness of world connections. At a six-hour exhibition-cum-conferences on Tamil culture presented at Riverside Brookfield High School on 29 May 1993, which was jointly sponsored by the International Tamil Language Foundation, Federation of Tamil Sangams of North America and the Chicago Tamil Sangam, every participating Tamil family brought a non-Tamil friend, mainly native-born Americans, to learn about the seventy million Tamils who live in seventy-five countries and the ancient Tamil heritage.[21]

The other associations of Biharis, Rajasthanis, Sindhis, Oriyas, or Marathis have followed similar growth patterns as the Tamil Sangam. With the decline in language skills among the second generation, there is a distinct probability that these language-based associations will lose their significance and many will die off. That is why these associations take the question of language classes very seriously and conduct their own classes in addition to those being conducted at the temple. The philosophy of these associations is that a specific environment, replete with cultural accouterments, is essential to the true understanding of a language and it cannot come from a temple that caters to so many different language groups.

The East African Cultural Organization

Among the various associations in Chicago that cater to the social and cultural needs of Indian immigrants, one is unique because it brings together Indians who had a homeland outside of India. Immigrants of Indian ancestry who have lived in East Africa for generations have their own informal association, the East African Cultural Organization, consisting of twenty-five to thirty dues-paying members and their families.[22] Its focus is primarily social and its main organized events are the annual picnic, a *Divali* celebration, and a *Garba* dance function.[23] The organization is "at least twenty years old," said one of the members, but its membership comprises only a fraction of the Indian immigrants of East African origin in Chicago. He estimated the total number to be about one thousand—"between 150 to 200 families"— with 40 percent from Tanzania, 40 percent from Kenya, and only 20 percent from Uganda. According to him, "Most of the Ugandan Indians went to England or Canada, not many have come to Chicago."

The majority of the association's members are in business, though there were many professionals, such as doctors and dentists and academicians in the group. Immigration of Indians from Africa to the United States is an ongoing phenomenon. Some of the members at the annual picnic had landed in Chicago only in August 1995. Most of them are Gujarati Hindus from Tanzania. They took up Tanzanian citizenship at the time of Tanzanian independence, mainly under pressure from the nationalist government, fully believing that they would gain equal civil rights with Africans. In the late 1960s, however, the nationalization policies of Julius Nyerere were perceived by Indians as threatening to their private interests. Their ancestors had come over in the nineteenth century, either to build the East African railroad for the British or as petty traders and grocers to furnish provisions for the Indian population. One of the immigrants estimated that 70 percent of Tanzanian business and industry was in the hands of Asians. However keen the nationalist African leaders may have been to bring about Africanization, Africans were not ready to take their economy into their own hands. The Indians felt more and more insecure and looked for ways to get out of the country. The fact that Indians remained exclusive and never married into the African community also kept them alienated. "The real turning point for Ugandans came when Idi Amin sent a proposal to the rich Indian widow Madhwani and was spurned because he was told that Indians widows don't remarry," said one immigrant. "We never let our women mix with Africans, so we could never be fully accepted in their eyes. That was enough to keep us perpetually insecure." The very rich chose to stay on to protect their vast investments, but the middle and lower classes who had the opportunity to leave Africa came to North America, sponsored by relatives already in Canada or the United States, or as professionals who qualified for preferential visas. One such immigrant with an East African background spent her early years in East Africa, went to school in England, got married in India, and now operates an Indian grocery store in Westmont.

Many of the immigrants had relatives in Africa, India, England, and other parts of Europe. The connection to India was very strong for some who had been educated there, or went regularly for *yatras* or religious pilgrimages, but almost negligible for others who had never visited the country; nevertheless, their Indian cultural identity remained powerful. The same was true of the connection to East Africa. For some immigrants, all their relatives had left Africa, so they had no cause to go back there, but others continued to maintain ties with their remaining brothers and sisters in Africa by visiting often. The general trend for Indians in East Africa was to send their children abroad for their studies. "There were no good schools or colleges we could attend in Africa," said one immigrant. "The rich sent their kids to England, the middle classes sent them to India for an education. Many of us chose our spouses in India, and most often we chose others whose background was also East African." The marriages were generally arranged through family or religious networks operating out of India but serving an international clientele.

Asked why they thought it necessary to maintain a separate identity as East African Indians and why they could not merge with other Gujaratis or Indians from other regions, most of the immigrants said they *felt* different. "Indian Gujaratis would hear us speak and immediately tell that we were not directly from Gujarat, that we were from East Africa," said one. "At every Indian gathering, I found myself seeking out and gravitating toward Indians from East Africa." Another said that East African Indians felt they were "superior." "We are also more well traveled than the average Gujarati from India. Our horizons have expanded because we have moved in international circles. We are equally comfortable with Africans and whites, and don't have the same prejudices as the Indians from Gujarat. Also, many of us have had a more comfortable life. "[24]

Back in Africa, these immigrants had had a close-knit life. "Everyone knew everyone else, like in a village. Also, we had no outside influences, like the media in the United States. Our customs were preserved because we continued to practice what our ancestors had brought over from India, even though many of us could not afford to go back frequently. Here, our children are constantly being subjected to American influences, and we are in danger of losing our heritage."

Many among the second generation, even those who did not visit their relatives in Africa or India regularly, felt that their East African origin would always be a part of them. "We have so many cousins here and we maintain such close family ties that the special awareness of our past will not go away," said one teenager, who visited his relatives in England frequently, but had never been to India. A member of the older generation, however, was more skeptical and perhaps more realistic. "Our numbers are too small for us to maintain a separate distinct identity for long," he said.

> We are not in an East African cocoon and, ultimately, we do call ourselves Indians. The time will come, maybe twenty years from now, when we will lose all our connections to Africa. Then we may lose our East African identity and merge with other Indians. As an organization, we doubt that we will survive into the second generation. Those who want to hold on to their culture will have to join the larger Indian groups. We will remain African only for so long. Then we will become "Indian" in America.

Interestingly enough, though many East African Indians liked to think of themselves as more "broad-minded" and "liberal" than the Indians from

India, there were others in the group who saw them differently, as more clannish and insular. Among the interviewees were Parsi and Sindhi women who had married men from East Africa, and they thought that the East African Indians were even more conservative than the Indians from India. They pointed to their more rigid observance of the caste systems, their strict vegetarianism, and their desire to marry only within their own narrowly defined parameters. "A Lohana will marry only a Lohana," admitted one East African Indian in the group. "We have preserved this for four generations in East Africa and are not about to lose it here if we can help it."

For the most part, these East African Gujarati Hindus did not mix as a group with the Muslims, though some of them had personal friends among the Ismailis. "The Ismailis who speak Kutchi are closer to us Gujaratis, more tolerant and relaxed about their religion than the Ithna'Asheri Muslims whose devotion to Islam is more fundamentalist and closer to the Middle East variety," said an immigrant. "But Hindus and Muslims generally keep each to themselves, even amongst the Gujaratis."

Some of the families interviewed said their social circle was full of other Gujarati Hindus from East Africa, while others, because of their professional connections or their spouses who were not from East Africa or their association with religious organizations, had many friends who were immigrants from other parts of India. They felt they had a common vocabulary and a strong enough ethnic identification to merge with the larger Indian community in Chicago. Certainly among the second generation, there was no compelling desire to maintain an East African identity by taking over the organization from their parents, once they themselves came of age. But for now, the association serves a felt need amongst its members to set themselves somewhat apart from the larger Indian immigrant community, at least in certain social settings.

One of the most interesting questions that the growth or demise of these language-based associations can help us answer is, how large an ethnic subgroup is required to maintain a separate culture? Economics has always determined to some extent the viability of the options available to immigrants. As international transport and communication become more affordable, the "importing" of culture from India may continue to be possible even for a small group of immigrants. Chicago's Indians can always enjoy this imported culture as passive spectators but that culture can survive in the new land only if they actively recreate it in new forms. Such recreation is partially dependent on the numerical strength of a group. Given the Chicago area Indian immigration population of approximately sixty thousand, and given that some linguistic groups such as the Rajasthanis or Biharis may be no more than 3 percent or 4 percent of this population, a numerical strength of two thousand or so seems to be sufficient to sustain a language-based association. The reason they exist and continue to thrive is that they serve a critical need at this point in the history of Indian immigrants in Chicago.

Arts Organizations

One of the most appealing and popular ways of preserving the cultural core of an immigrant community is through dance and music. Both classical and popular Indian dance enjoy the patronage of Chicago's Indian immigrants. The patterns of development in each area have differed according to the motivation of the patrons, the nature and extent of demand among the "consumers," and the commercialization possibilities. The variety in the institutions also reflects the varied art forms and the diversity of the immigrant population. Some hold rigorously to the classical traditions, anxious to pass on the purity of the art forms as they existed in India, but others freely mix classical, folk, and popular forms, both from lack of their own expertise as performers and creators as well as from a desire to appeal to a less rigorous audience in Chicago than back home. Innovative use of new technology and blending of cultural styles have taken place in response to the immigrants' need to evolve new identities in a new land.

The two main schools of classical Indian dance that have found loyal patronage in Chicago are *Bharatanatyam* and *Kathak*. *Bharatanatyam* is said to have a 3,000-year-old tradition in South India and interprets Hindu mythology through precise hand gestures, rhythmic movements and facial expressions. Its essential goal is to bring the *atman* or soul closer to *moksha* or union with God. *Kathak* is a dance of North India that evolved from the courtly Mogul traditions of entertainment for royalty. Both are performed to the accompaniment of live classical vocal music and sophisticated percussion.

Natyakalayalam Dance Company

In the person of Hema Rajagopalan, artistic director of the Natyakalayalam Dance Company and in her work, one finds elements of the immigrant experience that are common to many other immigrants striving to create something meaningful in a new environment without discarding the old.

Like other women in the Chicago area, she followed her husband as an immigrant to the United States in 1972. Though she had a Master's Degree in nutrition and could have sought a career in that field, she turned to her first love, *Bharatanatyam*, when she saw new opportunities opening up for her. As an accomplished dancer in India who had been performing professionally since the age of thirteen, she could entertain Indian audiences in Chicago who were starved for Indian cultural shows. She began a dance school in the basement of her home in Lombard in 1974 when she saw second-generation Indian children turning more and more to Western ways and losing touch with their Indian culture. She accurately estimated that Indian parents who were fighting the trend toward Westernization and looking desperately for ways to keep alive Indian values in their children would be committed to the dance school. According to Rajagopalan, her students have a variety of motivations for learning dance. Some seek release from life's pressures, some come in search of their ethnic identity, yearning to get to their roots, while others hope to gain a clearer insight into themselves through dance. In addition to the culture-retention factor, parents are driven by the ambition to see their children perform on stage, and don't mind driving two to three hours for an hour-long lesson, weekend after weekend, if it results in an on-stage performance.

Besides training her students in the rigorous classical discipline, Rajagopalan is known in the community for putting up dazzling dance-dramas that depict themes on the universality of religions. Her shows involve large ensembles of dancers with elaborate sets, a scintillating array of costumes, and symmetrical and eye-catching group formations. While orthodox purists decry such showmanship as "commodification" of culture, Rajagopalan sees this as coming through to fulfill the expectations of a Chicago audience and benefiting a noble cause. Her shows have raised as much as $150,000 for community endeavors such as temple building and installation of a bronze statue of Swami Vivekananda at the Hindu Temple of Greater Chicago.

Rajagopalan firmly believes that it is her immigrant condition that has helped her shake off the "burden of tradition," and saved her dancing from "decay." It was a painful experience to come out from under the shadow of the great orthodox teachers from whom she learned her art, such as the late Dandayudapani Pillai, but by being forced to accommodate to the demands of patronage in a new environment, she has fulfilled a unique vision, possible only in her particular historical context—that of establishing an ancient classical dance form as a way of nurturing one's culture and maintaining continuity of Indian values in a new land. She has done this without becoming trapped in tradition, even while mixing, matching, blending, and synthesizing in ways that have resulted in new dance forms. Her annual trips to India, both to enhance her own repertoire and subject herself and her students to the rigorous scrutiny of critics back home, exemplify the phenomenon taking place in other immigrant spheres of activity, such as business, academics, sports, and fashion, where the environment in both countries constantly influences the evolution of a new culture. In each one of these areas that Indians are happy to include under the banner of "culture," the immigrants straddle many worlds (and sometimes the entire globe), physically moving back and forth, feeding off one source and constantly giving back to it from another, so that the immigrant experience is not a one-way or two-way street but a continuous and endless cycle of interaction.[25]

Other Dance Forms

Other dance schools have sprung up in Chicago that cater to different needs. The Dilshad Dance Academy is the center for *Kathak*, while the Vision of India presents dance dramas using the talents of those who find classical dance too heavy or demanding. The Natraj Dance Akademi teaches a variety of dance forms including *Mohini Attam* and *Kuchipudi*. Many talented people teach dance or music in the basements of their homes to a handful of children as a way to make extra money. The names of these schools suggest the existence of full-fledged institutions with phrases such as "Dance Foundation" or "Center for Performing Arts" but their advertisements don't even carry an address, only a phone number. Some of these may grow into larger institutions, depending upon the commitment of the individual and the demand for what they offer, but for the time being, few qualify for the status of an institution the way Natyakalayalam does.

A new trend that has emerged in the immigrant community is the popularization of the *Raas-Garba* and *Disco-Dandia* dances, both of Gujarati folk origin. These are group folk dances that used to be performed mainly in the villages and were brought to the stage in India's big cities by professional "folk" artists. They are not particularly favored by the middle or upper class in India in the same way as *Bharatanatyam* and *Kathak* but have caught on in Chicago and become a public expression of cultural identity, especially for Gujaratis. Just as in America rock-and-roll bands play live music so teeny-boppers can bump and grind on the dance floor, imported Indian bands play *garba* and *dandia* music for Indian teenagers in locations such as Naperville North High School or Inland Center in Westmont. These are especially popular in September–October or Navratri Festival time. This can hardly be called "transplantation" of culture since the practice is not prevalent in India at all, but one devised for and by the immigrant community in response to their need for participatory dance. The same trend is seen with the *Bhangra*, a Punjabi folk dance of extraordinary vigor that has also caught on with amazing rapidity among the second generation. Westernized versions of these dances incorporate disco beats, Caribbean rhythms, and rap music, representing a melange of black, white, and brown, and reflecting a history that dates back to the indentured emigration of Indians to the Caribbean and their mix of Creole culture. Some Indian parents see this as a healthy substitute for rock-and-roll, while others are dismayed at the corruption of simple village dances and the distortion of "ethnicity."[26]

Music

The music scene is also fairly invigorating with two main organizations, the India Classical Music Society and the Chicago Thyagaraja Utsavam, catering to the needs of music lovers in the area. The main purpose of the India Classical Music Society is to sponsor concerts of top-notch performers from India, such as Hariprasad Chaurasia, L. Shanker, and Pandit Birju Maharaj, in both Hindustani and Carnatic styles. Starting in 1983 with a single concert performance, it ushered in its second decade in 1993 with a record twenty-one performances. It also sponsors an annual youth forum that enables the teachers of classical music in Chicagoland to showcase their students' talents. Concerts are funded by the $150 annual family membership fee, which gives the entire family access to all concerts, as well as grants from the Illinois Arts Council, Chicago City Arts, and the ILA Foundation.

Aficionados of South Indian music formed the Chicago Thyagaraja Utsavam in Villa Park in 1985. Core organizers or a large number of patrons appear to be from the AT&T company, since the brochure asks "AT&T employees to report their tax deductible contributions directly." They conduct an annual three-day music festival in honor of the eighteenth-century Carnatic music composer-saint Thyagaraja, drawing audiences from the entire midwest region, including Michigan, Ohio, Indiana, and Wisconsin. The idea of Chicago as a magnet for the arts for surrounding states and even the globe, seen as far back in its history as the Columbian Exposition of 1893, is played out in the everyday lives of Chicago's Indian immigrants. The goal of the Utsavam is to "nurture Carnatic music literacy and expose music to as many people as possible," especially to the second generation. Its

1993 "Chronicle" carried reports of a grand festival in May with "22 hours of programming, 1200 people in attendance, 160 performers and 70 volunteer cooks (preparing vegetarian meals served on site)." Its activities are reported in the mainstream media in Chicago and the arts press in India. Its annual report listed a modest income of $17,514 from donations, concert income, and tape and book sales, and assets of $16,380. Though of limited financial means, organizations such as this one serve a sizable number of people.[27]

The India Music Ensemble of Chicago is another private institution, started in 1983 and run by Patric Marks, which trains about 175 students in various disciplines of Indian music, including instrumental and vocal. Music patronage also occurs outside the institutional framework. The musical "soiree" or "evening of *ghazal*" is an event where large groups of Indians gather in the suburban home of an affluent host, sometimes for a fee of $25 to $50, and enjoy the performance of a musician from India. Such gatherings are meant only for the well-heeled, of course. Culture for the masses is provided only by the various ethnic organizations and associations.

Film

Besides music and dance concerts sponsored by these organizations, the other significant source of entertainment comes from Bombay (Mumbai). About eight hundred movies are made in India each year and the latest releases are played in theaters on the North Side, such as the Gateway theater on Lawrence and the Adelphi theater on Clark, as well as in the west and northwest suburbs. The General Cinema theater in Woodridge screens Tamil and Hindi movies on Sunday morning. (Indeed, the screening of Hindi movies in theaters all over the world has become a significant source of foreign exchange for India. Besides the traditional markets in the United Kingdom, the United States, and Canada, producers have seized opportunities in South Africa, Australia, Thailand, Hong Kong, and the West Indies for modern, slickly produced blockbusters.) Pirated or unauthorized video versions of films find their way into the homes of Chicago's immigrants long before they are released on video in India. The array of Indian language videos offered on Devon Avenue and suburban Indian video shops is truly astonishing. Parents who scorn Hindi movies as too trashy for viewing in India actually urge their children in Chicago to watch them just so they become familiar with the language. The result is that the second-generation Indians have become avid fans of Indian film stars and flock to see their heroes and heroines in person when they visit Chicago at least once or twice a year. "Superstar Nites" are organized by the merchants of Devon Avenue who team up with agents who sponsor global tours for screen idols such as Aamir Khan or Madhuri Dixit or whoever is the current rage on the Indian screen. Performances, which typically include several song and dance numbers from movies and in which both actors and actresses as well as the playback singers are featured, are staged at giant stadiums such as Rosemont Horizon or UIC's Pavilion. Tickets sell for $40 to $100 apiece, and performances are sold out well in advance. Six thousand spectators, including grandmothers and teenagers and babes-in-arms, came to one such concert in May 1994.[28] The "Live In Concert" tours are a peculiar creation of the immigrant situation. In India, such concerts are a rarity; they are held regularly only in major cities all over the world where expatriate Indians are concentrated. Their increasing popularity has spawned other related ventures such as "Cruise with the Stars," where, as the name suggests, fans can spend a ten-day vacation cruising with their favorite film stars, or glamorous beauty pageants or Independence Day parades at which film stars are invited to be chief guests and serve as crowd-pullers.

Films made by Indians living in the United States and dealing with the issue of bicultural identity and the lives of ordinary people are not disseminated as widely as the Hindi movies but more and more of them are being made. *Praying with Anger*, shown at a private fund-raiser in Chicago, deals with the confusion and frustration of an Indian American boy visiting Madras (Chennai) as an exchange student. The movie won the 1993 First Feature Award from the American Film Institute. Mira Nair's *So Far from India* deals with the issue of coming to the United States and the conflicts that immigration creates. Nair is a Hollywood director who has enjoyed considerable commercial success and popularity with her film *Mississippi Masala* (starring Denzel Washington), which deals with the travails of an Indian family transplanted from South Africa to the deep South. The Asian American Film Festival, which used to feature an odd Indian film or two, devoted an entire section to Indian film makers in 1995.[29]

In the thirty years of Indian immigration since 1965, there has been an increasing professionalization within the arts because Indian immigrants have set high standards for themselves both as consumers and purveyors of art. "Commodification" has also occurred because state and government funding is meager and the arts can hardly be expected to survive among immigrants without financial backing from the community itself. The word "professional" now defines not only those Indians who work in white-collar jobs in the mainstream but those who make a living by serving the special artistic needs of their own community.

The next chapter tells the story of religious institutions in Chicago which, like the cultural ones, play a vital role in helping Indian immigrants preserve and nurture their roots even as they shape them into new forms.

9

BUILDING INFRASTRUCTURE
Religious Institutions

> Although religious identity is often a significant aspect of ethnic
> culture, it is difficult to establish the exact relation between the
> two, whether the religious affiliation is essential to the ethnic
> community or if religious orientation is only ancillary to ethnic
> identity ... the two are not identical. Indeed, immigrants use
> different aspects of their various religions to develop new patterns
> of adaptive strategies.
> —Raymond B. Williams, *Religions of Immigrants from India and*
> *Pakistan: New Threads in the American Tapestry*

Of all the ways in which Indians maintain continuity with the home culture,
religion stands out as one of the most important and innovative. The Chicago
survey revealed that religion was very important to the immigrants, but it
also revealed variations in their approach. The ways in which religion has
been transmitted and transplanted in the United States depend in large
part on which religious group is involved, which part of India they are from,
how long they have been in the United States, and their personal approach
to religious issues. Nor are Indians in the United States averse to celebrating
American religious and social functions. Turkey is served, American-style,
with great enthusiasm in many an Indian home at Thanksgiving and the
tree decorated for Christmas in a participatory and celebratory spirit that
gives these events a uniquely Indian social and cultural significance.[1]

Thus the religious institutions that the immigrants have created respond
to a variety of needs and different aspects of the identity building process.
But they were all created in a conscious, planned move as a strategy to cope
with conditions in the new land. Because they represent a minority religion
in a new setting, they function in a very different way than they do in the
homeland. Most of the Indians who live in Chicago have not been part of

organized religion in India. Religion is "in the air" in India, a living, breathing tradition, which Indians do not have to make a conscious effort to imbibe. The lighting of a lamp at an altar in the home, sometimes in as simple a setting as a kitchen counter, infuses an Indian home with a religious aura. Religion is everywhere—on TV, in the movies, in street processions, and at family gatherings. Temple visits in India are usually reserved for very special occasions, unless there happens to be one located down the street from home, in which case one just makes casual visits to the temple now and then. In Chicago, the Indians feel impelled to enforce their religious identity in structured ways, for example, by visiting the temple every Sunday to pray. Perhaps this is because, without a peg on which to hang their religious identity, many Indians fear that it might be lost irretrievably, especially for the second generation.

In a major study of the religious traditions of Indians in Atlanta, Georgia, from 1979 to 1988, John Fenton notes that unlike many European immigrants who came to America seeking a religious haven, Indians were secular, urban, and technologically inclined. In the beginning, individual and family religious practices had greater significance for them, but as they changed from sojourners to permanent residents and began to put down roots, religion moved to the center of community life. Fenton distinguishes between "religious" Hindus who take part in temple and group activities primarily for religious reasons and "cultural" Hindus who do it primarily for social contact.[2] Since religious houses of worship in Chicago were built in response to community needs, they tried to appeal to as broad a base as possible, and accommodated the deeply religious as well as those who sought only social contact. So the temples, mosques, and *gurdwaras* are more than just places to conduct religious services, they are centers of culture propagation and community centers as well. Large community halls that accommodate several hundred people, a raised stage with professional lighting arrangements, a public address system, and a large scale kitchen available for family, social, and cultural activities are standard features.[3] So many houses of worship with these features have been founded in Chicago in recent times that some of the early immigrants worry about whether these institutions will be supported in later years by the second generation, when fresh immigration from India might slacken or be cut off completely. Other critics decry the use of such large sums of money in "meaningless ritual" and "dangerous superstition," advocating instead that these funds be channeled into providing services for the poor in Indian villages. But such counsel generally goes unheeded. For now, the need for religious services in each group is higher than ever before, and the majority of immigrants them-selves seem to be caught up in the excitement of building.

Hindu Religious Organizations

All the religions that are represented in India are also to be found among Chicago's Indian immigrants—Hindus, Muslims, Christians, Sikhs, Jains, Zoroastrians, and Jews—but the significant majority, between 75 percent and 80 percent, are Hindus. In the Chicago area, Hindus are estimated at roughly 100,000 (nationwide adherents are estimated at 1 million).[4] As with the cultural associations, Indians at first grouped under a Pan-Hindu iden-tity, without differentiating between the worshippers of different deities, but as their numbers grew and their finances permitted it, Indians began to regroup according to narrower preferences. Sometimes the splintering was due to personality conflicts, sometimes due to sectarian or philosophical differences. Generally, divisions expressed ideological differences and the survival of Indian regionalism.[5] And the remarkable organizational and fund-raising skills of the professional and economically successful elite have enabled them to lay strong foundations for several religious institutions within a short span of thirty years.[6] One writer has observed that "green-backs for the gods are streaming in almost as fast as the Ganges in spate."[7] *Hinduism Today*, a monthly magazine published from Hawaii, lists 80 tem-ples and ashrams in North America, while a booklet from Nashville lists 125 temples. There is no doubt that whatever the number, it is steadily growing. In the last twenty-five years, an estimated $375 million have already been used for temple building or pledged for new construction, with each temple costing between 1 and 5 million dollars.[8] There are today more than a dozen Hindu places of worship across Chicagoland, with each one catering to a different Hindu sect or geographical area. The temple building frenzy continues unabated in Chicago in the 1990s. The latest institution to declare its intention to acquire its own million dollar building on a five-acre lot in Carol Stream is the Arya Samaj Society of Chicagoland. The Arya Samaj is a reform Hindu sect that eschews ritualism and what it views as superstitious practices. Each one of these temples has its unique features and special con-nections to religious sites in India.[9]

While splintering of groups is one phenomenon, there is a parallel, oppo-site phenomenon that is going on at the same time—the coming together of all these organizations under a common aegis, the Council of Hindu Temples of North America.[10] Also, the centenary celebrations of the World's Parliament of Religions held in Chicago in 1993 brought the many different faiths in Chicago to center stage under a single umbrella.

The Hindu Temple of Greater Chicago (HTGC) in Lemont

A detailed profile of the Hindu Temple of Greater Chicago, the oldest of the religious institutions built by the post-1965 immigrants, illustrates many of the patterns that are common to religious institutions. Registered as a not-for-profit organization in 1977 with the express objective of building an authentic Hindu temple and community center, the HTGC selected Rama as the main deity for the temple since he is known and worshipped all over India. The founding group, with Dharmapuri Vidyasagar as its first president, hoped to "bring all the Hindus from various parts of India, irrespective of their language and cultural differences" to worship under one roof and provide "a precious gift for our future generations, as well as to all other believers and admirers of the Hindu religion."[11] A seventeen-acre site (increased in 1985 to twenty acres) was purchased in Lemont in 1981 for $300,000. Besides budgetary concerns, what influenced the choice of location was its accessibility (near I-55) and its remoteness from residential areas. Unlike Christian churches that serve a local parish and are built in the heart of the community, the Indian temple draws its clientele from far and wide and does not betoken a heavy Indian population in Lemont. The temple project was undertaken with funds raised from a widespread Hindu community, with most of the donors being the rich doctors and upper-class professionals, the Indian-owned National Republic Bank of Chicago, and the State Bank of India in Chicago. The architectural plans for the temple were given by the Tirumala Tirupathi Devasthanam, who also sent *shilpis* or sculptors from India to construct authentic *murtis* or images according to 3,000-year-old traditions. On June 17, 1984, a dignitary from India, the Chief Minister of Andhra Pradesh, was invited to be guest of honor at the ground breaking ceremony for the first temple to Ganesha built on the site. On July 4, 1986, the formal dedication or *Kumbhabisekham* of the larger Rama Temple was held. A magnificent eighty-foot-tall Rajagopuram or main tower rises high atop the wooded bluff, a startling sight on a landscape dotted with church spires in a suburb known as the "Village of Faith" for its many houses of worship. The second floor of the temple consists of a large, open hall with the images of Rama, Lakshmana, and Sita in front, with small rooms on the sides to house the deities of Radha-Krishna and Venkateswara. The basement houses a kitchen and a community hall. The temple offers regular religious services conducted by priests trained in India following authentic Vedic traditions. The *Ramalaya Samachar,* HTGC's official news-letter, lists the fee schedule for the different services, which range from $10 for a simple *puja* to hundreds of dollars for more elaborate rites.

The Ganesh Temple was expanded in 1992 to house the deities of Shiva and Durga. The GSD complex, as it came to be called, followed a different architectural style of the Bhuvaneshwar Temple in Orissa, and was built in response to groups who demanded a separate sanctum sanctorum for their own favorite deities. A grand *Kumbhabisekham* for this section of the temple was performed July 6–10, 1994. A number of *homams* or sacred fires burned simultaneously on the temple grounds and the air echoed with the rhythmic chanting of scores of temple priests. Both North and South Indian styles of worship had been accommodated in unified surroundings and many tem-ple leaders saw it as an important symbol of Hindu unity in North America. Such accommodation of different deities under the same roof is considered nothing short of sacrilege by purists in India, while other devout Hindus find the phenomenon amusing and typical of American-style disregard for tradition.[12] Temple authorities are now pushing ahead to build a *Kalyana Mandapam* or marriage hall and a community center that will house an auditorium, dining hall, and multipurpose classrooms.

Though the temple leadership in earlier years appeared to be dominated by members from South India, more and more North Indians have taken over in recent years. The priesthood, however, is still dominated by South Indians, a carryover from the early days when the HTGC relied on the patronage of the South Indian Tirupati Temple. But the temple operations have had their ups and downs. The generating and management of funds has been controversial because a few powerful individuals are seen to con-trol the whole organization. Funds raised for a particular purpose, such as the building of a marriage hall, are spent for other purposes, and certain members feel that there is no accountability to the public that contributes 80 percent of the temple revenues. Patrons provide the other 20 percent. There has also been concern about the lack of representation on the board of the thousands of devotees who only pay small sums of money for services . Trusteeships are generally reserved for the big donors and loan guarantors, and there are multiple category memberships according to the size of one's contribution.[13] The temple is also experiencing financial hardships in the mid-1990s as the donor pool slowly dries up. The generation that contributed handsomely in earlier years is now worried about sending their children to college or planning for their retirement. The second generation is still too young or too busy concentrating on career and material well-being to worry about spiritual needs or get deeply involved in temple affairs. At least, that is the explanation offered by one insider for the current crises in temple finances. Financial woes are bound to affect institutions that are still in the capital intensive stage, especially when it involves millions of dollars. The cost of the HTGC is estimated at $3.1 million. Many immigrants feel that the temple leaders are caught up in physical expansion projects when they should be more concerned about the spiritual crisis that is confronting the second generation.

Another area of controversy is the attempt by some fundamentalists to politicize the organization and make it appear supportive of the Vishwa Hindu Parishad (VHP), which has political ties to the Bharatiya Janata Party (BJP) in India. In the early 1990s, the temple allowed the VHP to hold joint events on its premises, but when some board members wanted the temple to officially felicitate certain politicians visiting from India, the temple decided to draw the line and dissociate itself from the VHP.[14] After the Babri Masjid incident in 1992, temple authorities became particularly wary of charges that they were supporting the BJP-VHP combine in Chicago and consciously steered away from activities that would make them vulnerable to such accusations.[15] The student wing of the Vishwa Hindu Parishad are the Hindu Students Councils (HSC) which have sprung up in universities with sizable Hindu populations. They have thrived especially where Catholic or Jewish or Muslim councils have set precedents for religious-based organizations. The HSCs are not to be confused with Indian students' associations, which are often dominated by Hindus and are so involved in celebrating Hindu cultural festivals that members of the other Indian religious groups feel left out. The Hindu Student Councils are specifically dedicated to helping Hindus understand their religious heritage on campus and "developing a bond of an extended Hindu family relationship that practices the universal ideals of Hindu Dharma." They also make their presence felt at the community association meetings and are actively supported by some temple groups. The transition from the local Hindu temple to the university level Hindu Council is an easy one for the Indian growing up in America and looking for a familiar support structure in a new university environment. The HSC was started in May 1990, had thirty campus chapters by January 1994 and claims to be the largest Hindu student and youth group outside India.[16] Its "Vision 2000 Global Youth Conference" held in Washington, D.C., in August 1993 to commemorate the centenary of Swami Vivekananda attracted "2,100 participants from Denmark, Malaysia, South Africa, Fiji, Trinidad, Kenya, UK, Germany, Netherlands, Guyana and other countries."[17] The organization keeps its VHP connection low-key and stresses the universality of its message of peace and brotherhood. Many students who belong to the HSC have no idea of its VHP political connections.

In trying to understand what Hinduism means to the second generation, and how the institutional infrastructure has shaped these concerns, some scholars juxtapose them with the concerns of the first generation, and see it as an "Indian = first generation = traditional" versus "American = second generation = modern" dichotomy.[18] In the case of Hindus in the United States, one needs to go beyond that and see that religion is a process of rediscovery for both generations as they each struggle to relate to their religion in new ways and redefine its significance for themselves. The first generation of Hindus instinctively felt that without the outward physical structures of the temples, the priests and the rituals, they would not be able to practice their religion or hand it down to their children. They had accepted their Hinduism somewhat unquestioningly in India but could hardly practice it in the United States unless they built the infrastructure. Most of their energies were thus directed toward the physical reconstruction of outward forms. Fenton has also noted the importance of the physical structure is showing the vested interest of the community in a stable, permanent presence in the adopted land, and consequently attracting even more support from other community members. Even the installation of a deity in a new location gives symbolic assurance that the new location is acceptable, and "by symbolic extension, the worshipping community is also transplanted with its god to its new home."[19]

Some members of the second generation who had no temple activities to influence them in their growing years in the 1970s and early 1980s had become young professionals in the 1990s and were confused about what Hinduism meant to them. They grew up in the United States believing in individualism, trained to be skeptical of received wisdom, and feeling uncomfortable with the elaborate ritualism associated with the temple. They took nothing for granted and questioned everything. In 1994, about thirty of them formed a discussion group called "Akshaya" and sought answers to some of their religious concerns. The Hindu priests at HTGC, many of whom were fluent in English, tried hard to explain Hinduism in terms of philosophy and lifestyle and give meaning to the rituals, but could not always satisfy the youth whose questions demanded answers more suited to a Western context.[20] For instance, a young female lawyer said she had come to the temple because when she was asked about her religion at work, she couldn't give satisfactory answers. Her company was willing to donate funds to her religious group but first she wanted answers to questions such as How is your religion structured? Are your priests intermediaries between humans and Gods? What is the significance of ritual prayer? What is the importance of personal faith in your religion? Another young man said he had taken many academic courses on Hinduism and still felt as though he didn't know enough about it. "None of the courses had the '*masala*' [spice] I was looking for." Another woman said that Hinduism sometimes seemed too flexible and sometimes not flexible enough. Could Hinduism survive in the translation into English? inquired another. She had been told that the power of the mantras lay in their enunciation, but the mantras meant nothing to her if she could not understand them in English. The search for the elusive is basic to all religions, but particularly acute for an inquiring generation searching for its roots and looking for elements it can identify with. The Hindu Temple is the center for ritual worship, but it also attempts to address such issues and explain itself to its devotees. In his study of Indians in Atlanta, Fenton predicted the survival of traditional ritual forms even if future generations were "mystified" by them.[21] Lack of full understanding of their significance has never prevented a Hindu from observing the most elaborate of rituals!

The HTGC has a Hindu Dharma and Philosophy Committee whose avowed mission is to "conduct and coordinate religious and spiritual discourses on the temple premises and serve as a resource to other institutions on subjects related to Hindu dharma." It conducts monthly open forums where experts are invited to talk on issues facing Hindus in this country and answer questions put to them by the audience. Swami Brahmanupananda of the Vivekananda Vedanta Society conducts a monthly class on the *Bhagavad Gita* on HTGC premises.[22]

Those Indians who are still in their teens in the mid 1990s have been the true beneficiaries of the temple and its infrastructure in the way their parents envisioned it for them. One happy outcome for Indian parents has been that the youth who frequently interact at temples have found marriage partners from within their own group. They have formed a group called "In the Wings" which is very similar to the youth groups in churches, in that they are encouraged to hold their own talent shows or song and dance events with minimal supervision by the adults. The name of the group also emphasizes that the youth are the next in line to take over the running of these temples. They are being carefully watched and groomed by their first-generation parents to take on this responsibility. They take active part in all the major Hindu festivals that are celebrated at the temple with pomp and splendor, including *Mahashivratri* (the birth anniversary of Lord Shiva), *Holi* (a boisterous festival heralding the end of winter), *Janmashtami* (the birth anniversary of Lord Krishna), *Hanuman Jayanthi* (the birth anniversary of Hanuman, the monkey-god), *Ganesh Chaturthi* (the birth anniversary of Lord Ganesha), *Dussehra* (the ten-day festival celebrating the triumph of good over evil), and *Divali* (the festival of lights celebrating the return of Lord Rama from exile and his victory over the evil King Ravana). The *Greeshma Mela* or summer fest is a popular annual event that features regional food stalls, clothing, jewelry, and art and craft sales as well as free health screening. On an average weekend, attendance at the temple is between three hundred and five hundred, but on spectacular occasions such as *Holi* with its color throwing and merrymaking, and *Divali* with its fireworks displays, the crowds are so thick (up to four thousand strong) that the Lemont police have to be mobilized to regulate traffic. Cars have to be parked in remote parking lots and a shuttle service arranged to bring worshippers to the temple site. Events that are not considered strictly religious such as *Baisakhi* (the Hindu Solar New Year Day, of particular significance to the Sikhs who celebrate it as a harvest festival) are also celebrated at the temple. Many Indian children in Chicago are growing up taking some of the cultural and ritual elements of Hinduism for granted in the same way that their parents did growing up in India. But while their parents may also have received their cultural influences from school or the general society in India, here in the United States, it is the temple alone that gives them the opportunity to participate actively in their cultural heritage. Temple activities have thus evolved into a potpourri of cultural, religious and social events in response to the needs of the first and second generations.

In another gesture of adaptation, Indians have taken to visiting temples only on weekends. The work week is too busy and distances too great to allow for participation on weekdays, so religious occasions that fall in the middle of the week are moved, in typical American style, to a Friday or Monday, as these are also the most auspicious days in the week. "Sunday school" at the temple consists of activities for the children such as language classes, discussion groups divided according to age levels, and teaching of the scriptures. Other diverse activities such as arts and crafts, meditation, and academic coaching are added to the list to cater to every conceivable need of the second generation that is deemed to be in tune with true "Hindu values." Other than these small group activities within the precincts of the temple, the youth are offered the opportunity to attend summer camps in out-of-state retreats such as Ganges, Michigan. These camps are important in enabling the second generation to create their own identity because it is also the time-honored and acceptable American way of self-identification. The children are also able to take part in other temple-related activities that are similar to church activities, such as volunteer and charitable work at a Thanksgiving feast for the poor and homeless. Feeding the poor and homeless is a natural function of temples in India as it is of churches in the United States.

Though the worshippers at the Hindu Temple are mostly Indians, the suburban Hindus who run the temple are well aware that Hinduism has a special appeal for many Americans, especially the "flower power" generation of the 1960s. For the less initiated, the Hindu Temple offers guided tours and a video presentation explaining the basic precepts of Hinduism and why it was that a group of immigrants found it necessary to recreate their religious traditions in a new land. Such efforts are directed toward countering the bad propaganda generated by the cult scares of the 1970s and 1980s that resulted in local opposition to temple building in many areas in the United States.

While the HTGC offers a shining example of the efforts of a pioneering immigrant group to preserve the unity of Hinduism and adopt a holistic approach to their religion, other Hindu institutions in the Chicago area offer Indians alternative methods of following their religion in alternative suburbs. Each and every one of them, such as the HTGC, has a large and loyal following, testifying to the remarkable diversity of Hindus in Chicago.

The Sri Venkateswara Swami (Balaji) Temple of Greater Chicago in Aurora

The delays caused by differences within the founding member group over plans for the HTGC led to the formation of a separate group in 1983 who undertook the construction of a second temple at Aurora. This group consisted of Telugu professionals, again, mostly doctors, and they picked a twenty-acre site to build the Sri Venkateswara (Balaji) Temple in a purely South Indian style.[23] On May 11, 1985, Morarji Desai, India's former Prime Minister, was chief guest at the groundbreaking ceremony. Built at a cost of $4 million by 1995, the temple's history is very similar to that of the HTGC. Money was raised by the same kind of fund-raising banquets and cultural programs, the building houses a main shrine and is surrounded by smaller shrines to other deities, it has a kitchen and community hall in the basement and it offers programs and rituals that are similar to those offered by HTGC.

The big question throughout the 1980s was, Would the community be able to build and support two separate temples in such close proximity, and sustain them in later years? Could it afford such duplication of efforts? The initial construction for both temples was successfully completed, which testifies to the fund-raising skills of the community. The Balaji Temple appeared to have the greater difficulty in meeting its financial burdens because of a smaller clientele. Its income for the year ending 30 September 1986 was $887,387, but in 1992 that figure had dropped to $600,000, though that was said to be a 15 percent increase over the previous year. By the mid-1990s, both temples seem to have a bright future by virtue of acquiring distinctive features of their own and catering to distinctly different sections of the community. The Rama Temple has broader support among all members of the community, especially the Hindi-speaking crowd, while the Balaji Temple appeals more particularly to the South Indians whose culture is connected to the South Indian languages. The Balaji Temple prides itself on the "authenticity" of its rituals, which are performed to please a generally more fastidious and orthodox South Indian population. Being located farther west, the Balaji Temple draws its devotees from that region, including Minnesota and northwest Illinois, especially Rockford, which has a large Indian population. It placed its "membership"—meaning those who come to worship, not necessarily a "paying" membership since temples do not have such requirements of their devotees—at "25,000 or more."[24]

The method of recruitment and the lifestyle of the Balaji Temple priests serve to illustrate the national and global connections of the Hindu temple organizations. The differences between the older generation of priests and the newer recruits serve also to highlight the changes that are taking place as a result of increased communication and interaction between Chicago and temple authorities in India. The older priests are more likely to come without their wives, tend to interact only with other South Indian families and may have less formal training in the priesthood than the younger priests. All the priests speak at least three South Indian languages, some also speak Hindi and English.

Mr. Narasimhachar, one of the four priests on the staff of the Balaji Temple, came to the United States in 1992 on a R1 or religious personnel visa. He had applied for a priest's job as an "independent" to five different temples in Houston, Boston, New York, Washington, and Pittsburgh. Since 1992, he had spent four months in Pittsburgh, six months in New York, one year in Atlanta and the last one and half years in Chicago, each time sent onward by the temple he had worked for last. Asked why he moved around so much, he replied that he went as and when the need for him arose in the Indian "community." Compared to the "small stipend and living expenses" received by earlier priests, he was given free housing (he shared an apartment with another Balaji Temple priest who was also here without his family), medical insurance, and an annual salary of $12,000. He had a 34-year-old son who worked as a Marketing Manager in Muscat, and a 30-year-old pharmacist son in Hyderabad. Asked about the differences between his job as a priest in India and here in the United States, he said that in India he worked from dawn till dusk and was totally involved in the lives of the people he served whereas here he had an eight-hour day and a six-day work week and was not expected to do more than conduct services. The temple did not receive more than ten to fifteen visitors on a weekday, though the weekends were busy with two hundred to three hundred visitors a day. On the first Sunday of each month there was an *Abhisekham* ceremony (the ritual bathing of the diety with milk, honey, and curd) and a cultural program at which attendance was heavier. Most of the functions held at the temple were religious, not social. The most popular outside services performed by the priests were *Grihapravesam* (house-warming), *Upanayanam* (sacred thread initiation), and *Satyanarayana Puja* (prayer to invoke the blessings of Satyanarayana or Lord Vishnu). South Indian brahmins in the United States still consider the *Upanayanam* a very important life stage ritual and conduct it in great style. Like the Bar Mitzvah for the Jews, it has special significance as an "initiation into adulthood" for males. The brahmin who has not undergone this ceremony cannot perform the major rituals expected of him in later years. Memorial rites or *Shradham* ceremonies were most often performed by individual families in the temple. According to the priest, rites and rituals were always performed without compromise except for the time factor because of the "fast life" here.

The newest recruit at the temple was a 27-year-old priest named N. P. S. Sankaramanchi who could speak Telugu, Tamil, Kannada, Hindi and English, though he wished his English was more fluent so he could interact more easily with Americans. He had got his job through a personal recommendation to the Balaji Temple Committee Chairperson who had come to Rajamundry in South India from Chicago and interviewed him for the job. The priest found the interview process quite rigorous and was astonished that his lay interviewer from Chicago knew all the *slokas* and *mantras* so intimately himself. He was the eldest son in a family that had been in the priesthood for nine generations and had received his formal training at the Tirupati Temple. He was confident that Hinduism had a bright future not only among Indians but Americans, too. He had recently traveled all the way to Fairfield, Iowa, to conduct a marriage ceremony for a Chinese couple according to Hindu Vedic rites and saw no limits to the spread of Hinduism. When asked whether there was a lack of interest among second-generation Indians in religious matters, he said it was not realistic to expect teenagers to be steeped in religion. "Let them become householders themselves, they will automatically turn to their temples. Give them time." He loved being in the Chicago area, interacted easily with the local Americans in Montgomery where he lived, and was looking forward to having his wife join him in a short while. He was most taken with "freedom in this country," and was enjoying the fact that "all our community members belong to the well-to-do, intelligent class and give me respect." The Balaji Temple priests knew of colleagues who had jobs in the Gulf, Australia, and Canada and said that foreign assignments were much sought after among the priests in India "because you can't save money in India the way you can abroad."[25]

The business manager at the temple was a 34-year-old *stapathi,* that is, a head planner or architect, who had received his training in temple architecture at Mahabalipuram in South India. Tamilians are the temple builders, he said proudly. He had come with twenty-one other *shilpis* to build the Rama Temple and after the HTGC was completed, he found himself out of work. He made a living by sculpting figurines for private homes until he got this appointment at the Balaji Temple in 1991. His wife was a computer science major at Northeastern University and he himself hoped to go back to school one day to learn about how he could integrate his traditional building methods with modern architectural techniques.

From the interviews with the temple personnel, it seemed that however temporary they might consider their own assignments, they saw a long-term future for the temple and for Hinduism in America. They felt that they belonged to an international community, and could feel at home in the Chicago area as much as in South India. Like the rest of the Indian immigrant community, they were here primarily for economic reasons, and felt privileged to be able to provide authentic religious services to Hindus so far away from home.

Other Hindu Organizations

Also known as the Akshar Purushottam Swaminarayan group, the Bochasanwasi Swaminarayan Sanstha (BSS) of Glen Ellyn has a holy book or *Granth* written by Lord Swaminarayan over 150 years ago that describes the rules, disciplines, and ethical standards to be practiced in day-to-day living. The organization is based on the "affirmation of the regional, linguistic, and sectarian ties" among its members, who are almost exclusively Gujarati. As followers of the "Pramukh Swami," they emphasize the importance of spiritual discourses, singing of *bhajans* and worshipping of saints in building a strong community. In 1983 the group purchased a former Veterans of Foreign Wars building and converted it into a temple. Images of Lord Swaminarayan and Gunatitanand Swami were installed in 1984.[26] The other main deities worshipped are Lord Rama and Krishna whose birth anniversaries are celebrated with great enthusiasm. In May 1995, the BSS played host to twenty representatives from other American "congregations" from the midwest.[27] Like the other Hindu temples, this one has its own youth wing, cultural wing, and Sunday discourses to serve a wide range of devotee needs.

The Swaminarayan Temple in Wheeling, Illinois, patronized almost exclusively by Gujaratis, was built in 1991 at a cost of $1.7 million and is maintained at an annual cost of $15,000 by the International Swaminarayan Satsang Organization of Chicago (ISSO).[28] There are other smaller Swaminarayan temples in Texas and New Jersey run by the ISSO. In sharp contrast to the ornate decor and intricate styling of the other Hindu temples, the Swaminarayan Temple is a cream-colored, square-shaped, flat-topped building with three squat domes adorning the front. It is set in a light industrial area and is hardly distinguishable from the surrounding buildings except for the domes. The single, large hall contains no idols, only huge, framed, golden trellis bordered pictures of all the manifestations of Narayana, including Vishnu, Krishna, Rama, and Shiva. The inspiration for the sect is said to be a revelation that happened on *Baisakhi* Day in 1882, so *Baisakhi* is celebrated with great fervor. The temple's main regular activity is the *satsang* or group worship every evening between 7:30 P.M. and 8:30 P.M. with men and women sitting on separate sides of the hall. The hall is also used for marriage parties and the basement for birthday ceremonies. The secretary of the temple, who owns a printed circuit board factory in the Chicago area, said the temple was run entirely by volunteers and served an almost 40,000-strong community of Gujaratis in the area. Their saffron clad priests were monks who came from temples in India on a two- to three-year rotational basis. The atmosphere in the temple was stark and spare and simple, with none of the opulent style of the HTGC or the Balaji Temple.

The influx of Gujarati immigrants in Chicago has resulted in a proliferation of temples to gods who are particular favorites on the west coast of India. It has also meant the coming together of huge crowds for mega-events such as the *Ashwamedha Yagya* (literally translated as "rituals to make the earth more eco-friendly") that was conducted at Chicago's Soldier Field stadium in July of 1995. The *Yagya*, said to be the 26th in a series of 108 to be performed between 1992 and 2001, supposedly drew a crowd of ten thousand, according to eye-witnesses. It was held in authentic style, stretched over three days, replete with chanting of Vedic *mantras* around 1,008 *kunds* or individual fires, and the releasing of the *Yagyashwa* or sacred horse. The sponsors were Gayatri Pariwar Yugnirman of Chicago, a Niles-based Gujarati religious organization with its headquarters at Shantikunj, Hardwar. The organization claims to have "4,000 branches in India and 500 branches in 76 countries." The Chicago event was the fourth such event to be performed outside India, the other three having been held in Leicester, Toronto, and Los Angeles. Such public displays of religious faith and their interconnection with similar events around the globe would not be possible if it were not for the considerable size and financial strength of the Chicago Indian immigrant population, the concentration of Gujaratis in it and their global connections to the Indian *oikumene*.[29]

Another important Hindu organization that serves the needs of Hindus in the North Side is The International Society for Krishna Consciousness (ISKCON) in Chicago. The Hare Krishna movement had already acquired a reputation as an "undesirable" cult among Indians in India long before the immigrants arrived in Chicago. It was seen as an organization that gave Hinduism a bad name and is dismissed by the more devout Hindus as an unfortunate result of Western distortion. ISKCON's Hare Krishna center in Evanston, whose membership was mostly American, was forced to move when it ran into trouble with the local authorities, but in 1980 after the temple moved to North Chicago, it began increasing its contacts with the Indian community and now its worshippers are mostly Indian.[30] It sponsors the annual Jagannatha Ratha Yatra parade, where a 40-foot-tall cart bearing the images of the gods is drawn down Devon Avenue and culminates in a festival of music, plays, and dance at Warren Park on Western Avenue.[31] The Indians of the Rogers Park–West Ridge neighborhood patronize the Hare Krishna Temple and have made it their own because of its excellent location in their midst. Earlier fears that the temple might decline in importance once the authentic Hindu temples in the suburbs had been built have proved to be unfounded. The temple is also connected with a Vedic Day Center on Devon Avenue, which is run on the ancient *gurukula* style and exposes the children to Vedic culture when they are still very young.[32]

The Brahma Kumaris are another sect in the Hindu tradition with a branch in Chicago. They celebrated the birth anniversary of their founder,

Brahma Baba, in January 1995 in Itasca. Founded in India in 1937 and administered mainly by women, the Brahma Kumaris World Spiritual University encourages women to take leading roles as spiritual teachers. It has 1,800 centers in fifty countries, and the Chicago branch has recently become more active and visible in its attempts to reach out to the Indian immigrant community. Another Hindu sect, the Sathya Sai Baba organization, is also active in Chicago, which serves as the center for seven states in the Midwest region. Members meet regularly in Oak Park and plan social service activities such as feeding the homeless every Sunday or running soup kitchens in the Polish and African American communities.[33]

Other important temple organizations in the Chicago area are the Manav Seva Mandir, supported mainly by the Gujarati community, which claimed an attendance of 12,000 at its grand three-day *Murti Pratistha* celebrations in July–August 1993, and 7,000 at its *Kalash Sthapan* ceremonies on August 5, 1995, and the Hari Om Mandir in the northwestern suburb of Medinah.

The Vishwa Hindu Parishad of Greater Chicago (VHP)

The history of the VHP in North America goes back to the 1970s, but the Chicago chapter is comparatively new, having been founded only in 1991. The VHP-USA has one hundred centers spread across forty-one states and provincial chapters throughout Canada.[34] It draws its membership from those Hindus who already belong to one or other of the temple organizations. It relies on voluntary contributions from its members who are supposed to donate one-twelfth of their earnings as *guru dakshina* (offerings to the guru), so the organization doesn't lack money. Its global reach ("Vishwa" means world) and its proselytizing philosophy set it apart from the other institutions which are more geared to providing Hindus with day-to-day religious and cultural services. It provides a banner for ideologues and demagogues to preach Hinduism abroad and gives political parties and Hindu groups in India such as the BJP, the RSS and Sangh Parivar a platform from which to launch their propaganda. The VHP echoes the BJP on all religious issues. Its mega-jamboree was Global Vision 2000 held in August 1993 in Washington, D.C., ostensibly to celebrate the centenary of Vivekananda's visit to Chicago. But Vivekananda was all but forgotten in the political controversy generated at the conference by secularist-minded anti-BJP demonstrators and the excitement over the mosque destruction at Ayodhya.[35] The VHP was banned by the Indian government for unlawful action in inciting rioting mobs to tear down the Babri Masjid in December 1992.[36] Such politicoreligious controversies are more the rage in other parts of the United States, particularly the West Coast, than in Chicago, where the VHP works more quietly behind the scenes with immigrants who have gained respectability as businessmen or "community leaders." The VHP makes news in Chicago innocuously when it celebrates Indian Independence Day or Vivekananda Jayanti Day, but its list of speakers and award honorees, usually heads of other organizations in Chicago, shows the extent of its reach in the community.[37] The VHP has tried to wrest control of temple activities in Chicago, but as described earlier, secular-minded trustees of the board have successfully resisted the move so far.

The Philosophical Hindu Organizations

The Chinmaya Mission in Hinsdale was established in 1979 to spread Vedantic understanding, based on the eternal values of Sanatana Dharma. Its worldwide network of institutions touches all levels of activity, including music, dance, and discourse involving service to all sections of humanity, from the very young to the senior citizens. It takes its inspiration from Swami Chinmayananda (1916–93) who founded the first mission in Madras in 1953. The Chinmaya International Foundation has organizations in major cities of the United States besides Chicago such as Washington, Flint, Orlando, Houston, Philadelphia, San Jose, and Los Angeles. It conducts weekly adult study groups, and Bala Vihar (children's) and Yuva Kendra (teenage) classes on the teachings of the Vedanta and the Gita, and summer camps. The Mission purchased 6.5 acres of land at Route 83 and Stevenson expressway in October of 1987 and has since built its permanent home there, consisting of the Dhyan Mandir, library, and classrooms. Its future plans call for the construction of a retreat center with dormitory-type rooms for spiritual camps and Vigyana Mandir, a congregation hall for discourse, and space for wedding and cultural activities.

The teaching and organizational concepts of the Chinmaya Mission are very similar to those of the Vivekananda Vedanta Society of Chicago, which caters more to an American than an Indian immigrant clientele. The Vedanta Society, established in 1938 in a Hyde Park mansion, is a branch of the Rama-krishna Math and Mission, which has its headquarters in Belur Math, India. Its mission is "to promote the truths of the Vedanta as expounded by Swami Vivekananda and help people study religion in its universal aspects." It maintains a temple, monastery, and guest houses in Chicago and a monastery with retreat facilities in Ganges, Michigan. Its 293 members (as of 1992) are mostly American, and though it does not have much appeal for the Indian immigrant community who prefer their homegrown, colorful, ritualistic version of Hinduism to the austere, meditation-, and philosophy-laden message of the society that is geared toward a western audience, it interacts with their religious institutions through joint sessions for youth at its Ganges township. Its leader Swami Bhashyananda also lectures to the Hindu groups in Chicago on Hindu philosophy.

Muslim Religious Organizations

There are 4 million Muslims in the United States, of whom African American Muslims number approximately 1.3 million.[38] The Muslims of Chicagoland number approximately 250,000 and worship at mosques scattered throughout the city and suburbs.[39] Estimates of South Asian Muslims in Chicago vary widely, but a figure between 20,000 and 25,000 is probably close to the mark, based on two elements: the fact that the 1990 Census counted 9,085 Pakistanis in Illinois and 263 Bangladeshis (and almost all of these may be taken to be Muslims), and the premise that the Indian Muslims number around 10 to 15 percent of the total Indian immigrant population in the Chicago area. In India, Muslims numbered 75.4 million or 11 percent of the population in the 1981 census. It is difficult to tell whether Muslims have left India in disproportionately large numbers for the United States. The earlier arrivals tended to be Hyderabadi Muslims but more and more of the Indian Muslims are coming from Gujarat, the state that continues to send large numbers of new immigrants to the United States. In any case, the Indian and Pakistani Muslims are far outnumbered by other Muslims, among whom are Arab, Albanian, Bosnian, and African American Muslims.[40]

Before the 1960s, the main Muslim organizations in the Chicago area were the Muslim student groups active on college campuses. They represented most of the Muslims who had come to the area after World War I and World War II, mostly of Arab, Turkish, Bosnian, and Iranian origin. Muslims from the Indian subcontinent did not arrive in Chicago until after the partition of India in 1947 and the breakup of Pakistan in 1971.[41] It was during the 1960s and 1970s when all Muslims regardless of their national or linguistic origin started to come together under one umbrella for prayer or to discuss global issues of Islam. Thirty-three Islamic organizations, estimated to represent 90 percent of the Muslims of Chicago, have united under the umbrella of the Council of Islamic Organizations of Greater Chicago. But it is the mosques at which Muslims pray on a day-to-day basis and gather for special events that influence their thinking and reinforce their identity as Muslims. Though mosques are open to all, leaders of certain mosques and their participants tend to be from particular areas of the world. In this kind of categorization, India, Pakistan, and Bangladesh tend to be treated as one geographical unit.

Thus, when talking of the Muslim community of Chicago, it is difficult to separate the Indians from the Pakistanis. Indeed, this is one aspect in which the term "Indo-Pak" is used to imply the existence of a community that considers national identity subordinate to its religious identity. Matters are complicated by the fact that Indian Muslims have relatives in Pakistan, and there is a division within the Muslim community between those who advocate loyalty to one country or another. Incidents such as the tearing down of the Babri Masjid in 1992, and the sporadic outbreak of riots and terrorist bombings in India inflame passions in the Muslim community. For some Chicago Indians, their Muslim identity is created in conscious opposition to Hinduism, as it was in the subcontinent, while for others it is in conscious alignment with the secular state of India. Both groups exist, and while one speaks a political language, the other speaks the religious, social, and cultural language of Islam, and is particularly important in helping the Indians forge their ethnic Muslim identity. There also exists a divide between the Punjabi Muslims, who consider themselves racially superior and prefer to identify with Punjabis of other faiths, and the non-Punjabi Muslims. In matters not directly related to religion, such as business and politics, Indians and Pakistanis, Hindus and Muslims of Chicago are able to cooperate quite well, especially when they recognize that they have common problems such as racism and discrimination. What they have in common in Chicago generally outweighs their differences in South Asia, at least for the time being.

The Muslim Community Center of Chicago (MCC)

The Muslim Community Center, first established in 1969 on North Kedzie Avenue in Chicago and since relocated to 4380 North Elston Avenue, has been the parent organization for several neighborhood centers. Some of the founding members of MCC were also members of the Muslim Student Associations. According to a Muslim community worker, the leadership of the MCC is "90 percent Indian, because Indians have a strong background in administration and organization."[42] Many of the leaders of suburban mosques in Villa Park, Naperville, Elgin, Rolling Meadows, and Glendale Heights have come from the Center and helped duplicate its programs in the suburbs. The MCC has a membership of 2,000 and serves 6,200 Muslims in the city. It runs evening and weekend Islamic schools, with several shifts each, and a full-time school in Morton Grove with an enrollment of 184 in 1994. The school is accredited by the State of Illinois with grades kindergarten through seventh grade and caters to Muslims of all nationalities, but its staff consists mostly of Indians. Other full-time schools in Villa Park, Lombard, and Bridgeview also offer education through high school, combining Islamic studies and Arabic language studies with regular state required courses.

The Islamic Foundation of Villa Park

The Islamic Foundation was formed in 1974 in Villa Park to serve the Indo-Pak Muslim families, many of whom were from Hyderabad in Central India, who had moved to the western suburbs. After facing some local opposition and legal difficulties in setting up their own mosque, the Foundation purchased a school and adjacent property for $550,000 in 1983 and began holding Friday noon prayers and religious school for children on the weekends. The highest priority item on the agenda of the community is the religious education of the second generation, so youth camps and summer schools dominate the agenda. In 1990, a full-time school was started with classes from K through 7. The teaching of Arabic and Urdu is considered very important, though religious classes are also conducted in English. Religious occasions such as *Eid* and *Ramadan* are observed in conjunction with the larger Muslim community, sometimes on a grand global scale in the huge McCormick Place.

Other organizations narrow the scope of Muslim identity still further. The Ithna'Asharis, the Hussaini Association, the Dawoodi Bohora Jamat, and the Nizari Ismailis are all organizations that bring together Muslims based on the narrowest of sectarian interests. They have memberships of a few hundred people, who meet once or twice a month, but they also conduct the whole range of activities that the bigger groups provide.[43] Other Muslim associations have a more social thrust. The Gujarati Muslim Association of America, founded in 1990 with a 1993 membership of about one hundred, counted among its goals the "socio-economic upliftment of Gujarati Muslims, especially those living in Gujarat and in America." Besides arranging social get-togethers, it raises money for riot victims and gives financial help to students in Gujarat.

The Consultative Committee of Indian Muslims in the United States and Canada (CCIM)

The CCIM, as its name suggests, identifies its members with the nation of India, in conscious distinction from Muslims of other countries. The Chicago chapter is only one of several spread across the United States and Canada. It tries to promote unity between Indian Muslims and Indians of other religious faiths by celebrating such events as the birthday of the avowed secularist Jawaharlal Nehru.[44] In an effort to be even-handed in its dealings with Indians of all faiths, it held a public meeting "to condemn the desecration and destruction of places of worship following the Babri Masjid incident," taking care to condemn destruction in principle, whether perpetrated by Hindus or Muslims. (Both temples and mosques were destroyed in the aftermath of violence that racked Hindu and Muslim communities in England, Bangladesh, and Pakistan.) Many other professional, business and service organizations in the Indian immigrant community joined hands with the CCIM in expressing their dismay at the religious violence.

The different approaches taken by the Chicago organizations that represent the Muslim and the Sikh communities show that while some Indian Muslims can still express their faith in the Indian government, the Sikhs, as a religious group, do not support the Indian state. The political differences that the Sikhs have with the Indian government at the present time preclude any such public show of solidarity as the CCIM is able to display whenever events in India provoke the need for such unity.

Christian Religious Organizations

Christianity came to India with Saint Thomas the Apostle, who is said to be buried in Madras (Chennai). Christians form a small but significant minority (2.5 percent) of India's population. The number of church groups that Indian Christians call their own is out of all proportion to their actual numbers, with as few as thirty or forty families getting together to form a group. The churches are based on denominational and linguistic differences. Most Indian Christians are from the southern states of India and are employed in the medical field as nurses or technicians, though there are some Hindi- and Gujarati-speaking Christians also. Though a Federation of Indian Christian

Associations was founded in Chicago in 1978, its cooperative network does not compare in effectiveness to that of other Indian religious groups. Neither have they enjoyed the attention of the denominational and ecumenical executives in the Chicago area.[45] Unlike other Indian religious groups, they have not had to construct their houses of worship but have been able to use existing structures. The India Mission Telugu United Methodist Church purchased its own worship center in Oak Park in 1993 for $300,000.[46] In India, it may be noted, the Telugu Methodists are submerged with all other Protestants in the Church of South India, and the only other significantly large church is Roman Catholic.

The India-Christian Fellowship Church of Oak Park was registered in 1973 as an interdenominational and multilinguistic church to serve Christians from all parts of India. Tensions developed in 1976 leading to the formation of breakaway groups. It interacts with the other Indian community organizations and stresses its Indian cultural heritage though its programs are similar to those in other American churches: Sunday worship, bible study, and summer vacation bible school.

The Emmanuel United Methodist Church in Evanston was originally a Swedish and Norwegian Church, but in the 1960s its aging white congregation began to include a variety of other ethnic groups, including Gujarati- and Hindi-speaking Indians. The church conducts services in Hindi, Gujarati, and English and its "congregation represents a multicultural body with members from Jamaica, Guyana, Trinidad, India, Pakistan, and Puerto Rico, as well as the United States."[47] The church declared its 1993 membership to be 180. In the late 1980s, the congregation included about 25 Gujarati- and 20 Hindi-speaking families.[48]

There are several Orthodox and Catholic churches in the Chicago area that faithfully replicate traditional practices and are closely governed by church politics from back home. The First Indian Church of the Nazarene in Oak Park, established in 1982, conducts its services in Malayalam and includes many Syrian Christians from the state of Kerala. A large Malayalee Christian congregation, numbering almost 350, is the Mar Thoma Church of Chicago, which purchased its own church building in 1986 in Des Plaines.[49] Other groups in the Chicago area include Malankara Orthodox, Syrian Christian, and Pentecostal. The Roman Catholics from India worship in the local parish churches but the India Catholic Association of America, founded in 1960, sponsors social enterprises and special masses for its members. It calls itself a "community of several sub-cultural constituents from a variety of professional areas" and celebrates five major festivals each year—the Cardinal Bernadin Mass, Easter, an annual picnic, Halloween, and

Christmas. It has also been sponsoring the Indian segment of "Christmas Around the World" at Chicago's Museum of Science and Industry since 1982. The Catholic Friends of India League is an umbrella organization that comprises the India Catholic Association of America, the Kerala Latin League Syro-Malabar, Syro-Malankara, and the Tamil Catholic and Goan Overseas Associations.

The history of Indian Christian associations in the Chicago area suggests that Indian Christians, like other Indian religious groups, do not wish to uphold a religious identity that is independent of a cultural identity. The importance of language, at least for the first generation, has led to the formation of small church groups distinct from other neighborhood church groups, but because services can be conducted in English for the second generation it is uncertain how long the cultural distinctiveness will be necessary to uphold the religious identity. Fenton predicted that, compared to Indians of other faiths, Indian Christians would most likely lose their Indian identity after the second or third generation and were also the most likely to intermarry and assimilate into Indian culture.[50] Racism, however, could affect such a trend, and since race and ethnicity have always been important factors of identity, it is possible that they will keep the Indian Christians somewhat apart from Christians of other races and ethnic groups and remain more in tune with their fellow Indians who belong to other religions. Unlike the other minority religious groups of Sikhs and Muslims, there are no political shadows cast over the Christians of India and their ability to come together with other Indians in order to preserve their ethnicity.

Other Religious Organizations

The Sikh Religious Society of Chicago in Palatine

Religion serves as the center of identity for the Punjabi-Sikh immigrants of Chicago to an even greater degree than for Hindus. Assembling at the *gurdwara* or place of worship enables them to retain their language, dress, rituals, and other customs that define Sikhs and distinguish them from other Indians. In the wake of the political turmoil in Punjab following the Golden Temple incident and the demand for a separate Sikh state of Khalistan, the Chicago Sikhs have set themselves self-consciously apart from the other Indians. Thus religion and politics in the home country are unavoidably mixed in the group life of immigrants in a distant land.

Worldwide, the Sikh population is estimated at 18.8 million, with 250,000 in North America.[51] (India's Sikh population in the 1981 census was 13.1 million, constituting 1.91 percent of the total population.[52]) The first Sikhs who came to Chicago before 1965 were university students, some of whom got together to form the Sikh Study Circle in 1956. In 1972, this became reorganized as the Sikh Religious Society of Chicago, whose purpose was to serve the needs of the Sikh community that was growing rapidly in numbers along with the rest of the Indian community. In the mid to late 1980s, the Sikh families living in Illinois, Wisconsin, and Northern Indiana were estimated to be about 1,000.[53] Other estimates put the number of Sikhs in the Chicago area from "2,500 to 5,000."[54] A religious facility recently opened in Milwaukee and another one is planned in northwest Indiana where Sikhs reside in significant numbers. Following the pattern of all other religious groups, the Sikhs soon moved from rented facilities to constructing their own place of worship. A four-acre parcel of land was bought in the northwest suburb of Palatine in 1974, groundbreaking took place in 1976, and the first services started in 1979. The *gurdwara* is simple and uncomplicated, reflecting the simplicity of the religion itself, according to the architect who designed the building. Upstairs, there is a prayer hall with the *Guru Granth Sahib* or Holy Book in a centered canopy and glass on all sides for a clear unobstructed view, while the lower level houses a *langar* or community kitchen, a dining hall, meeting rooms, and offices.[55] In 1993, the president of the society announced plans to construct a new building adjacent to the *gurdwara* at a cost of $1.7 million to house a large kitchen, *langar* hall, and library.[56] What is especially striking to the non-Sikh visitor is the display of photos of the Golden Temple incident in the perimeter of the lower hall, and the sign proclaiming Khalistan as the "Sikh homeland." Among the services offered by the Palatine *gurdwara* are weekly worship services, which include *kirtan* (devotional singing), *gurbani* (reading of holy passages), and *ardas* (group prayers). The main events that it celebrates are the birthdays of the founder of the religion, Guru Nanak, and the tenth Guru, Guru Gobind Singh, and the martyrdom of its fifth Guru, Guru Arjun Singh. *Baisakhi*, which marks the beginning of the New Year and the gathering of the harvest is celebrated with much gaiety and abandon and *bhangra* dances. The religious identity of the Sikhs continues to be built around the possibility of turning a political dream into a reality. In the 1990s, Sikhs worldwide seem to have tired of the violence and become disenchanted with the separatist leaders, but they do not necessarily support the Indian government, so the situation still retains its potential for fostering troubled relations between Sikhs and the larger Indian community in Chicago.

The effectiveness of the *gurdwara* in reaching out to the second generation is greatly affected by factionalism within the temple organization and *gurdwara* election politics. Also the second-generation Sikhs are anxious to abandon the *kesh* (uncut hair and beard) and are more interested in spiritual issues, while the immigrant generation is still eager to cling to the outward symbols of their faith. The community leaders took the pains to invite Cook County State's Attorney Jack O'Malley to the *gurdwara* to explain to him how the turban and *kirpan* are part of their religious tradition.[57]

Given American prejudice against foreign dress, and the stereotyping of Sikhs as "terrorists" and "fundamentalists," many Sikhs wonder if they can afford a conspicuous profile. They are aware that even if they call themselves "freedom fighters" the American public will view them as fundamentalists. Educating the American public and generating "good PR" became a prime concern when a 4-year-old Sikh boy was tragically slain by a mentally disturbed Sikh outside the Palatine gurdwara on 18 December 1994.[58]

The isolation of the Sikhs is increased by the fact that they are alienated from other Indians as well as Americans. Within the community, too, there is the socioeconomic divide between the earlier, professional, suburban immigrants and the less well-off, city-dwelling newcomers.[59] But it is to the larger American society that they are reaching out, through their involvement in Asian American coalitions and participation in American civic life. The Chicago area Sikhs want to be recognized and appreciated as a distinct religious group in American society, and it is through the institutional infrastructure of the Palatine *gurdwara* that they are able to strive toward this goal.

One religious group, the Sant Nirankari Mission, dissociated itself from the rituals of Sikhism and separated from the Sikhs in 1929. Established in the Chicago area in 1973, the group made Carpentersville its national headquarters in 1986 and has a small following of a hundred or so Punjabis in the area who believe in "universal brotherhood" and peace to all regardless of "caste, creed, color and nationality."

The Jain Center and Temple in Bartlett

There are about 70,000 Jains in the United States and about 2,500 of them live in the Chicago area. Jains in India numbered only 3.2 million in the 1981 census and make up less than 0.5 percent of the Indian population.[60]

Though Jainism is an offshoot of Hinduism, it rejects ritualism and places great emphasis on austerity and penance. There is much concentration of wealth in the small community, which specializes in banking and finance. Jains in Chicago trace their history back to the first Jain to visit Chicago in 1893 to represent Jainism at the first World's Parliament of Religions. It is said that since the Jain religion prohibited its monks from traveling outside India, Gandhi (not the Mahatma), a young lawyer and practicing Jain, was trained to be the intellectual representative of Jainism to the Parliament. The Jain Society of Metropolitan Chicago was established in 1969, but it was not until 1987 that the land for a temple was purchased, 15.2 acres of it for $115,000. In 1993, the $3 million facility had been completed and an elaborate idol installation ceremony held in the presence of India's high commissioner to the United Kingdom, the mayor of Bartlett, and the Cook County president.

The Jain society is also part of the Federation of Jain Societies in North America (JAINA). JAINA conventions typically bring together followers of the Jain religion from all over the world, including Canada, England, Europe, India, and the United States.[61] The same agenda is followed as that of the other language and religion based conventions, including seminars, workshops, presentations for different age groups on different aspects of the Jain heritage, and its future directions. The eight-day biennial JAINA convention hosted in Chicago in 1995 is said to have drawn ten thousand Jains and cost an estimated $500,000. The Jain Society announced plans to build a school, a senior citizen center, and expand its present facilities.[62] The Young Jains of America organization was established in 1989 to "explore Jain philosophy, its science and its principles within a community of youth and foster new generation leadership."[63]

The Zoroastrian Association of Metropolitan Chicago

Zoroastrians trace their history in India to the seventh century when they fled persecution from Muslim Arabs in Persia and sought refuge on India's west coast. Their religion forbids intermarriage and they are a fast-dwindling community in India. They are, however, highly respected in India as a cultured and refined people . Some of India's most prominent industrialists and businessmen are Parsis. There were only 120,000 Zoroastrians or Parsis in India in the 1981 census. Zoroastrians number some 500 to 600 in the Chicago area and were the first among Indian religious groups to have their very own prayer house. The Zoroastrian Association of Metropolitan Chicago was formed in 1974 and met regularly at a church building until 1983 when a $250,000 brick and cedar structure in Hinsdale was presented to the community by a philanthropist after whom it is named the Arbab Rustom Guib Darbe Mehr Zoroastrian Center of Chicago.[64] The community donated funds and professional architectural and general contracting services to build a large meeting hall and a smaller prayer hall which serves as the "fire temple" and houses the sacred fire. The fire, however, does not burn continuously but is lit on occasion.

About three-quarters of the two hundred or so member families are from India. About 10 percent are from Pakistan, the remaining 15 percent from Iran. Most of them are from the academic community and because they are such a small group, they are more cohesive than the larger and more business-dominated Parsi communities of Los Angeles and New York. The same concerns that plague the community in India are also of concern to the Chicago community—to what extent can outside influences, such as Westernization or intermarriage be tolerated, since the community is already dwindling in size and cross-cultural marriages are becoming more and more common. The dominant language of communication and religious education for the second generation is English, though some Gujarati is spoken by first-generation Parsis.

The above examination of Chicago's Indian religious institutions reveals the variety of ways in which Indians use them to preserve their identity and adapt to the new society. They use their houses of worship to impart religious education to their children. While Hindus, Sikhs, Jains, and Zoroastrians provide this education in the form of Sunday school classes, the Muslims have gone a step further and founded full-fledged Islamic schools where, in addition to the scriptures, the Islamic way of life is taught to the second generation. Temples, mosques, and churches also provide immigrants an opportunity for social contact through the celebration of religious and nonreligious festivals. Another important function is the offering of regional language instruction. The physical infrastructure greatly facilitates the transmission of traditions and enables immigrants to focus nonreligious activities around a religious nucleus. Temples also fulfill a charitable function, organizing food drives, blood drives, and other community service activities. Whatever the need of the hour, immigrants shape their religious institutions to fulfill that need, sometimes using traditional forms that existed in the homeland, at other times striking out in innovative ways of their own.

The Significance of the Cultural and Religious Core

The diversity of cultural and religious organizations among Chicago's Indian immigrants lends new meaning to the word "multiculturalism." In the larger American context, the word is commonly applied to denote people of different nationalities; in the narrower Indian immigrant context, it applies to language, religion, geographic region, class, and a host of other factors that define the world of origin. It also demonstrates that what unites Indians is as important as what makes them different from each other. Fenton notes that Indians, despite their diverse religions, share many unifying characteristics, including a single national identity, a common spiritual and cultural heritage, differences from other Americans, and a minority status in America.[65] Whether they choose to emphasize their commonalties or celebrate their differences depends partly upon the context in which they operate. When they are among themselves, they concentrate on the task of cultural preservation. When interacting with the world around them, they forge new links connecting them to other groups in Chicago, the rest of the nation and the world beyond.

10

FORGING NEW LINKS
Business and Politics

The manipulation of Indian ethnic identity also depends on a
range of possible goals and constraints. These include both the
conditions of the host society, as well as the motivations and
resources of the immigrant Indian community.
— Richard Harvey Brown, "Migration and Modernization:
Theoretical Issues for Further Research"

Chicago's Indian immigrant community has been motivated primarily by
economic and professional considerations, but it has also sought to participate in public life while retaining much of its own culture and to achieve
equal status with the other ethnic groups within the prevailing pluralistic
environment. Its secular institutions often grew out of everyday negotia-
tions based on these interests, so they are remarkably flexible. They also
defy broad generalizations so that the story of their development can only
be captured by describing in some detail the variety of circumstances and
the role of various individuals in responding to change. The thriving business ventures on Devon Avenue provide an excellent example of how the
Indian community has connected with the larger community while keeping
territorial rights for itself. While some of the business institutions that
Indians rely on exist within this commercial hub, there is also a wider, invisible, global network that Indians have developed because of the international nature of their operations.

Business Organizations

Gone are the days when an ethnic business community consisted mostly of
easily identifiable corner shopkeepers or greengrocers who lived in the heart

of the ethnic enclave, or ran a small family business that catered exclusively to the ethnic community. Though such business enterprises do exist on Devon Avenue and elsewhere in Chicago, they are only one part of a wider business community that includes businesses of a totally different nature: physicians who own private clinics, lab facilities and investment firms, diamond merchants with international connections in London and Hong Kong; computer consultancy firms that get their software developed through consortia in India, wealthy housewives who use their husbands' excess earnings to set themselves up in the boutique business, Dunkin' Donuts and Pak Mail franchisees who serve the larger mainstream community, and the small time insurance agents who pound the streets in all kinds of neighborhoods to drum up their business. This is not to say that the Mom and Pop ethnic store is extinct; rather, it has been joined by a host of other businesses with different requirements of capital, labor, inventory, clientele, and location. The heterogeneous nature of the immigrants themselves is mirrored in the range and variety of their businesses. The business owners differ in education, employment skills, family history, financial resources, cultural and religious affiliation, and their attitude toward their business.

One characteristic of Indian immigrant business in Chicago in the 1990s is that business represents many things to many people. People are in business not necessarily because that is where they want to be, or because it represents their ultimate goal in life. Certainly, depending upon the educational qualifications and family background of the immigrant, being in business for oneself could mean a boost in status in the community. On the other hand, "opening shop" could be a fall from bigger and better things in the immigrant's own eyes or according to the standards of the Indian community. Sometimes involvement in business can be interpreted to mean a greater stake in society on the part of immigrants, or to engender a greater sense of permanence in the adopted land.[1] But for many Indians in Chicago, business is the choice of last resort or the only way to make some money before returning to the homeland. Sometimes, it is also the only avenue open to an immigrant victimized by racial discrimination in the larger society. Whatever the case, it is obvious that "success" in business has to be measured by something more than a profit and loss statement. The balance sheet has to take into account the varied, and varying, attitudes of the business owners themselves.

According to a study based on 1990 Census data by the National Bureau of Economic Research comparing the self-employment rate for sixty differ-

Table 9   Industry distribution of self-employed Indian
American men, 1990

Industry	Percentage
Health services	31.2
Food stores	8.9
Retail trade	7.9
Legal, engineering, and accounting	6.8
Transportation	4.5
Construction	3.8
Eating places	3.5
Personal services	3.0
Auto repair	1.4
Horticulture	0.6
Other	28.5

SOURCE: National Bureau of Economic Research. Based on 1990
census data, *Little India*, August 1995, 28.

ent ethnic groups in the United States, the self-employment rate for Indian
men at 11.7 percent was slightly above the national average of 10.8 percent.[2]
The self-employed rate for Indian women was 7.4 percent compared to the
national figure of 5.8 percent. Self-employment rates for Indians increased
since 1980, when it was 9.9 percent for men and 4.7 percent for women.
Still, Indians ranked only thirtieth amid sixty racial and ethnic groups
examined in the study. (Israeli men led with a rate of 28.6 percent self-
employed followed by Korean men at 27.9 percent. Koreans also led the
ranking in self-employment among women.)

The industry distribution of self-employed Indian American men shows
that nearly one-third are in the health professions, the highest concentration of any ethnic group and more than five times the national average. The
next most popular business among Indians is food stores, followed by retail
trade, and engineering and accounting services (Table 9).

In Chicago, the concentration of retail businesses on Devon Avenue has
led to the development of an institutional infrastructure that is heavily
involved in neighborhood matters, while businesses in the health or engineering industries are more likely to rely on professional institutions that
have a widely scattered clientele. There are at least five types of Indian business in the Chicago area and they rely on different kinds of institutions to
support their efforts. First, there are the smaller, readily identifiable, overtly

ethnic stores catering only to the South Asian immigrant community. Next are the larger-scale manufacturers, traders, and restaurateurs who also serve the immigrant community but have customers from the larger society and rely on international supply networks. A third category are the small-scale franchise operators who provide goods and services in the larger mainstream community. The "managerial, administrative, sales" type of business owners make up a fourth category. They have enough administrative and business acumen to run an independent operation and include the travel, real estate, and life insurance agents who need accreditation to conduct their business but do not necessarily have a college degree and may therefore be classified as "semi-professionals." And finally there are those who rely on their professional, mainly technological, skills to set up their own businesses. These last could be in trading, manufacturing, or consulting, providing medical, accounting, legal, management, or engineering services, and their operations could vary considerably in size. While there may be other businesses that do not fall exclusively into one of the above categories, most businesses in the Chicago area do have one or other of the characteristics mentioned above. The same person could also move from owning or operating one type of business to another, or he or she could be the owner of several businesses that fall into different categories. The formal institutions that these businesses depend upon to varying extent are of many kinds: the local business association, the financial institutions, be they local, national, or international, depending upon the nature of the business, governmental institutions ranging from the local alderman to a United Nations agency, and even academic institutions. The best way to describe the impact of these institutions on the local businesses is to examine how the different categories of business function and which particular institutions they rely on the most. Of course, marriage and family ties have tremendous impact on certain kinds of businesses, especially those owned by Gujaratis and Sindhis, and in terms of labor and capital resources are far more important to them than the financial institutions.

The Institutions of the "Shopkeepers"

The readily identifiable grocery, video, sari, and appliance store owners or restaurateurs serving the Indo-Pak community are located either in "India town" on Devon Avenue or in one of the outlying areas that have a sizable concentration of Indian immigrants, such as the western suburbs of Naperville, Downers Grove, Oakbrook, and Westmont or Elk Grove Village, Morton

Grove, Des Plaines, Schaumburg, and Skokie located in the northwest. These business owners own one or more establishments, but they are essentially small time operators or at least they started out as such. Many of them offer a combination of services, so that it is not unusual to find a store that sells grocery, rents videos, and arranges for personal services ranging from baby-sitting to airline tickets. Generally speaking, these businesses were started by individual initiative and may not represent a continuity of entrepreneurial background from India. Karen Leonard noted that there was little or no such continuity among small-scale Indian immigrant businesses in California.[3] In Chicago, too, the trend is somewhat similar, with many people venturing into business for the first time without any background in trade whatsoever. One grocery store at the corner of 63rd and Fairview in Westmont was financed by an immigrant who wanted to give his old parents something to do in Chicago. The father is a retired Indian government official who wanted to live with his son in America but was not prepared to sit at home idly. So he and wife operate the grocery store that their son bought for them. An upscale boutique in Westmont is run by a doctor's wife who decided to capitalize on two resources: a husband with an income in a high-tax bracket that warranted a commercial investment, and a sister in India in the boutique business who could act as her regular supplier. *Rivaz* and *Khazana* are boutiques at the corner of Cass and Ogden in Westmont run by wives of successful doctors in the western suburbs. Other entrepreneurs came from business families in India but with no great stock of capital. Uma Sari Palace located on Devon Avenue was started by a couple who opened shop with $500 in 1973. The wife was from a business family in Hong Kong and the husband a mechanical engineer from Delhi.[4] Most of the thirty or so restaurants on Devon Avenue are run by business owners with different backgrounds ranging from doctors and engineers to hotel management professionals and even college dropouts. More and more of these establishments employ unskilled or low-skilled workers outside the Indian immigrant community. It is not unusual to see bus boys or waiters from other ethnic groups, such as Russians or Mexicans, working the restaurants on Devon Avenue. But employees at the cash register or behind the counter of expensive goods such as jewelry are invariably other trusted Indians, generally family members. Many of these small stores attract customers who are not South Asians, especially the restaurants.[5]

The merchants of Devon Avenue often cooperate on large-scale ventures that may require greater capital or more organizational skills than they can provide individually. For instance, they jointly sponsor pop-culture activities that are big money earners such as bringing movies to the big screen. They also sponsor ticket sales for music concerts and dance troupes that are another big draw with audiences starved for popular entertainment from the homeland. Classical dance and music, however, find their patrons more among the professional upper classes. The Devon Avenue merchants have thus successfully "commodified" culture and turned it into a profitable venture through their mass marketing strategies.

A survey conducted by the author in October 1994 of the approximately one hundred businesses on Devon Avenue between Claremont in the east and California in the west showed that the average Indian family could find almost everything here to support a distinctly Indian lifestyle. The grocery, video, vegetable, and meat shops account for about 25 percent of the businesses, restaurants constitute 20 percent, sari and dress shops another 20 percent. Twenty-two-carat jewelry stores are another important category (10 percent), as are the appliance, luggage, and gift shops (10 percent). The remaining 15 percent of businesses are service agencies providing service in areas such as travel and banking.[6] Stores also come and go on Devon Avenue with amazing rapidity depending upon the viability of the venture or management skills of the entrepreneur. Some restaurants change hands frequently while other enterprises go from success to success. A large bookstore was opened in 1995 by an entrepreneur who felt that the demand for ethnic and English language books from the homeland had outgrown his capacity to supply from a corner kiosk. Patel Brothers, who started out as a small grocery store in the 1970s, now own a big chunk of storefront property on Devon Avenue and have become the nation's largest Indo-Pak food retailer. They have also diversified into electronics, travel agencies, restaurants, and video shops. They started their own branded products division of foods and spices, have thirty-two retail outlets nationwide and recently opened a 91,000-square-foot facility in Skokie. They use an advertising agency based in India to promote their products worldwide, and while consolidating their hold on the ethnic market, hope to make inroads into the mainstream market as well. They provide an example of a business that moved from small to big within a span of twenty-five years and owe their growth as much to their individual skills as to the growth in the size of the community. Another example of a small Indian business expanding and reaching out to the larger society is provided by the partnership between Arlington Park Hotel and Goyal Enterprises to provide authentic Indo-Pak cuisine, especially for weddings in the South Asian Community. Though the primary purpose is to meet a growing demand from within the community, the tie-up with an existing American infrastructure ensures that the South Asian community gets what it wants in a cost-efficient manner, and the American consumer has more options for a greater variety of cuisine. Such cooperation and interaction will increase as Indian businesses reach out more and more to gain a larger market.

Three of the most important institutions for the businesses on Devon Avenue are the National Republic Bank, the Devon Bank, and the North Town Business Association. The National Republic Bank, established in 1897, is the only Indian-owned bank in the Chicago area and was acquired in 1984 by a team of entrepreneurs headed by Hiren Patel and Dr. Nimmagadda.[7] The head office is on Harrison Street in downtown Chicago, but a Devon Avenue branch was opened to serve the Indian community in its own neighborhood. With a 1994 turnover of $65 million, the bank serves not only the Indian community but also the Hispanic, Jewish, and Russian immigrants in the area. Bank deposits are 65 percent from Indian customers, 35 percent from the Jewish community. Hiren Patel came to the United States on a student visa and used to operate the XYZ Electronic Appliance store on Broadway before he bought the bank, which was operating in the red at the time. He started out by helping Indians who had no credit rating because they had never borrowed money before or because they had no income tax returns to show. They were small personal loans given with no collateral, but Patel felt he knew his customers and the bank's money was safe with them. Even now, when the bank's customers are not very regular with their payments, they are not harassed because business is transacted on faith. Over the years, the bank has made loans ranging from $5,000 to $750,000, helping entrepreneurs who wanted to set up liquor stores, laundromats, motels, convenience stores, and newsstands as well as larger institutions such as the Hindu Temple of Greater Chicago, Manav Seva Mandir, Jain Temple, and the Congregation of South Indian Churches. Among the bank's customers are also doctors investing in nonmedical businesses such as apartment buildings or waste management companies. There is not much interaction with the Pakistani businesses in the area, estimated by the bank manager at 10 percent of Devon Avenue shops, or with the Jewish-owned businesses. The bank's owners felt they had a social mission above and beyond the commercial—to help the newcomers who were struggling to make it in a new environment. The bank's branch manager spoke of the exploitation of immigrants some of whom came illegally from Mexico, Panama, and Canada, from the Mehasana district of Gujarat and from the Ismaili communities in Karachi, Bombay, or East Africa. The going rate for a false passport and illegal entry into the United States was Rs.600,000 to Rs.700,000, and the immigrants would be working their fingers to the bone for years to pay back that amount. In this situation, they could hardly go to the regular banking institutions for help. It appears that the Chicago Indians have taken the lead in commercial and personal banking compared to Indians in other parts of the United States. Though the east and west coasts have larger Indian populations, there is no bank as yet in those areas owned solely by Indians.

The Devon Bank, located on Western Avenue and also in the heart of the Indian business district, is committed to serving the local residents.[8] Irving Loundy, vice president of the bank, is also in the happy position of heading the North Town Business Association, and has twice the opportunity to prove his commitment to the community. Indeed, with all the internecine rivalry between the different immigrant businesses in the area, Loundy promotes Devon Avenue as an "international" rather than an "Indo-Pak" marketplace and is anxious to keep the businesses focused on a common goal of unity and profitability. Political connections are also important to these businesses, especially at the aldermanic level. Fiftieth Ward Alderman Bernard Stone (who won his seat over and above the voters in his constituency who wanted an Indian to represent them) stays in close touch with the business community, and is said to be committed to working toward interethnic cooperation. The Indo-Pak businesses also work hand in hand with the social, religious, and cultural associations in supplying goods and services at the innumerable Indian events; they also make full use of the "old boy" type of immigrant network that is particularly important to small businesses.

The North Town Business Association (NTBA), whose 1993 membership list contained eighty-five area businesses, has a crucial role to play in keeping the peace and prosperity on Devon Avenue, and is even more important to the Indo-Pak businesses located there than the local business associations might be for suburban Indian store owners. When Jewish businesses moved out of the area in the 1970s, the Indian businesses who moved in had no sense of collective purpose. Few of them cared to subscribe to the local chamber of commerce that went bankrupt and had to close down for lack of funds to meet its payroll. The Lerner newspapers published damaging reports about the decay of Devon Avenue before the businesses took collective and corrective action, afraid that customers might move to the suburbs as a result of crime around Devon. The concentration of Indian, Pakistani, and Bangladeshi shops in a four- to six-block strip also has dangerous potential for communal, nationalism-based violence. It is ironic that in the very geographical area where distinctions between Indian and Pakistani are blurred and both communities can come together to serve a common South

Asian culture, chances of trouble erupting are also the greatest. Sometimes fairly straightforward instances of rowdyism are interpreted as "Indo-Pak" or "Hindu-Muslim" hatred by certain elements of the society who have been unable to leave their animosities behind in South Asia.[9] At other times, members of one community deliberately target those of another. The greatest danger is that trouble in the homeland, such as when the Babri Masjid was destroyed, could turn Devon Avenue into a crucible of religious and national violence. The restraining hand of the organizational leadership is very important in keeping matters under control, especially in a city like Chicago where the police are relying more and more on community involvement to combat crime. Realizing this, the NTBA and other concerned bodies promptly arranged a show of solidarity by marching together on Devon Avenue to protest the violence at Babri Masjid in December 1992.

The issues that are addressed by the NTBA include problems of violence, crime, safety, cleanliness, gangs, graffiti, and parking. Stories of "eve-teasing," physical molestation, purse- and gold-snatching, hold-ups, slashing of car tires and other acts of vandalism, even abduction, on Devon Avenue have sometimes frightened suburban shoppers into staying away. Hoodlums who roamed Devon Avenue, especially during 1993–94 were both white racist Americans of the "dot-buster" variety, and Indo-Pak boys molesting women of each other's community. There was an average of three criminal incidents a month when the NTBA decided it was time to take visible action. In a concerted effort that brought together the mayor, the alderman, the Business Association and the Homeowners' League, a "Cleanup Devon" project asked for increased number of beat officers and patrol cars, and urged the businesses and customers to preserve the beauty of the neighborhood. No gang activity has been reported among Indian American youth in Chicago of the sort seen in California where a fifty-member gang (most with the last name Singh) and calling itself the All India Mob has terrorized individuals in the Fremont Indian community.[10]

Devon Avenue attracts large crowds during the festival season in October-November. It is decorated with special lights and banners for *Divali*, which is an occasion of as much significance to Indian businesses as Christmas is to the American retailer. The business community opens new account books at this time and goes all out to promote sales. The Indian consumers are also at their free-spending best at *Divali* time when they buy themselves new clothes, spruce up their homes, and exchange gifts. Appealing to the self-interest of merchants to revive the area and keep it safe, the NTBA has been able to foster the feeling that even if city hall neglects them, they need to rally round and help themselves if they are to retain the patronage of the widely scattered Asian Indian community in the Midwest. Thanks to such organizational efforts, Devon Avenue is still in a position to boast that it is one of the largest shopping centers for Indians in all of North America.

The Institutions of the "Big Merchants"

There is a distinct set of business owners in Chicago for whom business in a particular line has been a way of life for generations. These are the jewelers and diamond merchants, the large-scale manufacturers and traders of food supplies, and some of those in the garment and clothing trade. The exigencies of capital and inventory in this trade are such that they need the backing supplied by kith and kin, so they may have family business connections not only in India, but East Africa, England, or the Far East. Many of them run both wholesale and retail operations, and rely on family networks for capital, labor and inventory. Intermarriage in such communities is also often closely linked to their business operations.[11] In this kind of business, migration networks also play a crucial role. These are defined as "sets of interpersonal ties that link migrants, former migrants, and nonmigrants in origin and destination areas through the bonds of kinship, friendship and shared community origin."[12] Both the immigrant networks and the larger socioeconomic and political issues, in the host society as well as the other countries in which collaborating kin operate, exert a strong influence on such businesses. These kinds of business have at least one thing in common with the smaller ethnic shops—their clientele is mostly within the ethnic community—but their scale of operations sets them in a world apart. Their family backgrounds may also be less diverse. Also their commitment to the business—and their staying power and ability to survive ups and downs in the economy—are usually greater than those of the smaller business owner. The "risk-diversification" strategy in migration helps businesses because good times abroad might help households survive bad ones at home. And vice versa, for example, if businesses in Chicago need help, they may be able to count on their networks in India or some other country to help them out.

The story of Vitha Jewelers in Chicago illustrates some of the above-mentioned phenomena at work. Harjivan Vitha comes from a family who have been craftsmen of gold jewelry for generations in Gujarat. He immigrated to the United States from Africa in 1972 and sold twenty-two-carat gold jewelry from his basement for ten years before opening his first showroom on Devon Avenue. Soon he had two more showrooms, Laxmi Jewelers and

Zaveri Jewelers, part of an eleven-store chain that includes stores in New York, New Jersey, Florida, Georgia, and California. Each one of these stores is operated by a family member. Vitha imports jewelry from other parts of the world besides India, including England, the Middle East, and Africa and many of the family members in Chicago hail from these countries in the global *oikumene*, including Fiji. In the beginning, Harjivan Vitha used to travel extensively, setting up exhibitions and displaying his wares in cities all over the United States, including those with a tiny Indian immigrant population. Now he uses his chain store setup to rotate merchandise, moving it from one city to another if it does not sell at one location. The jewelry business is a fast-paced, competitive business, always attuned to the fluctuating price of gold and demanding huge outlays in inventory, especially during festival season when sales are expected to hit their highs. Despite the mushrooming of jewelry shops on Devon Avenue, the jewelers are confident of survival. This is a niche market because the Indians' passion for twenty-two-carat gold and love of exquisitely hand-crafted designs keeps them coming to Devon Avenue. It also keeps them away from American jewelers who sell only fourteen- or eighteen-carat gold and go for machine-cut designs. According to the World Gold council reports, Indians are the biggest buyers of gold in the world, accounting for 415 tons in 1994, almost 50 percent higher than the second-highest consumers, the United States, at 283 tons. Gem and diamond exports are big business in India too. Seven out of ten diamonds sold in the world are said to be cut and polished in India.[13] The Vitha business has been so successful that two Vitha brothers, both qualified professionals, one a CPA and the other a computer science graduate, have preferred to join the family business rather than pursue professional careers. Nonresident Indians worldwide play an important role in this industry.

Another story of international connections and how they contribute to success in the local market is seen in the operations of India Sari Palace. The chairman of the company lives in Hong Kong and heads the parent company India Emporium which provides an umbrella for sister companies in Washington, Los Angeles, Dallas, and Chicago. In 1993, the company diversified into the restaurant business, opening a South Indian vegetarian restaurant on Devon Avenue called Udipi Palace. Stores are all run by members and friends of a Sindhi family, and heads of stores meet quarterly to review performance and plans. The Gujarati and Sindhi domination of the trading business on Devon Avenue must be attributed at least in part to their cultural and religious traditions. Gujarati groups abroad are known to have "rapidly reproduced their entrepreneurial and trading expertise established in India and Africa."[14] The availability of greater resources, both human and financial, with these particular ethnic groups is certainly a factor in their economic success. Given the importance of continuity and intergenerational support in this business, do the immigrants expect their businesses to be carried on by the next generation? The family involvement in the Devon Avenue businesses continues to be strong, as long as it is profitable and can support all the members. There is an entire second generation of Indian hoteliers who have inherited the business from their parents and are already applying new marketing techniques learned at American universities to diversify or expand their "Mom and Pop" establishments. The hold of tradition and family institutions in the business arena looks poised to continue, at least for the Gujaratis and Sindhis in Chicago, just as it has done in times past in Africa and England.

The Institutions of the "Independent Franchisees"

A third type of entrepreneurship is represented by those who buy or lease franchises for operations that range from the fast food business (e.g., Dunkin' Donuts) to automobile service (Meineke) or mail-handling (Pak Mail). Ownership of gas stations such as Amoco and Shell, has increased dramatically in the Chicago area with as many as 180 owners of gas stations in the area, most of them Malayalees from Kerala.[15] Hotel and motel owners would fall into this category, too. The Asian American Hotel Owners Association claimed there were eight thousand Asian hoteliers of whom four thousand were members of AAHOA. The market value of their businesses was estimated at $26 billion, with 720,000 franchised rooms and 175,000 independent rooms.[16] If the people who own these businesses also happen to operate these businesses themselves, they are conspicuous as minority business owners. However, some of them employ non-Indians to run things on a day-to-day basis, if they can afford it, and so are not always easily identifiable. By the same token, if an Indian were to be seen operating one of these establishments, it does not follow that he or she owns the place. He could be working for an Indian or non-Indian owner. A study of newsstand vendors in the New York area by Johanna Lessinger revealed that many of them who were working for investor-owned franchises had little control over their businesses. Their jobs were poorly paid, and often dead-end but the reason Indians continued to flock to such jobs was, according to Lessinger, because they were still focused on the dream of "having a business of one's own" and were "bedazzled" with the notion that it was an achievable goal, though the harsh fiscal realities told a different story.[17] There are quite a few newsstand concessions owned or operated by Indians in Chicago at train stations and street corners (as, too, in the New York subways), and the nature of the relationship between owner and operator is not always clear. Some of them are run by relatives or friends of the owners who want to help out those who would have no way of getting jobs in the open market. But benign intentions also turn into exploitative tendencies among these business owners.

The manager of the Devon branch of the National Republic Bank estimated that 65 percent of the Dunkin' Donuts franchises in the north and northwest areas were run or owned by Indians, either by groups or individuals, and 80 percent of these were Gujaratis. It would start off with an immigrant seeking the most menial job in a store, having no qualifications for employment elsewhere, not being able to speak even a word of English. In two years, the immigrant would learn enough of the business to be able to work as a baker, and he would try to pass the exam that Dunkin' Donuts requires of its managers. Many fail in the first attempt but they try again. When they are ready to invest in their own store—a starter store is usually a satellite store where no baking is done—they come to the bank for the 20 to 30 percent down-payment. The ultimate goal is to move on from the donut business, where the work is hard and the hours are long, to owning other businesses, such as a gas station. Most of them do not want their children to inherit these businesses. They would rather send them to college and have them pursue a professional career. The success stories of these immigrants has helped give the Indians a good name with Dunkin' Donuts management, which is eager to give franchises to Indians, but the question of prestige within the community looms large among Indians running these stores. Because the community was originally made up of highly paid professionals, the feeling persists that keeping shop is a comparatively unworthy occupation. Attitudes differ in the smaller ethnic community from those in the larger American society. One woman who owns a liquor store in the western suburbs has no problems with the American community she serves, but is ashamed to acknowledge that she runs a liquor store when she meets other Indians. She has to face the scornful attitude of her suburban Indian friends who are professionals and who make no secret of the fact that they consider her occupation a lowly one. Another Pak Mail owner-operator in Westmont said she would rather be employed as a professional in the computer software industry for which she was fully qualified but being unable to find work in that field, she was forced to operate a small business.

These businesses may be able to get financial support from an Indian-owned bank but they are generally dependent on the franchiser for other support. Being widely scattered geographically and usually located in the midst of other American businesses, they feel vulnerable and like to maintain a low profile. Stories of crimes against 7–11 and White Hen Pantry stores as well as gas stations owned by Indians or Pakistanis intensify these feelings of vulnerability. But the Indians in the hotel and motel industry have banded together as professionals and managed to avail themselves of the institutional support of the Asian American Hotel Owners Association.

The Institutions of the "Semi-Professionals"

Those who work in a sales or in a managerial or administrative capacity for themselves may be called "semi-professionals" since they are in businesses that do not require a full-fledged college degree but demand a certain level of education or expertise in a particular field. While many life insurance, real estate, and travel agents may hold professional business or other degrees, they are more often identified as being in a "business" than in a "profession." The emphasis is on their sales and administrative abilities rather than their professional skills, and while one may question the validity of this distinction, there is no denying the fact that they are distinguished from the doctors and the engineers who are clearly the "professionals" admitted in the first wave of immigration in 1965.

The Indians who own TV stations or newspapers in the Chicago area are primarily seen as businesspeople, though they would likely fall into this category of "semi-professionals." Where do they rank in the socioeconomic ladder of the immigrant community? Some of them have achieved such spectacular financial success and contributed so heavily to the temples and the associations that they are easily accepted into the community of the professionals. At the same time, their command of the English language may be inadequate, they may have been educated in a village or small town in India, and they themselves may not be quite at ease with the urbane, sophisticated professional world. It is their business acumen that is responsible for their financial success, and they know that it is their financial success that gains them entry into the upper reaches of Indian immigrant society. Some of them have professional degrees but chose to function as independent agents for reasons of their own. Motivations for their choice are many, but are generally economic. The people in such businesses are self-made and have developed their own network of contacts that is suited to their particular business. The ethnic institutions they rely on heavily are the numerous associations through which they widen their contacts.

The Institutions of the "Professional Businesses"

The fifth and last group of immigrant business owners are those who have used their professional skills as a basis for their business enterprises. Here the conventional dichotomy between "professional" and "business owner" becomes even more blurred. Many of these entrepreneurs serve the industrial and high-tech sectors of the mainstream economy, and are particularly vulnerable to global market conditions. The majority of Indians who came in the first wave of the post-1965 immigration are acknowledged to be highly skilled professionals who "made it" in their own fields, and never thought of a career in business. It may seem that those who came in the second wave, the less qualified, sponsored kin are the ones who went into business for themselves because they had no marketable skills. The situation however can be different for both first-wave and second-wave immigrants. The professionals of the first wave cannot be dismissed as the "nonbusiness" kind. Many of them have successfully pursued a corporate career, and then abandoned the salaried job to become entrepreneurs. It could be an engineer who sets up a manufacturing plant, or a computer expert who sets up his or her own software development firm, or a communications specialist who buys and sells specialized equipment. On the other hand, it is also possible that among second-wave immigrants there were some highly qualified professionals who failed to find a job in an economy that had turned highly competitive. The same educational and skill level that some of the second-wave immigrants possessed could have secured a job for them easily in the 1970s and early 1980s, but it became increasingly inadequate in the economic climate of the late 1980s and early 1990s.

Many professionals have set up manufacturing and assembly plants in India that develop products for export. Their profitability is also due to the incentives given by the Indian government to encourage the setting up of such enterprises. The link with India for these entrepreneurs becomes even stronger because it is both personal and business-related, and conditions in India have a direct impact on their businesses. The Nonresident Indians form a particularly powerful lobby who are constantly trying to wrest concessions from the Indian government in return for increasing their participation in the Indian economy. Indians are invited to participate in India's modernization not only because India needs their investment dollars—estimated by professional investment bankers at a potential $10 billion each year—but because Indians can earn much higher returns in India than in the United States. Another attractive aspect of India for business investment lies in its respect for the rule of law, its industrial infrastructure, and its enormous pool of skilled labor.

The institutions that this sector of the Indian immigrant economy rely on most heavily are their own professional organizations, whether American or ethnic, as well as governmental and policy making organizations, not only in India and the United States but even world bodies such as the United Nations. The India Business Conference in Chicago has been meeting annually since 1992, bringing together representatives from business, government and top universities. After the liberalization of economic policies by the Rao government, teams of businessmen representing different industries travel regularly between India and the United States, sponsored by organizations such as the UNDP (United Nations Development Program), USAID (United States Agency for International Development), or the J. L. Kellogg School of Management. Students from Northwestern Kellogg's Business School have traveled to India to meet with government and business leaders since 1982 to study the business climate there first hand. Week-long conferences attract as many as five hundred CEOs and executives. Representatives of institutions such as the State Bank of India and the India Investment Center as well as top public officials from the different Indian states visit Chicago and speak in glowing terms of India's emergence as one of the most promising manufacturing and marketing centers in the world, and the potential advantages of a middle-class population of 250 million. These organizations also help NRIs and U.S. executives face key hurdles to doing business in India, such as government bureaucracy and red tape.

There are even instances where regional and linguistic affiliations of Indians play a decisive role in business. Telugu immigrants in Chicago are wooed by the state of Andhra Pradesh to set up industries in their own home state in India, and similarly, Malayalis in Kerala or Gujaratis in Gujarat. Some of these multimillion dollar industrial ventures are the result of cooperation between teams of professionals, such as doctors setting up a hospital complex in India, or even multinational ventures such as Indian immigrants setting up a consortium for manufacturing computer chips. The industries that attract such investment are mainly power, energy, oil refining, transportation and telecommunications, food processing, bio-technology, pharmaceuticals, and financial services. Indians are motivated as much by their sentiment for their homeland as they are by the profit instinct. The organizations that Indians turn to for support thus depends in large part on why and where they decide to locate their businesses. The state-owned State Bank of India and international banks such as Citicorp, Grindlays, and Hong Kong Bank play an important role in channeling NRI funds into specific programs in India. For example, Citibank held a joint seminar with India Medical Association to acquaint Indian physicians with monetary programs specially designed for them. The Indo-American Business Forum in Chicago is an organization that tries to bring together business groups and draw the attention of prominent politicians in the United States to the need for policy changes and legislation to make the climate more favorable to the Indian business community. For Indian immigrants, the entry of multinationals in an Indian market that was previously protected has meant that those familiar with U.S. capitalism have an extra edge as interpreters of the new business culture.

It is apparent that there is a common thread that runs through all the different types of business identified above, whether they provide work for wages and services to fellow immigrants or to other Americans. Some issues may be more relevant or significant in certain contexts, some issues may be specific only to a few situations, but on the whole the same concerns arise over and over again, namely, capital, labor, inventory, skill levels, family structure, structure of the economy, clientele, and geographic location. How and when opportunities arise and if they can be seized and availed of fully by the immigrant depend on a combination of these factors, and the kind of support available to them from institutions, whether within or outside the ethnic community. Roger Ballard was investigating just these factors when he tried to show how "a specific set of politico-economic differences on the one hand, together with an equally specific set of religio-cultural differences on the other, have interacted with the changes in the state of the British labour market as well as in the immigration rules to produce a strikingly varied set of outcomes." The same approach that he applied to Punjabis in Britain can be applied, with modifications, to Indian immigrant businesses in Chicago.[18]

The participation of Indian immigrant women in the business sector is governed by factors that affect the special world of immigration as well as the special world of women. Indian immigrant women thus have double jeopardy as minorities. Traditional and time-honored barriers are sometimes broken down and sometimes held to advantage, but they have never kept women out of business. Participation in business is increased for women both due to economic pressures and increased opportunities available in Chicago, so that whether a woman is a professional or is totally unskilled, she could still be actively participating in the economy. Indian women work as sales clerks on Devon Avenue and they also run international trading and technology transfer enterprises, shuttling between Europe or Hong Kong and South America the way many men do. Their main concern, however, is to overcome domestic barriers to participation in the economy, and the institutions that they have developed to cope with their own particular situation are discussed in the section on women's organizations.

The emergence of a separate immigrant economy has to be considered side by side with increasing immigrant participation in the existing mainstream economy. Chicago's immigrants have contributed to both, and in many cases, their new immigrant economy has turned out to be a global economy as well. The interaction between immigrant business and the host economy leads to constant modifications in both. Chicago's immigrants have made Indians aware of opportunities in the United States, even while they have interpreted India and the rapidly changing Indian scene to Americans who are still largely ignorant and unsure of conditions in India. As entrepreneurs they have created jobs and increased their status in their own and in American society. Occasionally, some fraudulent business practice and other negative report about members of the Indian business community has come to light. For instance, a female immigrant attorney pleaded guilty to charges of counseling her clients to lie to immigration officers and was sentenced. In another incident, FDA agents seized contaminated pest-infested foods at the House of Spices in Elk Grove Village. But these are minor, isolated cases and have not been brought to the attention of the general press or those outside the immigrant community.[19] Chicago's Indian immigrant businesses have generally been good for the community and for the city. They have not only availed themselves of existing institutions in Chicago to achieve these ends, but have also created their own institutions in response to a changing global scenario. The conventional as well as the hi-tech businesses have taken full advantage of the linking up of the modern world by the airlines, communication satellites and microwave relays that are now a part of day-to-day life for Indian immigrants and the economic reforms of the Narasimha Rao government in India have enabled the Chicago immigrants to exercise new options unthinkable a few years ago.

Political Organizations

The politically inclined Indian immigrants in Chicago are mainly of two kinds—those who believe that Indians should get more involved in the politics of the homeland and make a contribution to the survival of their own ideals in India, and those who believe that they should get more involved in local politics and be part of mainstream America. Still others believe that an informed Indian American citizenry should be knowledgeable and active in both areas. None of these groups has community-wide support. They operate with a small set of committed individuals who often feel they are up against a brick wall but continue to work because of their faith in their cause. Knowing how special interest groups work in democracies such as the United States and India, and that political mobilization in Chicago is clearly along racial and ethnic lines, they see that their strength lies in numbers. But with no issues on their agenda that Indians can see as critical or immediately relevant to their everyday lives, they don't grab the attention of the entire community.

Chicago Political Institutions

The record of Indians elected to public office in the United States is pretty dismal. Though several candidates have stood for political office, there are only five elected Asian-Indian officials in the entire nation. By contrast, there are three Indians elected to the Canadian House of Commons and two British Members of Parliament of Indian origin. Among those who stood for office in the Chicago area are Ahmed Patel for circuit court judge of Cook County (1990 and 1994), Om Dewan for Wheaton City councilman (1993), and Satya Ahuja for Burr Ridge Village trustee (1995). Dr. Jalil Ahmed, an Arizona businessman announced his plans to contest for retiring Democratic senator Paul Simon's office in December 1995. On the national scene, Peter Matthews of California, Neil Dhillon of Maryland, and Ram Uppuluri of Tennessee lost their bids for congressional seats in the anti-Democrat wave that swept the country in 1994. Peter Matthews has already announced his intention to run again in 1996. The first Indian woman to be elected to public office in the United States is Republican Nirmala McConigley who was elected to the Wyoming House of Delegates.[20]

The only person elected to office in the Chicago area was a 26-year-old dentist named Raj Ambegaonkar who became alderman of the third ward in Darien in 1993. His election surprised the Indian community since he was competing in an affluent 98 percent white suburban constituency against a respectable Republican incumbent who had been in office since the 1960s, but he won by taking only forty more votes than the competition. Ambegaonkar identified two factors that were particular stumbling blocks in his own campaign—gaining the confidence of the Indian community and getting them to support him with time and money. In February 1996, Ambegaokar was campaigning for election to the county board and was calling himself "Ambay" because, according to him, the voters could not "get past" his Indian name. He also said he was appalled at the extent of prejudice still prevalent against his ethnicity in the suburbs. He attributed his own victory to a dogged, grass-roots approach.[21]

The Indian community has adherents in both the Democratic and Republican parties. Though city residents usually vote Democratic and Devon Avenue businesses are behind Mayor Daley, the suburban elite voted for Republican Governor Jim Edgar. Their attitudes also change over time. Many sections of the Indian community became disillusioned with President Clinton's foreign policy—the sale of F-16s to Pakistan had the entire community up in arms—and wary of his health policies, though they were heavily supportive of him when he was first elected. Indian physicians were prepared to consider supporting Republican candidate Dole and invited him to explain his stand on health issues. Indians also identify those in power whom they consider "Friends of India" and invite them to campaign at their national conferences. In India, Indians have traditionally aligned themselves with the Democratic Party. Democratic Presidents Kennedy, Carter, and Johnson were all seen as friendly to India while Republicans, especially Nixon, are perceived as anti-India. Among the Democrats who have earned the confidence of Indians in the United States are Senator Paul Simon and Congressman Stephen Solarz. Very often, members of the Indian community vote for candidates based on their individual qualities, regardless of party affiliation. Such uncertainties keep politicians courting the Indian community.

Politicians also have a healthy respect for the fund raising capabilities of Indians. Many of the associations are quite successful in getting politicians to make personal appearances at their annual events. Illinois Democratic senator Carol Moseley Braun was guest of honor at the annual dinner dance of the Club of Indian Women held in May 1993. Minor city and state politicians show up regularly at Indian functions, eager to become more visible in the Asian American community. But the real feather in the cap for the Indians in Chicago was when they were able to get President Clinton to be the featured speaker at the thirteenth annual conference of the American Association of Physicians of Indian origin (AAPI) held June 29–July 2, 1995. The price, however, was stiff. One hundred and twenty-two physicians presented checks, at $1,000 apiece, which they handed to the Democratic Party without any immediate or tangible returns. Instead, all they got was a short speech at which "the President spoke judiciously, sticking to protocol and promising nothing" as one editorial put it.[22] Other featured speakers were House minority leader Democrat Richard Gephardt and the chairman of the commerce committee, Republican senator Larry Pressler. Such high profile activities are not necessarily greeted with unmixed approval by the Indian community. Many participating physicians complained that the money the Indians handed over to the Democratic party "on a platter" was a waste. Clinton's fifteen-minute keynote address at the inaugural session merely reiterated his intention to revive health care reform and to include Indian physicians in the process. Such vague and noncommittal remarks made some members furious that AAPI had failed to establish clear and articulate goals and get a firm commitment from political leaders before making massive contributions to them. Others saw it as a step in the right direction since a professional association had favorably spotlighted the entire Indian immigrant community and set the stage for influencing policy. Observers have commented that the obsession Indians have for the "photo-op" makes them spend hundreds of dollars merely for the privilege of having their picture taken with a prominent politician. No effort is made to develop a political, issue-oriented platform on which Indians can unite and adopt a bargaining stance. Without knowing which specific causes to fight for or which grievances to air in a united, public forum, Indians are seen as throwing away their resources in gaining fleeting publicity when they would be much better off channeling it into service-oriented projects.

Besides disunity and apathy toward political issues, there are other reasons for the generally poor showing of Indians in this sphere. One is that their numbers are too few for them to have a significant impact on Chicago politics. They have to adopt a strategy of cooperation with other ethnic communities and coalition-building with other political organizations in order to make a difference, but this remains a difficult goal. The Asian American Political Action Committee (AAPAC) was born of the realization that Asians are too widely scattered geographically in the city and suburbs to benefit from the kind of district restructuring that has helped Latinos and African Americans in Chicago gain political representation, so they need to show their strength in other ways.[23] The main activity of AAPAC is to organize an annual lunar year celebration dinner at which one of the eight different Asian American communities that it represents plays host. (The Indian community hosted it in 1987 and 1994.) Though the AAPAC has no regular agenda or follow up activity, the annual event serves to send a signal to the political parties that the Asians in Chicago are united and must have fair representation in state and city councils. Coalition building has remained difficult because Asians tend to vote more like whites rather than along ethnic lines. Without consensus among themselves, cooperation with blacks or Hispanics seems an even more distant possibility. For years, the activists in the Indian community in Chicago have tried to get Indians interested in political issues but to no avail. "Indians are only keen on cultural extravaganzas, they are not interested in issue-oriented politics," lamented Ranjit Ganguly, founder member of the Indo-American Democratic Organization (IADO). "In fact, to most Indians here, politics is a dirty word. They don't realize that if you don't organize politically, you don't exist, at least in the eyes of the government."[24]

IADO was started in 1980 when members of the Indian community realized that no matter how active they were socially and culturally as a group, City Hall wouldn't pay any attention to them unless they were a political body. "Once when Zubin Mehta was chief guest at an India League of America function," said Ganguly, "City Hall sent a lowly clerk to represent the Mayor, and the clerk sat right up there with prominent members of our community. That's when we realized we would never gain the respect and recognition we deserved if we didn't create a political identity of our own." IADO was thus formed to gain legitimacy and recognition in the host society, not in response to some inner need felt within the immigrant community. It was registered as a not-for-profit political organization with a membership of two hundred. "George Dunne promised to help us only if it was a Democratic party organization, so we went ahead and registered ourselves that way," said Ganguly. "Anyway, Cook County, where most of us were at that time, was heavily Democratic, so it made sense." There is no corresponding Republican body among Indian immigrants though committees are formed on an *ad hoc* basis at election time. There has been some talk of making a united and focused nonpartisan effort to educate the community and develop a political agenda, but nothing has come of it so far.

Membership in IADO has grown to five hundred over the years, but is still far short of representing the strength of the community. Its merit lies in that it has forced people to sit up and take notice of Indians as an ethnic group. IADO prides itself on the fact that Chicago's political candidates actively seek its endorsement. It organized a candidates' forum where Dawn Clark Netsch, Ronald Burris, and Richard Phelan presented their stands on issues and sought the support of the community in December 1993. IADO members helped to register two thousand new voters in 1994 by making house calls on newly naturalized citizens, holding educational seminars, setting up booths on Devon Avenue and at *gurdwaras* and temples, and by working with other ethnic groups. They have worked with different groups on different issues, teaming up with the Latin American community for voter registration, with the African-American community on affirmative action and discrimination, and with other Asians on the issue of fair representation in civic bodies.

On the question of voter registration, Ganguly observed that Indians were naturalized at a fairly high rate. In the 1990 Census, approximately one-third of Indian immigrants were naturalized citizens. Between 1984 and 1993, 11,159 Indian immigrants in Illinois were naturalized. The only other countries of origin for immigrants with higher naturalization figures were Mexico (19,196) and Philipines (14,408).[25] Ganguly observed that the motives for naturalization among Indians are related to family reunification benefits, scholarship benefits for college-going youth, and Social Security benefits for the elderly. Indians were not particularly interested in the voting process. Many of them shied away from becoming registered voters because that would make them liable for jury duty. They didn't think that government policy affected them directly. They believed that if they had made good in America, it was through their own hard work and skills, not because of any government handouts. Only the businesses on Devon Avenue felt they were beneficiaries of the affirmative action programs and worried about legislation. Ganguly noted the anomaly in the behavior of Indians.

> Americans believe that greater education makes for greater participation in the political process. That's not so at all for Indians. It's strange but true that those with the lowest educational levels in Chicago, the Mexicans, have the same low voter participation as the most highly educated group in Chicago, the Indians. Indians don't realize that making political contributions and projecting an image of success is not enough. They have to get out and vote.

IADO bears testimony to the fact that while Indians in Chicago are not yet stirred to political action for a variety of reasons, they have made a beginning; if at any time they should choose to become more active in politics, they can count on IADO for support. The organization supports independent candidates and those who run on a bipartisan basis, especially in the suburban areas, if they are Indian American. As Ganguly points out, the first step to gaining political office is interacting with the community at the local level. Indians are so busy with their own ethnic organizations, very few have made the effort to interact even with their neighbors.

The excuse for political inaction that held good in the early years of immigration is, however, becoming obsolete in the 1990s. Back then, the argument was that Indians had no real problems. As an economically successful group, they had no need to fight political battles; the theory was that only the poor or dispossessed or those on the fringes of society needed to get politically organized. With the growth and heightened visibility of the Indian community have come a host of problems such as job discrimination, racial attacks, and restrictive immigration laws. The Indian community is slowly waking up to these issues; more and more of the conferences and association conventions take note of these trends and try to organize the community to tackle them effectively. The hate crime wave that rocked the Indian American community in 1994 was concentrated mainly in the New York–New Jersey area, but it served to sensitize Chicago Indians to the possibility that they could also become victims of similar racial attacks. Sixteen separate incidents of racially motivated violence against Indians were reported in a two-month period in New Jersey in 1994. In 1995, four fatal attacks on Indian businessmen were reported from Elizabeth, New Jersey. Attacks have been reported in many other cities of North America, including Toronto.[26] So far, there have been only a couple of incidents of alleged racism against Indians in Chicago reported in the ethnic press. An Indian family in Chicago filed suit against their neighbors for harassment and "insulting their ethnicity," and in another report, a gas station owner at Addison and California described how he was robbed frequently and subjected to ethnic slurs. Sometimes malpractice suits against doctors have been construed as evidence of racism and discrimination. Of the 222 hate crimes in Chicago reported by the Chicago Commission on Human Relations in 1994, 22 were in the North Town neighborhood, which was the leading city neighborhood for such crimes in one year (18 of these 22 crimes were against Jews, and consisted mostly of damage to their synagogues). Because Indian merchants of Devon Avenue are located in this area, they fear that they could become highly visible targets of hate crimes, should the public mood swing against them due to international events or other political developments beyond their control. Such fears have also prompted the AIA to plan a civil rights council called the Council on Education and Legal Action, based on the need to act collectively to combat racism.[27]

It is difficult to say whether increasing racism toward Indians is due to the increase in lower-class immigrants or the increased visibility of upper-class immigrants because of the overall increase in the numbers. Both are probably important factors since white- and blue-collar Indians have both experienced discrimination.. The economic success of Indians masks the discrimination and racial slurs that they have to endure, and blinds the public to the more subtle forms of job discrimination against them. There are, however, many studies to show that Asian Americans trail whites when it comes to achieving corporate, political, and academic power.[28] Indians in Chicago have documented instances of discrimination toward Indian medical graduates and academics. In a collection of papers presented in May 1995 to the Illinois Advisory Committee to the United States Commission on Civil Rights entitled "Civil Rights Issues Facing Asian Americans in Metropolitan Chicago," Dr. Kishore J. Thampy, past president of the American College of International Physicians, wrote of discrimination against medical professionals by way of visa hurdles, obstacles in training, licensing and employment, while Dr. Ashish Sen, professor of urban planning at the University of Illinois at Chicago wrote bitterly of being left out of the inner circle and excluded from high paying administrative jobs in academia throughout his career. For every "success story" of an Indian scientist or CEO, there are many unreported stories of deserving candidates being denied just rewards on account of their ethnicity. Sometimes, Indians have been emboldened to fight their case in court as in the case of a county engineer in Fairfax, Virginia, who was backed by the NAACP.[29] The problem has drawn congressional attention. Democratic Congressman Martin T. Meehan of Massachusetts urged Congress to pay more attention to "racial harassment, hate crimes and discrimination against Indian Americans in many parts of the country."[30]

If the anti-immigration mood prevalent in the United States in the mid-1990s were to grow, the future for renewed Indian immigration could be bleak. As in an earlier era of restrictive immigration (1917 and 1924), Indians are not well mobilized to influence policy changes in the government. Immigration attorneys who serve the Indian community in Chicago say that there is no lobbying or any collective action on the part of the Indian organizations to fight these trends.

Political Institutions Connected with the Homeland

Though Indians in Chicago are interested in happenings in the homeland, there are very few issues exciting enough for them to become aggressively involved. One reason why Indians are complacent is that they are generally supportive of the government in India and seek to work in cooperation with it rather than trying to change it from the outside. Unlike Iraqi or Iranian immigrants who may have strong antipathy toward the government in power in their homeland, Indians are generally approving of the Indian government and likely to defend its foreign policy even when it has assumed anti-American overtones. When Nixon's notorious "tilt" toward Pakistan was exposed during the Indo-Pak war, Indians in Chicago applauded Indira Gandhi's gutsy 'standing up' to a superpower, and roundly denounced the U.S. government's actions as unfair.

The one area in which politics in the homeland has great potential to be volatile is in the mix of religion and politics. But even the Sikh and Muslim communities in Chicago are comparatively trouble-free in this respect. The Sikh community in Chicago has had ongoing tensions with the Indian government after the Golden Temple incident but has maintained a low profile, without indulging in any inflammatory anti-India rhetoric of the kind that came out regularly from other predominantly Sikh areas around the world, such as Southall in England. In the mid- to late 1990s, however, both in England and in India, there was disenchantment among Sikhs with the self-seeking militants.[31] Criticism from the Muslim community in Chicago is directed more against particular political parties in India than the government. In a rare display of protest in Chicago, a plenary session at the World Parliament of Religions meet in 1994 "Voices of the Dispossessed" was disrupted by a Kashmiri Muslim and a Sikh who denounced the Indian state, but their protests were quickly subdued.[32]

One Chicago organization that is sharply critical of the Indian state is India Alert. Their mission is to monitor civil and human rights violations in India, but the Indian immigrant community is not much inclined to pay attention to them. Even when they highlight serious abuses in India such as bride-burning and dowry deaths, the Indian immigrants in Chicago see it as an "Indian" problem, not an "Indian American" one. This is notwithstanding at least one case of wife abuse related to dowry which has occurred in Chicago's Indian community, according to Apna Ghar workers. Members of India Alert could not make their voices heard in the general public above the din of complaints about far grosser violations in China or South America.

The Overseas Friends of the BJP, which was set up in New York in 1991 to disseminate party ideology, has branches in Los Angeles, Washington, and Chicago. The BJP-VHP combine as it is referred to in the Indian press (the "troika" also includes the RSS or Rashtriya Swayam Sevak Sangh) is a powerful mouthpiece because it has a large following within the Indian business community and top professionals in both Canada and the United States. The same Indian immigrants who espoused Nehru's ideals of secularism when they moved out of India are now being wooed by the BJP in the hope that they will rise to the defense of Hinduism if they can be convinced that it is threatened in its own homeland. The active BJP-VHP membership in North America is said to exceed twenty thousand. Some of the party's objectives, such as developing a common civil code and reserving the right to develop nuclear weapons for self-defense, have strong appeal for those who want a strong and united India. The BJP has also promised dual citizenship for NRIs.[33] Besides echoing the party line, Overseas Friends of the BJP makes arrangements for visits of party leaders to the United States. They ensure that they get a chance to meet U.S. government representatives such as State governors, Congressional leaders and State Department officials. After the Babri Masjid incident, BJP party leaders toured the United States, Canada, and the Caribbean "to acquaint people in the west with crucial facts about Ayodhya."[34]

One problem that capitalist NRIs have with the BJP is that the party is turning away from its once proclaimed ideology of a free-market economy and instead becoming increasingly protectionist. Its rhetoric against multinationals—"stop the rape of Mother India by Uncle Sam"—is dismissed by some Indians as a vote-getting ploy, but others see it as damaging to NRI business interests in India. The scrapping of the Enron power deal by the Maharashtra government (for which the BJP took at least part of the "credit") in July of 1995 shook the Indian investment community in Chicago. NRIs are also alienated when the BJP urges Indian businessmen to treat India as "a nation, not a market" and to be wary of collaboration with foreign companies.

It appears that Chicago's Indian immigrants have still to come of age, politically speaking. Their numerical strength is far greater than their political activity would indicate, but still not enough to make a dent in Chicago area politics. Their dispersed pattern of settlement works against them and their tax dollars go to benefit their particular neighborhood and the federal coffers rather than their own ethnic community. Indians have noticed that other ethnics such as the Latinos and African Americans who live in clusters are able to benefit from restructuring for better representation, but they have not yet developed alternate strategies to use the system to their own advantage. Given these conditions in Chicago, Indians are more likely to gain political prominence through nominated offices than through elected offices, at least in the near future.

11

PURSUING SPECIAL INTERESTS
Professional Groups and the Media

Ethnicity is not merely a static assumption. Instead, it provides a
strategy for managing individual and group impressions, so as to
accrue benefits and avoid sanctions.
    —Richard Harvey Brown, "Migration and Modernization:
        Theoretical Issues for Further Research"

One of the strongest links in the web of connections among Indian immigrants in Chicago is the professional one. Though Indians do belong to
mainstream professional organizations such as the American Medical Association or the American Society of Engineers, they have also grouped separately as ethnics in their professional capacity. Most of the professional
organizations were formed in the 1980s when Indians realized they needed
to go beyond informal networking in order to further their career and business interests. They also saw that by coming together as professionals, they
could contribute to the welfare of India by transferring their technological
expertise and material resources such as hi-tech equipment through organized channels. This was one way of giving back directly to the motherland
what they had received in high quality, government-subsidized education in
India, and also a way of maintaining emotional ties to the past. Also the
growing conservative climate in the United States in the 1980s alarmed
many Indians who felt they had to band together and network among themselves in order to be professionally successful. Like the pan-Indian associations discussed earlier, these organizations cut across linguistic, regional
and religious lines, giving Indians a chance to meet on purely professional
grounds, and to rally around issues that interest them rather than their

religion or language alone. There are state and regional chapters to these national associations, such as the Illinois Chapter of the Association of Scientists of Indian Origin in America. The big opportunity for all members to meet is, of course, the annual conventions that are held on no less grand a scale than the annual events of the other types of associations.

Some professional organizations have their headquarters in the East Coast, such as the American Society of Engineers of Indian Origin. But no matter where their administrative office might be located, they tend to be global in their reach. The Asian Indian Architects Association was founded in 1993 and has both Indian and American connections through its affiliation to the Indian Institute of Architects in Bombay and the American Institute of Architects in Washington, D.C. The Association of Indian Neurologists—there are an estimated five hundred neurologists of Indian origin in the United States—was also formed in 1993. It develops student and faculty exchange programs between India and America. The Association of Asian Indians in Ophthalmology, formed in 1981, also sponsors exchange students from India so they may learn the latest techniques through short courses in the United States.

Professional Medical Organizations

The medical profession is probably the best organized among all the groups with professional associations in the Indian community. Several factors have contributed to this. The medical community takes some inspiration, no doubt, from the American Medical Association, which certainly sets its own high standards as a powerful lobbying group. The financial resources available in the Indian medical community have helped. Last, Indian doctors are very much aware that they owe their success to a certain set of historical circumstances which enabled them to make good as immigrants and earn disproportionately high salaries compared to other Indian professionals, and present conditions could be quickly upset in the changing scenario of health care in the nation. Not being organized to combat hostile influences could cost them dearly. Bill and Hillary Clinton made such an issue of health care reform in the 1992 election campaign that Indian doctors became alarmed at policy changes that could affect their practice. Managed care facilities were being asked to make decisions affecting physicians and patients based on a new cost-consciousness. Though safeguarding their own interests and monitoring the Washington scene was always part of the agenda of professional associations, it acquired renewed urgency in the 1990s and helped the medical professional organizations grow in size and importance.

American Association of Physicians from India

Chicago-area Indian immigrant doctors belong to one or more of the following professional associations: India Medical Association of Illinois, American College of International Physicians (a mainly Asian group of international medical graduates), and the American Association of Physicians from India (AAPI). Using AAPI as a case study, since it is pre-eminent among Indian professional organizations, it is possible to illustrate how professional associations in the Indian community are shaped by local, national, and international concerns. AAPI (headquartered in Michigan) was formed in 1982 and, after thirteen years of existence, claimed to represent twenty-six thousand Asian Indian physicians in the United States. More than half of these physicians belong to AAPI either directly or through affiliation with its eighty-nine member associations. It has five thousand members, more than half of whom are patron members, and spacious executive offices in Oakbrook Terrace, acquired in 1994, with a full-time administrative staff and a toll-free number. In 1994, it reported a general operating account of $275,000, a cash balance of $40,000 and a patron fund of $200,000. Obviously, the organization is not hampered by budgetary constraints.[1]

AAPI's most spectacular coup was when it managed to get President Clinton to be the featured speaker at its thirteenth annual convention held at the Chicago Sheraton from June 30 to July 2, 1995. It was the first time ever that a sitting President had addressed an Indian professional organization. Notwithstanding the controversy over the fact that Clinton did make a quick, easy and substantial addition to his campaign coffers at the expense of the Indian community, his presence at AAPI 1995 had a symbolic significance for all Indians, and for Indian physicians in particular. It showed that between 1965 and 1995 Indians had made the transition from an "invisible, model minority" to an organized, visible group with problems that they could address only through political involvement. When Indian doctors first came to the United States in the 1960s, they were welcomed with open arms because they were filling a need in the American economy. But in the 1990s circumstances had changed. It is estimated that by the year 2000, there will be 164,000 surplus doctors in the United States, and Indians fear that foreign doctors like themselves will be the first to suffer. As early as the

1980s, the foreign medical graduates or FMGs were beginning to protest discriminatory laws that set tougher licensing standards for them than for domestic medical graduates. A coalition body, the International Association of American Physicians (consisting of five different but all mainly Asian medical groups, including AAPI), managed to get Congress to examine discriminatory licensing practices in 1992; but lack of follow-up action and ineffective leadership along with continued infighting among FMGs have hampered further progress. Complicating the scene is an anti-immigrant mood in the country that has led Indians to perceive the discriminatory laws as both racially and economically motivated. Physicians from India still feel vulnerable to the prejudices of American society and organizations such as AAPI continue to study the impact of political mechanisms related to health care policies. So far, there is not much evidence that high visibility and the relative affluence of the medical community have necessarily translated into effective lobbying for Indian immigrants.

Apart from their political agenda, Indian professional organizations have done much work in providing continuing medical education both for their members here and their counterparts in India. Experts give lectures and seminars at regular professional meetings, and sponsor the visits of physicians from India so they may catch up with U.S. technology in certain fields. AAPI has a Charitable Foundation which operates nine medical clinics in India and conducts eye camps. There is also much effort put into raising AIDS awareness, both in India and the United States, especially in light of United Nations reports that India will soon be leading the world in number of AIDS cases, and already has the highest rate of increase in the world. The India Medical Association has teamed up with the Indo-American Center, a social service agency on Devon Avenue, to provide free medical services to the under-insured and needy immigrants in the Chicago area. Like other Indian organizations in Chicago and in keeping with the need to look ahead, AAPI has a medical students and residents wing that addresses the needs of a younger generation.

Other Professional Organizations

The activities of professional organizations such as AAPI show that Indian immigrants are anxious to channel their gains back into the Indian community, both locally and internationally. Schools for NRI children are being built in Ahmedabad and the outskirts of New Delhi with funds from professional organizations. The Indian Professional Non-resident Association (IPNA) is an organization founded by doctors, engineers, journalists, and managers from the United States, Britain, and the Gulf countries. IPNA is committed to building schools, hospitals, housing, and other social projects in India that are of direct benefit to NRIs and at the same time strengthen the link with India. Just as there are global conventions of Indians belonging to different religions or speaking different languages, so too there are global conventions of Indians belonging to different professions. The Global Convention of Indian Nurses was held in New York in June–July 1995 and was attended by nurses from Canada, Europe, the Middle East, and India, besides the United States.[2]

An interesting offshoot of the professional nature of the Indian immigration to the United States is that so many immigrants graduated from a few select universities in India that it led to the formation of several alumni associations. Not only have colleges and universities in India sent record numbers of their graduates to the United States, there is even an American institution in the Chicago area that has graduated a sufficient number of Indians to warrant the formation of a separate Indian alumni association. The Illinois Institute of Technology (often referred to in Chicago as the "Indian Institute of Technology") formed its Indian alumni chapter in July 1995. Among the major Indian institutions that have their own alumni groups are New Delhi's All India Institute of Medical Sciences (AIIMSONI-ANS of America, founded in 1981) and Banaras Hindu University. The Baroda Medical College, which celebrated its second annual convention in Oak Brook in July 1993, has an estimated 1200 medical graduates in the United States. The BJ Medical College in Ahmedabad sent at least 1,000 of its 1,800 graduates to the United States and they have their own alumni association. The avowed mission of these alumni associations is to assist their members who are seeking jobs or who need help in setting up a business, to extend technology and education programs to their alma mater by sponsoring Indian students for additional education and training in the United States, and to supply Indian universities with updated research material. The fund-raising capacities of some of these organizations is quite formidable—the Baroda Medical College raised $45,000 for its alma mater in 1993—and they play an important role in keeping immigrants connected to the homeland in tangible and intangible ways.[3]

The Network of Young Indian Professionals (NETIP) is not really a professional organization as its name suggests but more of a social group where young men and women can meet others of similar socioeconomic backgrounds. Established in Chicago in 1990 with twenty members, it was the brainchild of a first-generation Indian immigrant who felt that second generation Indians had a different agenda and should organize separately from their parents. By 1995, NETIP had become a loose federation of four-teen chapters across the United States with a membership of one thousand. Its avowed aims of "fostering professional development, community service and political awareness" remain on a higher plane than its day-to-day activi-ties which consist of "wine and cheese get-togethers" and "bi-weekly lunches at downtown restaurants." The organization is still apparently in search of an identity, according to a past president.[4] The latest debate gripping the members was whether to call themselves "young Indian professionals" or "young Indian American professionals." In Houston, where more and more recent Gujarati immigrants have become members, the vote was for keeping the word "American" out of the title. Chicago NETIP members, who are mostly second-generation Indians born and brought up in the United States, wanted to call themselves "Indian Americans."[5] Many young Indian professionals in Chicago dismiss NETIP as no more than a dating ground that will outlive its usefulness as more sophisticated matchmaking networks take over, while others believe that it will find an appealing professional agenda and increase in strength.

Social Service Organizations

Long after the Indian community in Chicago had changed from an elite, highly skilled and affluent group to a more motley crowd that included non-English speaking, unskilled and often destitute immigrants, the community itself did not recognize the growing need for social services among its mem-bers. "Problems" were equated with "failure" and the early warning signs of trouble in paradise were at first greeted with denial. The only need for humanitarian aid that the Indian community acknowledged was for Indians in India. So the first service organizations that sprang up targeted the poor and underdeveloped villages of India. It was not until the late 1980s that the need for social services among Chicago's own Indian community surfaced and became so obvious that the community geared up to handle it. The 1990 Census shows that 10 percent of Asian Indians had income below the poverty level. The figure for those who entered between 1980 and 1990 is 14 percent compared to 5 percent for those who came before 1980, and the reduced prosperity in the national Asian Indian population is reflected among Chicago's Indians, too. The spreading unemployment in the depressed economy of the late 1980s affected not only the newer immigrants who lacked job skills but the skilled, white-collar managers, engineers, and scientists, some of whom were laid off *en masse*, as Chicago shifted gears from a manufacturing to a service-oriented economy. Indians in Chicago have not yet swelled the ranks of welfare recipients, but more and more newly arrived Indians, especially the elderly, need financial assistance, lack medical insurance, and live isolated lives. The circumstances were ripe for social service agencies and, by 1995 at least half a dozen had sprung up, most of them located in the north and northwest of Chicago including the South Asian Family Services, the Suburban Family Services, the Metropolitan Asian Family Services, the Kiran Foundation, the Hamdard Center for Health and Human Services, the Asian Human Services, and the Indo-American Center. Most of them provide a similar set of services to their clients ranging from family-oriented services such as health care and education for the elderly or parenting classes for single mothers to legal counseling, job training, and immigration services. Another common feature is that all these agencies operate with funding from a variety of sources including city, state, and federal grants, corporate funding, and private donations. The quality of service provided is usually proportional to the size of the staff—those with little or no funding rely mostly on volunteer help and stay open for just a few hours a day, and others, notable among them the Asian Human Services with enough funding to employ a full-fledged staff, manage to provide a wide range of services.[6]

The Indo-American Center

One agency that has responded to the growing needs of the community is the Indo-American Center located in the heart of India town on Devon Avenue. A nonsectarian, nonprofit center, it serves people of all ethnic groups—the entire South Asian community as well as Iranians, Russians, Assyrians and Arabs who live in the area. It has opened its doors to anyone who asks for help, regardless of ethnicity, religion, language or politics. The organization was founded in 1990 by M. K. G. Pillay (1924–94), an immigrant who came to Chicago when he was already fifty years old and struggled hard to establish himself in the early years. As a student, he had participated in the Quit India movement and had gained experience as an administrator in the Indian Air Force, but he found it hard to get a job in Chicago and worked at menial tasks for the first two years. He knew first-hand the difficulties faced by immigrants who are down and out, and he was determined to set up a community organization that would address their needs. Taking his cue from the other successful Asian organizations run by the Chinese, Japanese, and Korean communities in the area, he launched a variety of programs to address the concerns of the elderly, the unemployed, and the illiterate. He held various offices in community organizations including presidentship of the Federation of India Associations before launching the Indo-American Center. In 1992, he was honored by the City of Chicago when he was elected to its Hall of Fame for Senior Citizens, the only Indian to gain this distinction.

Among the most successful programs of the Center is the Citizen's Outreach program, which enables immigrants to become United States citizens. Instructional classes in English, U.S. history, constitution, and government are conducted by volunteers for immigrants who choose to become citizens. By 1995, the Center had processed over 4,000 citizenship applications and more than 1,200 persons had become U.S. citizens through its Outreach program. The Immigration and Naturalization Service conducted interviews at the Center's premises, making it easier for the immigrants to complete the citizenship process in their own neighborhood. The Center's adult literacy programs are also very popular and many older Indian immigrants who live in the neighborhood have availed themselves of its educational programs. The Center is part of the Northside Coalition through which it cooperates with other ethnic community organizations, especially the Asian ones, to avail of a pool of funds and implement its literacy and citizenship programs. In 1994, the Center became the venue for a free medical clinic run by the India Medical Association (Illinois) Charitable Foundation. The clinic is supported by a coalition that includes other organizations such as the Association of Indian Pharmacists and Ravenswood Hospital and Medical Center. Its goals are to provide basic and preventive health care, public health education, and support community health care research. Other programs of the Indo-American Center include an ethnic dialogue program that invites tourists, students, researchers, and anyone else who is curious about Indians in Chicago to engage in a conversation with representatives of the community and learn more about Indian traditions and the ways of Indian immigrants.

The Indo-American Center provides an example of how organizations grow from very shaky beginnings and the vision of a single individual to a broad-based institution that cooperates with other organizations in the host society and claims the devotion and loyalty of several members who can carry on the work beyond the span of a single lifetime. The Center passed an important milestone when it acquired a permanent building and a paid staff in 1996. According to its founder Pillay, what was holding back growth was a lack of awareness on the part of Indians about how to tap all the resources available to them for social service. Though the Koreans and Japanese were much fewer in number, their leadership was more organized and more aggressive about procuring funding and more service-oriented than the Indian leadership. The Indians in Chicago who busied themselves with career advancement and temple-building were not attuned to championing social causes. In an interview before his sudden death in 1994, Pillay expressed deep concern about the social and class divisions within the Indian community and the urgent need to bridge the gap. In its own way, the Indo-American Center provides an avenue for those who are well-off in the community to directly assist those who are less fortunate among them, brings together the suburbanites and the city-dwellers, and creates a sense of community that goes beyond geographical proximity and cuts across class, gender and generation gaps.

Other Volunteer Organizations

Among the social service activities of Indian organizations must be counted the help given by Indian cultural and religious institutions to the larger American population. The Balaji Temple contributes toward aid for the homeless, runs soup kitchens, and provides clothing for the needy in Aurora.[7] Mention has already been made of the Thanksgiving feasts that Indian communities host on a regular basis. This is not only done as part of the Hindu tradition of giving to the less fortunate; it is specifically aimed at countering the bad publicity and hostility toward temple building that Indians have encountered from the local population. Other organizations in Chicago focus on the needs of the poor in India. The North-South Foundation, taking a page out of American fund-raising methodology, conducts "bikea-thons" and "walkathons" to collect money for subsidizing the education of bright but needy students in India. It has a sister organization in India through which it disburses its scholarships called BREAD (Basic Research Education and Development Society) and encourages scholastic achievement among students by conducting its own spelling bee contests.

The India Development Society (IDS) calls itself the "largest volunteer organization in North America which supports sustainable development." It was started in 1974 by a group of Indians who wanted to promote change and encourage activism in India rather than merely hand out charity. Their strategy for change was to adopt and support projects in many different parts of India, especially the rural and impoverished areas, where villagers could avail themselves of modern technology through the help of specialists and integrate it into their own lives. Thus "improvement" and "development" would be engineered by the people themselves rather than foisted from without. IDS provides technical information and assists with startup costs with the ultimate goal of letting go at some point when the projects become self-sustaining. As "catalysts for change," they are also committed to educating their three-hundred-odd members about the development process. Visiting scholars and activists from India interact with Chicago's Indians at seminars and workshops, keeping them abreast of and involved in developments in India. The National Conference for Sustainable Development in India was held at the Illinois Institute of Technology in September 1994 and featured speakers from India on topics such as the environment, population, AIDS, and human rights. As in the other religious and cultural organizations, the second generation have formed their own subgroup in IDS called Action for India. They organize events of their own under the guidance of the parent organization.

Some organizations based in India could have some impact on the lives of Indians in the United States such as the Rajiv Gandhi Foundation, established in New Delhi in 1991. The foundation counts among its goals the "spreading of Indian values throughout the world" and has inducted prominent community members from the Indian American population to implement its programs. Many are from the Chicago area, including Sam Pitroda, a telecommunications expert who once served as advisor to Rajiv Gandhi and relocated to his home town of Chicago after Gandhi was assassinated. Efforts at this stage are at the policy-making and planning levels and have not trickled down to the day-to-day lives of the Indian immigrants. Individual efforts to do social service in India are also conducted under the banner of "foundations." For example, the Jyoti Children's Development Foundation, headquartered in Skokie in 1986, was started by a biochemistry professor at Northwestern University in order to fund a school for the deaf in Kanpur, India. While the activity conducted by most of these not-for-profit, charitable organizations is legitimate, there are a few that are no more than fronts for tax shelters and ploys to enrich certain individuals. Insiders say that there is some abuse of funds obtained for training and development from state agencies but no charges have been leveled and no fraud has as yet come to light. Those organizations that have broad-based support and look for funding beyond the sphere of private donations from a few select members of the Indian community are, of course, subject to rigorous scrutiny and are the ones that survive in the long term.

Women's Organizations

One might wonder why Indian women in Chicago would need organizations of their own when such a multitude of associations already exist within the Indian community. It would seem that they could find a way to express themselves and fulfill their needs through any one or more of the scores of cultural, religious, social service, and professional organizations. The women are regularly invited to hold office and serve on the committees and are as involved as the men in organizational activities. Their involvement, however, is at a generally subordinate level, befitting the Indian patriarchal tradition. Most women, no matter how hard they work and how hefty a donation they make to a temple or a building fund, rarely rise above the office of vice president or treasurer and generally wind up serving on the "cultural" or "publicity" committees. The outstanding exceptions are, as mentioned before, Dr. Sudha Rao, president of the Hindu Temple, Dr. Nayeem Shariff, president of Association of Indians in America (Chicago chapter), and Dr. Ann (Lata) Kalayil, president of Indo-American Democratic Organization.

Club of Indian Women

The only organization where women could be in complete control was one where the membership was entirely female. Though the Club of Indian Women hardly started out with the idea of empowering women in this fashion and giving them an opportunity for leadership they might not have access to elsewhere, that is just what it succeeded in doing. Many of the women who organize club activities, arrange for seminars, conduct workshops, and head the committees acknowledge that they might not have blossomed along these lines if they were not part of an ethnic women's group. The Club of Indian Women began as a social group in 1978, when lonely housewives got together to share their experiences as immigrants in a strange land. In 1982 it acquired formal status and became the first organization of Asian American women in Chicago. Over the years, it grew into an activity-oriented club, gaining in membership with two hundred members in 1995 and acquiring the respect of local women politicians who regularly grace its annual events. In 1983, it started an Indo-Crisis Line in response to the needs of women in distress; in 1986, it started the Network of Working Women to address the needs of professional women among its members; and in 1993, a senior citizens' group was formed to help the parents of immigrants adjust to life in Chicago. Its ability to respond to the need of the hour has been its main strength but it has not been able to draw the second generation into its fold. The club's attempts to start a second-generation youth wing in 1995 met with no success. Indian women of the second generation who are caught up with career and marriage issues and don't feel alienated from the mainstream to the same extent as their mothers don't see the club as particularly relevant to their needs. The club's main events are an annual ethnic fair—the Meena Bazaar—that helps raise money for scholarships for needy Indian women, and a glittering annual dinner-dance at which luminaries such as Illinois Democratic senator Carol Moseley Braun and Illinois state comptroller Loleta Didrickson are chief guests. The Club donates money from its fund raisers to other social service organizations such as Apna Ghar, India Development Society, and Asian Human Services. At one meeting that was especially called in 1991 to redefine the club's objectives and formulate a mission statement, some members expressed dissatisfaction with its elitist image as a group of rich Punjabi women who meet in expensive homes in Oakbrook and whose activities are confined to traditionally feminine areas such as cooking, decorating, and fashion. They were anxious to broaden their membership base, induct younger women and reach out to other socioeconomic levels of the Indian community by offering practical and useful programs. Other members, however, insisted that their social teas and slumber parties were a very enjoyable and important part of their programming and could not be given up for any social service agenda. They felt there were other organizations to meet those kinds of needs and the club should remain focused on the "self-growth" of its members and other broad areas such as "intercultural exchange" and "networking" as defined in its mission statement.

Other Women's Groups

Similar women's groups are based in other areas. The Indian Women's Forum, started in 1991, draws its membership from northern and central Lake County, Illinois, and is also dedicated to the "self-development" of its members. Invited speakers have addressed topics such as political empowerment, financial planning, gender bias in education, and parenting the younger child.[8] It has established ties with the National Organization for Women (NOW) and the American Association of University Women. One women's group formed in 1994, the Dharma Women's Club, focuses its efforts on providing support to unwed women in India and those who are victims of the dowry system. The South Asian Women's Society of America, founded in 1992, tries to bring together women from all the countries of the subcontinent.

While most of the women who came in the first wave of immigration after 1965 were well-educated, upper-class women, the scenario began to change in the 1970s and 1980s as more and more women entered the United States without even a high school education. Some were sponsored relatives, but many were innocent victims of elaborate scams. Indian men with green cards went back to India, married women from the villages, brought them over to the United States, and then abused them or abandoned them when they couldn't fit into the society. Other women, even if they were from upper-class families and had formal education, just could not make the adjustment to a new environment. The result was a rise in the number of divorces and broken homes in the Indian community. It was the Club of Indian Women that first noticed with alarm the increasing number of distress calls it was receiving on its crisis hot line. Even women from upper-class homes were reporting cases of domestic violence as well as emotional, physical, and sexual abuse. Prem Sharma, one of the founding members of the club, recalled those early days in an interview. "The calls varied in nature. Sometimes it was just a woman calling to vent her feelings about an interfering mother-in-law. Or it could be a woman with two infants calling from a Dunkin' Donuts shop at 4 A.M. because her husband had beaten her up. Ours was a new community with new problems and we had to come up with new solutions."

Apna Ghar

The solution was Apna Ghar (Our Home), the first shelter for Asian women in the United States. As president of Apna Ghar, Prem Sharma has seen the organization grow from its founding in 1989 by a handful of concerned volunteers to a major community organization, funded by government agencies, that has helped hundreds of Asian families in crisis. It offers multilingual, multicultural support services, but over 50 percent of its clients come from the South Asian community. In 1995 it purchased its own shelter facility that can accommodate twelve women and children. With a staff of seven full-time and two part-time workers, scores of trained volunteers and interns, the agency provides temporary shelter for women and children seeking protection from violence in their homes. It also has a 24-hour hotline telephone number, a facility for supervised child visitation with noncustodial parents, and an advocacy and assistance program geared toward reconciliation and rehabilitation of families.

Ranjana Bhargava, the executive director of Apna Ghar, said that the entire community was shocked at the extent of the problem in the Chicago area. In 1990 alone, Apna Ghar responded to the needs of 160 women. The initial reaction of the community was to deny that the problem existed at all. Indians have the lowest percentage of "female householders with no husband present" (5.2 percent) among Asian ethnic groups and also compared to the U.S. national average of 16.5 percent (see Table 2, page 58). But the fact that most of the Indian immigrant families consisted of married couples did not mean they were devoid of serious domestic problems. The victims of domestic abuse had remained hidden for a long time and some of them were so isolated that they had never left their homes, never traveled in a bus, never handled a checking account. They didn't know where to turn or what do to in an abusive situation. Without extended family around them or even a network of friends they could confide in, they allowed the situation to deteriorate to an extreme degree before seeking help. Also, seeking help outside the bonds of family and community was frowned upon and a social service agency was usually the last recourse. Even when the magnitude of the problem became apparent, so-called community leaders objected vehemently to what they perceived as the washing of dirty linen in public. Anxious to uphold the prestige of the community and depict it as a model community with firm family values, they preferred to pretend that it was devoid of such shameful problems as wife abuse. But the persistence of the Indian women and the increased awareness among the general public helped Apna Ghar maintain a high profile. Bhargava saw an increase in the number of women seeking intervention in the earlier stages of an abusive situation.

According to Bhargava, there is no pattern or characteristic profile that can be used to describe Indian immigrant women who feel traumatized enough to seek the help of a shelter. The long-time, well-established wealthy immigrant is just as likely to be a battered wife as a newcomer to Chicago. What might have remained minor problems given extended family support and the familiar environment in India turn into major crises in Chicago given the economic and cultural pressures, the adaptation demands, and the increased vulnerability of the immigrant. Also what may have remained a marriage of convenience and plodded along at an uneasy pace in India is not tolerated in Chicago because there is less social disapproval of divorce, greater economic independence for the women, and more opportunities for them to break out of constrictive, time-honored roles. The rapid growth and changes in the community have also provided the women with more examples to follow when attempting changes in their own lives.

The changing social structure of the Indian immigrant community has also given rise to new opportunities for exploitation of women. Besides spousal abuse, women suffer abuse from employers and from agents who promise to procure them green cards. Sometimes older women are abused by their own adult sons. Affluent Indian families in the United States bring domestic workers from India where labor is cheap and plentiful, pay them below minimum wages, keep them isolated and overworked, and threaten them with deportation or abandonment if they protest.[9] In other cases, young women from middle-class families in India are "smuggled" into the United States by agents who extort money from them both in India and after they arrive in the United States. These women have to work double shifts in donut shops and grocery stores to pay off their debts. They live in cramped quarters on Lawrence Avenue under unhygienic conditions, and continue to suffer in silence, afraid to go back to India as failures. Apna Ghar cannot even reach out to them because the victims are too afraid to connect with what they perceive as governmental authorities.[10]

Apna Ghar was the first in a long line of crisis intervention and social service agencies that have sprung up in other states including Connecticut (Sneha), California (Maitri), New Jersey (Manavi), New York (Sakhi), Pennsylvania (Sewa) and Washington, D.C. (Asha). Centers also exist in Canada—in Toronto, Montreal, and Vancouver—and Great Britain—in Southall. Apna Ghar interacts with other service agencies not only in Chicago and the United States but also in India.[11]

The two women's organizations described above thus cater to two very different needs in the community. One is a response to the need for self-development, the other a response to a growing problem within the community. The growth of women's shelters is also attributed by some women in Chicago to the availability of state and corporate funds for such purposes. The fact that Indian women are addressing the problem head on and helping their sisters in need attests not only to their own vitality as a group but also to the power of the organizational infrastructure.

Media Institutions

The development of the Indian ethnic English language press in Chicago is a testimony to the wide-ranging interests of Chicago's Indian immigrants and their desire to stay connected with the homeland and with Indian communities throughout the *oikumene*. Chicago's immigrants have several English language newspapers which give them news about India and the local Chicago area Indian immigrant community. Some, such as *India Tribune* and *India Light* (formerly Spotlight), have a greater Chicago focus and are published in the city or in the metro area. Others may be published in Chicago, like the *Indian Reporter and World News*, but as the name implies, take a more global approach. Still others, such as *India Abroad*, which is headquartered in New York and *India Post*, which is headquartered in California, publish Chicago editions which carry local advertisements and special pages of local community news. The Indian press in Chicago is less professional and well-staffed, with fewer resources for in-depth, analytical reporting than the Indian press on the east and west coasts. *India West* out of California and *News-India Times* out of New York have much wider and more balanced coverage of news from India as well as local news than do the Chicago newspapers. Chicago's Indians can also choose from network and cable television channels as well as AM and FM radio broadcasts for news and entertainment from India. A book store on Devon Avenue, India Book House, brings them the latest publications from India, including special North American editions of Indian magazines and newspapers. An in-depth look at select publications helps us understand the differing motivations of publishers and the appeal of their publications to different segments of Chicago's Indian immigrant population.

India Tribune

India Tribune, one of the five English weeklies available in Chicago, was started in 1977 as a fortnightly. The publication became a weekly in 1982 and branched out with a New York edition in 1993 and an Atlanta edition in 1994. It hoped to launch its India edition called *U.S. Times* in 1996, though the venture remained still-born as of 1998.[12]

The editor, Prasant Shah, said he started the *India Tribune* because he "smelled a business opportunity."[13] At the time he started it, there were already three English language and four Gujarati-language publications but none of them was, according to Shah, "professional."[14] They were mostly cut-

and-paste jobs of news about India that had already been published in other sources. Shah felt that the highly educated and skilled Indians in Chicago would be interested in a more professional production, so he bought his own typesetting equipment and tried to give his paper a look that set it apart from the others.[15] He was also determined to run his newspaper so that it would be commercially successful. According to Shah, Chicago subscribers now number 26,000 while the number of national subscribers for all three editions is 61,000.

The *India Tribune* is a tabloid variety pack with something for every one. The lead pages and editorials generally report and comment on political or economic events of direct relevance to Indians in Chicago, whether the events take place in India or the United States or any other part of the globe. Sections such as "States' Round-Up," "Politics," "Economy," "Legal Matters," "Sports," and "India and the World" are common to all editions as is the "Magazine Section" directed mainly toward women and children. The magazine section "Filmi Duniya" contains gossip from "Bollywood" (the Indian film capital of Bombay) and feature articles from Indian women's magazines. Readers are kept well-informed of what happens in India on a timely basis, while the "human interest" element is supplied by local interviews and regular columns. Most of the newspaper consists of wire service reports, a reprint of locally generated news releases, and a rehash of gossipy-style chit-chat. With the increase in the Gujarati population in Chicago, the newspaper has seen a marked bias toward coverage of local events of interest mainly to the Gujarati community.

What is different for each regional edition are the advertising pages and the content of the "Community Front" section, which covers local events. Sometimes Shah may decide that certain local events in New York or Atlanta have significance for all Indians in America nationwide, in which case these events get written up even in the Chicago edition. Part of Shah's rationale for launching other city editions in the East and South is to "unite" all Indians in America, give them a common platform, and enable them to find a common voice. Community pages routinely report on association meetings and celebrations, political fund-raisers, awards presentations, and outstanding achievements of Indians. Infighting among different groups is generally decried and editorials often turn into clarion calls for "unity" and "communal harmony," especially on occasions such as India Independence Day, or when a candidate for political office is of Indian origin.

The growth of *India Tribune* from a fledgling two-man venture to a national publication with seventeen staffers and part-time writers is due in part to the population growth of Indian immigrants, not only in Chicago but the entire United States. It is also due to the growing links between India and the United States in the 1980s and 1990s that have been sustained through telecommunications technology and political developments. These connections have been recognized, capitalized upon and fueled by multinational telecommunications giants such as AT&T, MCI, and Sprint, financial service companies such as Citibank, Hong Kong Bank, and American Express, and the airline companies that fly between India and the United States. According to Shah, they were the first to recognize the importance of the Indian ethnic market and provide him the advertising revenue he needed to survive. He also resorted to what he himself calls "marketing gimmicks" such as sale of "life member subscriptions" to raise much-needed capital initially. *India Tribune* has 6,500 lifetime subscribers—six families have since moved to Alaska and continue to receive news about Chicago in Juno! To finance the New York edition, he sold five-year charter subscriptions for $51.00 each and raised $165,000 in one and a half months. Without this financial backing, he thinks he would never have been able to withstand the competition in the New York market from entrenched newspapers such as *India Abroad, News India Times, India Monitor,* and *Asia On-Line.* Shah made a calculated business decision to stay out of the west coast because newspapers such as *India West* and *News-India Times* were well-established and had saturated the market.

Comparing journalism the way it is practiced in India and Chicago, the Assistant Editor of *India Tribune,* who came to serve in Chicago after twenty-five years as a newspaperman in India, said, "Indian newspaper staffers are highly paid and respected and even feared for their influence. Some newspapers lose money but are backed by big business houses and are happy to stay in business because of the clout they have with the public. Here, the imperatives are totally different. The population is still small, the ethnic newspaper here is a diversion, an amusement, a source of certain kinds of information, but not an influencer of public opinion. Also it has to be commercially viable, so catering to the readership is all-important." Shah conducts an annual event, the India Tribune Nite, featuring a dinner-entertainment show in which local Indian youth show off their talents and enjoy the spotlight. Both its profitability and its public relations benefits are important to the newspaper, and highlight the fact that it is, first and last, a commercial endeavor. A chemical engineer turned businessman turned into a newspaper figure because of his willingness to take risks in a fast changing global scenario. An amateurish fortnightly tabloid begun in a Chicago basement and serving a handful of immigrants is, in the span of two decades, a stable business enterprise with national reach and international aspirations.

India Abroad

India Abroad, the other weekly that enjoys wide readership among Chicago's immigrant Indians, professes to have a different thrust than the *India Tribune.* With its editorial and corporate headquarters in New York and five separate editions (Eastern, Midwestern, Western, Canadian, and European) it has a more national and global perspective than the *India Tribune* and is less concerned with the hurly-burly of the local politics of the Chicago immigrant community. Stories from local offices throughout the world are sent to New York where the pages of all editions are made up based on the relative importance of local stories to a national audience. Ramesh Soparawala, the Chicago representative of *India Abroad,* said that the Chicago office was started in 1981, had three permanent members and two free lancers on its staff, and was second in importance only to the New York office in terms of revenue generation. According to him the London office was losing money, the Toronto office barely breaking even, but the paper was in it for the long haul and was not worried about financial survival. The paper had a solid base of readers, correspondents and advertisers and unlike the *India Tribune* could afford to ignore local pressures and print only what it deemed newsworthy. "We print what is important to India as a nation and to the global community of Indians, not because someone in the local community wants us to. We are also the only Indian publication in North America to have its circulation audited by the Audit Bureau of Circulation." The paper claims a circulation of 50,000 plus (its Chicago circulation is 15,500) and a "pass-along" readership of 200,000. The paper also prides itself on the high level of prosperity of its readers, whose average age is thirty-nine years, 92 percent of whom have a college degree and whose annual household income is $58,000. Since ethnic newspapers generally tend to exaggerate the extent of their readership an audited figure is important to maintain credibility in the community. The professional elite in Chicago give far greater credence to news items published in *India Abroad* and prefer it for its wider coverage of national and international news.

India Abroad, too, has conceded the west coast market to newspapers such as *India West* which have the right mix of national and local news and are well entrenched in the area. But in Chicago, Saporawala feels, there is room for all. "We have so many TV stations, each one catering to a different need and a different audience. *Chitrahaar* (the UHF television program) tries to bring the community together, *Bharat Darshan* (the cable television channel) concentrates on film-based entertainment Each one has a focus, so each one is thriving. But in the future we will have to change with changing conditions. The second generation is the audience we are gearing for. Right now, our India-based news and foreign-based news is a fifty-fifty split. That mix may have to change because the second generation is less interested in India and more concerned about what is going in their own community here. Only those who can make the transition to the new demands will survive."

Other Newspapers and Magazines

Changing conditions resulted in casualties in the Indian language newspaper market back in 1982. Pradyumna Mehta who started a Gujarati monthly in Chicago called *Hindustan Patrika* in 1977 stopped production in 1981.[16] As a compendium of news stories from India, it began to lose its relevance when the original newspapers and magazines became available in Chicago on a current basis. "Thanks to modern communications and transportation, I get Gujarati newspapers and periodicals direct from Bombay three days after it hits the newsstands in India. Why would anyone bother putting something together in Chicago?" he said. Two other Gujarati monthlies run along the same lines as *Hindustan Patrika* also failed in the 1980s. They were *Gujarat Vartman* and *Bharat Sandesh*. *India Abroad* explored the feasibility of a Gujarati paper in Chicago but dropped the project in 1994. Its New York Gujarati paper called *Gujarati Samachar*, with links to *Gujarat Samachar* of Bombay, is also sold in Chicago. Despite the size of the Gujarati community in Chicago which some observers place as high as 50 percent there has been no growth of a Gujarati language press for a number of reasons, the main one being that the most members of the Gujarati community are somewhat conversant in English and the English language press in Chicago caters to their needs adequately. The easy and prompt availability of Gujarati literature and periodicals from the homeland also discourages the growth of a local Gujarati language press. The same holds true for the other regional languages too, though Muslims from Hyderabad are said to have their own Urdu publication in Chicago called *Bazm-e-Deccan* and Malayalees from Kerala have the *Kerala Express* published by Grace Printing on Devon Avenue. Stores on Devon Avenue carry a wide variety of periodicals and newspapers in all the major regional languages of India.

Indian magazines in India have been quick to capitalize on the market among Indians abroad who are eager for news about India. *India Today*, the leading Indian weekly news magazine launched its international edition in 1981. In June 1992, it added a separate section to reflect the concerns, interests and achievements of Indians living in North America. A special section in the international edition also reports on prospects for foreign investment in India. In January 1994, the weekly started a special Gulf edition in Malayalam. The latest in *India Today's* string of special editions is the U.K. edition launched in April 1995. The perception in India is that Indians in the United Kingdom are not only more directly connected to their motherland than the Indians in North America, they are also more involved in the political and social life of their adopted country.[17] The weekly relies on stringers in North America to suggest which stories might be of interest to Indians abroad. Stories typically deal with issues of immigration, religious, cultural and political activities of immigrants, effects of the "glass ceiling," and discrimination. Success stories of Indians who make good abroad are staple fare. Other magazines that produce special editions for sale to Indians abroad include Bollywood film magazines, such as *Star & Style*. Indians in Chicago also have access to monthlies such as *India Worldwide*, whose North American edition is published in New York, and a magazine especially for second-generation IndianAmericans called *Onward*, started in 1994 and published in Dayton, Ohio.

Television and Radio Stations

Indian programming on Chicago's television broadcasting channels is still in its infancy. Programs come and go with amazing frequency, dying quickly for lack of professional management or staying power on the part of small investors. One program that has survived for more than fifteen years is *Chitrahaar*. Started by an enterprising housewife named Vichitra Nayyar with the dual purpose of "quenching the nostalgia for home, relatives and friends back in the subcontinent" and "to give the second generation a sense of belonging and pride in their unique heritage," *Chitrahaar* began with a Saturday morning live broadcast showcasing local talent featuring song and dance clips from Hindi movies. It uses an established transmitting channel that gives air time to many other ethnic broadcasts, such as the Chinese and Korean. The programming is usually woven around a particular topical or festive theme such as Gandhi's birthday or *Divali* or Christmas and all religions and linguistic communities are honored. Special efforts are made to give the show an "Indo-Pak" flavor. Also included is a calendar of community events and news footage from India. Occasionally, investors from India will appear on "interviews" and get an opportunity to plug their product on television. Though the reach of the broadcast may be widening, it has a long way to go before acquiring true polish and professionalism. It remains very much a "family-run" enterprise. "*Chitrahaar* Night" is an annual extravaganza, replete with a beauty pageant, fashion show and song and dance sequences from Hindi films performed by second-generation Indians. Like the events organized by the religious and cultural associations, it enjoys the patronage of Indian parents who are only too happy to see their children "imbibing Indian culture" instead of swinging at American joints.

Bharat Darshan, produced by Super Broadcasting in Skokie, offers its cable viewers all over metropolitan Chicago a melange of "current news from India, local news, activities and community events, talk shows and interviews, cooking shows, movie songs and live concerts, TV serials, and sports from India."[18] *TV Asia*, launched by Indian movie star Amitabh Bachchan in 1993, was the first big-budget attempt to use satellite technology to reach Indians in North America coast to coast. Broadcasts are primarily in Hindi, Urdu and English, and also in key regional languages. *TV Asia*, owned by its parent company Asia Broadcasting Network, is backed by an international consortium of businessmen and reaches homes in Chicago on a daily schedule via cable.

Ethnic radio programs are another popular source of entertainment for Chicago's Indians. *Jhankar* is an AM/FM radio show that broadcasts over a seventy-mile radius around Chicago from recording studios in Bloomingdale. Started by an electrical engineer as a hobby in 1976, the show plays popular Hindi film songs from the "good old days" of the 1950s, 1960s, and 1970s, an era which the pioneering Indian immigrants remember with nostalgia. Other AM radio shows that broadcast popular Hindi music are *Sangeeta* (the oldest radio show in Chicago and owned by Chitrahaar Broadcasting), *Tarana* and *Naubahar*.

The airwaves are also used by Indians for global communications. Internet activity has picked up with amazing rapidity among Chicago's electronically literate Indians. Unlike the earlier immigrants who came in the 1960s and 1970s and were mostly engineers and scientists, the professional Indians entering Chicago in the 1990s are computer software experts who are thoroughly comfortable in an electronic environment. *India-Net* is a global communications network of people of Indian origin outside India. Started in 1993 by a core group of about 250 volunteers, it includes two subsidiaries—*Action-India* and *Info-India*. *Action-India* uses the network to inform public officials and elected representatives about the Asian Indian community's views, while *Info-India* is directed toward the media and attempts to enhance the quality and content of their reporting on India and the global Indian community. *India-Net* held its first annual convention at the Loyola University in Chicago in September 1995. Session titles indicate the objectives of the organization: "United Action on Issues Facing Indian-Americans," "Grassroots Lobbying and Political Activism" and "Improving Media Perception and Foreign Policy Towards India."[19] It claims to have made its presence felt both in the United States and worldwide but it is too early to assess its impact on the lives of Indian immigrants. The Internet is an exciting, fast-growing arena that Indians will continue to use in innovative ways to connect with others in the *oikumene*. There is an Internet temple network that provides a calendar of Hindu religious events, spreads information about temple activities all across North America, and addresses questions on the finer points of Hinduism. It is aimed at the second-generation Indian Americans who are more hooked into electronic communication than their parents.

Letters and the Universities

A body of writing by Indians on their immigrant experience is slowly emerging that enables them to be better represented in scholarly texts than they were before. The voices of South Asian immigrant women are heard in *Our Feet Walk the Sky*, a collection of essays, fiction and poetry that reveals the many dimensions of assimilation and biculturalism especially as seen from the gender perspective.[20] Bharati Mukherjee is one novelist of international repute in North America, and new writers from New York, California, and even Tennessee are making their mark.[21] One Chicago writer, W. D. Merchant, has published an autobiography *Home on the Hill*, and is currently working on a second book, a novel.[22]

   Though individual Indians have long been part of faculty at most major universities not only in Chicago but throughout the United States, community or ethnic studies of the Indian immigrant group are still in the prenatal stage. The University of Chicago's Department of South Asian Languages and Civilization, which is steeped in the study of civilization in India and according to some Indian immigrants, wrapped up in its own elitism, did not concern itself much with the immigrants in the 1960s and 1970s. In the

1980s, there was a noticeable increase of second-generation Indians in its student body. These children of Indian parents were anxious to rediscover their roots and gain an intellectual understanding of a culture that they had already experienced on the inside but which they realized was different from the Indian culture in India. Still, the University of Chicago's South Asia programs are not fully in touch with the Indian community, though efforts are being made to build bridges through its outreach programs. At other universities, too, it is a similar story. The Asian American Advisory Board of Northwestern University has tried for five years to institute Asian-American studies classes in its curriculum.[23] Their efforts met with some success in 1995 when a course entitled: "Indians Abroad: South Asians in the United States" was offered for the first time. The University of Illinois at Chicago (UIC) has been offering courses on South Asian Civilization since 1970, but it was only in the early 1980s that any Indian students began to attend; before that, most of the students were American. In 1997, UIC established the Rajiv Gandhi Memorial Endowment in Indian Studies which was instrumental in offering the first course on "South Asians in Twentieth Century America" to undergraduate students in 1998. The Du Page Community College offers a Hindi language and Indian history class in acknowledgment of its sizable Indian immigrant population. Substantial monetary contributions from the Indian immigrant community in the Midwest are funneled outside the Chicago area to Bloomington University in Indiana (for a Bengali chair) and as far away as University of California in Berkeley (for a well-publicized Tamil chair). Strong connections between Chicago's Indian immigrant community and its academic world have yet to be made.[24] Meanwhile, on the national scene, organizations such as the Society of Indian Academics in America and the faculty of various universities with a South Asia concentration meet regularly at academic conventions to further the cause of teaching about Indian immigrants in the United States. A major convention on South Asian studies has been held for the past twenty-six years at the University of Wisconsin, and attracts dozens of Chicago-area residents.

Sports

First-generation Indian immigrants, especially the elite professionals, are not particularly sports-minded. Though they may take part in the office betting pool and are interested in professional team scores, they are not keen on playing sports themselves as an ethnic group. Their executive lifestyles are more attuned to participation in health clubs or tennis leagues than group sports. In fact, second-generation Indians frequently complain about their parents' lack of interest in their own sports activities at school. The first-ever sports festival held in the Indian community was by the Punjabis in May 1995. In India, too, it is the athletic and well-built Punjabis who dominate the sports scene. Volleyball, soccer, and *kabaddi* (a team sport native to India) teams competed in a playful atmosphere with food stalls and other vendor booths providing adequate distraction. Team names such as "Chicago Cabs" and "Shere-e-Punjab" suggested the identity and spirit of the participants.[25] Another interesting development is the attempt of second-generation Indians and Pakistanis to organize their own basketball teams. The Indo-Pak National Basketball Tournament (IPNBT) was started in 1989 to create "a fair, open, yet competitive tournament in Chicago for players of Indian and Pakistani descent" but was soon expanded to include teams from other states. The summer 1996 tournament had sixteen participating teams, ten of them from out of state. Players are between the ages of sixteen and twenty-four. Referees are volunteers and of non-South Asian descent, to ensure fair play.[26]

Cricket is the only sport that is played in the United States as part of the Indian immigrant legacy. In a way, it is also part of the British imperial legacy because it is the combined presence of immigrants from former British colonies and dominions that has given this sport a measure of popularity in Chicago. Teams of players, generally formed along national origin lines from India, Pakistan, Jamaica, and Barbados, compete in leagues on weekends in the Washington park area on the South Side of Chicago. There are almost three hundred cricket clubs all over the United States, half of them in New York, which is considered the Mecca of Indian cricket mainly because of the concentration of people from the Caribbean. The development of the sport has been hampered by the fact that the game requires a different type of ground, a special type of pitch and a wider field, than is usually available in sports grounds in the United States. The patronage, too, is not yet at the level which would ensure profits for organizers of cricket matches on a professional basis. A grand India-Pakistan cricket match which would have tested the waters was planned at Soldier Field for the summer of 1995 but fell through at the last minute. Cricket fans in Chicago are generally heartened by the availability of talent since there is a good pool of players who already have a good foundation from the homeland but feel the sport is languishing in Chicago for lack of funds from sponsors and because of haphazard administration.[27] Few see much hope of its surviving into the second generation unless changing demographics caused by in-migration of cricket-playing groups or cooperation among all those who come from other Commonwealth countries dictate otherwise.

Conclusion

The foregoing examination of the institutional infrastructure of Chicago's Indian immigrants falls short of including each and every organization but it does reveal certain key characteristics and factors in the growth of a community. It demonstrates that a community becomes identifiable, both to itself and to others, only when it becomes organized. Though the forms of these institutions may be loose and flexible—some have boards of directors and trustees, other don't, some are nationally affiliated, others are not, some are very narrow in scope with a handful of members, others are global in scope with hundreds or thousands of members, the variations are numerous—their value lies in helping the immigrants identify what aspect of their lives they want to explore and strengthen and how best they can achieve their aims and objectives. Sometimes their choices are based on inner needs which are so strong they help them overcome obstacles in an alien environment. The religious activity of Indian immigrants and the tremendous energy that has gone into the building of religious institutions are an example of such inner forces at work. But the temple building can also be seen as a reaction to the demands of an American society which identifies its population along religious lines as much as ethnic and racial lines. At other times, the exigencies of outside forces have propelled Indians into organizational activity, for example in the political sphere. Political activism on the part of Indians has still to acquire momentum and a reluctant electorate has yet to be galvanized, but given the conditions in Chicago and the historical background of the immigrants, Indian political organizations will acquire greater significance in the years to come.

Institutions have thus shaped, and been shaped by, the way Indians see themselves and how others see them. They go beyond the culturally colorful areas of art, religion, music and dance, and include the economic and political systems through which Indians have to move in their daily lives. They may have widely differing goals and their impact on individual lives may vary from the very important to the totally irrelevant, but they have an intrinsic value because they keep the Indians of the *oikumene* interconnected. For the vast majority who work in the mainstream with co-workers and clients who are non-Indians, these organizations provide a way to enjoy togetherness and celebrate their ethnicity with other Indians.

As far as individual leadership is concerned, no single figure has emerged as an authentic spokesperson for the entire community. Certain people are very active in certain circles and whenever individual achievers come to the forefront, the community applauds their success. By distributing awards and honors to them, the community plays them up as examples of good Indian American citizenry. What is significant is the development of the institutional infrastructure. Chicago's Indian immigrant institutions have taken the lead and shown the way in many areas: its women's organizations and its commercial and social service institutions are much better developed than those in other parts of the country. The diversity of these organizations reflects the diversity and traditions of India and the innovativeness of Indian immigrants in Chicago. Just as India is struggling to resolve the differences among its member states and maintain its unity and integrity as a nation, Indian immigrants, through these organizations, are struggling to maintain their unity and cohesiveness as an ethnic group without giving up on their separate regional identities. In a way, the evolution of these institutions tells the story that is at the heart of any richly diverse group of people: how to enjoy variety and multiplicity and connect with each other positively without losing sight of the essential oneness of it all.

In the struggle to adapt and survive, Indian immigrants have created a subculture and a subsociety through these organizations. They have created an identity that is distinct from and yet a part of their "Indianness" even as it is distinct from and yet a part of their emerging "Americanness." Most important, that identity is shaped by forces in the home country, in the host country, and indeed, the entire world, wherever Indians have formed an identifiable community.

Epilogue

Past Achievements and Future Challenges

Chicago's Asian Indian population has enjoyed more than thirty years of steady continuous growth. They are busy living up to the myth of the model minority and at the same time trying to face up to the challenges that threaten it.

—Padma Rangaswamy, "Asian Indians in Chicago: Growth and Change in a Model Minority"

All immigrants, regardless of their cultural heritage, search for synthesis and balance in their lives through a process of reconciliation that is much more self-conscious than it is for people who never leave hearth and home. For the post-1965 Indian immigrants of Chicago, this search began in independent India as a search for ways to be nationalist at heart but global in outlook, to be modern in practice yet devoutly traditional in spirit, to embrace the new without discarding the old—to be, above all, authentically Indian. That quest for an authentic Indian voice found a home in several different parts of the world, including Chicago, where it set down deep roots in a favorable economic and social climate. Like the American immigrants of the past—call them pilgrims or colonists or settlers—Indians coming to Chicago were also motivated by the overwhelming importance of individual and family interests, by the opportunity to participate in a market economy and to pursue their private lives in an atmosphere of social stability. But unlike many immigrants of yore who came to America fleeing tyranny or who yearned for precious liberty in a new land, Indians were leaving behind a system of government that they believed in, and a cultural heritage that they cherished. As subjects of a newly-independent country whose constitution guaranteed all its citizens equal status, they came to a new land taking basic civil rights for granted. Used to celebrating cultural differences among themselves back in the home country, they continued to observe and celebrate these differences in the new environment. The American ideals of "liberal individualism" and "cultural pluralism" were shared by these Indian immigrants who expected no less in the fabled land of opportunity. Once they arrived in the United States, most of the immigrants achieved remarkable successes while many experienced disillusionment and disappointment. Whatever their personal triumphs and vicissitudes, the continued immigration of Indians suggests that the lure of America still retains its hold on people from India.

A brief comparison of the profile of Indians in Chicago with the profile of Indians in some other countries of the *oikumene* helps us see the differences in the historic development of these communities and what factors are responsible for these differences. For instance, Indians in Trinidad also live in a multiracial, pluralistic society, but under very different circumstances from Chicago's Indians. Trinidad's Indians are in the lowest economic and social stratum of a highly structured society.[1] They have seen some progress in terms of educational advancement and occupational mobility in recent years, and some have even struck it rich in the recent oil boom. But for the most part, theirs remains a world of disadvantage, discrimination, and depression. Indians in Trinidad bear the weight of a century and a half of history compared to a three-decade-old history of Chicago's Indians, still it is possible to identify and compare some of the more important factors in the shaping of a historic identity. The nature of the original migration, whether it is indentured or free, colors the immigrant experience in profound ways. The indentured origin of Trinidad Indians, which confined them to the rural sector of the plantation economy, is only one of the many factors responsible for their present situation. Another important factor is the extent of links with the homeland. Trinidad Indians who came in the nineteenth century predominantly from one restricted area of India, the northern United Provinces, lost touch with their homeland, and drifted in the twentieth century without a comfortable identity. Chicago's Indians who come from all over India have, by contrast, developed an identity that encompasses their class status, their regional origin, and their religion, but manages to rise above and beyond that to accommodate their strong nationalist sentiments as well.

Other factors to consider in the historic development of an immigrant identity are the pressures and structure of the host society, which are very different for Trinidad and Chicago. Since the first shipload of Indians arrived in Trinidad on May 3, 1845, they were transformed by the proselytizing activities of Christian missionaries, so that a group that was 0.1 percent Christian in 1890 grew to be 20 percent Christian by 1946.[2] Christianity provided its converts with greater social mobility and material benefits, and became an important source of identity in a segmented, religiously defined society. The history of colonialism, too, played its part in shaping the lives of Indians in Trinidad who found themselves pitted against blacks in bitter and bloody labor struggles, racial and cultural antipathy, and political rivalry for representation, long before and after the state became formally independent in 1962. By contrast, Indians in Chicago have carved out a very different destiny for themselves, not only through their own efforts but also thanks to the comparative freedom they enjoy to pursue their legitimate self-interest.

Comparison of Chicago's Indians with another group in the *oikumene*, namely the Sikhs in Britain, highlights other interesting facets of the immigrant experience. As Arthur Helweg has pointed out in his study of Sikhs in England in the 1980s, the situation varies based on the time period in which an immigrant group is being studied, and also on the prevailing attitudes in the immigrant and host communities.[3] In the 1960s, when unskilled Indians started coming to Britain in large numbers to fill a void in the labor market, Indians still felt comparatively safe and secure in England. By the early 1980s, however, they were caught up in violent racial strife. What factors contributed to the change in circumstances and the change in attitudes? Unlike Indians in Chicago who are generally urban and settle all over the metropolitan area, the Sikhs in England clustered in pockets, and entire Punjabi villages were transplanted to specific locales in England in a system of chain migration. Coming as they did from small, peasant societies, they were unfamiliar with the English environment and found it difficult to adjust to the new society. The discrimination that they suffered at the hands of the British, who looked upon them as a conquered and therefore inferior people, helped fuel their sense of alienation. Back in India, the army assault on the Golden Temple in 1984 led many to believe that India was no longer a place they could return to and forced them to look at Britain as their permanent home. This altered the nature of the immigration. Whereas earlier it had consisted mostly of young single men who came as economic transients, it became predominantly female as young Sikhs returned to India and brought back brides, turning the community into a permanent, family-oriented one. At the same time, the British clamped down on unskilled labor migration, and attitudes toward Indians hardened considerably. The influx of Sikh refugees from East Africa in the late 1960s and early 1970s also contributed to the growth of the community and added to intra-ethnic tensions. Parminder Bhachu describes the East African Sikhs as highly conscious of their dual heritage, accentuating their traditions in matters of marriage and ritual observations, and setting themselves apart not only from the white majority but Sikhs who came directly from India.[4] Sikhs as well as other Indians made some economic progress into white-collar jobs, but there was no radical restructuring of their settlement patterns. They continued to be relegated to a secluded underclass and confined to segregated housing. It is always difficult for an immigrant community to dig themselves out of a weak position of marginalization and vulnerability. In this respect, Indians in Chicago are fortunate to have started out as a professional, well-to-do elite that is able to support and influence the new migration of lesser skilled immigrants.

Comparing Sikhs in England with Sikhs in California shows how the bond of religion can keep economically disparate groups connected across the *oikumene*. The American Sikhs provide an excellent example of a community that has developed worldwide connections in response to their own particular social need and their political history. There is now a wide global network of Sikh contacts, made possible by modern communications technology, which is important not only for family and social purposes such as intermarriage, but for political affiliation on issues such as the demand for a separate Sikh state. Sikhs travel back and forth frequently between California and the homeland and maintain contact with other overseas centers of Sikh life, such as England, Fiji, East Africa, and even New Zealand. The Canadian Sikh centers such as Vancouver, Toronto, Montreal, and Winnipeg also maintain close ties, with frequent marriage between Canadian and U.S. Sikhs.[5] Even though separatist politics have set them somewhat apart from other Indians, the socioreligious systems of the Sikhs are very much within the framework of a pan-Indian culture.

On the surface, it certainly appears as though Indian emigrants had it nowhere so good as they do in the United States. Compared to Indians in other parts of the *oikumene*, they seem to have fewer social barriers to integration at certain levels. Indians are still the most highly educated of all groups in the United States. The second wave of migration has diluted educational levels somewhat but not shaken Indians from their first rank. They enjoy one of the highest income levels and live in some of the richest suburbs. Their children out-perform other groups in American schools, identify strongly with other Americans in the classroom, and grow up to fit very comfortably into the workplaces of their choice. Unlike Indians in England or South Africa, who even after several generations behave in their enclaves as though they have never left India, Indians in the United States look poised, at first glance, to follow the well-worn path of other American immigrant groups as tracked by sociologists. As one sociologist put it, "It is a well-known fact among sociologists that the second generation of any immigrant group serves as a bridge to connect the old culture with the new. Likewise, it is always the third generation that adopts the customs and values of the new society and completes the process of assimilation."[6]

However, such "well-known facts" fail to take into account certain crucial factors in the American social experience. Indians, because of their race and color, can never achieve total acceptance into a white American society that has race and color bias. It is difficult to envision a period when race and color have not mattered in American history or will not matter in the future. Another stumbling block is the fact that Indian culture is very different from the Anglo culture and quite unlike the culture of earlier eastern and southern European immigrants whose experience popularized the assimilationist theories in the first place. Any attempts by the Indian immigrants in the United States to hold on to their own traditions or to reconcile the two disparate cultures may be seen as a threat and resisted strongly by both sides. Indians cannot follow the old "assimilationist" route but will have to work out new and innovative paradigms for their role in American society.

Another sociological theory that Indians put to the test says that racism survives only when the dominant group is successful in convincing a dominated group of its superiority.[7] Indians can be seen as "dominated" only because they are in a minority, but even as a minority group, they need to be convinced that the new American culture is somehow superior to the old Indian culture in order to *want* to assimilate. Because the vanguard of Indian immigration to the United States consisted of upper-class, affluent professionals, they were not only proud of their own rich and ancient heritage, many of them were convinced that it was superior to the Western culture and must be protected in an alien environment. Had the first wave of immigrants been economically or politically depressed in India, or had they not been so quick to achieve material success in the United States, they might have *felt* inferior and undergone greater pressure to work toward conventional assimilation. Credit must also be given to the hospitable climate in the United States, at least from the 1960s to the mid-1990s, toward Indian immigrants, which gave them room to grow and fashion their own immigrant culture.

As immigrants, Indians in Chicago have tried to mix the need for a certain modicum of privacy in their lives (also termed "insular" and "isolationist" tendencies by sociologists) with the need to be involved in the host society (also labeled "assimilation" and "acculturation" tendencies). Much of their time, energy and financial resources have gone toward building what is often denigrated as the "soft" or "colorful" aspects of ethnicity—religious customs, dress and cuisine, dance and music. Instead of trivializing these cultural aspects of immigrants' lives, one must see them as the foundation on which the self-confidence and self-esteem of Indians is built. Ultimately such outward cultural forms help the scientist and the doctor and the engineer to perform well at their jobs, and maintain the balance and equilibrium that all immigrants need to survive in a new land. The Indians have not neglected the "hard" issues either. They have guarded their professional and economic interests, have made a beginning in the political arena, and will no doubt fight for their place in the sun in America. There is an awareness in their community of the issues that must be fought over, and the rights and privileges that must be preserved in a democratic, pluralistic society. Like other Indians in the *oikumene*, they have developed values and techniques necessary for survival as an overseas community.

The growth patterns of the Indian community in Chicago are remarkably similar to patterns found in other Indian communities scattered across the United States. Whether it be the consecration of a temple, the election campaign of a political candidate, the proliferation of restaurants, the screening of Hindi movies, or the celebration of Indian Independence Day, the same phenomena can be traced in almost every major metropolitan area where Indians are concentrated. Variations do exist such as the dominance of Gujaratis in certain areas or the concentration of cab drivers in certain cities, but the overall pattern is the same. If there is a "Devon Avenue" in Chicago, there is a "Jackson Heights" in New York, and an "Artesia" in California, all of which act in the same way as magnets for Indian shoppers. Come Dussehra-Divali season, garba dance contests and disco dandia performances are held all over the United States, as are Independence Day celebrations or observances of Gandhi Jayanti Day. This is due in large part to the communication and interaction between the different regions, the existence of national and international organizations, and the common interests of an expatriate community. The commonalties and connections among Indians and the different ethnic groups in Chicago also show that Indian immigrants must be seen in the overall context of American history and not confined to the areas of "ethno-history" or "Asian studies," which automatically assign them secondary or peripheral status. When seen in the context of their global connections, it is apparent that they are an integral part of Indian and world history, too.

The values, customs and ideas that Indian immigrants brought with them to the United States as well as the physical setting of their lives in Chicago are important for understanding how immigrants make their choices. From the individual voices of immigrants, one can see how these choices are also driven by the complex interplay of human and nonhuman forces. But after all the analyses and explanations are in, there still remains what is unknowable and sometimes inexplicable in human affairs. Historians, however objective and inclusive they try to be, are alas! not gifted with that "all seeing" third eye of Shiva!

So it must be acknowledged that this particular story of Indian immigrants in Chicago has left many aspects unexplored or touched upon only briefly. The impact of Indian immigrants on Indo-U.S. relations and on American society has been hinted at but not examined in great depth. Such influences need more time to develop to a measurable extent, and from a historical standpoint, the story is still in its formative stages. For now, the best one can do to understand these forces is to see them at the level of individual experience. This study has also refrained from glorifying the achievements of Indians and their "contribution" to building America, or creating "great personae" out of community leaders. It is common for immigrant groups to claim their fair share of American history by highlighting the achievements of community "notables" in different fields of endeavor. Certainly the time has come to compile a comprehensive "Who's Who Among Indian Americans." But for every individual that this study has singled out by name, there are many others who have done their share of "building" the community who have remained unnamed. The general theme of contribution and leadership emerges from the story of how Indians in Chicago, over the course of three decades of steady and continuous growth, have organized themselves into an identifiable yet varied community. Because the story is told from the inside out, as it were, it lacks the perspective of the outsider looking in. How do other Americans view Indians and their ways? Do they appear as strange and as exotic as did the "ragheads" to the native Californians almost a hundred years ago? Do Americans know or care enough about the new Indian immigrants to form opinions about them? While Indians in Chicago are hardly shunned or stigmatized as they have been in other countries, it is not clear how well they are regarded by the rest of the population either. A separate study with a different focus would have to be undertaken to reveal that perspective.

Future directions for the Indian immigrants will be determined by the extent of continued immigration, public attitudes and policies toward immigrants, and conditions in India. In the fast-changing global scenario, it is possible that unforeseen patterns of immigration will emerge. In creating their new society, Indians traveled frequently back to India and to other parts of the world, weaving an international web of connections that opened up new options for pursuing a future outside the United States. It is estimated that about 195,000 United States residents emigrate each year.[8] There is no official estimate of how many of these are Indians, but return migration to India or to other lands remains a possibility. For many immigrants, memories of the homeland fade away with age but for others the connections to the homeland are intensified with the passing years; for still others, there remain unfulfilled yearnings, no matter what the time or place. Immigrants who live between cultures inhabit places and spaces where disparate values intersect or collide and they keep searching for the perfect balance. Perhaps it is in the nature of the immigrant experience that the quest for harmony remains a quest without end or becomes the end in itself.

NOTES

Prologue

1. Indians are generally referred to in scholarly works as "East Indians" or "Asian Indians," the latter term having been adopted by the U.S. Census Bureau so as not to confuse them with Native American Indians. In this work, they will be referred to as Indians, plain and simple. This is also the only term that they themselves are comfortable with. In the context of demographics derived from the census figures, they may occasionally be referred to as "Asian Indians."

2. *We, the American Asians*, U.S. Census Bureau, 1993, and *Indicators for Understanding: A Profile of Metro Chicago's Immigrant Community*, a study conducted by the Latino Institute, Chicago and Office for Social Policy Research, Northern Illinois University, Dekalb, Illinois, 1995, 45–52. See also Padma Rangaswamy, "Asian Indians in Chicago: Growth and Change in a Model Minority," in *Ethnic Chicago: A Multicultural Portrait*, ed. Melvin J. Holli and Peter d'A. Jones (Grand Rapids, Mich.: William B. Eerdmans, 1995), 438–62, for a more detailed statistical comparison of Chicago Indians and Indians in other areas such as New York, Atlanta, and Kalamazoo, Michigan.

3. Joan M. Jensen, "East Indians," in *Harvard Encyclopedia of American Ethnic Groups*, ed. S. Thernstrom (Cambridge, Mass.: Harvard University Press, 1980), 296–301.

4. Joan M. Jensen, *Passage from India: Asian Indian Immigrants in North America* (New Haven: Yale University Press, 1988); Brett Melendy, *Asians in America: Filipinos, Koreans & East Indians* (Boston: Twayne Publishers, 1977); Ronald Takaki, *Strangers from a Different Shore: A History of Asian Americans* (Boston: Little, Brown & Co., 1989).

5. S. Chandrasekhar, ed., *From India to America: A Brief History of Immigration: Problems of Discrimination, Admission & Assimilation* (La Jolla, Calif.: Population Review, 1982). See also Karen I. Leonard, *Making Ethnic Choices: California's Punjabi Mexican Americans* (Philadelphia: Temple University Press, 1992) for an ethnographic study of this early group of immigrants who married Mexican women.

6. I am deeply indebted to Professor Leo Schelbert for helping me develop the *oikumene* theme and apply it to Indian migration. Leo Schelbert, "Emigration from Imperial Germany, 1871–1954: Contours, Contexts, Experiences," in *Imperial Germany*, ed. Volker Duis, Kathy Harms, and Peter Hayes (Madison: University of Wisconsin Press, 1985), 127.

7. Roger Daniels, *Asian Americans: Chinese and Japanese in the United States since 1850* (Seattle: University of Washington Press, 1988), xiii.

8. Paramatma Saran, *The Asian Indian Experience in the United States* (Cambridge: Schenkman, 1985); Paramatma Saran and Edwin Eames, eds., *The New Ethnics: Asian Indians in the United States* (New York: Praeger, 1980); and Maxine P. Fisher, *The Indians of New York City: A Study of Immigrants from India* (Columbia: South Asia Books, 1980).

9. John Y. Fenton, *Transplanting Religious Traditions: Asian Indians in America* (New York: Praeger, 1988); Raymond B. Williams, *Religions of Immigrants from India and Pakistan: New Threads in the American Tapestry* (Cambridge: Cambridge University Press, 1988); and Raymond B. Williams, ed., *A Sacred Thread: Modern Transmission of Hindu Traditions in India and Abroad* (Chambersburg, Pa.: Anima Publications, 1992).

10. Arthur W. and Usha M. Helweg, *An Immigrant Success Story: East Indians in America* (Philadelphia: University of Pennsylvania Press, 1991); Richard Harvey Brown and George V. Coelho, eds., *Tradition and Transformation: Asian Indians in America*, Studies in Third World Societies 38 (Williamsburg, Va.: College of William and Mary, 1986).

11. Priya Agarwal, *Passage from India: Post-1965 Indian Immigrants and their Children* (Palos Verdes, Calif.: Yuvati Publications, 1991); Jean Leslie Bacon, *Life Lines: Community, Family, and Assimilation Among Asian Indian Immigrants* (New York: Oxford University Press, 1996).

12. Johanna Lessinger, *From the Ganges to the Hudson: Indian Immigrants in New York City* (Boston: Allyn & Bacon, 1995), 71–95. Also see Arjun Appadorai, "Patriotism and its Futures," *Public Culture* 5 (1993).

13. Colin Clarke, Ceri Peach, and Steven Vertovec, eds., *South Asians Overseas: Migration and Ethnicity* (Cambridge: Cambridge University Press, 1990); Ravindra K. Jain, *Indian Communities Abroad: Themes and Literature* (New Delhi: Manohar Publishers, 1993); Peter van der Veer, *Nation and Migration: The Politics of Space in the South Asian Diaspora* (Philadelphia: University of Pennsylvania Press, 1995).

14. Hugh Tinker, *The Banyan Tree: Overseas Emigrants from India, Pakistan and Bangladesh* (London: Oxford University Press, 1977), and *A New System of Slavery: The Export of Indian Labour Overseas 1830–1920* (London: Oxford University Press, 1974).

Chapter 1   The Indian *Oikumene* and Its Heartland

1. V. S. Naipaul, *An Area of Darkness* (New York: The Macmillan Company, 1964).

2. The effect of the communications revolution on Indian migration to the United States is one of the important themes in Arthur W. and Usha M. Helweg, *An Immigrant Success Story: East Indians in America* (Philadelphia: University of Pennsylvania Press, 1991).

3. Arjun Appadorai draws attention to the United States as a place where "people come to seek their fortunes but are no longer content to leave their homelands behind." Arjun Appadorai, "Patriotism and its Futures," *Public Culture* 5 (1993): 423–25, 427, quoted in David A. Hollinger, *Postethnic America: Beyond Multiculturalism* (New York: Basic Books, 1995), 151. See also Johanna Lessinger, *From the Ganges to the Hudson: Indian Immigrants in New York City* (Boston: Allyn & Bacon, 1995), 71–95.

4. See Prologue for an introduction to *oikumene*.

5. Ministry of Labour, Government of India Annual Report 1994–95, 120–26.

6. Colin Clarke, Ceri Peach, and Steven Vertovec, eds., *South Asians Overseas: Migration and Ethnicity* (Cambridge: Cambridge University Press, 1990), 1. See page 2 of Clarke et al. for a list of countries with overseas South Asian populations totaling 8,691,490 in 1987. It should be noted that some of the figures are outdated and others are inaccurate, such as those for Fiji and South Africa. See Figure 3, page 20, for more accurate figures.

7. Jagat K. Motwani, Mahin Gosine, and Jyoti Barot Motwani, eds., *Global Indian Diaspora Yesterday, Today and Tomorrow* (New York: Global Organization of People of Indian Origin, 1993), unnumbered page, "Comments From Co-Chairmen Dr. Thomas Abraham and Ram Lakhina."

8. The 1994 estimate for the Indian population is by the United Nations.

9. Clarke et al., *South Asians Overseas*, 1.

10. Motwani et al., in *Global Indian Diaspora*, also recognize an early third wave between the seventh and fourteenth centuries when trade links between India and East Africa and India and the Far East were established but the historical literature on this period is somewhat limited.

11. Hugh Tinker, *The Banyan Tree: Overseas Emigrants from India, Pakistan and Bangladesh* (London: Oxford University Press, 1977), 3.

12. Other destinations include Grenada, St. Vincent, Lucia, Martinique, Guadeloupe, and St. Croix. Roger Daniels, *History of Indian Immigration to the United States: An Interpretive Essay* (New York: The Asia Society, 1989), 8. Descendants of indentured immigrants later migrated to the countries of their colonial masters, e.g., from Surinam to the Netherlands, after Surinam's independence in 1975.

13. I owe thanks to John Kelly who brought this to my attention.

14. Hugh Tinker, *A New System of Slavery: The Export of Indian Labour Overseas 1830–1920* (London: Oxford University Press, 1974), 40–55; Chandra Jayawardena, *Conflict and Solidarity in a Guianese Plantation* (London: The Athlone Press, 1963), 14.

15. Tinker, *New System of Slavery*, 55–59; Donald Wood, *Trinidad in Transition, The Years After Slavery* (London: Oxford University Press, 1968), 107.

16. For a more detailed account of patterns of migration from India and statistics on Indian populations in each of these countries, see Padma Rangaswamy, "The Imperatives of Choice and Change: Post-1965 Immigrants from India in Metropolitan Chicago" (Ph.D. diss., University of Illinois at Chicago, 1996), 82–121.

17. Burton Benedict, *Indians in a Plural Society* (London: Her Majesty's Stationery Office, 1961).

18. See Adrian C. Mayer, *Peasants in the Pacific: A Study of Fiji Indian Rural Society* (Berkeley and Los Angeles: University of California Press, 1973) for a broad account of Fiji political history, and V. Lal, "Marooned at Home," in Clarke et al., *South Asians Overseas*, for an account of the 1987 coup that robbed Indians of their democratically won political gains. Another work by John D. Kelly, *A Politics of Virtue: Hinduism, Sexuality, and Countercolonial Discourse in Fiji* (Chicago: The University of Chicago Press, 1991) throws light on the role of the colonial masters in setting the stage for political conflict. See also John D. Kelly, "*Bhakti* and Postcolonial Politics: Hindu Missions to Fiji," in *Nation and Migration: The Politics of Space in the South Asian Diaspora*, ed. Peter van der Veer (Philadelphia: University of Pennsylvania Press, 1995), 43–72.

19. *Europa World Yearbook, 1995* (London: Europa Publications), 1410.

20. Raymond T. Smith, "Race and Political Conflict in Guyana," in *Race* 12 (April 1971): 417–27. For Indians in Trinidad, see John La Guerre, ed., *From Calcutta to Caroni: The East Indians of Trinidad* (London: Longmans, 1974), and Colin G. Clarke, *East Indians in a West Indian Town, San Fernando, Trinidad, 1930–70* (London, Allen & Unwin, 1986).

21. *India Tribune* (Chicago), 5 November 1994.

22. Hugh Tinker, "Indians in Southeast Asia," in Clarke et al., *South Asians Overseas*, 39–55.

23. Barton M. Schwartz, ed., *Caste in Overseas Indian Communities* (San Francisco: Chandler Publishing Company, 1967). R. K. Jain, *Indian Communities Abroad: Themes and Literature* (New Delhi: Manohar Publishers, 1993), 17.

24. Steven Vertovec, "Oil Boom and Recession in Trinidad Indian Villages," in Clarke et al., *South Asians Overseas*, 89–112.

25. "Coolie" in India is, and used to be, a straightforward term meaning "one who transports a burden." Only in the context of indentured labor has it acquired demeaning overtones and been used to devalue the social status of an entire people. See Tinker, *New System of Slavery*, 42, for a fuller account of the origin of the word.

26. Tinker, "Indians in Southeast Asia," 39–55. See also David West Rudner, *Caste and Capitalism in Colonial India: The Nattukottai Chettiars* (Berkeley and Los Angeles: University of California Press, 1994), 79–85.

27. Michael Twaddle, "East African Asians Through a Hundred Years," in Clarke at al., *South Asians Overseas*, 154.

28. See Parminder Bhachu, *Twice Migrants: East African Sikh Settlers in Britain* (London: Tavistock, 1985), and Arthur Helweg, *Sikhs in England*, 2d ed. (Delhi: Oxford University Press, 1986).

29. D. R. Rajagopal, "Hong Kong Indians Retain an Affluent Stronghold," *India Tribune*, 11 December 1993.

30. Vaughan Robinson, "Boom and Gloom: the Success and Failure of South Asians in Britain," in Clarke et al., *South Asians Overseas*, 274.

31. Study conducted by Virender Singh Kerala and Roger Ballard, "Indians Making Steady Climb on Britain's Social Ladder," *India Tribune*, 26 February 1994.

32. Norman Buchignani, Doreen M. Indra with Ram Srivastava, *Continuous Journey: A Social History of South Asians in Canada* (Toronto: McClelland and Stewart Ltd., 1985), 128–42.

33. Charles E. Waddell and Glenn M. Vernon, "Ethnic Identity and National Identification. The Social Construction of Commitment Among Indian Immigrants to Australia," in *Migration and Modernization: The Indian Diaspora in Comparative Perspective*, ed. Richard Harvey Brown and George V. Coelho, Studies in Third World Societies 39 (Williamsburg: College of William and Mary, 1987), 13–23.

34. John Perry, "Indian Israelis: Making Giant Strides in the Promised Land," *India Worldwide* (New York), January 1995, 4–10.

35. *India Tribune*, 25 February 1995.

36. Myron Weiner, "The Indian Presence in America: What Difference Will It Make?," in *Conflicting Images: India and the United States*, ed. Sulochana Raghavan Glazer and Nathan Glazer (Glenn Dale, Md.: The Riverdale Company, 1990), 249.

37. Many fine books have been written on the occasion of India's fiftieth anniversary of independence. Among the more readable is Shashi Tharoor's *India: From Midnight to the Millennium* (New York: Arcadia Publishing, 1997).

38. *Harvard Business Review*, November 1993, 66–79.

39. Weiner, "Indian Presence in America," 251.

40. Richard Harvey Brown, "The Migrating Self: Persons and Polities in the Process of Modernization," in Richard Harvey Brown and George V. Coelho, eds., *Tradition and Transformation: Asian Indians in America*, Studies in Third World Societies 38 (Williamsburg: College of William and Mary, 1986).

41. Alan Roland, "Indians in America: Adaptation and the Bicultural Self," *Committee on South Asian Women Bulletin* 7, nos. 3–4: 23–28.

42. Norman Brown, the Sanskrit scholar, analyzes the basic underlying unities that define Indian civilization, and identifies one of the values of Hinduism as "duty and the unusual stress put upon correct action." W. Norman Brown, "The Content of Cultural Continuity in India," *The Journal of Asian Studies* 20 (August 1961): 427–34.

43. Milton Singer, *When a Great Tradition Modernizes: An Anthropological Approach to Indian Civilization* (Chicago: The University of Chicago Press, 1972); David G. Mandelbaum, *Society in India: Continuity and Change* (Berkeley and Los Angeles: University of California Press, 1970); Pauline Kolenda, *Regional Differences in Family Structure in India* (Jaipur: Rawat Publications, 1986); Pranjal Sharma, Soutik Biswas, and Rohit Brijnath, "Change Amidst Continuity," *India Today*, 15 July 1994, 80–92.

44. M. N. Srinivas, *Religion and Society among the Coorgs of South India* (London: Oxford University Press, 1952).

45. Bernard Cohn, "Regions Subjective and Objective: Their Relation to the Study of Modern Indian History and Society," in *Modern India, An Interpretive Anthology*, ed. Thomas R. Metcalfe (New Delhi: Sterling Publishers, 1990), 135–36.

46. Jawaharlal Nehru, *The Discovery of India* (New Delhi: Oxford University Press, 1989), 62; first published in 1946 by The Signet Press, Calcutta.

Chapter 2   The American Context: From Pariah to Elite

1. S. Chandrasekhar, "A History of United States Legislation with Respect to Immigration from India," in *From India to America: A Brief History of Immigration: Problems of Discrimination, Admission & Assimilation*, ed. S. Chandrasekhar (La Jolla, Calif.: Population Review, 1982), 12.

2. Joan M. Jensen, *Passage from India: Asian Indian Immigrants in North America* (New Haven: Yale University Press, 1988), 12–15.

3. Joan M. Jensen, "East Indians," in *Harvard Encyclopedia of American Ethnic Groups*, ed. S. Thernstrom, A. Orlov, and O. Handlin (Cambridge, Mass.: Harvard University Press, 1980), 296. See also Surinder M. Bhardwaj and N. Madhusudana Rao, "Asian Indians in the United States," *South Asians Overseas: Migration and Ethnicity*, ed. Colin Clarke, Ceri Peach, and Steven Vertovec (Cambridge: Cambridge University Press, 1990), 197–98.

4. The story is told of how the Swami arrived in Chicago without a guide or a place to stay and was taken in by Mr. and Mrs. George W. Hale of 1415 N. Dearborn Street. Thereafter, he made the Hale residence his base for his midwestern tours on his frequent visits to the United States. *Vedanta in Chicago Golden Jubilee Souvenir* (Chicago: Vivekananda Vedanta Society, 1980), 12.

5. I cannot help but think of the agent who came to the steel township of Ranchi in eastern India where I lived with my engineer husband in 1967, touting, probably in the very same fashion, the economic opportunities open to skilled engineers in the United States. I have no idea if he was paid for his efforts, and if so, by whom.

6. Jensen, *Passage from India*, 31.

7. Harold S. Jacoby, *A Half-Century Appraisal of East Indians in the United States* (Stockton, Calif.: The Sixth Annual College of the Pacific Faculty Research Lecture, 23 May 1956), 28.

8. Brett Melendy, *Asians in America: Filipinos, Koreans and East Indians* (Boston: Twayne, 1977), 231.

9. Melendy, *Asians in America*, 232.

10. Karen Leonard, "Marriage and Family Life among Early Asian Indian Immigrants," in *From India to America*, ed. S. Chandrasekhar, 67–74. Takaki, *Strangers from a Different Shore*, 312.

11. Takaki, *Strangers from a Different Shore*, 307. See also Karen I. Leonard, *Making Ethnic Choices: California's Punjabi Mexican Americans* (Philadelphia: Temple University Press, 1992) for a sympathetic account of the Sikh struggle for human rights.

12. Takaki, *Strangers from a Different Shore*, 299–300.

13. *New York Times*, 24 April 1973.

14. Takaki, *Strangers from a Different Shore*, 306, 367.

15. Jensen, "East Indians," 296.

16. Roger Daniels, "United States Policy Towards Asian Immigrants: Contemporary Developments in Historical Perspective," *International Journal* 68 (spring 1993): 325.

17. Karen Leonard, "Ethnic Identity and Gender: South Asians in the United States," in *Ethnicity, Identity, Migration: The South Asian Context*, ed. Milton Israel and N. K. Wagle, South Asian Studies Papers 6 (Toronto: University of Toronto Centre for South Asian Studies), 169. In other countries of the Indian *oikumene*, too, there exists a feeling of hostility between descendants of the old colonial immigration and the post-1965 immigrants.

18. Lavina Melwani, "The Fruits of Labor," *Little India* (Reading, Pa.), August 1995, 10–22.

19. David M. Reimers, *Still the Golden Door: The Third World Comes to America* (New York: Columbia University Press, 1992), 81.

20. Roger Daniels, *History of Indian Immigration to the United States: An Interpretive Essay* (New York: The Asia Society, 1989), 41.

21. Reimers, *Still the Golden Door*, 89–90.

22. Padma Rangaswamy, "The Imperatives of Choice and Change: Post-1965 Immigrants from India in Metropolitan Chicago" (Ph.D. diss., University of Illinois at Chicago, 1996), table 3: "Indian Immigration as Percentage of Total Immigration to the United States," 145.

23. My own father-in-law, who had been sent in his youth to the United States by the Indian Railways to study the latest in railroad technology, was so taken with this country that he would have loved to stay beyond the allotted year, but he had to return to India. Years later, when it was time for his own grown son (who later became my husband) to seek technical training abroad, he carefully avoided exposing him to the United States, and maneuvered to send him to the USSR instead. He was afraid that his son would fall under the "spell" of America, as it were, and never return to his native land! It was not until after my father-in-law's death in 1965 that we even entertained the idea of coming to the United States. This personal story provides one more example of how several factors have to come together at a certain point in time to make immigration possible.

24. Arthur W. and Usha M. Helweg, *An Immigrant Success Story: East Indians in America* (Philadelphia: University of Pennsylvania Press, 1991), 26–44.

25. See Gerald E. Dirks, "International Migration in the Nineties: Causes and Consequences," *International Journal* 48, no. 2 (spring 1993): 191–214, for a summary discussion of what causes people to migrate from the less developed to the more industrialized countries.

26. Sunita Wadekar Bhargava, "Curry and Calypso," *India Today*, 31 January 1993, 48c–d.

27. Myron Weiner, "The Indian Presence in America: What Difference Will It Make?" in *Conflicting Images: India and the United States*, ed. Sulochana Raghavan Glazer and Nathan Glazer (Glenn Dale, Md.: The Riverdale Company, 1990), 247–48. While Indians in India complain of the brain drain, Weiner notes that neither the Indian government nor the Indian people would like to see any restrictions placed on emigration.

28. Ibid., 243.

29. Eight out of ten immigrants were already married when they came. Juan L. Gonzales Jr., *Racial and Ethnic Families in America* (Dubuque, Iowa: Kendall/Hunt Publishing, 1992), 129.

30. Rangaswamy, "The Imperatives of Choice and Change," table 4: "Relative Regional Concentration of Asian Population in U.S. compared to Total U.S. Population, 1980 and 1990," 159.

31. Bhardwaj and Rao point out that states such as South Carolina, Alabama, Mississippi, Tennessee, Arkansas, Kentucky, and West Virginia do not attract Indians who see them as regions of "racial prejudice, poverty, and little opportunity." But states such as Texas, Georgia and Florida are attractive as centers of "engineering, commerce, tourism and real estate." "Asian Indians in the United States," 201.

32. Statistical Abstract of the United States, 1990–1994, "Immigrants Admitted by Leading Country of Birth and Metropolitan Area of Intended Residence," table 8.

33. Harry H. L. Kitano and Roger Daniels, *Asian Americans: Emerging Minorities* (Englewood Cliffs, N.J.: Prentice Hall, 1988), 167.

34. Bhardwaj and Rao, "Asian Indians in the United States," 209.

35. Daniels, "United States Policy Towards Asian Immigrants," 333.

36. The main source for comparative statistics in this chapter are the two excellent special reports on Asian Americans by the Census Bureau that handily summarize socioeconomic characteristics. *We, the Asian and Pacific Islander Americans*, 1980, and *We, the American Asians*, 1993, both from the U.S. Census Bureau.

37. Bhardwaj and Rao, "Asian Indians in the United States," 199.

38. Gonzalez commends the Indian culture's emphasis on family ties, and sees that as the main reason they are able to maintain strong community ties in spite of the fast pace of life in the United States. Gonzalez Jr., *Racial and Ethnic Families*, 125.

39. Daniels, *History of Indian Immigration*, 43.

40. Kitano and Daniels, *Asian Americans*, 174. Elliott R. Barkan, "Whom Shall We Integrate? A Comparative Analysis of the Immigration and Naturalization Trends of Asians Before and After the 1965 Immigration Act (1951–1975)," *Journal of American Ethnic History* 3 (1983): 29–57.

41. Reimers illustrates this migratory pattern with the aid of a chart that shows how one student non-immigrant acquires immigrant status, then becomes a citizen and within the span of a few years induces the migration of at least fifty relatives. Reimers, *Still the Golden Door*, 95.

42. Bhardwaj and Rao, "Asian Indians in the United States," 200.

43. Parmatma Saran noted in 1985, "Only a few years ago, one rarely saw an Indian working at a gas station, driving a cab, working in a restaurant or in any manual job. In recent times, in the larger cities in the United States, especially in New York, Washington, Chicago and Los Angeles, this is not uncommon." Paramatma Saran, *The Asian Indian Experience in the United States* (Cambridge: Schenkman, 1985), 100.

44. Lavina Melwani, "Dark Side of the Moon: Some Indians Live the Great American Nightmare," *India Today*, 31 January 1994, 60c.

45. Based on personal observation about new arrivals in the Indian community in Chicago.

46. *India Today*, 30 June 1995.

47. Gopal Krishna Singh, "Immigration, Nativity, and Socioeconomic Assimilation of Asian Indians in the United States" (Ph.D. diss., Ohio State University, 1991). Only native-born Asian Indian women had reached earnings parity with whites.

48. Other research also supports this finding. Kwang Chung Kim, a Korean American sociologist at Western Illinois University, found that Asian American workers had greater education and worked longer hours to achieve the same income as whites in their profession. *Chicago Tribune*, 7 August 1994. *The Asian and Pacific Islander Population in the U.S., March 1991 and 1990*. Bureau of the Census, Current Population Reports, Population Characteristics, P20-459, figure 7.

49. *We, the American Asians*, Figure 3.

50. Daniels, *History of Indian Immigration*, 4.

Chapter 3   The Attraction of a Metropolitan Region

1. For a summary overview of Chicago's Indian population, see Padma Rangaswamy, "Asian Indians in Chicago: Growth and Change in a Model Minority," in *Ethnic Chicago: A Multicultural Portrait*, ed. Melvin D. Holli and Peter d'A Jones (Grand Rapids, Mich.: William B. Eerdmans Publishing Company, 1995), 438–62.

2. Cynthia Linton, ed. *The Ethnic Handbook: A Guide to the Cultures and Traditions of Chicago's Diverse Communities* (Chicago: The Illinois Ethnic Coalition, 1996).

3. U.S. Census Bureau, 1990 Census of the Population, General Population Characteristics, Illinois, table 6.

4. Harold M. Mayer and Richard C. Wade, *Chicago: Growth of a Metropolis* (Chicago: The University of Chicago Press, 1969), ix.

5. U.S. Census Bureau, 1990 Census of Population Illinois, Social and Economic Characteristics, tables 4 and 5, pp. 22–23.

6. Gregory Squires, Larry Bennett, Kathleen McCout, and Philip Nyden, *Chicago: Race, Class, and the Response to Urban Decline* (Philadelphia: Temple University Press, 1987), 28, 34.

7. Squires et al., *Chicago*, 36.

8. From personal interviews with engineers affected by layoffs.

9. John Miller and Genevieve Anderson, eds., *Chicago Stories* (San Francisco: Chronicle Books, 1993), xii; Squires et al., *Chicago*, 97.

10. Dominic Pacyga, "Ethnic Neighborhoods," in *Ethnic Chicago*, ed. Holli and Jones, 606, 617.

11. Chicago has a long history of racially motivated violence. Race riots were sparked in 1919 when whites stoned a black youth to death for accidentally swimming into the white sector of an unmarked beach in Lake Michigan. Allan H. Spear, *Black Chicago: The Making of a Negro Ghetto, 1890–1920* (Chicago: The University of Chicago Press, 1967), vii. Incidents of attacks against blacks for being in the wrong place at the wrong time continue to be reported in the press even in the 1990s.

12. Dominic A. Pacyga and Ellen Skerrett, *Chicago City of Neighborhoods Histories and Tours* (Chicago: Loyola University Press, 1986), 467–73.

13. Squires et al., *Chicago*, 94.

14. Mike Royko, *Boss: Richard J. Daley of Chicago* (New York: Penguin Books USA, Inc., 1971), 6. The neighborhood concept was guarded most fiercely by none other than Chicago's political icon and its most famous mayor.

15. See Madhulika S. Khandelwal, "Indian Immigrants in Queens, New York City: Patterns of Spatial Concentration and Distribution," in *Nation and Migration: The Politics of Space in the South Asian Diaspora*, ed. Peter van der Veer (Philadelphia: University of Pennsylvania Press, 1995), 178–96. There are striking similarities in the spatial distribution of Indians in New York and Chicago.

16. *Indicators for Understanding: A Profile of Metro Chicago's Immigrant Community*, study conducted by Latino Institute, Chicago and Office for Social Policy Research, Northern Illinois University, Dekalb, 1995.

17. Squires et al., *Chicago*, 97.

18. Pacyga and Skerrett, *Chicago City of Neighborhoods*, 87–163.

19. Colleen Taylor Sen, "Incense and Spice: Traveling to that Exotic Crossroads Called Devon Avenue," *Chicago Tribune*, 9 September 1993, sec. 7, p. 1.

20. Interview with Mr. Rattan Sharma, 27 September 1998.

21. Khandelwal, "Indian Immigrants in Queens," 85.

22. In a move meant to please all the major ethnic groups in the area, city officials have named the street at various sections as Golda Meier Avenue, Gandhi Marg, Mohammed Ali Jinnah Marg, and King Sargon Boulevard. Chicagoans have survived the confusion generated by this terminology by generally ignoring the different names and by continuing to refer to it as Devon Avenue.

23. William Cronon, *Nature's Metropolis: Chicago and the Great West* (New York: W. W. Norton & Company, 1991).

24. Padma Rangaswamy, "The Imperatives of Choice and Change: Post-1965 Immigrants from India in Metropolitan Chicago" (Ph.D. diss., University of Illinois at Chicago, 1996), table 24: "Distribution of Asians in Census Tracts 205 to 209 in Chicago in 1990," 533.

25. *Chicago Tribune*, 23 September 1991, sec. 1, p. 6.

26. Squires et al., *Chicago*, 41–42.

27. Cynthia Linton, "Immigration and Immigrants: How They are Portrayed in the Chicago Press," in *One City*, ed. Lucretia A. Bailey (Chicago: The Chicago Council on Urban Affairs, spring 1997), 20–23.

28. See Vijay Prashad, "Crafting Solidarities," in *A Part, Yet Apart: South Asians in Asian America*, ed. Lavina Dhingra Shankar and Rajini Srikanth (Philadelphia: Temple University Press, 1998), 105–26.

29. David Hollinger calls this "distinctive system of classification by descent-defined communities" America's "ethno-racial Pentagon." David A. Hollinger, *Postethnic America: Beyond Multiculturalism* (New York: Basic Books, 1995), 23.

30. Squires et al., Chicago, 98.

31. Jean Leslie Bacon, "Hierarchy Transformed: Intergenerational Change in Chicago's Asian Indian Community" (Ph.D. diss., University of Chicago, 1993), 2.

Chapter 4   The Quantitative Profile: Responses to a Survey

1. Horace Kallen, *Culture and Democracy in the United States* (New York: Arno Press, 1924).

2. Milton Gordon, *Assimilation in American Life: The Role of Race, Religion, and National Origins* (New York: Oxford University Press, 1964), 234. One theory formulated by David Hollinger in *Postethnic America: Beyond Multiculturalism* (New York: Basic Books, 1995) suggests an alternative "cosmopolitanism" that would permit Americans to choose their affiliations according to personal preference. Gordon sees such an ideal situation prevailing only in scholarly, artistic or intellectual circles.

3. Gordon, *Assimilation in American Life*, 242.

4. The division is as follows: low income—those earning up to $50,000 (31 percent); middle income—between $50,000 and $100,000 (28 percent); and high income—above $100,000 (37 percent). The first immigrants are those who came before 1980 and the second wave are those who came after 1981.

5. For comprehensive information on methodology, lines of inquiry, and the statistical approach used in the analysis of survey data, along with survey questionnaire and detailed tabulation of responses, see Padma Rangaswamy, "The Imperatives of Choice and Change: Post-1965 Immigrants from India in Metropolitan Chicago" (Ph.D. diss., University of Illinois at Chicago, 1996), 485–518.

6. Paramatma Saran, *The Asian Indian Experience in the United States* (Cambridge: Schenkman, 1985), 109.

7. There are now eighteen official languages in India.

8. Myron Weiner, "The Indian Presence in America: What Difference Will it Make?," in *Conflicting Images: India and the United States*, ed. Sulochana Raghavan Glazer and Nathan Glazer (Glenn Dale, Md.: The Riverdale Company, 1990), 244.

9. Arthur W. and Usha M. Helweg, *An Immigrant Success Story: East Indians in America* (Philadelphia: University of Pennsylvania Press, 1991), 263.

10. Sunita Sohrabi, "Accent on Assimilation," *India Today*, 31 March 1992, 52e–f.

11. Though many Indians do not see "culture-by-translation" as desirable, they accept it reluctantly and see it as the only alternative to total extinction of Indian culture in the new land.

12. Robert Hardgrave, "Rediscovery of India," *India Today*, 31 August 1992, 60h. Hardgrave discusses the range of motivations for second-generation Indians to study their mother-tongue— from urging of parents to their own desire to write to relatives at home and gain a formal understanding of their own roots.

13. Kamala Viswesaran, "Predicaments of the Hyphen," in *Our Feet Walk the Sky*, ed. Women of South Asian Descent Collective (San Francisco: Aunt Lute, 1993), 303.

14. Helweg and Helweg, *An Immigrant Success Story*, 262.

15. A more specific question such as "Did you vote in the last election?" may have elicited a more interpretable response.

16. Tania Anand, "Breaking a Barrier," *India Today*, 30 September 1992, 52c–d.

17. Alan Roland, "Indians in America: Adaptation and the Bicultural Self," *Committee on South Asian Women Bulletin* 7, nos. 3–4: 23–28.

18. Helweg and Helweg, *An Immigrant Success Story*, 262.

19. *India Tribune*, 25 March 1995.

20. Joseph Ahne, "Koreans of Chicago," in *Ethnic Chicago: A Multicultural Portrait*, ed. Melvin J. Holli and Peter d'A. Jones (Grand Rapids, Mich.: William B. Eerdmans Publishing, 1995), 485.

21. There is ample evidence from other sources such as media reports and the *Report of the Illinois Commission on Civil Rights (1995)* that Indians, even the most highly skilled, face discrimination on the job.

22. This is borne out by the observed significance levels in the correlations procedures. The weak significance levels showed that there is no correlation between experiences of social discrimination and gender, income level, and length of stay. See Rangaswamy, "The Imperatives of Choice and Change," 487–88.

23. See John Y. Fenton, *Transplanting Religious Traditions: Asian Indians in America* (New York: Praeger, 1988), 106, and Helweg and Helweg, *An Immigrant Success Story*, 263.

24. Karen B. Leonard and Chandra S. Tibrewal, "Asian Indians in Southern California: Occupations and Ethnicity," in *Immigration and Entrepreneurship: Culture, Capital and Ethnic Networks*, ed. Ivan Light and Parminder Bhachu (New Brunswick: Transaction Publishers, 1993), 141–57.

25. Fenton, *Transplanting Religious Traditions*, 50.

26. For details regarding the analysis of variance testing that led to this conclusion, see Rangaswamy, "The Imperatives of Choice and Change," 485–90.

Chapter 5   Astride Many Worlds: The Women

1. Ludwik Fleck, *Genesis and Development of a Scientific Fact*, ed. Thaddeus J. Trenn and Robert K. Merton, trans. Fred Bradley and Thaddeus J. Trenn (Chicago: University of Chicago Press, 1979), 47. Fleck places what he calls the "thought collective" in a certain time and place in history.

2. See Padma Rangaswamy, "The Imperatives of Choice and Change: Post-1965 Immigrants from India in Metropolitan Chicago" (Ph.D. diss., University of Illinois at Chicago, 1996), 508–18, for profile of those who participated in the group discussions, the questions that were posed to them, and the analytical approach.

3. Karen Leonard, Jean Bacon, and Priya Agarwal are some of the writers who have explored the Indian ethnic experience from the intergenerational point of view.

4. Over 1981–91, the number of females per 1,000 males declined in India from 934 to 929. In developed countries, the ratio is around 1,060 females for each 1,000 males. Karen Brandon, "Born into Uncertainty," *Chicago Tribune*, 28 January 1996, 1.

5. K. M. Kapadia, *Marriage and Family in India*, 3d ed. (Calcutta: Oxford University Press, 1966), 254. Margot I. Duley and Mary I. Edwards, eds., *The Cross Cultural Study of Women: A Comprehensive Guide* (New York: The Feminist Press, 1986), 149.

6. Manu 1, 149; see R. C. Majumdar, *Ancient India* (Delhi: Motilal Banarsidass Publishers Private, Ltd, 1994), 474.

7. Quoted in Duley and Edwards, *Cross Cultural Study of Women*, 181.

8. Emily C. Brown, "Revolution in India: Made in America," in *From India to America: A Brief History of Immigration: Problems of Discrimination, Admission & Assimilation*, ed. S. Chandrasekhar (La Jolla: Population Review, 1982), 42.

9. Harold S. Jacoby, *A Half-century Appraisal of East Indians in the United States* (Stockton, Calif.: The Sixth Annual College of the Pacific Faculty Research Lecture, 23 May 1956), 12.

10. Gary Hess, "The Asian Indian Immigrants in the United States: The Early Phase, 1900–1965," in *From India to America*, ed. S. Chandrasekhar, 32–33.

11. The Committee on South Asian Women (COSAW), supported in part by Texas A & M University's Women's Studies program, has published a bulletin since 1982. Also see Women of

South Asian Descent Collective, ed., *Our Feet Walk the Sky* (San Francisco: Aunt Lute, 1993). There are also several movies made by Indian women based in North America that add to the rich and varied primary sources on Indian women immigrants.

　12. "Trapped in Tradition," *India Today*, 30 September 1992, 52f–g.

　13. Interview with Marilyn Fernandez, social service administrator in Chicago, 9 February 1992.

　14. Paramatma Saran, *The Asian Indian Experience in the United States* (Cambridge: Schenkman, 1985), 97.

　15. Saran, *The Asian Indian Experience*, 136–75.

　16. Ibid., 109.

　17. Sathi Das Gupta, *On the Trail of an Uncertain Dream*, (New York: AMS Press, 1989), 160.

　18. Bharati Mukherjee, *Wife* (Boston: Houghton Mifflin Company, 1975); *A Middleman and Other Stories* (New York: Grove Press, 1988); *Jasmine* (New York: Grove Weidenfeld, 1989).

Chapter 6　Caught in Limbo: The Youth

　1. *India Tribune*, 8 July 1995.

　2. 1990 U.S. Census, Household and Family Characteristics of Selected Asian and Pacific Islander Groups by Nativity, Citizenship and Year of Entry, table 2.

　3. Satinder Bindra, "Living on the Edge: Punjabi Teenagers Defy Parents and Gurudwara and Create a New Swinging Culture," *India Today*, 15 August 1992, 48b–c.

　4. *India Tribune*, 26 June 1993.

　5. R. K. Radhakrishnan, "NRI Medicos' Fees Augment College Facilities," *India Tribune*, 27 January 1996.

　6. Little India Data Service, Reading, Pa., quoted in *India Today*, 28 February 1994, 60c–d. Though it is not clear what exactly is meant by "race," when Indians speak of people of a different "race," they generally mean "non-Indians."

　7. Cover story, "Shades of Love. Insights into Intercultural Marriages," *Onward* (Dayton, Ohio), vol. 1, no. 3 (1995): 17–24.

　8. *India Tribune*, 10 June 1995.

　9. *India Tribune*, 20 November 1993.

　10. From personal interviews with Indian youth.

　11. From personal interviews with Chicago's youth. Also see Anupama Chandra, "Marriage, Indian Style," *Reader*, vol. 21, no. 5 (1 November 1991), sec. 1; and Priya Agarwal, *Passage from India: Post-1965 Indian Immigrants and Their Children* (Palos Verdes, Calif.: Yuvati Publications, 1991).

　12. Lavina Melwani, "Brown or White? A Brave New Generation of Inter-racial Children Emerges," *India Today*, 28 February 1994, 60c–d. See also Jean Walsh, "The New Indian Americans," *India Currents* (San Francisco) September 1992, M16.

　13. Sunita Wadekar Bhargava, "Curry and Calypso: Child of Two Cultures, the Community Adapts to a Third," *India Today*, 31 January 1995, 48c–d.

Chapter 7　In Search of Security: The Elderly

　1. Papers presented by Rashmi Gupta, "Asian Indian Elderly and Caregiving: Problems and Prospects," and Mono Ranjan Sen, "Problems and Future of Senior Citizens of Indian

Descent," at the First National Indian-American Conference, Montclair State University, New Jersey, 16 September 1995. The 1990 U.S. Census shows 2.8 percent or 23,000 Indians in the "65 years old and over" category.

2. Carol Jouzaitis, "Immigrants Force U.S. Self-exam. Legal Residents Could Face Loss of Benefits," *Chicago Tribune*, 21 May 1995, sec. 1, p. 13.

3. *India Tribune*, 14 August 1993.

4. In comparing notes with researchers in the New York/New Jersey area, where the Indian population is much larger than in the Midwest, I found that the elderly South Asians are much better served in the Chicago area. Mono Ranjan Sen, who has been working with seniors in the east since the 1970s, reported that most Indians did not avail themselves of the balanced meal programs in the New Jersey area because the meals were only Western-style and usually included meat.

5. Jyotsna Mirle Kalavar, "Life Satisfaction of Immigrant Asian Indian Elderly in the United States of America" (Ph.D. diss., University of Maryland College Park, 1990). See also Maxine P. Fisher, *The Indians of New York City: A Study of Immigrants from India* (Columbia: South Asia Books, 1980), 93–97, for an analysis of six case studies of parents of Indian immigrants.

6. *India Tribune*, 2 January 1993. Rohini Nilekani et al., "When They Are 64, Will They Get Their Children's Support?" in *India Tribune*, 12 June 1993.

Chapter 8   Preserving the Core: Cultural Institutions

1. Raymond B. Williams, *Religions of Immigrants from India and Pakistan: New Threads in the American Tapestry* (Cambridge: Cambridge University Press, 1988), 10. Williams notes that Michael Leonardo (1984, 134) "points out that labeling a collection of humans as a community or a social category confers upon it a hoped-for alliance of interest, solidarity, and tradition."

2. See Jean Bacon, *Life Lines: Community, Family, and Assimilation Among Asian Indian Immigrants* (New York: Oxford University Press, 1996), 60–63. Bacon contends that Indian parents deliberately demonize American society and insist that Indian values are "superior" to American values as a strategy to prevent their children from becoming too Americanized and to hide an underlying inferiority complex. The truth may be somewhat simpler. Many Indians do truly believe in the superiority of their own culture.

3. Bacon, *Life Lines*, 22–58. Bacon discusses the personality conflicts in organizations and the intergenerational conflicts in families in detail, but not the divide between the well-heeled professional suburbanites and the less well-to-do, nonprofessional city dwellers.

4. See Maxine P. Fisher, *The Indians of New York City: A Study of Immigrants from India* (Columbia, Mo.: South Asia Books, 1980), 117–33, for a detailed account of the AIA's fight to get Indians recognized as a separate group in the 1980 census.

5. Phone interview with Dr. Shariff conducted on 2 September 1995.

6. *India Tribune*, 17 October 1992.

7. *India Tribune*, 3, 10 September 1994. The media itself is not above getting embroiled in power and personality politics and is accused by its readers of "yellow journalism."

8. The Federation of India Associations is a Chicago-based organization and also claims to be "the largest umbrella organization in the USA, with a membership of about 100 associations." *India Tribune*, 18 February 1995.

9. Sanjay Nambiar, "We Deserve Visionary Leadership, Not Squabbling Fools," *India Tribune*, 22 January 1994.

10. *India Tribune*, 30 July; 6 August 1994.

11. *India Tribune*, 3 December 1994.

12. Fisher, *The Indians of New York City*, 127.

13. See Bacon for a detailed discussion of "ego" problems in Indian organizations, *Life Lines*, 36.

14. Fisher, *The Indians of New York City*, 83.

15. *India Tribune*, 27 August 1994.

16. *India Tribune*, 6 August 1994.

17. A notice announcing the Annual Convention of Tamils in Toledo Ohio, 1–4 1995, listed fourteen different colleges in South India for members to identify with and organize alumni meetings.

18. *India Tribune*, 1 July 1995.

19. The Federation of Gujarati Associations of North America (FOGANA) held their fifteenth dance competition on September 3, 1995, at the Chicago Theater in downtown Chicago and featured twenty-seven competing teams.

20. *India Tribune*, 11 March 1995.

21. Fifty-five million Tamils live in India, the rest in Sri Lanka, Malaysia, Singapore, Mauritius, South Africa, Indonesia, Fiji, Australia, Canada, the U.K. and the United States. *India Tribune*, 5 June 1993.

22. The organization is not formally registered.

23. Most of the data in this section comes from my meeting with members of the East African Community Organization at their annual picnic at Katherine Legge Memorial Park, Hinsdale on August 20, 1995.

24. This same interviewee said that he was "born with a golden spoon" while Gujaratis from India were "closer to want and poverty."

25. From personal interviews and published sources. *India Tribune*, 30 October, 1993. Sanjay Nambiar, "Pioneering a Renaissance in Bharatanatyam, " *India Tribune*, 30 July 1994. Susan Kreimer, "Preserving Indian Heritage," *Chicago Tribune*, 13 August 1995, 1B.

26. *India Tribune*, 23 September 1995.

27. *India Tribune*, 11 June 1994. *Chicago Tribune* (Du Page edition), 28 June 1993. *Daily Herald* (Du Page County), 16 May 1993. *Sruti* (Madras, India), July 1992.

28. Reshma Memon Yaqub "Indian Stars of Many Talents Wow Audience of Many Tastes," *Chicago Tribune*, 31 May 1994, sec. 1, p. 18.

29. Lavina Melwani, "Angst of a Diaspora," *India Today*, 15 August 1995.

Chapter 9   Building Infrastructure: Religious Institutions

1. David Firestone, "How Immigrants Find Their Role in U.S. Holiday," *The New York Times*, 26 December 1993, 1.

2. John Y. Fenton, *Transplanting Religious Traditions: Asian Indians in America* (New York: Praeger, 1988), 101–67.

3. *India Today*, 30 April 1995, 64C.

4. *Chicago Tribune Magazine*, 20 August 1993, 16.

5. Fenton, *Transplanting Religious Traditions*, 176.

6. Raymond B. Williams, *Religions of Immigrants from India and Pakistan: New Threads in the American Tapestry* (Cambridge: Cambridge University Press, 1988), 226.

7. Arthur J. Pais, "For God's Sake," *India Today*, 15 March 1993, 60b.

8. Ibid. The $375 million is broken down as follows: $150 million from the International Society for Krishna Consciousness, $125 million already used and $100 million still being raised.

9. A Badaga (South Indian) architect in Cleveland designs nothing but Hindu temples and shopping malls. His temples have areas for both Saivite and Vaishnavite deities.

10. *India Tribune,* 17 October 1992. The Council, headquartered in New York brought together the heads of fourteen temples nationwide at a meeting in September 1992 in Chicago. The members discussed pooling of temple resources, standardization of management practices and sharing of expertise. Temples for different deities tend to be built in different cities so that almost every major god and goddess (as well as many minor ones) in the Hindu pantheon are fully represented in North America.

11. Urmilla Chawla and Sudha Rao, "A Historical Review" (brochure from Temple archives).

12. *India Tribune,* 4, 23 June; 22, 30 July 1994.

13. *India Tribune,* 1 January 1994.

14. The Second Annual Hindu Youth Conference conducted by the Vishwa Hindu Parishad, Greater Chicago Chapter was held on the temple premises on August 1, 1992.

15. Board members of the temple vehemently denied any connection with the VHP but a researcher in the Chicago area, Lisa McKean, believes that temple boards are successfully "infiltrated" by the VHP. According to McKean, the VHP's avowed strategy is to use respectable Hindu organizations as a front for their own extremist activities. "Political Capital and Spiritual Camp: The Hindu Nationalist Movement and Front Organizations in the United States," Paper presented at South Asia Conference, University of Wisconsin at Madison, November 1993.

16. *India Tribune,* 15 January 1994, 21.

17. *HSC Brochure,* January 1994.

18. Jean Bacon's *Life Lines* takes this limited approach.

19. Fenton, *Transplanting Religious Traditions,* 172.

20. Interview with Akshaya members at HTGC on 19 February 1995.

21. Fenton, *Transplanting Religious Traditions,* 226.

22. *India Tribune,* 20 November 1993.

23. The first South Indian temple which sought to reproduce traditional architecture in the United States was dedicated to Lord Venkateswara, and was built in Penn Hills, Pennsylvania, in 1976. Until similar temples were built in other parts of the country, this temple attracted devotees from all over the United States and Canada. Vasudha Narayanan, "Creating the South Indian "Hindu" Experience in the United States," in *A Sacred Thread: Modern Transmission of Hindu Traditions in India and Abroad,* ed. Raymond B. Williams (Chambersburg, Pa.: Anima Publications, 1992), 148–49.

24. Williams, *Religions of Immigrants,* 232–33. *India Tribune,* 12 December 1992.

25. Interview with temple personnel, 11 August 1995.

26. Williams, *Religions of Immigrants,* 233.

27. *India Tribune,* 20 May 1995.

28. Williams, *Religions of Immigrants,* 234. In the 1980s this group was very small and was meeting once a month in homes.

29. *India Tribune,* 5 August 1995; 23 September 1995, 33.

30. Williams, *Religions of Immigrants,* 234.

31. *India Tribune,* 23 July 1994.

32. *India Tribune,* 27 August 1994.

33. From personal interviews with Sister Pratima of the Brahma Kumaris and the head of the Midwest region of the Sathya Sai Baba Organization who wished to remain anonymous, September/October 1995. For more detailed information on these branches of Hinduism, see Lawrenace A. Babb, *Redemptive Encounters: Three Modern Styles in the Hindu Tradition* (Berkeley and Los Angeles: University of California Press, 1986).

34. *India Today,* 11 October 1992, 48c.

35. Tania Anand, "Gift-wrapping Hindutva," *India Today*, 31 August 1993, 48c–d. Also 25 August 1993, 56g.

36. *India Tribune*, 12 June 1993.

37. *India Tribune*, 29 October 1994.

38. *Europa World Yearbook 1995* (London: Europa Publications), 1,477.

39. *Chicago Tribune Magazine*, 29 August 1993, 16; *Europa World Yearbook 1995*, 1,477, 3,289.

40. Williams, *Religions of Immigrants*, 242.

41. *25th Anniversary Volume of the Muslim Community Center* (Chicago, 1995).

42. Phone interview on 3 January 1996 with Sher Rajput, a Muslim community worker and a board member of several Chicago area Muslim organizations.

43. Williams, *Religions of Immigrants*, 245.

44. *India Tribune*, 3 December 1994.

45. Williams, *Religions of Immigrants*, 246–52.

46. *India Tribune*, 4 September 1993.

47. Church brochure.

48. Williams, *Religions of Immigrants*, 247.

49. Ibid., 250.

50. Fenton, *Transplanting Religious Traditions*, 234–35.

51. *1993 Statistical Abstract of the United States*, Table 90.

52. *Europa World Yearbook 1995*, 1,477.

53. Williams, *Religions of Immigrants*, 240.

54. Paul Numrich, "Sikh Religious Society of Chicago" (unpublished narrative paper written for the Immigration Congregations Project of the University of Illinois at Chicago, Office of Social Science Reasearch, 1995).

55. Williams, *Religions of Immigrants*, 240, and Numrich, "Sikh Religious Society."

56. *India Tribune*, 16 January 1993.

57. *India Tribune*, 8 May 1993, 24. Numrich ("Sikh Religious Society") recounts the case of a young man from the Palatine *gurdwara* taking his case for wearing a turban with his military uniform all the way to the U.S. Congress.

58. *India Tribune*, 12 December 1994. *Chicago Tribune*, 25 July 1995.

59. Numrich, "Sikh Religious Society."

60. *Europa World Yearbook 1995*, 1,477.

61. *India Tribune*, 12 June 1993.

62. *India Tribune*, 22 July 1995.

63. *India Tribune*, 14 May 1994.

64. Information on the Zoroastrian community was obtained through a phone interview with Mehroo Patel of the Zoroastrain Association on 27 January 1996.

65. Fenton, *Transplanting Religious Traditions*, 153–57.

Chapter 10   Forging New Links: Business and Politics

1. Robin Ward and Richard Jenkins, eds., *Ethnic Communities in Business, Strategies for Economic Survival* (Cambridge: Cambridge University Press, 1984), 1.

2. The study was conducted by Robert W. Fairlie of the University of California at Santa Cruz, and Professor Bruce D. Meyer of Northwestern University, Evanston, Ill. Achal Mehra, "What's Up, Doc?" *Little India* (Reading, Pa.), August 1995, 28–29.

3. Karen B. Leonard and Chandra S. Tibrewal, "Asian Indians in Southern California: Occupations and Ethnicity," in *Immigration and Entrepreneurship: Culture, Capital and Ethnic*

Networks, ed. Ivan Light and Parminder Bhachu (New Brunswick: Transaction Publishers, 1993), 141–62.

4. *India Tribune,* 6 November 1993.

5. Terry Wilson, "Saris Become Sheer Success," *Chicago Tribune,* 14 April 1996, MetroDupage section, p. 1. The report says that "some of the best customers of these (sari) stores are American women who simply like the unusual look of the sari."

6. The survey counted every Indo-Pak store on either side of Devon Avenue between Claremont and California, an area that has the highest concentration of South Asian businesses in Chicago.

7. This account of the National Republic Bank is based on an interview with Rohit Maniar, Devon Branch Manager on 5 November 1995.

8. In a recent review of seventy-seven Chicago neighborhoods to see how well local financial institutions conformed to the Community Reinvestment Act that pushes them to lend to residents in their neighborhoods, West Ridge, where "India town" is located, was ranked fourth. Rogers Park, the adjacent neighborhood, was ranked thirteenth. *Chicago Tribune,* 30 April 1995, Business Section 7, p. 1.

9. *India Tribune,* 11 September 1993. According to the news report, Pakistani youths "teased" the wives of Indian store owners and got into a fist fight with the Indian men. Tension was defused when police intervened quickly.

10. *India West,* 8 September 1995, sec. A, p. 34.

11. See Pnina Werbner, *The Migration Process: Capital, Gifts and Offerings among British Pakistanis* (New York: Berg Publishers, 1990). Many of the phenomena that Pnina Werbner has observed among the Pakistani immigrant community in Manchester are at work in Chicago also, such as the accumulation of capital, sharing of labor and exchange of gifts.

12. Douglas S. Massey, "Economic Development and International Migration in Comparative Perspective," *Population and Development Review* 14 (1988): 396; quoted in *Immigration and Entrepreneurship,* ed. Light and Bhachu, 25.

13. *India Tribune,* 22 April, 28 December 1993; 6 May 1995.

14. Ivan Light, Parminder Bhachu, and Stavros Karageorgis, "Migration Networks and Immigrant Entrepreneurship," in *Immigration and Entrepreneurship,* ed. Light and Bhachu, 40.

15. From a conversation with a Malayalee gas station owner who said that their business association was planning on adopting the nozzle as its logo, 13 November 1998.

16. *India Tribune,* 9 December 1995.

17. Johanna Lessinger, "The Tyranny of the American Dream: New York's Indian Immigrants as Workers and Investors." Paper presented at the American Anthropological Association, Washington, D.C., November 1989.

18. Roger Ballard, "Migration and Kinship: the Differential Effect of Marriage Rules on the Processes of Punjabi Migration to Britain," in *South Asians Overseas: Migration and Ethnicity,* ed. Colin Clarke, Ceri Peach, and Steven Vertovec (Cambridge: Cambridge University Press, 1990), 246.

19. *India Tribune,* 6 March, 1993; 6 November 1993.

20. *India Tribune,* 20 November 1993; 2 January, 1993; 24, 22 January, 1994; 1 April 1995; 5 August 1995. *India West,* 8 September 1995, sec. A, p. 38. *India Today,* 30 April 1995, 64c.

21. Phone interview with Ambegaokar, 25 February 1996.

22. *India Tribune,* 8 July 1995.

23. Chinatown was divided to accommodate creation of the first Latino congressional district and a legally required black district as well as maintain a predominantly white 11th ward. *Chicago Tribune,* 7 August 1994, 4.

24. Most of the information on IADO is from an interview with Ranjit Ganguly in September 1995.

25. *Indicators for Understanding: A Profile of Metro Chicago's Immigrant Community* (Chicago: Latino Institute; and DeKalb: Office for Social Policy Research, Northern Illinois University, 1995), 37.

26. *India Tribune*, 5 March 1994; 4 March 1995; Ajit Jain, "Immigrant Gas Station Worker Savagely Beaten," *India Abroad*, 1 September 1995.

27. *India Tribune*, 20 March, 20 May 1995; 8 May 1993.

28. *Chicago Tribune*, 7 August 1994, 6.

29. *India Today*, 31 December 1993, 48k.

30. *The Hindu* (Madras), 30 May 1995, 4.

31. Khushwant Singh, "In Search of Sikh Identity," *India West*, 24 November 1995, A5–6.

32. Lisa McKean, "A Global Spiritual Bazaar: The 1993 Parliament of World's Religions in Chicago" (unpublished paper).

33. Sanjay Suri, "Advani for Secularism and Dual Citizenship," *India Abroad*, 1 September 1995.

34. *India Tribune*, 30 January 1993.

Chapter 11 Pursuing Special Interests: Professional Groups and the Media

1. *India Tribune*, 10 June 1995. Published interview with AAPI President, Dr. Gopal Lalmalani, 17 July 1995.

2. *India Tribune*, 7 November 1992; 29 July 1995; 1 July 1995.

3. *India Tribune*, 6, 27 March 1993; 24 July 1993; 2 April 1994.

4. Phone interview with a past president in October 1995.

5. *Spotlight*, 7 July 1990, 14.

6. The sources for information on social service agencies are personal interviews with the key members of the agencies and the literature published by the agencies themselves.

7. *India Tribune*, 2 January 1993.

8. *India Tribune*, 12 June 1993.

9. Lavina Melwani, "Of Human Bondage," *India Today*, 15 February 1995, 239.

10. Personal interviews with Dunkin' Donuts employees.

11. *India Abroad*, 31 January 1992. Also from personal interviews, annual reports, and literature supplied by Apna Ghar.

12. Data pertaining to *India Tribune* was obtained from an interview with the publisher Prashant Shah and its associate editor, J. V. Lakshmana Rao, on 18 August 1995, at the newspaper's offices on Peterson Ave in Chicago.

13. Shah has a chemical engineering degree. The other partner in this venture was Rajiv Desai, who had a journalism background. Desai has since gone back to India and is running his own successful public relations firm in New Delhi.

14. The English language publications were *India Times, India Post* and *Image India*.

15. In the early years of publication, the *India Tribune* did not even have a competent copy editor, its stories were written in sloppy English and the newspaper was full of printer's devils.

16. Interview with Mehta on 12 September 1995. Mehta now runs a grocery store, Apna Bazar, on Devon Avenue.

17. Interview with Monisha Dubey, Senior News Coordinator at *India Today's* Editorial Offices in New Delhi on 18 July 1995.

18. From interview with Yogesh Shah, owner of Super Broadcasting Company, 21 July 1992.

19. *Spotlight*, 22 September 1995.

20. Women of South Asian Descent Collective, ed., *Our Feet Walk the Sky* (San Francisco: Aunt Lute, 1993).

21. Ajit Kumar Jha, "Creating Homelands: Four Second-Generation Indians in the U.S. Sidestep Clichés to Redefine Immigrant Writing," *India Today*, 31 March 1995, 211–13.

22. W. D. Merchant, *Home on the Hill: A Bombay Girlhood* (Washington, D.C.: Three Continents Press, 1991).

23. *India Tribune*, 18 February 1995.

24. A Tamil industrialist from the Midwest contributed $65,000 towards a total of $400,000 to Berkeley for establishing a Tamil chair. *India Today*, 15 August 1995, 60m.

25. *India Tribune*, 29 April 1995.

26. Interview with players and official Glen Steiner of IPNBT Tournament at Walther Lutheran High School, 28 July 1996.

27. *India Tribune*, 30 October 1993.

Epilogue

1. Colin G. Clarke, *East Indians in a West Indian Town San Fernando, Trinidad, 1930–70* (London: Allen & Unwin, 1986).

2. Ravindra K. Jain, *Indian Communities Abroad: Themes and Literature* (New Delhi: Manohar Press, 1993), 23.

3. Arthur W. Helweg, *Sikhs in England* (New Delhi: Oxford University Press, 1986).

4. Parminder Bhachu, *Twice Migrants: East African Sikh Settlers in Britain* (London: Tavistock, 1985), and Arthur Helweg, *Sikhs in England.*

5. Bruce La Brack, "Immigration Law and the Revitalization Process: The Case of the California Sikhs," in *From India to America, A Brief History of Immigration: Problems of Immigration, Admission, and Assimilation*, ed. S Chandrasekhar (La Jolla, Calif.: Population Review, 1982), 59–66.

6. Juan L. Gonzales Jr., *Racial and Ethnic Families in America* (Dubuque, Iowa: Kendall/Hunt Publishing, 1992),138.

7. Harry H. L. Kitano and Roger Daniels, *Asian Americans Emerging Minorities* (Englewood Cliffs, N.J.: Prentice Hall, 1988), 7.

8. Priscilla Labovitz, "Immigration—Just the Facts," *The New York Times*, 25 March 1996.

INDEX

Aathimoolam, Mr. N., 233
Abhisekham ceremony, 256
acculturation, 98–99. *See also* assimilation
Ackerman, Congressman Gary, 225
Action for India, 310
Africa, Indians in, 20, 234–37. *See also* East
    Africa; South Africa, Indians in
Agency for International Development
    (U.S.), study by, 51–52
Ahmed, Dr. Jalil, 291
Ahuja, Satya, 291
AIDS, 304, 310
Akshar Purushottam Swaminarayan. *See*
    Bochasanwasi Swaminarayan Sanstha
    (BSS)
Alien Land Acts of California (1913), 44
Alliance of Midwest Indian Associations
    (AMIA), 226–27
All India Institute of Medical Sciences, 305
Ambegaonkar, Raj, 291–92
American Association of Physicians of
    Indian Origin (AAPI), 117, 293,
    303–4
American Association of Retired Persons
    (AARP), 212
American Federation of Labor, 3
American Film Institute, 243
American Institute of Architects, 302
Americanization, 61, 99, 128, 166
American Medical Association, 301, 302
American Society of Engineers of Indian
    Origin, 302
Amin, Idi, 25, 235
Amritsar, 33
Andhra Pradesh, 230, 288
apartheid, 22. *See also* race

Apna Gar (Our Home), 118, 153, 205, 298,
    313–15
Appadorai, Arjun, 338 n. 3
Arabic language, 264
ardas, 268
arranged marriages. *See* marriage: arranged
Art Institute of Chicago, 41
arts, performing, 223, 243. *See also*
    organizations: arts
Arya Samaj Society, 247
ashrams, 247. *See also* temples
Ashwamedha Yagya, 258–59
Asia, South Asians in, 18
"Asian, " use of term, 7–8, 337 n. 1
Asian American Film Festival, 243
Asian American Hotel Owners Association,
    284
Asian American Political Action Committee
    (AAPAC), 293–94
Asianet, 36
Asian Human Services, 195, 312
Asian Indian Architects Association, 302
Asiatic Exclusion League, 3
assimilation, 5, 98, 116–17, 128, 333. *See also*
    Americanization
Association of Asian Indians in
    Ophthalmology, 302
Association of Indian Neurologists, 302
Association of Indian Pharmacists, 308
Association of Indians in America (AIA),
    220, 224–25, 227, 228, 297
Association of Rajasthanis, 220
Association of Scientists of Indian Origin,
    302
associations. *See* institutions; organizations
atman, 238

Australia, Indians in, 27
Ayodhya, 233, 260, 299. *See also* Babri Masjid

Babri Masjid, 250, 260, 263, 265, 281, 299
Back of the Yards, 86
Bacon, Jean, 338 n. 11, 348 n. 2, 348 n. 3
Bagai, Vaisho Das, 44
Baisakhi, 253, 258, 268
Balaji Temple, 116, 135, 254–57, 258, 309
Ballard, Roger, 289
Banaras Hindu University, 305
Bangladesh, Bangladeshis, 18, 90, 262, 265
banking, 248, 288–89
Baroda Medical College, 305
Barred Zone Act (1917), 43, 46
Bazm-e-Deccan, 320
BBC, 36
Bengali Association of Greater Chicago, 231
Bengali language, 29, 103
Bhachu, Parminder, 332
Bhagavad Gita, 252, 261
bhajans, 123–24
Bhangra, 241, 268
Bharatanatyam, 133, 238, 239, 240
Bharat Darshan, 320, 322
Bharatiya Janata Party (BJP), 250, 260, 299
Bhardwaj, Surinder M., 341 n. 3, 342 n. 31
Bhargava, Ranjana, 314
Bhashyananda, Swami, 262
Bhuvaneshwar Temple, 249
Bihar Cultural Association, 220, 221
Biharis, 234, 238
bindi, 54
BJ Medical College, 305
Bochasanwasi Swaminarayan Sanstha (BSS), 257
Brahma Baba, 260
Brahma Kumaris, 259–60
Brahmanupananda, Swami, 252
brahmins, 37, 38, 50, 256
"brain drain," 4, 51, 342 n. 27
BREAD (Basic Research Education and Development Society), 309
Britain. *See* Great Britain
British colonialism. *See* colonialism: British
British Columbia, 42
Brown, Norman, 340 n. 42
Brown, Richard, 9
"brown sahibs," 218
Buddhism, 20

Burma (Myanmar), Indians in, 17, 20, 22, 24, 39
Burris, Ronald, 295
Byrne, Mayor Jane, 74, 138

Calcutta, 21
California, Indians in, 3, 39, 42–43, 44, 45, 46, 54, 94, 123, 332
Cambodia, Indians in, 20
Canada, Indians in, 27, 39, 40, 42, 291
"capitation" fees, 175
Caribbean, Indians in, 7, 18, 25, 39, 51, 190, 241
Carnatic music, 241–42
Carter, President Jimmy, 292
caste system, 25, 37–39, 237
    disintegration of, 23
    and marriage, 37, 232
    Untouchables, 37
Catholic Friends of India League, 267
Catholicism, 266, 267
Census of the United States. *See* U.S. Census Bureau
Ceylon. *See* Sri Lanka, Indians in
chain migration, 61
Chandrasekhar, 111
Charotar Patidar Samaj, 180, 232
Chaurasia, Hariprasad, 241
"Chicago," defining, 77–78
Chicago City Arts, 241
Chicago Commission on Human Relations, 296
Chicago Department of Aging, 195
Chicago Tamil Sangam, 117, 221, 230, 232–34
Chicago Thyagaraja Utsavam, 241
child rearing, 35, 152, 153, 159, 167–70, 205, 207, 208. *See also* family
Chinatown, 227, 352 n. 23
Chinmaya International Foundation, 261
Chinmaya Mission, 261
Chinmayananda, Swami, 261
Chitrahaar, 320, 321, 322
Christianity, Christians, 123
    missionaries, 331
    religious organizations, 265–67
Church of South India, 266
Citibank, 289
citizenship, 44–45, 58, 64, 107–8
Clinton, Hillary, 302
Clinton, President Bill, 292–93, 302, 303

Club of Indian Women, 138, 292, 311–12
CNN, 36
Coca-Cola, 32
Coelho, George, 9
Cohn, Bernard, 38
colleges and universities, 323–24. *See also*
  education; *individnal names of colleges*
  and universities
College of Du Page, 106, 232
colonialism, 4, 18, 20–21
  British, 22, 24
  other than British, 21
"colored," 26, 94
Committee on South Asian Women
  (COSAW), 346 n. 11
commodification of culture, 239, 243–44, 278
"community," defining, 218–19, 348 n. 1
Community Reinvestment Act, 352 n. 8
constitution, India's, 30, 33, 146
Consultative Committee of Indian Muslims
  (CCIM), 265
Cook County, 80, 83, 84, 91, 92
"coolie," 24, 339 n. 25. *See also* indentured
  labor
Council of Hindu Temples of North
  America, 248, 350 n. 10
Council of Islamic Organizations of Greater
  Chicago, 263
Council of Kerala Churches of Chicago, 232
Council on Education and Legal Action, 297
cricket, 325
cultural pluralism, 98–99, 330

Daley, Mayor Richard J., 74, 344 n. 14
Daley, Mayor Richard M., 74, 292
dance, classical, 36, 133, 238–41
Daniels, Roger, 8
Darshan, Bharat, 320, 322
Das, Taraknath, 43
dating, 119–21
  computerized, 180–81
  See also marriage
Dawoodi Bohora Jamat, 264
Dayal, Har, 43
Deepavali, 233. See also *Divali*
Delhi Cloth Mills (DCM), 28
Democratic Party, 292, 293
demographics, 2, 53–54, 56–62, 64–65,
  78–80, 95, 101–7, 347–48 n. 1. *See also*
  U.S. Census Bureau

Desai, Morarji, 254
Desai, Rajiv, 353 n. 13
Devon Avenue, 30, 32, 54, 74, 195, 226, 231,
  281, 296, 344 n. 22
  building of, 88–89
  as commercial center, 95, 273–78, 283, 290
  decay of, 280
  growth of, 90–91
  and politics, 136, 138, 295
Devon Bank, 280
Dewan, Om, 291
dharma, 34
Dhillon, Neil, 291
diaspora, 7. See also *oikumene*
Didrickson, Loleta, 312
diet, 36, 195, 237
Dilshad Dance Academy, 240
Disco-Dandia, 240
discrimination, 33, 114–16, 146, 224, 346 n.21
  based on caste, 37, 38, 50
  based on race, 43, 51, 228, 296. *See also*
  racism
  based on religion, 50, 269
Divali, 74, 233, 234, 253, 281, 321, 334
divorce, 33, 146. *See also* marriage
Dixit, Madhuri, 243
Dole, Bob, 292
Doordarshan, 36
"Dotbusters," 54
dowry, 33, 146. *See also* marriage
dress, traditional, 231, 269, 351 n. 57. *See also*
  sari
Dunkin' Donuts, 85–86, 285
Du Page Community College, 324
Du Page County, 79, 80, 81, 83, 84
Durga, 249
Durgu Puja, 231
Dussehra, 74, 253, 334
Dutch colonies, 21

East Africa, 21, 22, 24, 25, 27, 39, 40, 235–36,
  237, 339 n. 10
East African Cultural Organization, 234–38
economic growth, distribution of, 80–81,
  84–86
economic liberalization, 32, 287–88
Edgar, Governor Jim, 292
education, 31, 51–52
  British influence on, 29
  and caste, 37

education (*continued*)
  and income, 99–100
  in India, 29, 167
  levels of, 59, 64, 65, 66, 68, 69, 110, 343 n. 48
  of Muslims, 264
  religious, 271
  of women, 68, 165
  of youth, 167, 168, 174–75
Eid, 264
elderly, 145, 193–213, 347–48 n. 1, 348 n. 4
  changing attitudes about, 198, 205
  employment of, 201–2, 209–10
  and grandchildren, 205, 207, 208
  numbers of, 193–96, 197
  role of, 202
  values of, 204–5
Elkhanialy-Nicholas survey, 228
emigration, 7, 9, 10, 17–20, 26, 45–47, 65
  as "brain drain," 4, 51, 342 n. 27
  destinations. *See individual names of countries*
  as effect of British colonialism, 18, 20–21
  and the elderly, 197, 199, 201, 202
  factors in, 3, 47, 49–52, 342 n.23;
    economic, 4, 5, 26, 27, 32, 103, 235;
    expulsion, 25; political, 31–32, 50
  and indentured labor, 20–24, 40, 51, 330, 339 nn. 12 and 25
  history of, 9, 18, 20, 39, 41–47, 147, 229, 339 n. 10
  numbers, 17–18, 24
  and women, 148–52
  and youth, 177–79
  See also immigrants; immigration
Emmanuel United Methodist Church, 266
employment, 49–50, 52, 59, 64, 108–12
  of elderly, 202, 209–10
  patterns of, 85–86, 93
  self-, 274–76
  of women, 152–53, 154
England. *See* Great Britain
English language, 29–30, 31, 104–6, 114, 286
Equal Rights Amendment, 146

family, 58, 61, 64, 101, 152–53, 191, 218, 343 n. 41
  child rearing and care, 35, 152, 153, 159, 167–70

and the elderly, 202, 205, 207, 208, 213
and generation gap, 169, 177, 190
and immigration laws, 61, 196
importance of, 33–34, 152, 156, 159, 343 n. 38
roles in, 152–53, 164–65
and "sandwich generation," 211
structure of, 34–35, 159, 208
Far East, 339 n. 10
farming, 43–44, 46
Federation of Gujarati Associations of North America (FOGANA), 133, 349 n. 19
Federation of India Associations (FIA), 226–27, 308, 348 n. 8
Federation of Indian Christian Associations, 266
Federation of Jain Societies in North America (JAINA), 270
Federation of Tamil Sangams of North America, 230, 233–34
Fenton, John, 246, 251, 252, 272
Fermi National Laboratory, 111
Fernandez, Dr. Marilyn, 156
festivals, 231, 253
Fiji, Indians in, 7, 17, 20, 21, 22, 25, 39, 40, 104, 229, 283, 338 n. 6, 339 n. 18
film industry, 242–44
First Indian Church of the Nazarene, 266
Fleck, Ludwig, 346 n. 1
foeticide, 33, 145
FOGANA. *See* Federaration of Gujarati Associations of North America
fundamentalism, religious, 250, 269

Gandhi, Indira, 32, 33, 136, 298
Gandhi, Mahatma, 4, 23, 146, 321
Gandhi, Rajiv, 32, 310
Gandhi Jayanti Day, 334
Ganesha, 248, 253
Ganesh Chaturthi, 253
Ganesh Temple, 249
Ganges, Mich., 254, 262
Ganges River, 36
Ganguly, Ranjit, 138, 294, 295, 296
Garba, 234
Garba Raas, 231, 240. See also *Raas-Garba*
Gayatri Pariwar Yugnirman, 259
gender, 100, 129. *See also* men; women
generation gap, 169, 177, 190
Gephardt, Richard, 293

Ghadr party, 43
ghazal, 242
Global Convention of Indian Nurses, 305
gods. *See* temples: worship; *names of individual gods*
Gold Coast, 76, 91
Golden Corridor, 81
Golden Temple, 33, 267, 268, 298, 331
Gonzalez, Juan L., Jr., 343 n. 38
Gordon, Milton, 98–99, 118, 345 n. 2
Gosine, Mahin, 338 n. 7, 339 n. 10
Granth, 257, 268
Great Britain
    colonialism, 20, 24–25
    immigration restrictions in, 47
    Indians in, 17, 20, 22
    land-tenure system of, in India, 42
    Sikhs in, 40, 331–32
    violence in, 265, 331
green card, 57, 107, 194, 197, 198
Greeshma Mela, 253
Grenada, 339 n. 12
Grihapravesam, 256
Guadeloupe, 339 n. 12
Gujarati language, 103, 104, 106, 195, 266, 271
    publications, 316–17, 320
Gujarati Muslim Association, 232, 264–65
Gujaratis, 29, 86, 89, 212, 231–32, 276, 279, 349 n. 24
    and business, 20, 90, 283, 284, 285, 288
    dance forms of, 240
    in East Africa, 234–38
    in Kenya, 15
    and marriage, 180
    Muslims, 232, 264–65
    religious organizations, 135, 258, 259, 260
Gujarati Samachar, 320
Gupta, Anjali, 169
Gupta, Sathi Das, 165, 166
gurbani, 268
gurdwara, 168, 246, 267, 268, 269, 295, 351 n. 57
Guru Arjun Singh, 268
guru dakshina, 260
Guru Gobind Singh, 268
Guru Granth Sahib. See Granth
gurukula, 259
Guru Nanak, 268
Guyana, Indians in, 17, 20, 21, 22, 229

Hale, Mr. and Mrs. George W., 341 n. 4
Hanuman, 253
Hanuman Jayanthi, 253
Hardgrave, Robert, 345 n. 12
Hare Krishna movement, 259
Hare Krishna Temple, 90, 259
Hari Om Mandir, 260
hate crimes. *See* racism
health care, 302–3
    and the elderly, 194, 196, 200, 201, 212
Helweg, Arthur W. and Usha M., 9, 331
hierarchy
    of caste system, 37
    and family structure, 35
Hindi language, 29, 103, 106, 195, 266
Hinduism, 23, 253, 259–60
    in Fiji, 40
    and Islam, 263
    and politics, 299
    rituals, 36, 38, 252
    and second generation, 251–52, 257
    values of, 34, 197, 340 n. 42
    and women, 146
    worship, 134, 135. *See also* temples: Hindu
Hinduism Today, 247
Hindus, 123, 247
    conflicts with Muslims, 30
    "religious" versus "cultural," 246
Hindustani music, 241
Hindustan Patrika, 320
Hindu Students Councils (HSC), 250, 251
Hindu Temple of Greater Chicago (HTGC), 134, 221, 222, 239, 248–54, 255, 257, 258, 279
Hindu Youth Conference, Second Annual, 350 n. 14
Holi, 253
Hollinger, David, 345 n. 2
homams, 249
Home on the Hill, 323
Hong Kong, 26
human rights, 298. *See also* racism
Hussaini Association, 264
Hyderabad, Hyderabadis, 262, 264, 320

identity, 170
    collective, 23–24, 29–33, 217–18, 219, 220–21
    creating, 5–6, 9, 231
    cultural, 226, 235–36, 237, 243, 267

identity (*continued*)
and dance, 239
East African, 235–37
historical, 8, 29–33
"Indianness," 16, 38, 39, 213, 218, 327
linguistic, 30–31. *See also* language groups
national, 40, 272. *See also* nationalism
pan-Hindu, 247
pan-Indian, 220, 229
public, 231
Punjabi-Sikh, 267
religious, 263, 264, 267, 268–69
and youth, 170–74, 190
ILA Foundation, 227–29, 241
Illinois Advisory Committee to the United
States Commission on Civil Rights, 297
Illinois Arts Council, 241
Illinois Institute of Technology, 305
immigrants, 17, 20
in business, 273–90
classification of, 8, 47–48, 76–78, 94, 224
demographics on, 56–62, 101–8. *See also*
demographics
distribution of, 54–56, 78–80, 81–84, 85,
86–93, 94–96, 221
economic prospects for, 80–81, 84–86
education of, 51, 62, 68, 69, 104–5, 110
geographical origins of, 51. *See also*
emigration; *names of individual countries*
and India, 24, 163, 298–300
numbers, 1–2, 3, 17, 20, 21, 22, 26–27, 47,
78–79
other than Indian, 47
political activity of, 31–32, 136, 138,
291–300, 303–4, 326
Punjabi, 42–45, 52
social sphere of, 112–19
values of, 33–34, 35–36
and Western values, 33–34
See also emigration; *names of immigrant
groups*
immigration
post-1965, 9, 29, 45–47, 49, 56, 147, 343 n. 41
states that attract, 53, 342 n. 31
waves of, 3, 65, 68, 89–90, 105–6
Immigration and Naturalization Service
(INS), 3, 41, 308
immigration law 3, 43, 44, 45–47, 70, 110, 147,
197
family reunification clause, 61, 196

Immigration Reform Act (1965), 7–8, 45–46,
47–48, 110
income, 2, 60, 65, 67, 69, 92, 99–100, 101, 102,
107, 128–29, 343 nn. 47 and 48, 345 n. 4
indentured labor, 20–25, 40, 51, 330, 339 nn.
12 and 25
Independence (1947), 146, 317, 334
celebrations of, 226, 227, 243, 261
effect on emigration, 18, 26–27, 29–30
India, 26, 33, 37, 340 n. 42, 345 n. 7, 346 n. 4
constitution of, 30, 33, 146
costs of emigration, 51–52
culture of, 33–39, 345 n. 11, 348 n. 2
(chap. 8)
economic policies, 288
importance to immigrants, 124–27,
298–300
independence. *See* Independence
investment in, 28, 287–88
partition, 30, 262
recent political history, 29–33
relations with Pakistan, 30
India Abroad, 107, 110, 316, 319–20
India Alert, 298
India Book House, 316
India Business Conference, 288
India Catholic Association of America, 266
India-Christian Fellowship Church, 266
India Classical Music Society, 233, 241
India Development Society (IDS), 309–10,
312
India Forum, 220
India Investment Center, 288
India League of America. *See* ILA
Foundation
India Light, 316
India Medical Association, 289, 303, 304,
308
India Mission Telugu United Methodist
Church, 266
India Music Ensemble of Chicago, 242
"Indian," use of term, 104, 337 n. 1
India-Net, 323
Indian government
demonstrations against, 30
on emigration, 342 n. 27
External Affairs Ministry, 18
Ministry of Labour, 17
and Muslims, 50
and Sikhs, 32, 50, 265, 268–69

Indian Institute of Architects, 302
"Indianness," 16, 38, 39, 213, 218, 327. *See also* identity; *oikumene*
Indian Professional Non-Resident Association (IPNA), 305
Indian Reporter and World News, 316
Indian values, 33–34, 199, 220, 239. *See also* Hinduism: values of
Indian Women's Forum, 312–13
India Sari Palace, 89, 138, 283
India Today, 321
"India town," 86, 276
India Tribune, 316–19, 353 n. 15
India West, 316, 319
India Worldwide, 321
individualism, 33, 34
Indonesia, 20
Indo-American Business Forum, 289
Indo-American Center, 195, 304, 307–9
Indo-American Democratic Organization (IADO), 222–23, 294–96
Indo-Crisis Line, 312
"Indo-Pak," 30, 263
Indo-Pak National Basketball Tournament (IPNBT), 325
infanticide, 33, 145
Info-India, 323
institutions, 212, 326–27
    business, 80–81, 84; franchisees, 284–86; merchants, 282–84; professional, 287–90; semi-professional, 286–87; shopkeepers, 276–82
    cultural, 217–44
    defining, 219, 221
    media, 316–19
    political, 291, 298
    religious, 123–24, 186, 212, 245–72, 326. *See also* temples
    social service, 195
    See also organizations
International Association of American Physicians, 304
International Society for Krishna Consciousness, 259
International Swaminarayan Satsang Organization (ISSO), 258
International Tamil Language Foundation, 233–34
Islam, 263. *See also* Muslims
Islamic Foundation of Villa Park, 264–65

Ismailis, 104, 237, 264, 279
Israel, Indians in, 27
Ithna'Asharis, 237, 264
Ivy League, 2, 91, 227–28

Jagan (Cheddi), 23
Jagannatha Ratha Yatra parade, 259
Jainism, 270
Jains, 123, 269–70
Jain Society of Metropolitan Chicago, 270
Janmashtami, 253
jatis, 37
Jhankar, 322
Johnson, President Lyndon, 45–46, 47–48, 292
Judaism, in India, 27
Jyoti Children's Development Foundation, 310

Kalamazoo, Mich., 8, 104, 123
Kalash Sthapan, 260
Kalayil, Dr. Ann (Lata), 223, 311
Kali, 146
Kallen, Horace, 98
Kalyana Mandapam, 249
kangani system, 22. *See also* indentured labor
Kannada Kuta, 117
Kannada language, 103
Kashmir, 30
Kathak, 238, 240
Kennedy, President John F., 292
Kenya, Indians in, 15, 25, 234
Kerala, 266
Kerala Association, 231
Kerala Express, 320
kesh, 269
Khalistan, 40, 267, 268
Khan, Aamir, 243
Khandelwal, Madhulika, 89
Kim, Kwang Chung, 343 n. 48
kin relationships. *See* family
kirpan, 269
kirtan, 268
Krishna, 253, 258
kshatriyas, 37
Kuchipudi, 240
Kumbhabisekham, 248, 249
kunds, 259
Kutchi language, 237

labor practices. *See* employment; indentured
    labor; *kangani* system; occupations
Lakshmana, 248
Lakshmi, 146
langar, 268
language-based organizations. *See*
    organizations: language-based
language groups, 29, 103–6, 117, 195, 238,
    255
    preservation of, 22, 30, 105–6, 345 n. 12
Latin America, South Asians in, 18
Latino Institute, 87
Leonard, Karen, 277
Leonardo, Michael, 348 n. 1
Lerner newspapers, 280
Lessinger, Johanna, 284
Loundy, Mr. Irving, 89, 280
Luce-Celler Bill (1946), 45
Lucia, 339 n. 12

Madras (Chennai), 21, 265
magazines, 320–21
Mahabharata, 36, 220
Maharaj, Pandit Birju, 241
Maharashtra Mandal of Chicago, 230
Mahashivrati, 253
Malayalam language, 103, 266
    publications, 320, 321
Malayalis, 231
    and business, 288
Malaysia (Malaya), 17, 20, 21, 22, 24
Malthusian theory, 50
Manav Seva Mandir, 260
Manchester University study, 26
Mandela, Nelson, 22
mantras, 256, 259
manufacturing, shift from, 85
Manusamhita, 145
Marathi language, 27, 29
Marathis, 234
Marks, Patric, 242
marriage, 35–36, 56–57, 119–21, 146, 180–82,
    218, 342 n. 29
    arranged, 57, 119, 120–21, 132, 181–82,
        235
    and caste, 37, 232
    child, 145
    interracial, 44, 180
    and matchmaking, 180–81, 306
    premarital sex, 121, 181–82

    and women, 145, 152, 159, 165, 181–82,
        190–91
    See also divorce
Mar Thoma Church, 266
Martinique, 339 n. 12
matchmaking. *See* marriage: and
    matchmaking
Matthews, Peter, 291
Mauritius, Indians in, 17, 20, 21, 22, 229
Mayor's Office, City of Chicago, 226, 227
McConigley, Nirmala, 291
McDonald's, 32
McKean, Lisa, 350 n. 15
media, 36, 316–23, 348 n. 7
Medicaid, 194, 212
Medicare, 212
Meehan, Congressman Martin T., 297
Mehta, Pradyumna, 320
men
    behavior of, 118
    role of, 197
Merchant, W. D., 323
methodology, 10, 98–100, 100–101, 144
Michigan Avenue, 135, 226
Middle East, Indians in, 17, 27
Mississippi Masala, 243
Mohini Attam, 240
moksha, 238
Mombassa-Uganda railway, 22
Moseley-Braun, Carole, 138, 292, 312
mosques, 263
    violence at, 265
mother-tongue, 105–6. *See also* language groups
Motwani, Jagat K., 339 n. 10
Motwani, Jyoti B., 339 n. 10
Mukherjee, Bharati, 166, 323
multiculturalism, 39, 272
Murti Pratistha, 260
murtis, 248
Museum of Science and Industry, 267
music, classical, 36, 233, 241–42
Muslim Community Center of Chicago
    (MCC), 263–64
Muslims, 123, 237, 262
    conflicts with Hindus, 30
    discrimination against, 50
    identity, 263, 264
    Indian, 23, 30, 264–65
    and Indian government, 32–33, 50, 298
    religious identity, 263, 264

religious organizations, 262–65
  and Sikhs, 265
Myanmar. *See* Burma, Indians in

NAACP, 297
Naipaul, V. S., 15
Nair, Mira, 243
Narasimhachar, Mr., 255
Narayana, 258
National Conference for Sustainable
    Development in India, 310
National Federation of Indian American
    Associations (NFIA), 225
nationalism
  African, 235
  Burmese, 24
  immigrants and, 40, 43, 124–27
  in India, 4, 229
National Origins Quota Law, 46
National Republic Bank, 248, 279
nativism, 25. *See also* racism
Natraj Dance Akademi, 240
naturalization, 61, 295
Natyakalayalam Dance Company, 238–40
Naubahar, 322
Navratri Festival, 241
Nayyar, Vichitra, 321
Nehru, Jawaharlal, 4, 15, 31, 38, 265, 299
neighborhood, concept of, 74, 86, 94
Nepal, 18
Netherlands, 339 n. 12
Netsch, Dawn Clark, 295
Network of Working Women, 312
Network of Young Indian Professionals
    (NETIP), 305–6
News-India Times, 316
newspapers, 116–17, 316–21. *See also individual
    names of newspapers*
New York, Indian population in, 164–65, 344
    n. 15, 348 n.4
New Zealand, Indians in, 27
Nimmagadda, Dr., 279
Nixon, President Richard, 298
Nizari Ismailis, 264
Non-Resident Indians. *See* NRIs
Northern Illinois University, 87
Northside Coalition, 308
North-South Foundation, 309
North Town Business Association (NTBA),
    280–81

Northwestern University, 85, 288, 324
NRIs (Non-Resident Indians), 27–28, 140,
    305
  and the BJP, 299
  as business lobby, 287–88
  children of, 175
  education of, 304–5
  investment in India, 28, 32, 289
Nyerere, Julius, 235

occupations, of immigrants, 26, 42, 59,
    62–63, 64–65, 110–11, 201–2, 273–75
O' Hare International airport, 76
oikumene, 10, 26, 28, 40, 45, 213, 259, 283,
    316, 323, 327, 330, 331, 332, 334, 341
    n. 17
  definition, 7, 16–20
O'Malley, State's Attorney, 269
Onam, 231
On the Trail of an Uncertain Dream (Gupta),
    165
Onward, 321
Opium Wars, 26
Oprah Winfrey Show, 181
organizations, 26–27, 219–22
  all-India, 223–29
  arts, 238–44
  business, 273–90
  caste-based, 232
  language-based, 117, 220–21, 223, 229–32,
    234, 237
  leadership in, 222–23, 228, 327
  medical, 302–4
  political, 291–300
  professional, 116, 117
  religious, 232, 249–72; Christian, 265–67;
    Hindu, 247–62; Jain, 269–70; Muslim,
    262–65; Sikh, 267–69; Zoroastrian,
    271
  social service, 306–11
  state-based, 220–21, 223
  volunteer, 309–11
  women's, 311–15
  See also institutions
Oriyas, 234
Orthodox Church, 266
Our Feet Walk the Sky, 323
outlier communities, 16, 17, 40, 45. See also
    oikumene
Overseas Friends of the BJP, 299

Pacific Islanders, 69
Pakistan, Pakistanis, 26, 90, 262, 352 nn. 9
    and 11
    breakup of, 262
    relations with India, 30
    violence in, 265
Pandit, Dr. Sakharam Ganesh, 44
parades, importance of, 74, 136, 226–27, 228,
    243, 259
parochialism, 230
Parsis, 237, 270, 271
partition, of India, 30, 262
Patel, Ahmed, 291
Patel, Hiren, 279
Patel Brothers, 139, 278
Paul, Swaraj, 28
Penn Hills, Pa., 350 n. 23
Phelan, Richard, 295
pilgrimages. See yatras
Pillai, Dandayudapani, 239
Pillay, M. K. G., 307–8, 309
Pitroda, Satyen (Sam), 32, 310
pluralism, 98–99, 118, 128, 330
Pongal, 231, 233
Population Research Center (Dharwad,
    India), 198
poverty, 65, 67, 69
Praying with Anger, 243
Pressler, Senator Larry, 225, 293
property ownership, 106–7
Protestantism, 33, 266. See also Christianity
Punjabi language, 103
Punjabis, 29, 42–45, 46
    and business, 289
    identity, 267
    Muslims, 263
    traditional dance forms, 241

Quit India movement, 307
quotas, 22
    educational, 227–28
    national origin, 3, 45–46
    See also immigration law

Raas- Garba, 133, 231, 240. See Garba Raas
race
    definitions of, 8, 26, 44, 93–96
    and marriage, 180
    meaning of, to Indians, 347 n. 6

racism, 8, 25, 26, 39, 292. See also
    discrimination
    violence and, 3, 22, 43, 54, 296–97, 344 n.
    11
radio, 316, 321–23
railroads, Indians building, 22, 42–43, 235
Rajagopalan, Hema, 238–40
Rajasthanis, 234, 238
Rajiv Gandhi Foundation, 310
Rama, 248, 253, 258
Ramadan, 264
Ramalaya Samachar, 249
Rama Temple, 248, 255
Ramayana, 36, 145, 220, 233
Ramgoolam, 23
Rao, Dr. Sudha, 222, 311
Rao, Narasimha, 32, 288, 290
Rao, N. Madhusudana, 342 n. 31
Rashtriya Swayam Sevak Sangh (RSS), 260,
    299
Reimers, David M., 343 n. 41
religion, 186–87, 247
    and the arts, 36, 239
    importance of, 35–36, 121–24
    and politics, 23, 250, 260, 265, 269. See also
        Bharatiya Janata Party (BJP); Vishwa
        Hindu Parishad (VHP)
    See also organizations: religious
Republican Party, 292
Reserve Bank of India (RBI), 28
Réunion, 21, 104
ritual, 21, 35–36, 104. See also temples:
    worship
Rogers Park neighborhood, 90, 352 n. 8
Roman Catholic Church. See Catholicism

Sanatana Dharma, 261
"sandwich generation," 211
Sangeeta, 322
Sankaramanchi, N. P. S., 256
Sant Nirankari Mission, 269
Saran, Paramatma, 8–9, 164–65, 343 n. 43
Sargent & Lundy, 85
sari, 231, 352 n. 5
Sathya Sai Baba, 260
satsang, 258
Satyanarayana Puja, 256
Saund, Dalip Singh, 45
Schelbert, Leo, 17, 337 n. 6

sectarianism, 26–27
Sen, Dr. Ashish, 297
Sen, Mono Ranjan, 348 n. 4
Shah, Prasant, 316–17, 318, 353 n. 13
Shanker, L., 241
Shariff, Dr. Nayeem, 224–25, 311
Sharma, Mr. Rattan, 89, 138
Sharma, Prem, 313
shilpis, 248
Shiva, 249, 253, 258
Shradham ceremony, 256
Sikh Religious Society of Chicago, 267–69
Sikhs, 7, 123, 267, 268, 269
    in Britain, 15, 40, 331–32
    in California, 3, 42–43, 44, 45, 46, 54, 332
    in Canada, 40, 42–43
    discrimination against, 50, 269
    in East Africa, 22
    and the Indian government, 34–33, 50,
        265, 267–69, 298
    and Muslims, 265
    religious identity, 46, 267–69
Sikh Study Circle, 268
Simon, Senator Paul, 292
Sindhis, 26, 234, 237, 276, 283, 284
Singapore, Indians in, 22, 39
Sita, 145, 248
Skokie Association of Indians, 221
slavery, 21. *See also* indentured labor
slokas, 256
Smrtis, 145
Social Security benefits, 194, 196, 205, 295
So Far from India, 243
Solarz, Congressman Stephen, 292
Soparawala, Ramesh, 319
South Africa, Indians in, 17, 20, 21, 22, 25,
    229, 338 n. 6
sports, 324–26
Sri Lanka, Indians in, 17, 18, 20, 21, 22
Sri Venkateswara Swami Temple of Greater
    Chicago. *See* Balaji Temple
stapathi, 257
Star & Style, 321
State Bank of India, 248, 288, 289
St. Croix, 339 n. 12
Stone, Alderman Bernie, 95, 280
structural pluralism, 99, 118, 128
St. Vincent, 339 n. 12
Suburban Family Services, 195

sudras, 37
Supplemental Security Income (SSI), 194, 212
Surinam, 21, 339 n. 12
Sutherland, Justice George, 44
Swaminaraya, Lord, 257, 258
Swaminarayan Temple, 135, 258
Syrian Christians, 266

Tamil Association, Tamil Sangam, 231
Tamil language, 29, 103, 104, 117
Tamil Nadu, 104
Tamils, Tamilians, 232, 233–34, 242, 349 n.
    21, 354 n. 24
    Annual Convention of, 349 n. 17
Tanzania, Indians in, 25, 234–35
Tarana, 322
television, 36, 137, 316, 321–23
Telugu Association of North America
    (TANA), 230
Telugu language, 103, 230
Telugus, 231, 232, 254, 288
Telugu United Methodist Church, 266
temples, 124, 246, 258, 271
    building of, 247, 248–49, 257, 254–55, 326
    Hindu, 134, 135, 212, 221, 248–60, 350 nn.
        10, 15, and 23
    social function of, 252–53
    violence at, 265
    and women, 260, 311
    worship, 248–49, 256, 258
Thailand, Indians in, 20
Thampy, Dr. Kishore J., 297
Thyagaraja, 241
"Tikka" ceremony, 132
Tipu Sultan, 36
Tirumala Tirupathi Devasthanam, 248
Tirupati Temple, 249, 256
Tobago, 21
Topinka, Judy Barr, 136
trade, 20, 24–25, 339 n. 10
transnationalism, 9
Trinidad, Indians in, 15, 17, 20, 21, 22, 23,
    229, 330–31, 339 nn. 15, 20, 24
Truman College, 227
TV Asia, 137, 322

Uganda, Indians in, 25, 234
Uma Sari Palace, 89
United Nations, 288, 338 n. 8

United States Agency for International
    Development (USAID), 288
United States v. A. Kumar Mazumdar (1923), 44
United States v. Balsara (1910), 44
United States v. Bhagat Singh Thind (1913), 44
University of Chicago, 106, 323, 324
University of Illinois at Chicago (UIC), 324
Untouchables, 37. *See also* caste system
Upanayanam ceremony, 256
Uppuluri, Ram, 291
Urdu language, 104, 106, 264, 320
U.S. Census Bureau, 57
    1900 Census, 41–42
    1980 Census, 1, 2, 9–10, 53–54, 56, 57, 68,
        69, 70, 94, 224
    1990 Census, 1, 2, 9–10, 52–54, 56, 57, 61,
        63, 68, 70, 77, 78–79, 91, 101, 110, 168,
        262, 274–75, 295, 306–7
    definitions of "Indian," 218, 337 n. 1
    See also demographics
U. S. Commission on Immigration Reform,
    70
U.S. government
    U.S. Immigration Service, 47–48
    immigration policy, 31, 46–47, 147, 297. *See
        also* immigration law
    Indians serving in, 45, 291
    policy toward Pakistan, 292, 298
U.S. Supreme Court, 44. *See also* immigration
    law

vaishyas, 37
varnas, 37
Vedanta, 261
Vedanta Society of Chicago, 41, 252, 261
Vedic Day Care Center, 90, 259
Vedic tradition, 249, 259
vegetarianism, 237. *See also* diet
Venkateswara, Lord, 350 n.23. *See also* Balaji
    Temple
Vidyasagar, Dharmapuri, 248
Vishnu, 256, 258

Vishwa Hindu Parishad (VHP), 250, 251,
    260–61, 299, 350 nn. 14 and 15
Vision of India, 240
Vitha, Harjivan, Vitha Jewelers, 282, 283
Vivekananda, Swami, 41, 239, 251, 260, 261,
    341 n. 4
Vivekananda Jayanti Day, 261
voting, 107, 295

Washington, Mayor Harold, 74
Weiner, Myron, 342 n. 27
Werbner, Pnina, 352 n. 11
Western Electric, 85
West Ridge neighborhood, 352 n.8
We, the American Asians (1993), 57
Williams, Raymond B., 348 n. 1
women, 56, 143–66, 260
    in business, 289–90
    careers and, 152–53
    education of, 64, 66, 68, 165
    films made by, 346–47 n. 11
    images of, 145–47, 166
    income levels of, 343 n. 47
    and India, 33, 146, 163, 346 n. 4
    and marriage, 145, 165, 181–82, 190–91
    organizations for, 311–15
    rights of, 33, 146
    role of, 145, 146, 147, 152, 153, 156, 159,
        164–66, 202, 222–23
World Columbian Exposition, 41, 241
World Gujarati Samaj, 230
World Parliament of Religions, 41, 248, 298
worship. *See* temples: worship

Yagyashwa, 259
yatras, 235
youth, 144, 167–91, 221
    education of, 167, 168, 174–75
    generation gap, 169, 177, 190
    and self-identity, 190

Zoroastrians, 270–71